Eclipsed Cinema

EDINBURGH STUDIES IN EAST ASIAN FILM
Series Editor: Margaret Hillenbrand

Available and forthcoming titles

Independent Chinese Documentary
Dan Edwards

The Cinema of Ozu Yasujiro
Woojeong Joo

Eclipsed Cinema
Dong Hoon Kim

Memory, Subjectivity and Independent Chinese Cinema
Qi Wang

Hong Kong Neo-Noir
Edited by Esther C. M. Yau and Tony Williams

www.edinburghuniversitypress.com/series/eseaf

Eclipsed Cinema

The Film Culture of Colonial Korea

Dong Hoon Kim

EDINBURGH
University Press

Edinburgh University Press is one of the leading university presses in the UK. We publish academic books and journals in our selected subject areas across the humanities and social sciences, combining cutting-edge scholarship with high editorial and production values to produce academic works of lasting importance. For more information visit our website: edinburghuniversitypress.com

© Dong Hoon Kim, 2017

Edinburgh University Press Ltd
The Tun – Holyrood Road
12 (2f) Jackson's Entry
Edinburgh EH8 8PJ

Typeset in 10/13 Chaparral Pro by
IDSUK (DataConnection) Ltd

A CIP record for this book is available from the British Library

ISBN 978 1 4744 2180 5 (hardback)
ISBN 978 1 4744 2181 2 (webready PDF)
ISBN 978 1 4744 2182 9 (epub)

The right of Dong Hoon Kim to be identified as author of this work has been asserted in accordance with the Copyright, Designs and Patents Act 1988 and the Copyright and Related Rights Regulations 2003 (SI No. 2498).

Contents

List of Figures	vii
Acknowledgements	ix
Introducing *Joseon Cinema*: the Question of Film History and the Film Culture of Colonial Korea	1
1 The Beginning: Towards a Mass Entertainment	13
Film Culture Begins: the Development of Early Film Culture	19
Film Production Begins: Moving Picture Unit of the Office of the Governor General	30
2 Joseon Cinema, Cinematic Joseon: on Some Critical Questions of Joseon Cinema	55
Desperately Seeking the Joseon Image: *Arirang* (1926) and the Making of Joseon Film Aesthetics	59
Joseon Film Lyricism: Joseon Colour and Joseon Films 'Exported' to Japan	82
3 Migrating with the Movies: Japanese Settler Film Culture	103
The Formation and Characteristics of Settler Film Culture	110
'A Film Practice Distinctly Joseon': the Ethnic Segregation of Movie Theatres	129
4 Colonial Film Spectatorship: Nationalist Enough?	144
Korean Spectators, or How they Learned to Stop Worrying and Love Hollywood	147
Performing Colonial Identity: the Transcolonial Practice of *Byeonsa/Benshi*	167

5 Film Spectatorship and the Tensions of Modernity	184
Modern Girls and Boys go to the Movies: Cinema, Modernity and the Colonised Nation	190
Mobility, Movie Theatres and Female Film Spectatorship	210
Conclusion: Integrating into the Imperial Cinema	229
Notes	236
Appendix	264
Bibliography	273
Index	284

Figures

1.1	Danseongsa advertisement	15
1.2	Audiences gathered at mobile film screenings	20
1.3	DeVry advertisement	40
1.4	MPU officers hosting a mobile screening	45
1.5	Screening of MPU films at the 1922 Tokyo Peace Exposition	47
1.6	Tōyō Katsudō Shashinkan at the 1922 Tokyo Peace Exposition	48
1.7	Seeing off drafted soldiers in *Joseon at the Home Front*	54
2.1	Cover art for *Arirang Hill*	66
2.2	Musical score for the theme song of the film *Arirang*	69
2.3	Advertisement for *Arirang*	79
2.4	Na Un-gyu as madman Yeong-jin in *Arirang*	81
2.5	Promotional still for *Han River*	92
2.6	Advertisement for *The River*	97
2.7	Promotional still for *The Wayfarer*	99
3.1	Young Tokunaga Kumaichirō	104
3.2	Hisagokan Theatre in Incheon	117
3.3	Advertisement for Sakuraba Shōkai	119
3.4	Serial novel adaptation of *The Broken Coin*	125
3.5	Bandō Tsumasaburō and Makino Teruko in Seoul	128
3.6	Hon-machi in South Village	133
3.7	Japanese-language preview of *The Four Feathers*	141
3.8	Advertisement for *The Four Feathers* and *Fast Company*	142
4.1	*Jisang yeonghwa* featuring the film *Shoes*	149
4.2	Report on Paramount's 1923 deal with Joseon Geukjang	151
4.3	Advertisement for Gisin Yanghaeng	152
4.4	Advertisement for *Peter Pan*	155
4.5	Moving Picture Band of the Tongyeong Youth Association	159
4.6	A theatre listing with the photos of *byeonsa*	170
4.7	Early *byeonsa* stars	175
5.1	'Mimicry of Others'	191

5.2	'Things that crawl out when the autumn leaves are falling'	192
5.3	Emperor Gojong (circa 1900)	195
5.4	Clara Bow, the 'It Girl'	197
5.5	Trends in modern girls' hairstyles	198
5.6	'Modern Boy's Stroll'	200
5.7	'The Scenery of Late Autumn'	201
5.8	'The Sin of Spring Day' and 'This Is How I Lost My Leg'	215
5.9	Ae-sun in *Sweet Dream*	218
5.10	*Gisaeng* perform at the 1929 Joseon Exposition	223
C.1	Preview of *Romeo and Juliet*	231

Acknowledgements

This project has time and again humbled me. When I embarked on this research for my dissertation, I was discouraged by many who thought I had engaged in a risky topic that could not be dissertation-length research owing to the few surviving film prints and the lack of materials I could work with. To confess, I shared the same concern when I first conceived a germinal idea for the project. Days and months spent at archives, however, constantly proved this early speculation wrong, making me realise that the imminent problem was not the absence of resources but working out where to start with the mountains of materials I excavated, how to interweave them to discover forgotten accounts and relate new stories, and when to curb my addiction to the act of archival research. Every time I tried to close my research, I ended up with new findings that challenged me with new sets of questions. I have to admit that this seemingly closure-less process sometimes wore me out but, more often, excited me for thoughts of new future projects that would allow me some day to draw up a bigger picture. In this regard, this book marks not the end of one research but the beginning of a much larger one.

Without the unfailing support of so many people, I would not have been able to send this work off into the world. My first appreciation is due to my two mentors/friends. This project could have never been initiated without the unwavering confidence entrusted in me and my project by David James. As my adviser, he sustained me and my project with his astute guidance and enthusiastic support, and he was a continuous source of encouragement throughout the project's evolution. Daisuke Miyao provided me with much needed mentorship and friendship from the moment this project started taking the form of a book to the end of the tunnel. I found a lifelong colleague and friend in him.

As this project is built on extensive archival research, I have accrued debts to many scholars, colleagues, friends and institutions that generously supported my visits to archives and libraries in the United States, Korea, and Japan. A research fellowship from the Oregon Humanities Center at the University of Oregon enabled me to focus on my research in spring 2014. I gratefully acknowledge the Japan Foundation which supported my research for Chapter 3 in Japan in the summer of 2014. I appreciate Chika Kinoshita and Tokyo Metropolitan University for hosting me during my tenure as a Japan Foundation fellow. With a grant from the Center for Asian and Pacific Studies of the University of Oregon, I was able to obtain some important materials at the last phase of the typescript. A travel grant I received from the Stanford East Asia Library in spring 2015 granted me access to its Korean and Japanese collections, allowing me to final-check reference matters and take care of loose ends. I am indebted to Kyungmi Chun who kindly found a time to assist me during my stay in Palo Alto. I offer my sincere gratitude to Itakura Fumiaki, Itatsu Yuko, Sasagawa Keiko, Tomita Mika, and Yang In-sil for sharing their insights with me about research in Japan. Kirsten O'Connor and Itatsu Yuko always made my sojourns something more than professional ones, giving me opportunities to take breaks from the piles of papers with delightful chats, culinary adventures, and museum visits.

I express my earnest gratitude to those who read the typescript at its various stages and gave me constructive criticism. I must first thank Hye Ryoung Ok who closely read both early and final drafts of the typescript. The book benefited tremendously from her perceptive suggestions. I owe a great deal to Priya Jaikumar and Akira Lippit, my dissertation committee members at the University of Southern California, for providing me with their intellectual insights and personal support as well as professional examples. I am thankful to the participants at the Fifth Rising Stars of Korean Studies Workshop held at the University of Southern California in October 2013 for their healthy criticism on the earlier draft of the book. I particularly appreciate the encouragements by Hye Seung Chung, John Duncan, Theodore Hughes, Eun-Young Jung, David Kang, and Sunyoung Park. I am grateful to Patricia Ahn, James Cahill, Stephanie DeBoer, David Desser, Hideaki Fujiki, Nam Lee, Sachiko Mizuno, Abé Markus Nornes, Scott Nygren, Jia Tan, and Qi Wang for reading different parts and versions of my project and providing feedback that helped me refine and augment my arguments.

My colleagues at the University of Oregon supported me in various ways. I genuinely thank Roy Chan, Rachel DiNitto, Maram Epstein, Leah Foy, Lisa Gillis, Luke Habberstad, and Kaori Idemaru for their collegiality and friendship; Michael Anderson, Sangita Gopal, Alison Groppe, Kathleen Karlyn, Yoko Miyao, Omar Naim, Yunjung Oh, Priscilla Ovalle, Jennifer Presto, and Bish Sen for stimulating conversations about film, media, and culture; Glynne Walley and Nobuko Wingard for their help with the translation of tricky Japanese texts; and Lucien Brown, Jeff Hanes, Gyoung-Ah Lee, Susanna Lim, Lori O'Hallerin, Bokim Youm, and Kyu Ho Youm for their constant support for my research on Korean film and culture.

The editors and staff at Edinburgh University Press were a great pleasure to work with. Margaret Hillenbrand's interest in my research spurred this project and was instrumental in turning the typescript into print. Gillian Leslie's remarkable patience and tireless advocacy guided me through the completion of my first book. I also thank my copy-editor Elise Hansen for her careful work which significantly improved the accuracy of the typescript. Modified versions of my previously published articles are included in the book, and I thank the Oxford University Press, Taylor & Francis and BFI/Palgrave Macmillan for allowing me to reprint them. 'Performing Colonial Identity: *Byeonsa*, Colonial Film Spectatorship, and the Formation of National Cinema in Korea under Japanese Colonial Rule', an earlier version of the second part of Chapter 4, was originally published in *The Oxford Handbook of Japanese Cinema*, edited by Daisuke Miyao (Oxford and New York: Oxford University Press, 2014), pp. 172–87. It is reproduced by permission of Oxford University Press, global.oup.com. Portions of Chapter 3 were published in 'Segregated Cinemas, Intertwined Histories: the ethnically segregated film cultures in 1920s Korea under Japanese colonial rule', *Journal of Japanese and Korean Cinema*, 1.1, 2009, pp. 7–25. It is reprinted by permission of Taylor & Francis Ltd, www.tandfonline.com. Portions of Chapter 1 were published in 'Film Audiences without Movie Theaters: Early Film Culture in Korea, 1897–1919', *The Korean Cinema Book*, edited by Nikki J. Y. Lee and Julian Stringer (British Film Institute/Palgrave Macmillan, 2017). It is reproduced with permission of BFI/Palgrave Macmillan.

My heartfelt thanks go to my parents, family members, and friends in Korea who supported me at every point along the way. I deeply thank Hye Ryoung Ok and Kangmin Kim for offering me diversions from the pains of writing and for their love, patience, understanding, and laughs. Lastly, I should like to conclude with my warm memory of Jaime Nasser whose academic rigour, critical spirit, and kind-hearted friendship seeped into various parts of this book. I dedicate this book to the memory of my dearest friend who left us too early.

Introducing *Joseon Cinema*: the Question of Film History and the Film Culture of Colonial Korea

When approaching the film culture in Korea under Japanese colonial rule (1910–45), we are quickly led into a vast site of absences and voids which requires us patiently to carry out an archaeological unearthing and excavating of the remnants across historical, social and cultural terrains. The lack of actual celluloid images is generally seen as the primary form of absence that confronts scholars because only about a dozen feature films from the colonial period, along with a handful of propaganda films and newsreels produced by the authorities, remain, and no single commercial film produced prior to 1934 survives. Scholars consider the limited availability of 'Korean' films from this period as the major burden in their attempts to reconstruct colonial film history. As a Korean film historian recently noted, owing to this limitation few scholars have offered a comprehensive study of colonial film culture in Korea, leaving a most noticeable void in Korean film history.[1] Yet, if we walk further into this concealed chapter of film history, we begin to wonder if the lack of available film texts can really be deemed the sole problem posed for efforts to understand colonial film culture. It is estimated that only about two hundred commercial films were made in the colonial period, accounting for, at best, 5 per cent of all the films screened at cinemas beginning in the early 1920s when local film production began; before the 1920s, all the films projected on to the silver screen in pre-colonial and colonial Korea were foreign imports. According to the film censorship record of the colonial government, for instance, of the 931 submissions the board censored during its first six months of activity between August 1926 and February 1927, 482 were American and European films, 441 were Japanese, and only eight films were locally produced.[2] Ironically, despite the conspicuous dearth of 'Korean' films, which comprised an extremely small portion of colonial film culture, and their unavailability today, existing studies focus exclusively on 'Korean' films and film-makers and consider them as the central (and often only) pieces in narrating colonial film history. If we ground our historical perspective on the overemphasis on Korean films and film-makers, however, we are bound to a provincial aspect of colonial film culture. Figuratively speaking, by employing the censorship statistics cited above, the master narrative of colonial film history created with this narrow historical perspective would narrate colonial cinema with eight 'Korean' films, their creators, and Korean spectators' interaction with them, while disregarding and marginalising stories of more than nine hundred films – Japanese, Hollywood, European, propaganda, and educational films – and their varied overall impacts on colonial film culture. If we continue to consume ourselves with the obsession over one facet of colonial cinema, how can we possibly attempt to explore other hidden areas of colonial film culture? What truly created the void in film history is not necessarily the non-existence of 'Korean' film texts, in this regard, but the absence of a historiographical and conceptual framework that could allow us to create an inclusive account that sheds light on all the films, agents, and issues in colonial film history.

In its effort to develop a comprehensive picture of the film culture in colonial Korea, *Eclipsed Cinema* offers a critical perspective on the associations among colonialism, film historiography, and national cinema. I am principally interested in questioning the histories that are accepted as natural, and to which we have grown accustomed, and in unearthing the histories, facts and individuals that have been ignored, excluded and forgotten by conventional historiographical frameworks. Thus, my interrogation of colonial film culture opens with evoking an established but often ignored and even forgotten fact: the cinema of colonial Korea was not a national cinema, and thus employing theories and histories of a Korean national cinema constricts our understanding of colonial film culture. In fact, both the historical and the theoretical figurations of colonial cinema are helplessly trapped in the rubric of national cinema. Whether seen as an occupied cinema that struggled (and often failed) to maintain its filmic sovereignty or the *ur*-form of *minjok* cinema (Korean national cinema) that is characterised as the decades-long tension between Korean film-makers' nationalist impulses and oppressive colonial realities, almost all the historical accounts of colonial cinema are based on a common presupposition that it is the opening moment of Korean film history and thereby should be understood within the purview of Korean national cinema. It should be noted, however, that only certain features of colonial film culture have been embraced by film historians and thus became the basis for North and South Korean national cinemas. That is, film historians have placed their endeavours on discovering the elements that could constitute a connection between the film culture in the colonial period and postcolonial cinema in order to create a seamless cinematic tradition while disregarding other components that present disruptions for a historical trajectory of the Korean national cinema they have struggled to design. The problem is that these efforts inevitably colour colonial cinema in a particular manner, as Susan Hayward insightfully argues, a critical formation of a national cinema depends on the discourses of what to include and what not to.[3] In other words, any attempt to look at colonial film history through a bias of the Korean national cinema framework is destined to highlight only a limited portion of colonial film culture such as 'Korean' films, Korean film-makers and their sufferings and nationalist desires, a framework that ultimately benefits the politics of postcolonial film historiography while hurling the rest into historical oblivion.

As such, the national cinema paradigm assumes an uninterrupted development of film history from the colonial period to the contemporary Koreas. To make this historical narrative look unproblematic, it relies on the discourse of 'purity': Korean national cinema's essential standard to decide what to include and what to exclude. Film historians in the two Koreas, for example, are still debating which film counts as the first 'authentically' Korean film: *The Border* (*Gukgyeong*, 1923), *The Vow Made under the Moon* (*Wolhaui maengse*, 1923) or *Loyal Vengeance* (*Uirijeok guto*, 1919). Among these three productions made during the colonial period, in South Korea *Loyal Vengeance* is officially designated as Korea's first film although many film historians still contest this decision. Since 1962, South Korea has celebrated its annual national film day on 27 October, the day when *Loyal Vengeance* was premiered in 1919. In a strict sense, *Loyal Vengeance* is not a film; it is a chain drama, a hybrid genre between film and stage drama, which used documentary-like filmed sequences in key scenes – a car chase, changes in backdrops and scenes, and so on – of live stage performance. The logic behind this official designation is that *Loyal Vengeance* was the first film produced by Koreans, Kim Do-san and his theatre group, and its casts were mostly Koreans, while the other two films *The Border* and *The Vow Made under the Moon* were financed by Shochiku, a Japanese film studio, and the Office of the Governor General respectively.[4] Consequently, the degree to which a film is untainted by Japanese hands – or how pure it is – has become the sole standard for determining the first Korean film. Quite ironically, however, *Loyal Vengeance* embodies a distinctive Japanese influence: the cinematographer and editor of the film were Japanese and, more importantly, the chain drama or *rensageki* was a genre invented in Japan which gained popularity in colonial Korea from the late 1910s to the mid-1930s after it had been imported from Japan.[5]

In the meantime, North Korea views *The Vow Made under the Moon* as the first Korean film because 'although the film was produced by the Office of the Governor-General to effectively exploit Korean capital by promoting the use of bank accounts, the director Yun Baek-nam and his crews had a different intention . . .

the film has its significance as a cultural enlightenment movement'.[6] Through imagining the film-makers' resistant position without offering any concrete evidence, North Korean film criticism insinuates that the degree of Japanese intervention in *The Vow under the Moon* is tolerable, and thus it is safe to regard this film as the very first Korean film. The contradictory understandings, standards, and historiographical methods of North and South Korea over the designation of the first Korean film evidently reveal the arbitrary nature of postcolonial film historiographies and the vain attempt to define pure Korean-ness or Korean films. If we adhere strictly to the purity paradigm, no single film qualifies as a Korean film because no film from the colonial period was completely free from Japanese intervention in one way or another. This inconsistent definition of what constitutes a pure Korean film in Korean film histories has allowed many questionable films to be categorised as Korean films while dismissing and branding others as 'lesser' Korean films. As a result, such unreflexive positions have fuelled a seemingly never-ending series of debates concerning the nationalist film historical paradigm. The task of discovering and preserving Korean-ness can be achieved only through the manipulation of history which inevitably edits out substantial aspects of colonial film history.

To map the compound topography of colonial film history, therefore, it is essential to move beyond the framework of national cinema and to excavate aspects that are now deemed unimportant or unnecessary and to reassess them. Colonial cinema was a hybrid construct at the discursive juncture of national, colonial and regional cinemas, and thus the way in which it was formed and functioned cannot be sufficiently explained with a theory of national cinema. Rethinking colonial film history requires a different conceptual method that enables us to pursue the multifaceted nature of colonial film history without being tied to the confines of Korean national cinema. Thus, I propose to employ the term *Joseon cinema* for this purpose. Recently, some film historians in Korea and Japan have begun to use Joseon cinema (K: *Joseon yeonghwa*; J: *Chōsen eiga*) instead of 'Korean cinema under Japanese occupation (*iljesidae* or *sikminjisidae yeonghwa*)' because Joseon cinema was the term used to describe colonial Korean (Joseon) cinema during the colonial period. The term has been restored, however, mainly as a matter of convenience to indicate a particular moment in Korean film history,[7] and there has been little effort to define critically what Joseon cinema is. Joseon cinema should not be simply deemed equivalent to the early history of Korean national cinema because it refutes an easy theorisation or categorisation and, instead, raises some intense critical and historiographical questions that I shall attempt to unpack.

On 29 August 1910, the Meiji emperor of Japan promulgated that Korea was 'put under protection of Japan' through an agreement with the Korean government to 'eternally maintain the peace of Asia and the safety of the empire in the future' and 'protect Korea from disasters and secure its peace'.[8] With this rhetoric used to justify Japan's forced colonisation of Korea, the short-lived Korean Empire (Daehan Jeguk, 1897–1910) disappeared into a chapter of history. Upon colonisation, the Emperor Sunjong was demoted to king and turned into a member of the Japanese royal family, and the name Joseon was restored by the empire to designate the new colony, replacing Hanguk (Korea).[9] The Korean Empire had been established by Gojong, the twenty-sixth king of the Joseon dynasty (1392–1897), as part of top-down efforts to modernise Korea and cope with increasing imperial threats in the last decades of the nineteenth century. As a means to improve the image of Joseon as a modern state and show off its serious determination to maintain independent sovereignty, on 12 October 1897 King Gojong acceded to the emperorship and, on the following day, the emperor declared that he had named his empire The Empire of Great Korea (the Korean Empire). From that year until Japan's colonisation in 1910, the nation was officially referred to as Daehan Jeguk (The Empire of Great Korea), Daehan (Great Korea) or most commonly, Hanguk (Korea). Korea's belated modernisation ultimately fell short, however, as Japan, after defeating China, Russia, and other imperial powers in the competition to acquire control of Korea, turned the Korean Empire into its protectorate in 1905 and then into its colony five years later. The change of the name to Joseon upon colonisation per se represents the abolition of Korea's sovereign rights, its subsumption into the Japanese Empire, and the violent nature of this process. Also importantly, at a symbolic level, the restoration of the old name Joseon by the coloniser sent a clear message to Koreans that their efforts to create a modern, independent state had turned out to be futile. Despite its apparent demeaning connotation, however, it is also true that Joseon had been the title of the nation employed by Koreans to designate themselves and their nation for five hundred years. In fact, because of the obvious connection between the Joseon dynasty and the Korean Empire, Joseon continued to be popularly used among Koreans after the establishment of the Korean Empire. Though the state ceased to exist, Joseon was still imagined as a collective being by Koreans who continued to develop their distinctive, shared characteristics even after colonisation. But Koreans' efforts to build their modern identity now had to take into account the discontinuity between the old Joseon and the colony Joseon, that is, their stateless situation and colonial realities.

The film culture that developed under colonial rule reflects the conflicting identity problem raised by the colony Joseon. The concept of *Joseon cinema* is useful in this sense because it enables us to navigate through the multilayered relationship of the cinema to Korea's colonial modernity that cannot be properly addressed with the restraining notion of Korean national cinema. For the empire and colony, Joseon cinema meant the films or film culture of Joseon, not those of the Korean people or the colonised. In other words, the 'Joseon' in *Joseon cinema* was understood as a geo-cultural notion, denoting a locally specific film culture within the imperial territory rather than an ethnically specific film culture. In this regard, Joseon cinema can be viewed as a colonial film culture developed in relation to the film culture in Japan proper or a regional film culture of the empire. Yet it is mistaken to presume that Joseon cinema was a mere subcategory of imperial cinema and devoid of any distinctiveness. Though there were some parallel developments between Joseon cinema and Japanese cinema, Joseon cinema developed its own characteristic film practices and operated largely independent from Japanese cinema for much of the colonial period, making it difficult simply to reduce it to a provincial film culture. If anything, as I shall explore in the following chapters, its autonomous nature made Joseon film-makers, industry professionals, film critics, and filmgoers imagine Joseon cinema as if it were a national cinema. The unique character of Joseon cinema emerges from the very recognition of these interlocking and mutually influencing aspects of Joseon cinema.

Looking at Joseon Cinema Differently

Reclaiming the marginality and obscurity of film history, I came to embrace the notion of historical writing as an act of widening historical knowledge. As a result, my analysis of Joseon cinema willingly invites complexities, contradictions, ambiguities, and heterogeneities rather than suppressing them to iron out history. In an attempt to reconstruct lost intricacies of Joseon cinema and weave an inclusive historical narrative, I have designed several specific historiographical strategies. Most crucially, the terms *film culture* and *cinema* in my study include the entire practices of cinema, ranging from film production, distribution, exhibition, spectatorship, policy, and censorship to social receptions of film texts and the film medium. Rather than placing films and individuals at the centre of my account, I pursue an intertextual discourse analysis to draw a film history across social and cultural terrains. Consequently, my primary sources of inquiry are not the surviving film prints or lives and careers of film-makers. In interrogating the ways in which Joseon film culture informs the complicated interrelations among cinema, modernity, colonialism, identity construction, and film history and finding a way, in the absence of actual film texts, to develop a picture of what film cultures in colonial Korea were like, I consider the entire range of 'texts' such as films, literary works, newspapers, magazines, industrial accounts, promotional materials, and governmental documentation that have allowed me to unearth a densely textured account of colonial film history. Naturally, exploring archives and digging up historical materials have been fundamental components of my effort to construct discursively the film culture in colonial Korea. *Eclipsed Cinema* brings together materials collected at various libraries and film archives in South Korea, Japan, Europe, and the United States and, by carefully interweaving these seemingly unrelated documents scattered across the globe, the book sheds much-deserved light on the forgotten aspects of early East Asian film history.

As noted earlier, for decades the history of Joseon cinema has been written exclusively about films by Korean film-makers and Korean spectators' responses to them. To develop a broader picture of Joseon cinema, however, it is imperative for multiple reasons to look beyond the films produced by Koreans and Korean spectators' loyal devotion to them. Korean filmgoers' interactions with locally produced films or Joseon films were rare occasions at best and quite special events because they account for only a small portion of the film culture in colonial Korea. By simply highlighting the relationship between Joseon film and Korean spectators, we would end up completely losing sight of the manner in which the scarcity of local productions and the dominance of foreign films affected the formation of Joseon film culture. It is, therefore, intrinsically limiting to discuss Joseon cinema only with a highly limited number of film texts and by considering an entire film culture based solely on local productions, the Korean film-makers who produced them, and the Korean film fans' engagement with them. Also, perceiving film history merely as the mode of production has straitened the understanding of Joseon cinema. This restrictive historical perspective proves to be quite resilient because, even today, it still appears to dominate colonial film historiography. Since the discovery in the 2000s of about a dozen films from the late 1930s and 1940s, colonial cinema has garnered renewed scholarly attention in Korea and Japan, and a good number of scholars in the anglophone world have published essays about colonial film-making. These scholars employed the newly discovered films as a new lens through which they could look into the workings of Joseon cinema. Nevertheless, this new surge of interest in the last phase of colonial cinema does not deviate from the conventional approach, in that most film historians continue to locate at the centre of their research the film texts, Korean film-makers, and the magnitude of political realities that directed local film production while still assessing individuals and filmic elements in view of their contributions to the development of a Korean national cinema or in collaboration with the imperial agenda.

Eclipsed Cinema ventures into neglected areas of colonial film history by breaking away from this prevalent historiographical problem. Instead of framing colonial film history as the tension between the colonising forces and colonised, this book seeks to interrogate the convoluted relationship between the cultural institution of cinema and the colonial and modern experiences of Korea. Typically, histories of Joseon cinema have been written to redeem Korea's colonial past, underscoring Korean film-makers' struggles to maintain a Korean identity and mobilise emerging nationalism. Thus, efforts to locate and identify film-makers and films that endeavoured to address colonial realities despite the oppressive colonial occupation are tethered to the text-based approach that creates the historical narrative around films and film-makers. This nationalist historical writing actively mitigates and even conceals the apparent presence of Joseon cinema in the contact zone between Korean and Japanese film histories. As Nick Deocampo eloquently argues in his study on the history of early Filipino cinema under the influences of multiple imperial forces, 'Film historians who trace the beginning of a national cinema to a time of fierce nationalism may only be too tempted to investigate history through the rose-coloured glasses of a nationalist, but this may be achieved at the expense of history'.[10] Likewise, because of the nationalist historiography which is inclined only to underline nationalist efforts in the postcolonial Koreas, 'any interpretation that lies outside the nationalist framework, let alone one that dares to challenge the relevance or validity of the framework itself, is often ignored as unimportant or castigated as morally deficient, regardless of the evidence', as Carter J. Eckert so insightfully remarks.[11] In Korea and other former colonies of Japan, the ideals of a nationalist perspective have been overemphasised but privileging the nationalist paradigm has tended to stifle other possible stories and withhold material historical accounts.

To conceptualise adequately Joseon cinema and its dual nature as a colonial and pseudo-national cinema against the colonial backdrop, therefore, it is indispensable not only to examine the Korean elements but also to consider the Japanese elements embedded in Joseon cinema, such as the film culture of the Japanese settlers. The Japanese Empire was fundamentally built on settler colonialism – sending a considerable number of Japanese to its colonies, as well as colonial subjects to various parts of the empire, to carry out concurrently modernisation in the empire and in the colonies. Towards the end of the empire, nearly a million Japanese took up residence in Joseon. Their presence and influence in metropoles, cities, and towns considerably affected the development of modern culture in the colony, including cinema. Yet the Japanese settlers' film culture has been pushed on to the margins of colonial film history, often simply dismissed as another form of exploitation or overbearing imprint of imperial cinema left on the colonial cinema of Korea, for Japanese migrant film-makers, exhibitors, distributors, critics, and spectators were consequences of colonialism. The 'Japanese-ness' in Joseon cinema, however, should not be merely equated to Japan proper, Japanese people or Japanese film. Living in the colony as immigrants for generations, settlers developed a distinctive identity that shaped the relation between their film culture and that of their homeland as an ambivalent one. The settler film culture's in-between-ness was one of the chief elements that determined the course of Joseon cinema. Settler producers and film-makers were involved in the majority of Joseon productions, collaborating with Korean film-makers; exhibitors managed more than two-thirds of the movie theatres in colonial Korea that were geared towards Japanese settlers; distributors served as agents of Japanese studios but also distributed Hollywood pictures for Korean filmgoers; film critics and journalists often joined in their efforts with their Korean counterparts to develop theories about Joseon cinema and to try to find ways to defend 'our cinema'[12] from the increasing influx of Japanese film capital. Owing to their ambivalent location on the conceptual border between Korean and Japanese national cinema, Japanese settlers' multiple contributions to Joseon cinema have not been adequately explored in Korean and Japanese film histories. Taking into consideration these forgotten figures and their film practices, as well as the interaction between the film cultures of local Koreans and settlers, is a key to understanding the film culture in colonial Korea. To bring settler film culture into my account of Joseon cinema, I make a distinction between the words *Joseon* and *Korea* with regard to Joseon cinema. I employ Joseon as a comprehensive term; that is, when I use phrases such as 'Joseon film-maker', 'Joseon film', or 'Joseon film culture', *Joseon* in these terms includes Japanese settlers and their film culture as well. At the same time, I use the words *Korean* or *Japanese* to designate an ethnically specific aspect of Joseon cinema, such as 'Korean movie theatres', 'Japanese movie theatres', 'Korean film-makers', and so on.

Thinking about film history beyond the oppressor–oppressed binary frame will also enable us to tackle the insularism that directs studies of Joseon cinema, because it allows us to locate Joseon cinema in a broader historical development of film. Understanding the development of Joseon cinema against the global film historical context certainly makes it possible to envisage a richer account of Joseon cinema. By placing Joseon cinema in a global film network through comparing it to the functions of other colonial cinemas and probing the impact of Hollywood's global business, European art cinemas, and pan-Asian film enterprises of the Japanese Empire on Joseon cinema's development, *Eclipsed Cinema* joins in the efforts to extend the critical scope of early cinema and modern visual cultural studies.[13] These fields of studies have been very productive in film studies and cultural studies since the late 1970s, producing many groundbreaking works that introduce innovative historiographical methods and theoretical approaches. Yet their main discourses have seldom deviated from Euro-American contexts. In the same vein, the cinema's role and function in projects of imperialist expansions still remain understudied. European modernity cannot be divorced from its histories of imperial aggression and expansion in its political, economic and cultural dimensions. Therefore, the role of the cinematic medium as one of the overriding engines that propelled European modernity and imperial mechanisms cannot be overlooked. Considering that, since its inception, the development of cinema has been indebted to the commodification of 'Others', the commercial advantages of various imperial wars, and the uses of penetrative powers of imperial networks for developing film distribution and exhibition systems, the marginalised status of this issue effectively eclipses one of the formative aspects of the medium's early history.

My effort to redefine the concept of Joseon cinema and expand a historical understanding of colonial film culture is elaborated in the following five chapters. This theoretical, macro-historical exploration is firmly grounded in a detailed, microscopic study of varied aspects of Joseon film culture. Though the chapters revolve around different thematic focuses, they considerably overlap as the narrative of my inquiry constantly interweaves different areas of Joseon cinema in order not to lose its intricacies. Nevertheless, the chapters could be broken down into three parts as the principal focus shifts across these chapters. Whereas the first two chapters interrogate Joseon cinema with a focus on the aspects of film production – film business practices, film companies, film-makers, Joseon films, and film criticism – the last two chapters situate the film culture within theories of film reception and spectatorship. Organised chronologically at first to detail the development of film practices and culture, Chapters 1 and 2 inquire into the varied efforts of film-makers and film-making entities to develop Joseon film culture and define what Joseon film is from around the late 1910s until the late 1930s. Moving beyond the conventional approach that privileges a group of selected 'Korean' films, I consider a wide variety of films, ranging from commercial productions to educational and propaganda films, in my attempt to explore a range of thematic concerns, stylistic patterns, and critical questions film-makers considered when they tried to cinematise their respective versions of a Joseon image. Rather than fixating my discussion on the filmic images and film-makers' intentions, I place it within broader social, cultural, and film industrial contexts, putting films in dialogue with both the cinematic and non-cinematic factors that influenced the representational politics of Joseon films.

In Chapters 4 and 5 my critical and historiographical concerns draw on theories of film spectatorship and reception to extend the landscape of Joseon cinema. In looking at social perceptions and accounts of colonial film spectatorship,

I examine them in the nexus of Joseon's colonial and modern experiences. In Chapter 4 I consider colonial film-viewing practices as a political domain in which various forms of colonial tensions were represented and mediated. Unlike the conventional studies which overstate the Joseon film–Korean viewer relationship, my discussion of this political dimension of film spectatorship focuses primarily on Korean film spectators' engagement with American cinema. Taking the dearth of local productions and predominance of Hollywood productions into consideration, I argue that any attempt to relate Korean spectators' movie-going and film-viewing patterns only to local productions is bound to be a reductionist understanding of Joseon film culture. Therefore, I examine colonial film spectatorship by exploring film-viewers' reception and consumption of not only local but also imported films. My interrogation of film spectatorship and reception continues in the last chapter, expanding the scope of the inquiry. Preoccupied with the cinema's relation to the subjects of colonial exploitation, nationalism, and national identity, few scholars acknowledge that colonial film viewing was a much more compound activity marked by the range of political, cultural, and historical components that defined Korea's overall modern experience. In particular, in standard Korean film history, the fascination Korean film fans had with the cinema has yet to find its place. The novelty of the cinema, however, the pleasure of film viewing, and the liberating effect the cinema could offer were crucial in nurturing varied social perceptions and debates surrounding this prominent modern culture. My study of film spectatorship in the final chapter, therefore, explores the manner in which film spectatorship mediated and represented Korea's compound modern experiences. And it particularly focuses on the association between the cinema and politics in gender and sexuality, the issue subjected to the most intense form of social debates in relation to movie-going.

Chapter 3, which analyses Japanese settler film culture, functions as a bridge between the first two chapters and last two. As I strive to integrate Japanese settlers into my account of Joseon cinema, I make a conscious effort to uncover some key figures from historical obscurity and narrate their stories in order to describe their seminal role in the advancement of Joseon film practices. As the chapter progresses, however, the discussion gradually expands to probe an overall settler film culture, including movie theatres, film programs, film criticism, and spectators, and its interactions with both Japanese film culture and the local Korean film culture. By organising the flow of my inquiry in this manner, I highlight the heretofore forgotten Japanese settlers' pervasive influence across different aspects of Joseon cinema.

Taken collectively, the chapters present a chronological trajectory that charts an evolution of film culture in colonial Korea from a privileged cultural experience of selective groups of people in the mid-1910s to the most dominant, unchallenged popular culture casually referred to as 'the sole entertainment institution in Joseon'[14] in the late 1930s. Colonial film history is often perceived as a singular entity, but Joseon cinema was never a stagnant concept. In response to the industrial, cultural, and political changes that influenced the film culture, Joseon cinema's definition and nature accordingly underwent transformations over almost four decades of Japanese colonial rule. Though I bring in film practices prior to or after the aforementioned two decades whenever relevant, *Eclipsed Cinema* primarily engages with the middle stage of Joseon cinema that not only saw the most drastic growth of film culture but also demonstrated most tellingly the manifold dynamics of Joseon cinema outlined thus far. A critical observation of Joseon film culture in the two decades traversed by this book thus brings to light the eclipsed stories of Joseon cinema.

Note to readers: Throughout this book, including the notes, bibliography, and appendix, all Korean and Japanese names (except those which have been published in English) are presented in the East Asian order of family name first. All translations from Japanese and Korean materials are mine unless otherwise noted.

Chapter 1
The Beginning: Towards a Mass Entertainment

The winter night is getting longer, and the snow-covered ground makes us feel truly desolate. If you come to our theatre when all these sorts of winter feelings stir you up, the hearth would warm your body, and every time marvelous pictures you have never seen before are projected on the snow-white screen, you would suddenly find yourself thinking, 'This must be the real paradise'. Hence our belief that you would not find a better evening's entertainment than this. (From an advertisement for Danseongsa Theatre's reopening, *Maeil sinbo*, 21 December 1918)

The 1920s in colonial Korea dawned in a maelstrom of apprehension, unrest, and uncertainty. Social tensions became palpable in January 1919 when Gojong, the twenty-sixth king of the Joseon dynasty and first emperor of the Korean Empire who was dethroned by Japan in 1907 when Korea was the protectorate of Japan (1905–10), passed away. His sudden and untimely death generated a rumour that he might have been poisoned by Japanese officials which many Koreans accepted as a fact at the time of the death. It ignited an explosion of the tensions between the colonisers and colonised that had been escalating for decades since even before Japan's official colonisation of Korea in 1910. Just a couple of months after Gojong's death, the March First Independent Movement, the first nationwide nationalist movement organised by nationalists, ensued and soon swept Joseon with a nationalist fervour that took over half a million demonstrators into the streets within a couple of months. This first national-scale uprising was swiftly countered by the colonial authorities' ruthless measures that led to the arrest of tens of thousands of demonstrators. A month later, the Provisional Government of the Republic of Korea, a Korea government in exile, was established by exiled nationalists in Shanghai, China. Seeing the deterioration of the situation in the colony, Tokyo realised that the military-led colonial rule, built on coercion and overtly discriminative policy, had failed and thus reached the decision to replace high-ranking officials of the colonial government of Korea, including Governor General Hasegawa Yoshimichi, and initiate major reform in the colonial rule. When reminiscing about this challenging time for the empire, Mizuno Rentarō, who led the reform as civil governor of the colony Joseon along with the newly appointed Governor General Saitō Makoto, wrote, 'It was the most challenging event in governing Joseon'.[1] Mizuno experienced the severity of the situation first-hand immediately upon his arrival in Joseon on 2 September 1919 when Saitō and he were greeted at the South Gate railway station by sixty-five-year-old Korean nationalist Kang U-gyu's bomb attack in broad daylight which injured more than thirty officials, policemen and onlookers. For the next few years, the Saitō and Mizuno administration was charged with the task of overhauling governing strategies.

Though often overshadowed by these boiling political tensions at the time in historical accounts, the equally critical perils posed for colonial Korea around 1920 were two pandemics. Arriving in October 1918, the Spanish flu that killed at least fifty million across the globe infected almost 40 per cent of the entire twenty million population in Joseon and claimed 140,000 lives.[2] 'The so-called Spanish flu', *Maeil sinbo* later reports, 'was even worse than the pest and cholera'.[3] This 1918 flu pandemic was immediately followed by the outbreak of cholera that victimised over fifteen thousand lives in 1919 and twenty-four thousand in the following year.[4] In the few years' span between the late 1910s and early 1920s, as I have shown, Joseon was fraught with unsettling events that profoundly affected the lives in the colony. Rather incongruously, however, it is during this same period that the film epidemic spread from film production to exhibition, engendering a seismic transformation in film practices as well as the remarkable growth of film culture in scope and popularity; cinema finally matured into the most popular, unrivalled form of mass entertainment.

In this chapter's epigraph from the Danseongsa advertisement announcement of its reopening, the upbeat tone that reads seemingly at odds with the bleak social milieu, though it may sound like a publicity cliché, emanates an enthusiasm of the emergent Joseon film world. With this poetic ad, Danseongsa Theatre (Figure 1.1), originally built in 1907 for traditional performing-art spectacles, publicly announced its reopening on 21 December 1918, after a six-month-long renovation to turn it into a theatre solely devoted to film screening. The theatre remained one of the most prominent movie houses in Joseon throughout much of the colonial period until it was sold in 1937 because of financial difficulties. Danseongsa's conversion from a theatre that accommodated various performing arts and occasional film screenings into a permanent film venue at the threshold of the decisive decade of the 1920s is an emblematic

The Beginning: Towards a Mass Entertainment 15

Figure 1.1 The Danseongsa advertisement that announces its reopening as a movie theatre. (*Maeil sinbo*, 21 December 1918)

event that represents a breakthrough, a major one, in the development of film culture in colonial Korea. The reopening of the theatre attests to film's rapidly growing popularity or 'thriving prosperity' in the late 1910s, as a *Maeil sinbo* report put it.[5] Importantly, its film-historical ramifications are far more than a mere statistical matter, and the ad for Danseongsa demonstrates several key changes which took place at the time that would shape the burgeoning Joseon film culture of the following decade: the advent of Korean film patrons, institutionalisation of movie theatres (and film-viewing practices), and overall expansion of the film business. A closer look at the manner in which a theatre space and film-viewing experience are characterised in the ad will illuminate these major changes that triggered the evolution of Joseon cinema.

Seen from a publicity perspective, this ad cannot be a model advertisement because its overly general description of a film-viewing experience does not efficiently articulate the new theatre's distinct merits. Rather it seems to be more concerned with vividly delineating what a film-viewing is like for potential patrons. Indeed, when the theatre opened, there was not much competition for Danseongsa, as one of the only two movie theatres catering for Korean clientele in Seoul. With only one competing theatre to consider, a more imminent challenge seems to be about educating prospective filmgoers about the act of film-spectating inside the theatre building through the meticulous and lyric depiction. Placed in a film-historical context, therefore, the ad leads us to ruminate on an important historical fact. In the second half of the 1910s, movie theatres finally began to emerge, though slowly, as a main site for film consumption, which means a theatre still remained largely new to the majority of the population in Joseon. In this sense, it is not surprising that the ad goes into greater detail in accounting for what a cinema experience is like and promotes the visit to a movie theatre as an unrivalled 'evening's entertainment', employing the term globally used to designate film's rise to a major mass entertainment. In fact, the decade of the 1920s in Joseon not only witnessed the rapid growth of film culture but also the emergence of other new, modern cultural and leisurely activities, such as revues, stage dramas, sports, amusement parks, and expositions. Nonetheless, it was cinema that became the predominant popular culture in colonial Korea; from the 1910s onwards, the popularity of the cinema continued to grow and, towards the end of the colonial period, filmgoers made up half of the entire number of visitors to all entertainment venues.[6] When Danseongsa was converted into a cinema, however, theatre was a new modern cultural institution unavailable to the majority of the population and films were still mostly consumed at temporary or non-theatrical venues. This explains why the delineation of what it is like to watch a movie in a movie theatre becomes the main promotional point the ad highlights.

Another important facet of film culture that the ad demonstrates is that it was targeted specifically to Korean film patrons. With its renovation, Danseongsa became the second movie theatre that served Korean filmgoers after Umigwan Theatre (1913), leading the gradual appearance of movie theatres that catered exclusively to Korean spectators in the 1920s. So-called Korean (K: *Joseonin*) theatres slowly appeared in major cities such as Seoul (Joseon Guekjang, 1922), Daegu (Mangyeonggwan, 1922), Pyongyang (Jeilgwan, 1923), Incheon (Aegwan 1926), and Mokpo (Mokpo Geukjang, 1926). The appearance of these Korean movie houses signalled another significant shift in Joseon cinema. Until the late 1910s, film culture in Joseon was largely developed by Japanese emigrants who built, owned and managed entire movie theatres in Joseon; and, with the exception of Umigwan, all the theatres served Japanese settlers while the film-viewing experience of Korean patrons was principally irregular and fragmentary owing to the absence of a permanent venue for them. In this regard, it was not fortuitous that commercial film production in Joseon took off only with the emergence of a sizeable number of Korean spectators in the early 1920s. Joseon films were produced solely for Korean spectators and thus released only at Korean theatres, not even considering Japanese settlers as their potential viewers. The rise of movie theatres for Korean filmgoers and Joseon films was also associated with the urbanisation during the 1920s, prompting a major migration of the Korean population from the countryside to urban areas. In port cities, such as Gunsan and Mokpo which were developed by Japanese settler merchants, the migration of Koreans in this period altered the structure of the ethnic composition as Koreans began to surpass the number of Japanese settlers, and theatres in these towns and small cities had to find ways to attract these new residents to their theatre originally built to serve Japanese migrants.

This ethnic segregation at movie theatres, which took place in the 1920s, presents us with an important clue in analysing the language of the Danseongsa ad. The contrast between the interior of the cinema space and the exterior of the real world constructed in the ad considerably underscores the escapist nature of film-viewing activities. This effect that the act of film-viewing may offer spectators is nothing unique but what is intriguing is that the ad describes the cinema space not as an escape or distraction from the drudgery of one's everyday life but, instead, as something of an emotional sanctuary where one could momentarily restore her or his troubled inner world. Considering the gloomy social environs at the time, as described at the beginning of the chapter, it is hard to avoid speculation that the illustration of the cinematic experience as an emotional shelter in the Danseongsa ad is somehow related to the harsh realities ('the winter time') Joseon faced at that moment. Whether it be a colonial reality, escalating tensions between Japanese and Koreans, police brutality or ongoing pandemics, the ad promises that the cinema could provide an emotional comfort, however temporary. It is an indication that a film-viewing experience was tethered to what was going on outside the darkened theatre, and the formation of film culture could not be divorced from social realities.

A commonplace of the 1920s in Korean film history has it that this is the crucial period in terms of the foundation of a national cinema because it was the decade that witnessed the beginning of local film production and industry, the earliest masterpieces, and the first film authors and stars. This sort of configuration of the decade's importance in the development of Joseon cinema is based on a historical approach that understands film history primarily as the mode of production. As I have discussed, however, the transformation of Joseon cinema encompassed all aspects of film culture and, in fact, such changes first occurred in film exhibition and distribution. To be more specific, the first major breakthrough for Joseon cinema began not with local film production but with the institutionalisation of movie theatres, the arrival of a massive movie audience, and the collective and regular film-viewing experience that movie theatres made possible. An exploration of the sites of film exhibition, such as movie theatres, movie-going patterns, film fans and spectatorship, and film reception, therefore, must be incorporated into one's observation of the rise of Joseon cinema because the advent of theatres and increase in film patronage were the true catalysts for the start of film production and evolution in the film business. The significance of the 1920s can thereby be sought not only from an increase in film productions but also from the emergence of mass audiences as well as the changes in how films were exhibited, viewed, consumed, and received – in other words, a new way of movie-going and film-viewing activities engendered by movie theatres. The commencement of local film production and discursive developments of Joseon cinema cannot be thoroughly examined without looking closely into the changes that transpired in the overall film culture from the late 1910s onwards.

The main narrative of this book begins from the second half of the 1910s when the film culture underwent a series of changes and cinema began to develop into a prominent form of mass entertainment in Joseon. This chapter looks into the cultural and industrial factors and forces that brought about a major transformation of Joseon film culture in the late 1910s through an examination of various aspects of Joseon film culture, ranging from shifts in film exhibition and distribution practices to the first local film production. To offer a detailed historical background for my exploration of Joseon cinema from this period onwards, the chapter begins with tracing the historical development of early film culture leading up to the reopening of Danseongsa and then further interrogates the changes in Joseon cinema at the dawn of the 1920s which I just discussed concerning the Danseongsa ad. Rather than trying to be merely informative by probing individuals' careers and listing theatres and film venues in their order of appearance, the following discussion critically scrutinises sociopolitical and cultural conditions that influenced the construction of early film culture. Equal attention is given to the collective efforts of early film entrepreneurs and exhibitors in creating film exhibition sites, including movie theatres, defining social and cultural functions of theatre space for a society devoid of an adequate theatre culture, and cultivating film audiences.

The second part of the chapter focuses on another important film historical event that greatly affected the emergent Joseon film culture at this time: the establishment of the first film-making entity. Formed in 1920, the Moving Picture Unit (MPU) of the colonial government began to produce films several years before the start of commercial film production. Owing to its political nature, this governmental film unit has been nearly forgotten in standard colonial film history. As the first film production entity and state-managed film unit of Joseon, however, the MPU made multilayered contributions to the emergent Joseon film culture, from film production to exhibition. Instead of confining the MPU's activities to the fields of politics and governance, therefore, I aim to develop a rich account of the MPU that reconstructs its considerable influence on early formation of colonial film culture. Though my discussion primarily considers the MPU's activities in its early years, I shall also trace the evolution of this prominent governmental film unit throughout the colonial period in my effort to include it in my account of Joseon film culture.

Film Culture Begins: the Development of Early Film Culture

Due to the lack of records, film historians still struggle to reach a consensus with regard to the question of where and when the first film screening took place in Korea but, according to existing documents, film screening began to develop into a form of mass entertainment from 1903 when two theatres, Hyeobryulsa and East Gate Moving Picture Site (*Dongdaemun Hwaldongsajinso*), built up a rivalry. When the latter initiated film screening, the former also acquired a film projector and included a motion picture in its programme; and, according to a newspaper report, the two theatres attracted 'waves of spectators'.[7] Upon this rivalry, *The Korean Review*, an English journal published by American Methodist's Korean Church, reported, 'It may not be generally known that along with other products of modern civilization, such as electric lights and cars, two railroads, postal and telegraph services, &c. [sic], Seoul rejoices in a theatre. On the evening of Buddha's birthday, a very popular holiday in Korea, an amusing conflict occurred between two of these enlightening forces.'[8] The journal then related in full detail that the Seoul Electric Company, which managed East Gate Moving Picture Site, had requested the loan of the troupe of acrobats from Hyeobryulsa but the latter declined the request as it had also planned a show that night, and that evening, while the troupe performed on the Hyeobryulsa stage, the electric lights 'happened to' go out.[9] Though the rivalry was abruptly ended when the government banned Hyeobryulsa from programming any entertainment for fear of the theatre's ill effects on the public, the two theatres were immensely popular among early Korean spectators. This rivalry was somewhat unavoidable as the two theatres were actually the only two theatres Korea had in 1903. Established in 1902, Hyeobryulsa was Korea's first permanent indoor theatre and East Gate Moving Picture Site was developed from a promotion screening that Hanseong (Seoul) Electric Company held at the company's warehouse outside the East Gate in June 1903. Before these two theatres which occasionally projected films, there was no single permanent indoor theatre in Korea.

My account of film culture for the first two decades in Korea starts with this historical absence of a mass entertainment venue, as it fundamentally directed the formation of film culture in pre-colonial and colonial Korea. When looking into Joseon film culture, it is difficult to miss the dearth of film and entertainment venues. Noticing the scarce number of movie theatres in Japan and its colonies, for instance, a Hollywood trade journal reported that the colony Joseon only had around thirty-five movie theatres while Japan had 1,413 cinemas as of 1932.[10] The report continued that the number of movie theatres in Japan was very small compared to other industrialised countries, as it represented one theatre for fifty thousand people, and contended that this shortage of film venues had become one of the major obstructions that had hindered the development of film culture in Japan. But the situation in Joseon was even worse. Considering the Korean population (twenty million), which was approximately one-third of the Japanese population (sixty-five million), thirty-five movie theatres meant one cinema for about 600,000 people. Movie theatres appeared at an extremely slow rate in Korea, and it took more than twenty years for a theatre to become a major site of film consumption. The number of theatres only began to increase sharply around 1940, reaching close to two hundred,[11] when the colonial administration built small theatres that accommodated one to two hundred audience members for screenings of propaganda films and wartime newsreels. Travelling exhibitors wandering all across the peninsula to screen films for residents in areas without a theatre and special screenings organised by newspaper companies, religious groups, various social organisations, and governmental offices were still the chief methods of experiencing the wondrous world of movies for many, and both practices continued to exist throughout the colonial period, and even after the Korean War in the 1950s. (Figure 1.2)

Figure 1.2 Audiences gathered at mobile film screenings (*sunhoe yeongsa*) organised by a newspaper company to watch a newsreel that documented the disastrous flood which swept Joseon in 1934. Screenings were held at a youth association centre, a school playground and a park (left to right).
(*Donga ilbo*, 29 July 1934)

One of the obvious reasons why Joseon had such a small number of movie theatres is the unstable political and economic state of Joseon as a colony, and this affected not only the growth of the film business but the culture industry overall. The unusual scarcity and considerably delayed development of movie theatres also stemmed from the innate cultural background, that is, the complete absence of a permanent indoor theatre practice in Joseon. In his article 'A Theory on Joseon Cinema', written in 1941, Yim Hwa, a leftist KAPF (Korea Artista Proleta Federatio)[12] writer and literary critic, who contributed to several film productions in the 1930s, discusses a couple of key social and cultural conditions that impeded the early development of cinema. Yim notes:

> But the bigger problem lies in the weak stage drama tradition . . . the stage drama was the most fundamental base that nurtured the first phase of film medium, and the fact that the stage has the weakest tradition among all the artistic forms is one of the crucial cultural conditions that delayed film production in Joseon.[13]

Yim's argument, which singles out the weak stage tradition as the most pressing issue the development of Joseon cinema faced, illuminates how much the lack of stage tradition affected film production, style, and even the course of film history. Indeed, the performing arts and stage drama were never considered nor institutionalised as legitimate art forms for hundreds of years in Korea because they were seen rather as indecent forms of lowbrow entertainment. Social abhorrence against the performing arts during the Joseon dynasty, built on the ideals of orthodox Confucianism, was so strong that a theatre did not even exist. As a result, the absence of stage tradition influenced not only filmmaking, as Yim points out, but also the ways in which movies were exhibited and consumed. As I briefly mentioned earlier, before Hyeobryulsa opened in 1902, the national theatre run by the government, there was no single permanent indoor theatre in Korea. In this regard, it was not just the cinema that Korea imported but theatre per se came together with film as a brand new cultural institution. All theatres, including movie theatres, were newly built, most of them established only after Japan colonised Korea. Therefore, before movie theatres competitively appeared around 1920, the movie-going experience was not really tied to theatres but occurred at various sites which were not typically associated with film, and was often limited to a small group of spectators. Going to movie theatres which offered regular film programmes and mingling with strangers from an array of social backgrounds were experiences few Koreans had known before the 1920s.

In the absence of the theatre culture, early film screening replicated the traditional practices of performing arts exhibition. Until 1902, when Korea's first theatre opened, Korea had only temporary outdoor theatres – traditionally, public spaces were temporarily turned into performing spaces. There was no national theatre, either. Instead, dance and other performances for the aristocrats and the royal family were held at gardens and courtyards inside imperial palaces which were turned into open, outdoor, and temporary theatres only on special occasions. Traditional Korean theatre scholar Sa Jin-sil categorises these temporary outdoor theatre spaces for the performing arts into four distinctive performance spaces that were formed towards the end of the Joseon dynasty.[14] According to Sa, all these spaces functioned as temporary performing spaces only for special occasions; they were divided by the nature of the audience and the physical conditions of the spaces; and the characteristics of spaces and audiences were essentially tied to the class and social background of the audience members. Sa names each space according to the degree of openness to the audience, and labels the first of the four spaces as 'the closed performance space' which was the royal palace. Sa explains that royal courtyards at imperial palaces were used for various performances by musicians and female dancers who were hired exclusively for the government to celebrate national events or feasts for royal family members. Performances at this closed performance space, as the name itself suggests, had extremely limited numbers of people in attendance with pre-designated seats in keeping with attendees' official ranks and social positions. The next type of space, 'the semi-closed performance space', was also associated with the royal family but what distinguishes this space from the closed space was its slightly broader audience as well as its location. The performances at the semi-closed space were held to show off publicly the kings' dignity during selected national events near the palaces. Though members of the audience were controlled, ordinary people could enjoy the performances as they were intended as an opportunity for the public recognition of the kings' power. The third space, 'the semi-open performance space', was organised by government officials and aristocrats when they threw personal and official parties or feasts. Though shows featuring dances and singing were hosted by upper-class people for their entertainment, people outside this class – servants, maids, helpers and just onlookers – were allowed to enjoy the shows, even though invitations were not officially extended. Lastly, there was 'the open performance space'. Held in an open public space, typically a marketplace, travelling troupes of performers delivered unscheduled performances in front of random audiences, mostly composed of middle- or lower-class persons. These types of shows, which featured mask dance, circus, acrobatics, and singing, did not have fixed entry fees. Instead, audiences decided how much money they were willing to pay based on their own judgement of the quality of the show.

For nearly two decades after the arrival of cinema, film screening and viewing in Korea/Joseon largely followed these four distinctive open-theatre patterns because of the extremely limited availability of permanent theatres and other venues for public gathering. More specifically, the class segregation that characterised each and the different performance types and spaces or their degree of open-ness with regard to their intended audiences are what defined film-viewing experiences in early film culture. Concerning film spectatorship, early cinema historians tend to associate the first decade of film history mainly with working-class audiences. As many scholarly works demonstrate, for instance, in the United States film was a popular and cheap entertainment geared mainly towards the working class and immigrants until the mid-1910s when the film industry sought to expand and 'upgrade' its patrons by way of producing sophisticated epics, spectacles, and features with complex narratives as well as introducing new theatre venues such as lavish movie palaces. In Korea, however, the new medium attracted people of different social and class strata because film was not a simple entertainment but the very distillate of Western modernity, an 'astonishing development of Westerners' scientific technology',[15] that piqued the curiosity of people of all social status. The immense interest did not quickly turn the cinema into an entertainment for mass consumption because of the unavailability of proper venues and peoples' indifference to a modern form of entertainment. Instead, early film culture was largely monopolised by the aristocrats, the affluent, and government officials who could afford the expense and effort involved in film screening. Newspaper reports on early film exhibition before the 1910s abound in these individuals who personally purchased a film camera/projector and arranged film screenings at their residences to entertain their guests or to educate the general public. Yet there were even more traditionalists who thought of the theatre as a symbol of modern (and Western) decadence, where people came to enjoy lowly performing arts. This resistance towards modern cultural venues, coupled with traditional denouncement of the performing arts, continued to hamper the institutionalisation of theatre as well as the development of film culture. Hyeobryulsa ceased to programme any kind of entertainment, including film screening, for example, because of the demands from officials and intellectuals who feared the detrimental effect on the public of Korea's first theatre; and, when the government tried to reopen it in 1906, the effort was met by public outcry against the motion. Therefore, in the first decade of film culture, the series of special screenings were held at a controlled, exclusive space for extremely limited members of audiences.

The most distinctive form of screening exemplifying the exclusivity of film screening is that hosted inside the royal palace. Following their stage or dance-viewing tradition, the emperor and royal family arranged special screenings and brought in screening crews into the palaces rather than venturing out to movies. The earliest record of this kind of film screening at the palace dates back to circa 1899. A Chicago-born traveller Elias Burton Holmes (1870–1958), the inventor of the travelogue, who travelled around the world and gave lectures on his travels with vast numbers of photos and films he shot, published his travelogues, *The Burton Holmes Lectures*, in 1901. In the tenth volume of *The Burton Holmes Lectures*, which documents his trips to Korea and Japan, Holmes recounts an anecdote related to a film screening for Emperor Gojong.

We entertain His Highness [Prince Lee Jae-sun] with our portable machine for showing miniature motion-pictures, the like of which he has never seen before. He grows enthusiastic and begs us to allow him to take the instrument to the palace to show it to the Emperor. We gladly acquiesce, and after teaching him how to operate the instrument, we resume our tramp through the suburban villages and along the country roads all submerged in sunshine.[16]

As for the new palace, where the Emperor now lives, venturing out only once or twice a year, we gained admission to its precincts through the influence of our little motion-picture machine. As I have already told you, it was taken to be shown to the Emperor by the 'Fat Prince', Ye Chai Soon [Lee Jae-sun]. It was retained two days at the palace and sent back in the dead of night by imperial messengers, who came with torches and lanterns through the streets, roused the hotel, and delivered the magic-box accompanied by several presents from his Majesty, including twenty yards of rich green silk and half a dozen fans, together with an explanation of the delay, due to the fact that the baby prince, youngest son of the Emperor and actual palace tyrant, had been fascinated by the toy and had wept when they attempted to take it from him, falling asleep still gripping it firmly in his chubby hands.[17]

The story of Holmes's 'magic-box' continues as 'the Fat Prince' asks him to see it again, and this small projector finally ends up being Holmes's gift for the baby prince. It is difficult to determine whether the screening involving Holmes's projector at the palace was the first movie experience for the Emperor Gojong but Holmes's travelogue is the oldest existing record that recounts a story of film screening at the palace – the closed screening space – and also the imperial members' fascination with movies. From the first decade of 1900 throughout the 1910s, newspapers continually reported screenings held at the royal palaces or 'the emperor's moving picture viewing' (K: *hwaldong sajin eoram*; J: *katsudō shashin goran*),[18] detailing the time, space, attendants, projectors, and often a brief introduction of films screened. The reports indicate that these screenings were done solely for the emperor and other royal family members.[19] Royal families often invited guests over to the palace and enjoyed movies with them. The following newspaper item minutely reconstructs how this slightly different type of screening at the palace, as it were, a screening at the semi-closed space, was held.

The Korean Headquarters of the Patriotic Housewives' Association received an order from the Deoksu Palace and watched films with His Majesty at the Dondeok Royal Court from 8pm on the 15th, and about a hundred, including His Highness and Her Highness, royal families, cabinet members, and female officials, joined the screening. As His Highness sat on his chair, wearing formal Korean attire, at 8 sharp, the head of the Headquarters explained, and Mr Seo Byeong-hyeop translated, such films as the training of firefighters, brothers in a snow storm, war in the Japan Sea, army drills, and some comedies. They also screened a film that documents the Royal Prince and Jukjeon Prince playing with ducks and fish in the Binri Palace and another documentary that shows the Royal Prince's trip with the demised Mr Itō [Itō Hirobumi] to the northeast region. His Majesty was very satisfied and every time film reels were being changed, His Majesty had pleasant conversations with others sitting next to him. The screening was over at 10pm, and people were served teas and cookies at a guest room as they left the screening.[20]

This record demonstrates that Gojong, now dethroned, and the imperial family hosted a special screening for a slightly bigger audience and employed it for the opportunity to socialise with people from outside the palace. Though the screenings in this case still occurred within the royal palaces for selected audiences, they were organised by royal family members in order to intermingle with 'ordinary' people and display their authority and dignity. With regard to 'showing off' the royal dignity, it is important to note the critical function of the media as these kinds of special screenings at semi-closed and at closed spaces were usually reported by newspapers so that the royal dignity could reach many more people.[21] In this manner, film screenings at imperial palaces had become an integral part of Korean royal court culture. This exclusive movie-viewing practice, specific to royal family members and a small group of invited guests, continued until Sunjong, the last emperor of the Korean Empire, whose favourite pastimes included moving pictures and billiards, died in 1926.[22] The practice of screening with a specific agenda for limited audience members became institutionalised over time. Diverse social and governmental organisations and individuals arranged special screenings for promotional and, more frequently, educational purposes. These screenings were sometimes limited to members of a specific organisation but, more commonly, they were open to the general public. These types of film screenings were held at various locales, including office spaces, performing arts theatres, schools, lecture halls, private residences, parks, and so on. Complementing commercial film exhibitions, these special screenings, hosted by various entities, continued until the early 1940s when the Office of the Governor General banned the use of the Korean language and implemented strict regulations regarding public exhibitions and social gatherings.

While the exclusive form of screening dominated the way films were screened and consumed for the first decades of film culture, screenings for the general public took place intermittently. The first commercial and public screening in

Joseon was a promotional event for Hanseong Electric Company in 1903. This first electric firm was initially founded in January 1898 as a joint-venture enterprise between American businessmen Henry Collbran and H. R. Bostwick and the Korean royal family. In December, the company began the construction of a single-track tramline operating between the West Gate and Hongneung, a mausoleum where the emperor's beloved late queen was buried, in Seoul. The opening ceremony for this first tramline in Asia was held on 17 May 1899, and the company completed its first power plant towards the end of the same year. The tram became a public attraction but incessant horrific accidents scared off people, and many were fearful of electricity as an apparition, calling the tram a monster craving human blood. As a result, the tram business was much slower than anticipated. To make matters worse, Collbran, who had taken advantage of the Korean government's unfamiliarity with international law when they documented the deal, constantly threatened the emperor to make up for the company's deficit; and the emperor finally gave up his shares and handed the company over to Collbran, as he feared unpleasant diplomatic tensions with the United States. This scandal infuriated the Korean public. Recognising Koreans' enmity towards him, Collbran created an amusement department in his company and then held a series of circus shows and operated a merry-go-round to promote his trams and electricity business and also to subdue the Koreans' escalating hostility against him. On 24 June 1903, the company placed an advertisement in *Hwangseong sinmun* to publicise its brand-new promotional event which featured the screening of motion pictures at the company's power plant.[23] *The Korean Review* reports on this monumental film screening in detail as follows:

> It is a pleasure to report the great success that certain members of the Electric Company are meeting with in entertaining the public. Two of the gentlemen connected with the Company have recently purchased an expensive Stereopticon and Moving Pictures Machine. Beginning about the middle of June they have been giving first-class exhibitions nightly from 8:30 to 10 on the grounds of the Company at the East Gate. The admission fee has been set at the modest sum of 10 cents Korean (about 3 cents US currency), so that all, even the poorest, might enjoy the show. A box car, made comfortable with car cushions, is run out on a switch to serve as a 'private box' for the foreigners who attend. Over 1100 tickets were sold at one exhibition.[24]

According to this account, the event combined magic lantern slides with film screening, a typical pattern of early film exhibition that programmed short films with other forms of entertainment. A spectator who attended this event later recollected that much of the programme was a magic lantern show, only several short films were screened near the very end, and he and other spectators had had a hard time understanding the content of both slides and films as no narrator was present and no explanation was given.[25] Another important piece of information which deserves our attention here is that, even though the films were screened at the company's power plant where trams were parked, American event organisers tried to replicate a theatre space within the power plant, creating designated seats for their special guests ('a private box'). Those who attended this film screening, therefore, encountered the film and, at the same time, first experienced what it was like being in a 'theatre' as they mingled with huge crowds and even with 'special spectators' (foreigners) whom they would probably not meet in other locations. Yuri Tsivian, in his classical study of social reception of early cinema in Russia, demonstrates that early film patrons were fascinated not just by the films alone but also by the exhibition environment which collectively contributed to the overall impression of cinema.[26] Going to a movie, in this regard, became a dual cultural experience that allowed early Korean spectators to experience films and the theatre space (or its replica) simultaneously, influencing their perception of two modern cultural institutions and their intertwinement.

This promotional film screening, however, did not quite change the public view on Collbran and his company, as public protests against the company continued even after the screening.[27] Even though Koreans were seriously concerned about the invasion of foreign capital and imperial aggression, as Collbran's case shows, it seems that they could not resist the powerful allure of movies. The power plant was eventually turned into a temporary movie theatre known as East Gate Moving Picture Site that occasionally screened movies. It later became Gwangmudae in 1907, a makeshift theatre; and, in the next year, American Korean Electric Co. sold the management of the theatre to Park Seulpil, who later rose to be one of the most influential film exhibitors as the manager of Danseongsa.

Commercialisation of Film Screening and Emergence of the Movie Theatre

Commercial film screenings for the general public finally began in 1907 when Korea saw its first professional film exhibitor, L. Martin. Unfortunately, nothing specific is known about this French film exhibitor but there remain newspaper reports and advertisements that include the location of the temporary movie theatre he managed near Seoso Gate in Seoul's central area, the film programmes – mostly French Pathé shorts – admission fees, and the screening hours.[28] Japanese entrepreneurs soon started their film-related businesses around this time, building theatres, distributing and exhibiting films, and selling film stock and equipment, and it was these Japanese settlers who systematically developed film exhibition into a commercial business. Towards the end of the decade, the Japanese built more theatres for kabuki, *yose*, and *shimpa* in Japanese residential areas to serve their fellow settlers and, finally, in 1910, Korea's first movie theatre, the Gyeongseong (Seoul) High Entertainment Theatre (K: Gyeongseong Godeung Yeonyegwan), was established by Japanese settlers in Kogane-machi (today's Second Euljiro Street), a borderline area between the Korean and Japanese residential areas in Seoul. The High Entertainment Theatre was a two-storey building whose second floor had Japanese tatami mats and whose first floor had only a small number of seats; thereby, the majority of the audience watched movies while standing. The theatre could accommodate six hundred people but, because most of the spectators had no seat, attendance was always over capacity, sometimes reaching an astonishing two thousand spectators. Its patrons were a mixture of Koreans and Japanese which was quite unusual as the separation between Korean and Japanese movie theatres was soon to begin with the establishment of theatres geared towards each ethnic group by the mid-1910s. Its programmes, predominantly French Pathé shorts, changed approximately every four days.[29] Over the next two years, two more movie theatres, Taishōkan (K: Daejeonggwan, 1912) and Koganekan (K: Hwanggeumgwan, 1913), were introduced specifically for Japanese audiences. These three early movie theatres were all owned by the Japanese which demonstrates the pivotal role of settlers in the advent of movie theatres and overall film culture in Joseon.[30] In the meantime, Umigwan, the first cinema targeting Korean audiences, opened in December 1912. The owner was Japanese settler Hayashida Kinjiro who ran Hayashida Trading Company based in Seoul.[31] Umigwan was even bigger than The High Entertainment Theatre, with a capacity of one thousand spectators but, when it was packed, the theatre could accommodate up to seventeen hundred viewers.[32] Unlike the other three movie theatres, which featured Japanese movies as a main attraction, Umigwan's programme consisted mainly of American and European films,[33] as the theatre sought to entertain Korean filmgoers. While the majority of movie theatres were concentrated in Seoul, other cities began to recognise the new entertainment. Finally, around 1915, the film culture took off as mass entertainment when multiple numbers of movie theatres opened in other major cities and enjoyed 'a booming business' as reported in 1916 by the Joseon correspondent for the Japanese film journal *Kinema Record*.[34]

Almost all the theatres and movie houses at the time, with the exception of Umigwan, were built and run by Japanese settlers primarily for their fellow settlers and were located in major cities. One intriguing exception to this trend which is worth noting is Geumganggwan Theatre (1913) in Gongju County (Gongju City today) of South Chungcheong Province. Geumganggwan was the first theatre built neither by the government nor by foreigners but by a Korean individual. When compared to other cities and towns which housed the earliest theatres for occasional film screenings or movie theatres in the 1910s, Gongju stands out. Unlike other cities, Gongju was a small rural county with only about ten thousand residents in 1913.[35] Thus, it is difficult to imagine that the theatre could yield decent revenue or present entertainment on a regular basis but what is important here is that the theatre was not built merely for commercial purposes. Kim Gap-sun, the owner of the theatre, was a self-made businessman who had served as a high-ranking official of the central government before the colonial period and continued to expand his business as a real estate developer, rising as one of the wealthiest men in Joseon. He built Geumganggwan as a philanthropic work for his community and the theatre functioned as more than an entertainment site. As the sole public space in the county, it was used as a venue for film, stage drama and performing arts and also functioned as a civic centre in which a range of community events was held. This multiple function assumed by the theatre is one of the defining qualities that characterised the essential nature of not only movie theatres but any kind of theatre in colonial Korea. Owing to the shortage of the institutionalised public sphere, public service was one of the important expected purposes of the movie theatre, serving the communities' interests. Even theatres in major cities, such as Danseongsa and Umigwan, were used for public events but the public function was particularly crucial for the cinemas located in smaller towns and rural areas where social institutions were rare.[36]

Becoming a Mass Entertainment

The rapid growth of the film business in Joseon in the latter half of the 1910s was impelled by the changes in the film distribution and exhibition systems. The first experiment with film production finally began in the early 1920s with the local production of chain drama, actualities and, eventually, theatrical fiction films which were made to capitalise on an increasing number of Korean patrons at cinemas. Commercial production became possible only after the film world cultivated a sizeable Korean film patron base. In this sense, it seems inevitable that those who first seriously explored film production were exhibitors and theatre owners/managers who produced the films as a sort of promotional measure to lure more Korean spectators into movie theatres. Danseongsa's Park Seung-pil, for instance, commissioned Kim Do-san Theatre Group in 1919 to shoot *Loyal Vengeance*, a short film for its chain drama, and *A View of Seoul City* (*Gyeongseongui gyeong*), an actuality that featured Seoul. Premiered at Danseongsa, these two films are deemed by many as the first Korean films. After witnessing the explosive responses to the Kim Do-san group's shorts and other chain dramas that followed, Hayakawa Jōtaro, a Japanese settler, who emerged as a major player in the Joseon film and entertainment world as the head of Hayakawa Entertainment from the early 1910s, realised the potential of Joseon films; in 1923, Hayakawa produced the fiction film *Tale of Chun-hyang* (*Chun-hyang jeon*) which became a phenomenal hit. With the success of these films, commercial film production finally took off in colonial Korea.

Yim Hwa notes in his essay discussed earlier that 'the moving picture phase' may not exist in Joseon film history because the first Joseon films were produced when the global film business was already in the process of maturing into the so-called evening's entertainment phase and a major form of mass entertainment, moving well past the one-reeler, cheap entertainment phase.[37] This statement appears to be a proper assessment of Joseon cinema's seemingly unorthodox development but still misses the point that the earliest film production of Joseon was first explored by exhibitors in a manner largely the same as other national cinemas' moving-picture phase; in fact, movie theatres continued to be deeply involved in film production in Joseon as late as the mid-1930s when germinal efforts to establish a studio system began to appear. Until then, neither production companies nor exhibitors possessed enough financial capabilities to develop a film studio. This situation left film-makers no choice but to maintain their close alliance with exhibitors who remained their major sponsors. In this sense, Joseon cinema did not necessarily skip the moving-picture phase but, rather, some of the practices that defined this early phase lasted longer than elsewhere.

The zealous responses to the first Joseon films soon drew new private investors to form the first film firms. Joseon Kinema, the first film production company opened in 1923, exemplifies yet another major turn in Joseon cinema. Established by four Japanese settler merchants who had no film background, this joint-stock company began its film production in the city of Busan. The era of commercial, independent film firms was finally inaugurated with Joseon Kinema. What is neglected in history, however, is that those who first recognised the potential of locally produced films were not commercial exhibitors but the colonial government. Institutionalised film production in Joseon, as a matter of fact, had started a few years earlier with the establishment of the Moving Picture Unit of the Office of the Governor General (K: *Hwaldong sajinban*; J: *Katsudō shashinhan*) that produced, distributed and exhibited propaganda and educational films. Formed in 1920 as one of the primary measures taken by the new Saitō Makoto administration for its reformist efforts, the Moving Picture Unit was the first film production entity Joseon ever saw.

Film Production Begins: Moving Picture Unit of the Office of the Governor General

It does not take long speculation to realise that the major reforms in colonial rule which ensued after the 1919 Independent Movement considerably affected the burgeoning Joseon cinema and its subsequent development. I shall discuss,

The Beginning: Towards a Mass Entertainment 31

therefore, whenever relevant in the following chapters, how these changes in administration, policies and legislation which occurred at the time interacted with the film culture. This section focuses on the more direct and immediate consequences the reform in colonial governance brought to Joseon cinema: the birth of the Moving Picture Unit of the Office of the Governor General (MPU hereafter). Cultural Rule (K: *munhwa tongchi*; J:*bunka seiji* or *bunka tōchi*), the new administration's governing strategy, was introduced in 1919 after the Independent Movement sent shock waves to Japan, to 'set up a foundation for what we call a civilised governance'[38] by replacing the Militant Rule of the previous administrations. The brute violence the Hasegawa regime had resorted to in order to subdue the demonstrations drew both domestic and international criticism, and the Hara Satoshi administration of Japan saw the coercive militant rule of the Terauchi Masatake (1910–16) and Hasegawa (1916–19) administrations not only as an inadequate governing strategy but one of the actual causes for the Joseon crisis. In tandem with the Taishō democracy of Japan that witnessed the augmentation of party politics and a bureaucrat-centred administration, Prime Minister Hara decided completely to overhaul the existing administration in Joseon by placing bureaucrats, instead of army officials, at the centre of governance. As the first step, Saitō Makoto, a navy admiral, was appointed Joseon's new governor general, and he was the first (and last) head of colonial government who was not an army general, an arrangement meant to reduce the excessive intervention of the army into the colonial governance.[39] The first task of the Saitō administration (1919–27)[40] was to implement a new governing method that better reflected the Hara administration's philosophy of ethnic assimilation for the colonial governance, which aimed to turn Joseon into 'an extension of Japan (*naichi*)'[41] as if it were a region of Japan, not just an overseas colony. Among the new policies and legislation introduced to carry out this major reform, a new administrative strategy, which directly influenced the decision to create a film unit, was the emphasis on propaganda. The campaign of 'Dissemination and Publicity' (J: *shūchi to senden*) was central to the Saitō administration's reform, as Saitō and his administration were convinced that the lack of mutual understanding between the empire and the colony was the root cause of the Korean resistance movements, as well as the previous colonial administration's failures. They saw the achievement of, and increase in, communications between the empire and colony as the key to success in integrating Japan and Joseon. Accordingly, the colonial government formed a variety of committees, units and offices to explore diverse methods and possibilities that could cement the relations between the colonisers and colonised and also properly inform people in Joseon, Japan, and beyond of the ideals of its reform plans. This entailed various forms of promotional efforts, including the use of media. In August 1920, the Office of the Governor General (OGG hereafter) unveiled its plan to convey the Joseon situation regularly and in a timely manner to Japan through pamphlets, posters, lectures and films. In particular, it hurriedly assigned a special extra budget item line to produce promotional films, an astonishing sum of 8,000 yen (roughly 4,000 dollars), with a plan to allot annually a budget for this specific purpose from that point on which allowed its film unit, established in April earlier that year, to make its first film.[42] The MPU was soon brought under the supervision of the Information Committee (J: *Jyōhō iinkai*; K: *Jeongbo wiwonhoe*) created in December 1920 to 'introduce Joseon affairs to Japan proper and foreign countries, and to introduce Japanese affairs to Joseon' and to propagate its administrative affairs.[43] Thus began the MPU, the first film production entity of Joseon.

Owing to its explicitly political nature, the MPU has been placed at the verge of film history and its films and activities have not received serious scrutiny. In the light of the slow development of cinema in Joseon, the Saitō administration's employment of cinema was radical enough to receive scholarly attention, albeit limited, but has been probed in complete separation from Joseon film culture and largely dismissed as a simple political manoeuvre.[44] The MPU's relationship to overall Joseon film culture, however, should not be pushed aside just because of the obvious political function of this film entity. Its extensive influence on the emergent Joseon cinema, ranging from film production to exhibition, as well as its film-historical implications in global film history invite more critical attention on the activities of the MPU. In fact, the film unit turned out to be the most prolific film-making entity in Joseon and became the sole film production organisation that survived for more than two decades until the end of colonial rule, producing more films than any other film company, studio or unit of colonial Korea. Most importantly, because the film unit appeared when Joseon cinema was undergoing a major advance, its activities influenced the burgeoning film culture at all levels, as I shall elaborate in the pages that follow. In addition, the historical significance which the MPU bears is not just confined to Korean film history. The MPU was the first governmental film production unit in the entire Japanese Empire, predating any film unit run by major governmental entities such as the Ministry of Education (1923),[45] Ministry of Agriculture (1923), and Ministry of Railway (1924) in Japan.[46] The colonial government of Taiwan produced its first propaganda piece in 1924, and the much-researched South Manchurian Railway Company's film unit (*Minamimanshū Tetsudō Kabushikigaisha eigaban*) was created in 1923 initially to make promotional movies and travelogues and then to produce newsreels and cultural films (*bunka eiga*) later in the 1930s. The MPU produced more films than any other governmental offices; by 1937, the MPU had produced 222 films while the two most prolific government film units of the Ministry of Education and Ministry of Railway had made 162 and 149 respectively.⁴⁷ Despite its seminal position in the state-managed film activities in the Japanese Empire, however, the MPU has been neglected in Japanese film history. Given that the so-called educational film (*kyōiku eiga*), including wartime propaganda and social edifice films, is a finely researched subject in Japanese film studies, the invisibility of the film business of the colonial government of Joseon in Japanese film historical accounts is quite noticeable. This lacuna is illustrative of postcolonial film historical tendencies that engage with drawing a boundary between Japanese and Korean national cinemas and actively playing down the intertwined early film histories. On this tendency to disavow the interwoven histories between the empire and its colonies in Japanese historiography, Leo Ching notes that Japanese historians tend to focus on Japanese imperialism as a problem of Japan in their attempts to understand the origins and failures of Japan's imperial enterprise. 'Precisely because the defeat of Japanese militarism occurred at the hands of Allied forces and not under the pressure of its empire's disintegration', Ching writes, 'the questions did not concern the universal validity of enlightenment or rationality', and thus 'the exigent concern was not that of Japan's relationship to its decolonised "others", but to itself'.⁴⁸ It is this historical perspective that dominates post-war Japanese film historiography, accounting for the limited efforts to engage with the colonial cinemas and especially the noticeable lack of attention to the complex associations between colonial film-making in Japan's former colonies and the concept of Japanese national cinema. According to this historiographical perspective, any form of film production in colonial Korea, including that of the colonial administration, is an issue of Korean cinema and the subject for Korean film studies which really do not concern Japanese film history.

Orphaned between the dismissal and negligence of Korean and Japanese film historians because of its place in a now-defunct contact zone between the two national cinemas, the MPU's significance in film history has never garnered serious attention. The MPU, as a matter of fact, was not only the first of its kind in the Japanese Empire but the first film-production unit established by any colonial government across the globe. Most imperial powers explored the use of cinema for educational and propaganda purposes in their colonies but none could compete with Imperial Japan which most vigorously mobilised the cinema for its colonial governance. For example, the British Empire's utilisation of film in its colonies is well known and quite extensively studied⁴⁹ but its colonial film enterprise was launched much later than the Japanese Empire's film units. The British Empire intermittently produced educational films for colonial populations from as early as 1920. But it was not until 1939 when the Colonial Film Unit, the first film-making unit managed by the colonial government in

Africa, was formed to produce educational and propaganda films for African populations, primarily in an attempt to mobilise them to join the empire's war efforts. Even the Bantu, the precursor to the Colonial Film Unit, produced its first film no earlier than 1935. The Film and Photo Bureau of the Belgian government, another significant example of imperial film production, was founded even later, in 1949, to produce films intended for the Congolese. Despite its rich film-making tradition, France did not even entertain the idea of employing the cinema for its colonial administration but, instead, Paris vehemently discouraged any kind of film-making activities in the colonies – including even location shootings pursued by French film-makers – as it feared the adverse effects it might bring to its colonial governance if the colonised learned to make films and raise their voices through this powerful medium.[50]

For its various film historical significances, the film unit of the colonial government of Joseon deserves a chapter not only in Joseon cinema history but also in global film history. To unveil the forgotten presence of the MPU, I shall discuss in detail the specific political context from which the MPU emerged and frame the birth of the film unit in the contexts of both Korean and Japanese film traditions and histories, especially trying to introduce the MPU into the discourses and politics of propaganda and educational film. This attempt allows us to integrate the role and function of the MPU into the burgeoning film culture in Joseon and to develop a more inclusive picture of Joseon cinema. This does not imply a disregard for the political nature of this official film unit but frees the critical analysis from merely binding it to political intentions and effects in order to explore its more multifarious film-cultural and film-historical implications. Most importantly, the beginning of the MPU cannot be comprehended solely with the colonial government's political considerations. Historians of colonial Korea who take notice of the Saitō administration's employment of cinema, however, tend to expound the MPU merely as a propaganda vehicle for new governing strategies, failing to explain why the colonial government decided to turn to the cinema as their main propaganda medium in the first place. This is an important question which has never been asked despite the contradiction that film had not even reached the majority of the Korean population at the time. The containment of the MPU to the realm of politics is yet another case that foregrounds the political condition as the sole determinant in assessing colonial culture. By reducing film history to a matter of politics, this sort of historical perspective proves to be problematically ahistorical, as it fails to situate the MPU at the more convoluted juncture among film history and culture, film-technological development, and the colonial milieu out of which the MPU was born. In addition, while the authorities' control of film practices, the state-sponsored films, and Korean film-makers' collaborations with the empire during the final years of colonial rule have been exhaustively studied and well recognised, little is known about the authorities' film enterprise prior to the 1940s. My effort to trace the MPU's development, therefore, begins with properly placing the film unit in a historical context.

Educational Uses of Visual Media in Japan and Joseon

There exists much evidence that demonstrates the authorities' interest in film even before the MPU. The earliest example would be the 1908 documentary *Tour of Korea* (J: *Kankokukan* or *Kankoku itshū*; K: *Hangukgwan*) which recorded the trip of the crown prince of Korea and Itō Hirobumi, the resident general of Korea (1905–9), across Korea.[51] The documentary was shot and distributed by Yokoda Shōkai, premiered at the Kinkikan Theatre in Tokyo for public viewing in 1908, and screened for the royal family of Korea at the palace in Seoul a few years later.[52] In 1915, the Railway Bureau of the OGG commissioned the Kansai branch of Japan's Nikkatsu Studio to shoot a promotional documentary featuring the 1915 Trade Fair held in Seoul.[53] In the meantime, several educational films were commissioned by the Taiwanese colonial government in the 1910s; the government sponsored the Patriotic Women's Association to make a couple of propaganda films in the mid-1910s. Thus, films were sporadically made by the authorities in Joseon as well as in Taiwan. But a more conspicuous example that exhibits the authorities' keen interest in employing visual media for educational and propaganda purposes in pre-colonial Korea and the colony Joseon is the magic lantern slide show.

Magic lantern shows started in Korea in the 1890s,[54] and the use of magic lantern slides for social edifice began as early as 1906, a year after Korea became the protectorate of Japan. Min Won-sik, a high-ranking official of Home Affairs personally bought a stereopticon and hosted magic lantern shows in Seoul in 1906 for public sanitary education.[55] Around the same time, the Bureau of Agriculture, Commerce, and Industry organised a magic lantern show for agricultural education and, in the following year, it dispatched a magic lantern unit to more than ten rural communities to introduce up-to-date agricultural technologies to farmers.[56] From 1908, magic lantern shows became widely available because they were held for both private and public entertainment. The magic lantern was favoured as a major educational and propagandistic medium not only by the authorities but also by religious and social reformist groups. In fact, employing magic lantern slides for instructional purposes was not specific to Korea; by the time it arrived in Korea, it had already been deemed an effective instructional tool across the globe.[57] The magic lantern show's format, combining slides with a lecture, enabled it to become a popular educational medium because it allowed lecturers to use still visual images to complement their lectures, making it easier for them to engage the audience. Though used for various types of education, instruction, public lectures, and propaganda, the magic lantern was most frequently employed for the purpose of sanitary education for the general public in Joseon. As mentioned in the earlier section, Joseon of the 1910s was plagued by a series of epidemics such as Spanish flu, cholera, typhoid, and pneumonia, and the Department of Sanitation relentlessly produced and screened magic lantern slides to educate the public about the importance of hygiene. Just a couple of months before the MPU began film production, for instance, the Department of Sanitation and the Gyeonggi Province co-produced magic lantern slides and a film about cholera and rented movie theatres in Seoul to screen them;[58] a month later, the department put together a magic lantern unit and dispatched it to arrange slide shows all across the peninsula.[59] At a meeting with the provincial governors held in September 1920, when cholera was still at large, Governor General Saitō praised highly the fact that sanitation education through magic lantern slides proved to be successful but he urged the governors to try other methods such as motion pictures, public lectures, and artwork exhibitions for more effective education of Koreans who 'still had an infantile understanding about sanitation' and often opposed a change in their customs by fervently resisting the authorities' instructions on the importance of sanitation.[60]

Placed in this historical context, the MPU was not entirely 'groundbreaking', nor completely new, because administrators already actively employed visual media for education, social edifice, and policy promotions. The creation of the MPU, however, still marks an important turning point as it indicates that the colonial government now fully embraced visual media and began to develop a centralised system with which it could more thoroughly integrate visual media into the governance. While functioning as the control tower for all kinds of cinematic propaganda activities, the MPU supported governmental offices, regional governments and social organisations to operate their own film units. In terms of media, the introduction of the MPU signalled that the preferred medium for propaganda purposes had now shifted from the magic lantern to film. In fact, film rather suddenly replaced the magic lantern as the main propaganda medium with the arrival of the Saitō administration. While the MPU made more and more films on a range of subjects beginning in the mid-1920s, the number of magic lantern shows arranged by the authorities fell sharply within just a couple of years after the MPU's establishment. The shows were virtually abandoned by the authorities after 1922, though they did not entirely go away, as religious organisations and social reformists continued to turn to the magic lantern as their main instructional medium, mostly for economic reasons. The magic lantern slide show ceased to be used as an official medium until the colonial government revived it in the 1940s after its two-decade-long hiatus because of the shortage of film stock caused by the war.[61] In 1942, because of an urgent need for the production and exhibition of wartime propaganda magic lantern slides, the colonial government even founded Joseon Cultural Magic Lantern Company (K: Joseon Munhwa Hwandeung Hoesa; J: Chōsen Bunka Gentō Kaisha) whose executives included such leading Korean film-makers as Choi In-gyu and Choi Wan-gyu. The company came to control the entire magic-lantern-related business such as the production and sales of slides and projectors.[62] In the final years of colonial rule, the magic lantern once again became a prominent propaganda medium, along with film and *kamishibai* (paper theatre), especially for rural areas that lacked theatres.

The question to ask here, then, is what led the new colonial government to go with moving pictures, instead of the magic lantern or other forms of visual media? Of course, the magic lantern was a vanishing art form as film's popularity was on a steep rise. Even so, this general trend still does not fully account for the trust the colonial government invested in the film medium, especially given that film still had not reached much of the population of Joseon in the late 1910s and thus was not 'mass' media just yet. Simply put, film became a main governing medium and educational tool because newly appointed bureaucrats from Japan entrusted unwavering faith in the potential of the medium as an effective governing apparatus. The rise of film as a chief political and educational medium at this time cannot be adequately explained without considering the developments in the governmental and educational usages of film in Japan that fundamentally affected the newly appointed bureaucrats' decision to form a film unit. The hiring of visual media for political and educational purposes has a long history in Japan, and the first such attempt can be traced back to 1874 when the Educational Magic Lantern Association began producing educational slides. Since then, visual media, such as magic lantern slides, *nishiki-e* (multicoloured woodblock prints) and, later, films were employed for social edifice, scientific education, and so-called civilisation and enlightenment (*bunmei kaika*) purposes; during the Russo-Japanese wars, they were also mobilised for newsy documentaries and promotion/propaganda of war efforts. The term *education* became more regularly associated with film beginning in 1911 when the Ministry of Education included a magic lantern and motion picture sector in its new committee for public education.[63] In response to the growing interest of the authorities in educational films, more and more private film companies and film-makers were eager to explore the commercial potential of educational film-making. Therefore, at first, the production and distribution of educational films were mostly done by private film firms that were occasionally commissioned by various governmental entities. Shortly after the colonial government of Joseon began to operate its film unit and produce its films, led by the Ministry of Education, which launched its film business after the Great Kantō Earthquake (1923), both the central and regional governments of Japan introduced their own film units that were in charge of the production, distribution and exhibition of educational films. By the mid-1920s, prefectural governments, public organisations and schools managed *junkai eisha* (mobile film screening) units and/or film equipment rentals, and the demand for educational films continued to grow every year.[64] Meanwhile, an increasing number of newspapers also operated their own film-making and exhibition units at this time, further nurturing this spark of interest in film's educational function. Thus, the production, distribution and exhibition networks for educational films came to be in place in Japan in the mid-1920s, resulting in the educational film's firm integration into Japanese film culture. The term *educational film* (*kyōiku eiga*) at the time was used as an umbrella term that included all kinds of non-commercial films intended for public enlightenment, moral suasion, social edifice and spread of information, ranging from newsreels, instructional films, and science films to governmental propaganda.

Noting the longstanding interest of Japanese authorities in the potential of the film as an educational medium, the *Journal of the Society of Motion Picture Engineers*, a Hollywood trade periodical, reported in length in 1932 that diverse government departments and media entities, such as the Ministry of Railway, the Ministry of Navy, All-Japan Motion Picture Education Society, Osaka Mainichi Shimbun, Asahi Shimbun, the Japan branches of the League of Nations and of the Red Cross Society, Buddhist temples and 'even the Korean government', produced motion pictures for propaganda purposes.[65] The journal concluded its section on Japan's educational films by anticipating:

> Everyone is convinced that the screen is the finest medium to inculcate knowledge or carry a forceful message to the public. The moment the government's budget and the various official funds will permit it, there is no doubt that important sums will be allotted to motion picture production and distribution.[66]

This comment, which forecasts a further growth of educational film production in the Japanese Empire, illustrates that a social understanding towards film as the most effective educational medium was universal. Hideaki Fujiki, in his article on the development of educational film in the 1920s, demonstrates that the social discussion surrounding film's potential for social edifice and moral suasion was in full swing by the early 1920s and had started winning over the attentions of bureaucrats. According to Fujiki, after witnessing the enormous popularity of the French crime serial *Zigomar* (1911–12) that had generated society-wide debates about the detrimental effects of cinema and the need to regulate film, Japanese authorities became fearful of, and fascinated by, the powerful nature of this emerging medium.[67] Naturally, theories to fathom the powerful nature of cinema emerged and, as Hideaki shows, those who first theorised film's innate nature in relation to its educational potential tended to view film's emotional effects and intuitive appeal as the primary features of cinema's medium specificity that make it such a powerful social and educational medium.[68] These pioneers' theory of film's intuitiveness and emphasis on the power of moving images, as well as their struggles to redirect cinema's powerful capacities to educate the public, travelled from Japan to Joseon through Japanese migrants, especially bureaucrats, educators and intellectuals. In his essay 'Demanding Exigent Establishment of Educational Moving Pictures Theatres', for instance, Kunii Izumi, a Japanese educator committed to education in colonial Korea,[69] called for a need to build a theatre for children's education by arguing that cinema would be an exceptionally powerful instructional material because films could appeal directly to the intuition of young students and film images are the closest representations of actual objects.[70] Another settler educator asserts that the audiences receive 'strong impressions unconsciously' from film which makes it possible easily to educate them.[71] Similarly, the Bureau of Educational Affairs of the colonial administration underscored the importance of film in its social edifice affairs, stressing film's exceptional capability in representing an object, to which 'the language, literature, or any techniques can't even try', and in immensely influencing audiences through its representational power and reaching them without the constraints of time and space.[72]

Echoing theories advanced by advocates of film's educational use in Japan, therefore, Japanese educators and bureaucrats residing in Joseon were confident that film's unique potential for public education lay in its powerful psychological, emotional, and sensorial impacts on audiences. This explains the logic behind the new colonial authorities' introduction of the MPU, a seemingly drastic measure, given that the development of film culture was still at its nascent stage in Joseon. After all, the Joseon film industry did not even produce commercial films at that time, and no other film company existed when the MPU produced its first films in 1920. In other words, film was a medium that was exposed to a highly limited number of people in Joseon. As we have seen, however, those who envisioned the educational use of the medium marvelled at film's mimetic power and, based on their own fascination, they presupposed film audiences would feel the same way as they did – film could easily captivate viewers and grasp their attention. Film was chosen by the authorities not because of its qualities as a mass medium but rather for its capacities to immaculately reproduce the real and engage the audience's attention.

40   Eclipsed Cinema

Though the educational possibilities of the cinema enthralled many, one of the most important factors that resulted in the major advance of educational film in the early 1920s was, in fact, a development in film technology. The empire-wide institutionalisation of educational film became possible when Okamoto Trading Company, based in Kobe, first imported DeVry's portable projectors from the United States in 1919, and their popularity led other importers competitively to import and distribute other overseas portable projectors.[73] Commonly referred to as 'Theatre in a Suitcase', DeVry projectors had been manufactured since 1912 by Dr Herman DeVry in response to the increasing demands from social reformists and educators who explored the educational potential of the motion picture. Since then, DeVry products had become a leading portable projector used for screenings at non-theatrical sites such as schools, religious gatherings, open air spaces and private residences in the United States, and eventually gained a global reputation. (Figure 1.3)

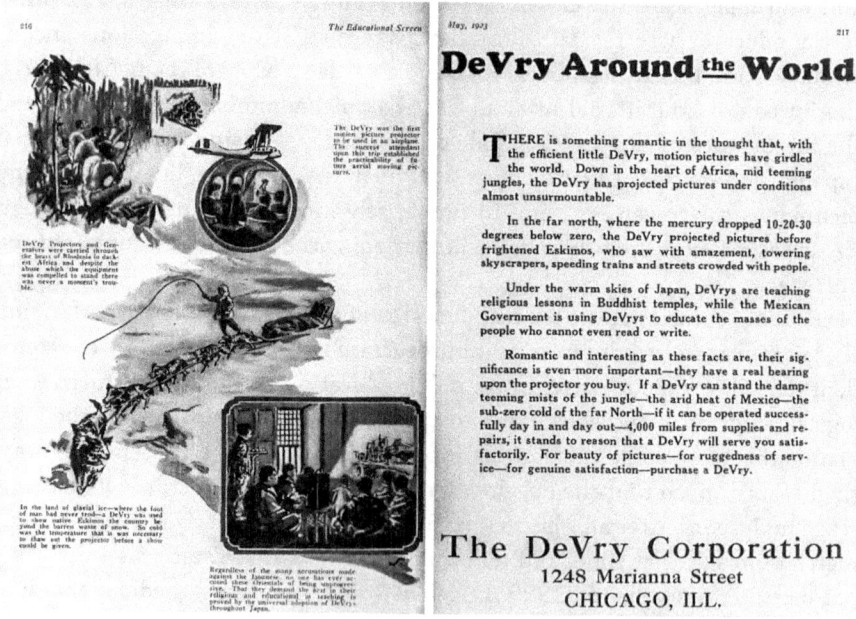

Figure 1.3   The DeVry advertisement that boasts its global popularity. (*The Educational Screen*, 2.5, May 1923, pp. 216–17) The illustration at the bottom right corner on the left page portrays a film screening at a private residence in Japan. The caption which accompanies the image reads, 'Regardless of the many accusations made against the Japanese, no one has ever accused these Orientals of being unprogressive. That they demand the *best* in their religious and educational in [sic] teaching is proved by the universal adoption of DeVry's throughout Japan.'

The arrival of DeVry's projectors to Japan finally enabled the authorities to put to the test their theories about film being the most fitting educational and promotional visual medium and pursue the production and exhibition of educational films. The availability of cheaper, lighter, and energy-efficient portable projectors allowed the bureaucrats, reformists, educators and journalists to resolve the main challenges that had obstructed the development of educational film, ranging from heavy screening equipment and insufficient electric power to expensive screening costs. Most of all, the greatly increased mobility of film made it possible for educational films to reach a much larger number of their intended audiences. Immediately after the introduction of portable projectors, such as the DeVry, the educational film business in Japan grew exponentially. According to the statistics compiled by the Department of Social Edifice of the Ministry of Education, by 1924, over two thousand educational films were available for hire and almost 1,400 projectors were ready to project these films.[74]

The establishment of MPU, in this regard, could be understood as part of the empire-wide efforts to employ the emerging media for non-commercial, educational and political purposes. It is true that the mass mobilisation of film for propaganda efforts of the Cultural Rule era was impressive but the colonial government's establishment of the MPU and its use of film for propaganda purposes were not necessarily 'out of the ordinary';[75] the MPU just happened to be one of the first governmental film units in the empire. The subsequent discussion, then, needs to be oriented towards the specific contexts of colonial Korea that gave birth to the empire's primary governmental film entity: what is the significance of the emergence of the MPU in the Joseon context? To begin with, it is useful to look into the Information Committee that supervised the MPU's activities in its formative years.

Representational Politics of Early MPU Films

The Information Committee was the significant entity in charge of the colonial government's publicity and propaganda through print media and film.[76] Owing to the gravity of its task, the committee's membership featured some of the key figures in the new Saitō administration as well as civilian advisers. The sixteen-member committee was chaired by Civil Governor Mizuno Rentarō (a post previously called vice governor general) who was the head of the civil administration that took care of administrative as well as judicial affairs. Mizuno is credited as the actual architect of the structural reforms in the colonial administration as well as of the governing strategies during the first years of the Saitō administration, and thus his impact was crucial despite his relatively short tenure. Mizuno, though he stayed in Joseon for only three years until 1922 when he was recalled to Japan to serve once again as the Minister of Home Affairs, laid the rudimentary foundation for the Cultural Rule that lasted until it gave way to the more coercive governance that emerged in the mid-1930s in the wake of the empire's total war efforts. As previously mentioned, Cultural Rule was referred to as 'civilised governance' by the new colonial government and its advocates,[77] and was based primarily on the recognition of locality, thus allowing Koreans a certain leeway they had not had before. 'Paying respect to the unique Joseon culture and customs' became 'one of the policies of the colonial government'.[78] Countering concerns raised against this leniency, Mizuno used his famous chimney analogy which stipulated that 'if you seal off the chimney when a furnace is lit, it will eventually explode', and to avoid that 'explosion', it is better to allow Koreans to let off a little steam.[79] In this way, while inferentially critiquing the coercive manner of the previous administration, Mizuno made it clear that his main agenda for the reform lay in overhauling the governing strategies, not in giving in to Koreans' demand for independence. In spite of all, Mizuno's reform, which was grounded on the rhetoric of mutual understandings and recognition of locality, was not an empty political slogan. The 'civilised' governance brought out major reforms in governmental strategies. For the first time, Korean-language print media, including newspapers and magazines, were allowed publication; Koreans were recruited into the governmental offices; Japanese officials were encouraged to learn basic Korean to communicate better with the locals,[80] and even Mizuno himself committed to learning Korean;[81] the same compulsory educational opportunities were guaranteed for Koreans; and the administration included Koreans as well as Japanese migrants into its policy-making process. The chief governing strategy, in this regard, transitioned from coercion to winning a consensus from Koreans concerning Japan's rule of Korea in a more 'civilised' manner. Therefore, accumulating knowledge about the colonial subjects and communicating better with them became a crucial business for the authorities. Indeed, the major purpose of the Information Committee was to 'introduce Korean affairs to Japan and overseas, introduce Japanese affairs to Korea, and publicise and propagandise the real status of colonial administration and policies'.[82]

The MPU's very first productions were intended for this purpose. The first pair of films the MPU produced and circulated were *Joseon Affairs* (J: *Chōsen jijō*; K: *Joseon sajeong*) and *Japanese Affairs* (J: *Naichi jijō*; K: *Naeji sajeong*) with which the newly appointed bureaucrats sought to educate people about the situations in Joseon and Japan. Though paired together, each film's intended audience was markedly different. *Joseon Affairs* was screened for those whom the MPU felt it needed to inform about Joseon, while *Japanese Affairs* was produced for the Korean population in Joseon. The former, a five-volume actuality shot by the MPU before its transfer to the Information Committee, was screened in major Japanese cities such as Osaka, Nagoya, Tokyo, and Fukui,[83] primarily for royal families, aristocrats, politicians, law-makers, and bureaucrats. Not everyone in Japan felt comfortable with the drastic reforms pursued by the Saitō and Mizuno administration, especially the new measures that warranted an unprecedented freedom of speech, assembly and association for the locals, as well as legislative desegregation between Japanese and Koreans in many areas.[84] The MPU's screening, therefore, served to counter the criticisms in Japan towards the new colonial government. In the meantime, *Japan Affairs* travelled across Joseon to 'introduce Koreans to Japanese affairs'.[85] Considering the urgent need to propagate new governing strategies, initial audiences for these two films were those, in Japan and Joseon alike, who could greatly influence public opinions and even make actual, important decisions but, eventually, the films reached the general population through mobile screenings.

The two separate target audiences in the MPU's formative years involved two different representational politics. The films produced by the MPU in its early years are all believed to be lost so it is difficult to assess directly the films' contents. Nevertheless, surviving documents, which record these films and their screenings, offer us some important details about the content as well as production and exhibition contexts with which we could look into the representational politics of early MPU films. As for films such as *Japanese Affairs* intended for Korean viewers, it was of the utmost importance to make the viewers realise the conspicuous differences between Joseon and Japan. The crews that filmed *Japanese Affairs*, for instance, took shots of Tokyo Station, skyscrapers in the Marunouchi area, the modern bridges, and other objects and areas that could most clearly represent 'Japan's advanced culture'.[86] These representational tactics, which stressed the insurmountable gap between Joseon and Japan, aimed to make Japan's colonisation look natural and inevitable and lead Koreans to accept being colonial subjects of the advanced Japanese Empire. '(Korean) spectators', an OGG yearbook documents, 'were awed at the development of the empire (*naichi*) projected on the silver screen right in front of their eyes, instilling them with respect and love for their motherland'.[87] This cinematic strategy was closely associated with the new administration's active promotion of *naichi sasatsu* or the 'Inspection Tour of Japan proper' programme that sent a massive number of Korean aristocrats, bureaucrats and educators to Japan in the hope that they would witness the differences between Joseon and Japan and become civil agents who, upon their return, could share what they saw with their fellow Koreans. In fact, the next project for the Korean population after *Japanese Affairs* was a documentary that recorded one of these tours. *The Inspection Tour of County Magistrates to Japan Proper* (1920), which documented county officials' journey from their departure to their visits to Kobe, Osaka, Kyoto, Yamada, Nagoya, Shizuoka and Tokyo, toured across Joseon to about 68,000 audience members in total. Those who attended screenings during its first tour included, but were not limited to, students at all grades, professional trainees, regional office workers and other bureaucrats.[88] When screened, the film was accompanied by the live narration of invited lecturers who were members of the trip. The presence of these narrators was a calculated effort by the authorities who wished to give more credentials to the film's content. This practice of presenting Korean narrators from local communities soon became a standard.[89] Screenings were also arranged for Koreans living overseas, especially those in Manchuria and Russia where exiled Korean nationalists actively carried out nationalist activities to which the colonial authorities paid concerned attention.[90] The MPU's films, along with the lecturers, were dispatched to educate Korean migrants in these areas. The carefully crafted cinematic rendering of the gap between Japan and Joseon again effectively contributed to the overseas screening campaigns. According to the official report by a Japanese consul of Russia, in a screening organised in Siberia, Russia, in May 1921, for example, a number of films, which featured both Japan and Joseon, were screened for over two hundred Koreans, along with one hundred Russian and Japanese guests, and this four-hour event concluded with a thirty-minute lecture in Korean by a Korean colonial government official who had hosted the screening.[91] The event left Korean attendees 'so moved', the consul documents, as they finally 'learned the real situation in Joseon and Japan', and thus the event turned out to be truly useful in further 'enlightening Koreans'.[92]

Another characteristic representational strategy, according to Tsumura Isamu, the long-term adviser for the MPU as well as the film censorship board who left a considerable amount of writings on the MPU, involves a film style. 'Films screened for Koreans relied on the simplest film techniques that did not interrupt an observer's perception', Tsumura writes, 'and the Japanese would find these films quite tasteless'.[93] This recollection reveals that the MPU did consider the fact that many Koreans lacked film experience. Though highly politicised, in this sense, we could see that the MPU's mobile screenings were a contributing factor to the proliferation and popularisation of film culture in Joseon. As the films of the MPU were screened in a compulsory manner, its screenings provided many Koreans with rare opportunities to experience an encounter with cinema. This was particularly the case for those who lived outside major cities and who did not have film-viewing opportunities. Along a similar line, MPU films offered female attendees unusual chances to enjoy the wondrous world of film and be present in a great number of audiences without being concerned about the social stigma placed on them. Female film spectatorship was severely critiqued because movie theatres were seen as a public sphere where women's presence was actively discouraged, a social attitude that continued to linger on even until the mid-1930s.[94] Given that many attendees at the screenings of MPU films had limited film-viewing experiences (or even none), the attraction did not necessarily derive from the film's content but instead from the very act of film viewing. In other words, though the exhibitions of MPU films were politically charged acts, the purpose was often changed into a cultural and even leisurely activity for the event attendees. Significantly, travelling exhibition units sent off to rural areas presented people with an exposure to the entirety of the film-viewing experience that entailed mass viewing – anywhere from five hundred to several thousand attendees – projectors, electric lights, generators and lecturers. The pleasure of experiencing modern technology, science, and culture through film viewing was certainly an integral part of the mobile film screenings but one should not overlook the political effect that this replica of the theatre experience wielded on the minds of people. Apart from the content of films, people's encounters with urban culture and modern technologies, brought to them by central government workers, also served an important function. While witnessing the power of the state, which solicited support from the provinces, cities and towns in mobilising thousands of people to come to a single event and urged offices in the vicinity to turn off lights to bring enough electric power to move the celluloid images on the screen,[95] a concrete relationship between the wonders of modern technology and the state was firmly established in people's minds. Those who attended these screenings were supposed to learn their relation to the empire not only from films but equally through their realisation of what the state was capable of doing for the film-screening events. (Figure 1.4)

Figure 1.4 MPU officers hosting a mobile screening.
(*Chōsen Sōtokufu Kinema*, 1936)

Films projected for the Japanese population relied on a completely different representational strategy which is well documented in the photographs that record the screening of the MPU films at the 1922 Tokyo Exposition. As shown in Figure 1.5, promotion of the new colonial administration's achievement was expanded into the physical space beyond the silver screen. An official report on this film exhibition held at Tōyō Katsudō Shashinkan, a theatre built for the screening of the MPU film at the exposition site, notes 'We tried to take advantage of every single space in the theatre, hanging posters on the walls next to the screen'.[96] The image painted on the stage curtain contrasts two images of Joseon, 'old Joseon' on the right side (a palanquin in the dirt) and 'new Joseon' on the left (an automobile on a metalled road) with a Korean woman located at the centre. Sixteen posters which surrounded the screen presented images and slogans for the governing agenda of *naisen yūwa* or 'Harmony between Japan and Joseon'. The representation of Joseon in this theatre space was meant to conceptualise the progress of Joseon under the new colonial administration and its endeavours to restore a peaceful relationship between the empire and the colony, informing their fellow Japanese of the kinds of achievements the colonial government had made in Joseon. Indeed, the rendering of Joseon's achievements was the key to the OGG's general publicity campaign in Japan. A report from *Joseon*, an OGG-published Korean-language magazine, introduces this effort:

> Joseon has made such progress in every area in recent years, and harmony between the Japanese and Koreans has been achieved. Yet it is unfortunate that people in Japan, except a small number of intellectuals, are still not adequately informed about the Joseon situation. Thus, the OGG decided to dispatch a group of lecturers who would more thoroughly introduce Joseon to Japan.[97]

Joseon's article particularises that lectures, films and other forms of propaganda intended for the Japanese focused on showcasing Joseon's progress as well as on the improvement in the Japan–Joseon relationship under the colonial government's new leadership.

This agenda also explains the OGG's serious dedication to exhibiting the MPU's films at various expositions and fairs held across the empire, which emerged as the main venues for the MPU films.[98] As expos and fairs were to commemorate the latest accomplishments of Japan, both as a modern nation and imperial power, the OGG was invited to put its achievements on display for the public, and the MPU's films became the major feature of the OGG at exposition and fair sites. The MPU films were screened at expositions and fairs every year from their first appearance at an exposition hosted by Oita, Japan, in 1921,[99] and these screenings saw 'considerable efficacy'[100] in drawing in a great number of visitors and 'educating' them about Joseon. (Figure 1.6)

The Beginning: Towards a Mass Entertainment 47

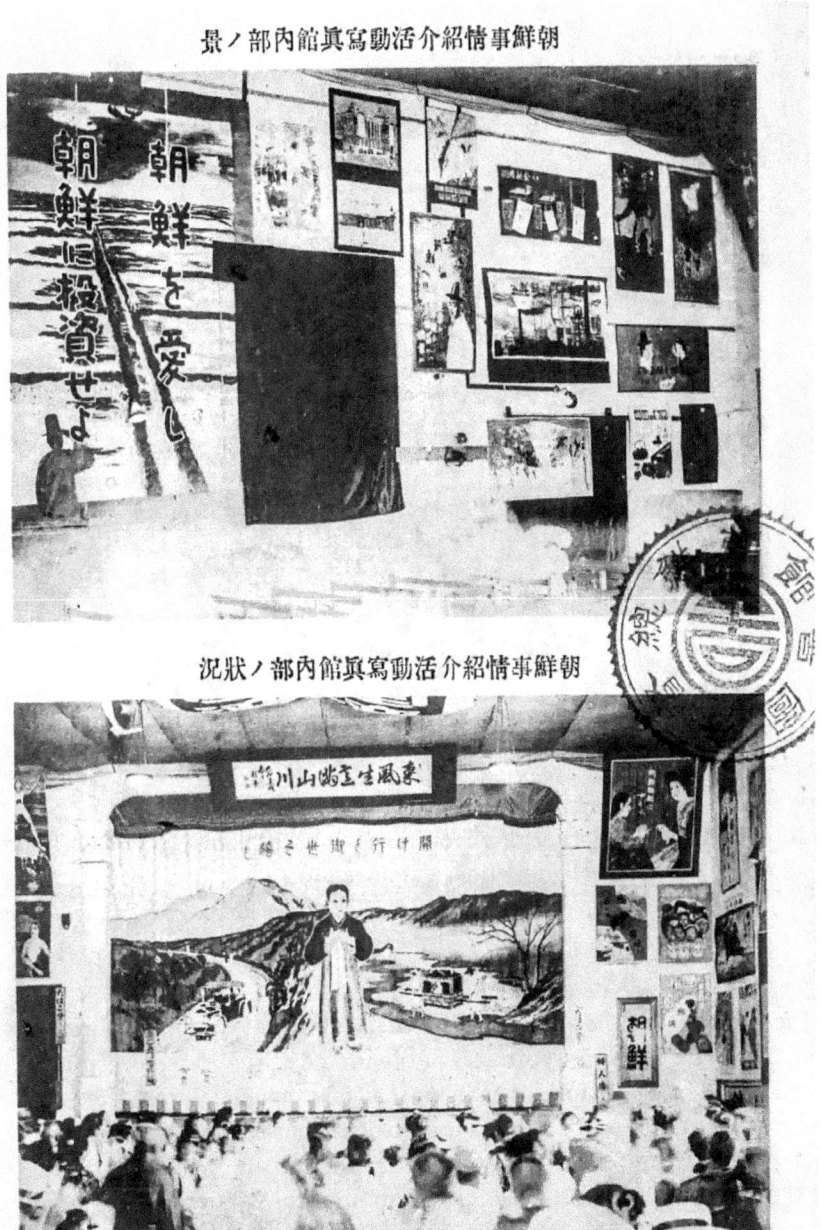

Figure 1.5 The screening of MPU films at the 1922 Tokyo Peace Exposition. (*Heiwakinen Tokyo hakurankai Chōsen kyōchanshakai jimuhōgoku* [Keijō (Seoul): Chōsen Kyōsankai], 1922)

Figure 1.6 The facade of Tōyō Katsudō Shashinkan, the movie theatre built by the colonial government of Joseon to 'introduce Joseon affairs' at the 1922 Tokyo Peace Exposition. (*Heiwakinen Tokyo hakurankai Chōsen kyōchanshakai jimuhōgoku*)

It is worth mentioning here that the MPU's film exhibition format which incorporated a lecturer, regardless of the intended audiences, was much closer to the magic lantern format than to that of commercial film screening, as a lecturer who possessed extensive knowledge about the subject matter narrated the screenings of MPU's films. Of course, film screening in Joseon and Japan at the time always featured *benshi*, a film narrator (K: *byeonsa*), who provided live narration for on-screen images, but their performance was part of the diegetic world rather than an expert giving a lecture about what was on the screen. Instead of hiring a professional *byeonsa/benshi*, the MPU's films were accompanied by the experts who had authority over the filmed subjects. As I discussed, the presence of these experts was considered important as it gave more credibility to the content and thus effectively dealt with many sceptical Koreans who questioned the authenticity of the filmed subjects as well as the political messages the images carried.[101] Occasionally, professional *benshi* were hired when the films were played at prestigious venues such as expos and fairs where films were screened for general Japanese audiences. Still, a solid knowledge of Joseon and the film's subject matter was the first qualification required when hiring *benshi* as they should be able to 'thoroughly introduce Joseon'.[102] Recruiting the right lecturer, who possessed both decent knowledge about the film content and performance skill, proved to be challenging and Tsumura Isamu argued for a need to train *benshi/byeonsa* specialised in educational films.[103]

The audiences of the MPU films were not limited to Koreans or Japanese but the MPU films were designed also to propagate the situation of Joseon to international communities.[104] Witnessing the brutality of the Japanese military police during the 1919 nationalist movement, American and Canadian Christian missionaries based in Joseon (and Christian associations in Japan as well) raised critical voices against the inhumane treatment of demonstrators. Intense criticism ignited, in particular with the ruthless massacre of thirty-two Korean demonstrators who were burnt to death at a Christian church by Japanese soldiers, an incident now known as the Je-am Village Massacre Incident. While Washington did not take any direct political action, despite Koreans' hope for American intervention, missionaries were highly outspoken, contributing articles to the American and European press to expose the violent nature of the Japanese rule of Joseon and, it was hoped, influence Western countries to take action. The Saitō–Mizuno administration took this issue seriously and pursued measures to counter the missionaries' efforts to support the Koreans.[105] With the intention of rectifying the misunderstanding, the authorities dispatched lecturers to America and Europe to arrange public lectures in which they tried to educate Westerners about the situation in Joseon and justify Japan's rule. Saitō himself published an essay for *The Independence* to account for his new policy in governing Joseon.[106] The MPU's films became part of this media warfare. Mizuno was involved in this overseas promotional campaign, and he personally commissioned the Japanese Reverend Yamamoto Tadami, who later migrated to Joseon for missionary work, to tour North America along with the MPU's films in 1920.[107] Yamamoto and his wife visited major cities in the United States, Canada and Mexico to give lectures and screen the films. Many of the events Yamamoto hosted occurred at churches, a conscious move (along with the dispatch of Yamamoto himself) to tackle the missionary problem. In addition to Yamamoto's tour, the MPU subtitled films and shipped them out to the United States (three films), United Kingdom (one), France (one) and Sweden (one) where Japanese embassies and other organisations screened the films for the general public.[108] After that, arranging special screenings for foreign visitors became a staple of the MPU's activities.

MPU and the Film Reformist Movement

In 1924, when the Information Committee was disbanded, the MPU was transferred to the Department of Social Affairs of the OGG's Home Affairs. The transfer had an impact on the MPU's status within the administration because it was changed from an organisation managed by a committee headed by the civil governor to a unit under the supervision of a department in the colonial office. Unsurprisingly, its budget was drastically cut in 1925.[109] Though, on the surface, the MPU's activities seemed to suffer, this change was actually a rational decision because the Department of Social Affairs was in charge of welfare, social care, and social edifice, the subjects that had emerged as the main genres of educational films. To put it differently, the transfer did not have an impact on the overall activities of the MPU as much as it did on the nature of the films the MPU produced. Evolving from a propaganda film unit, the MPU began to produce films on more diverse topics; while continuing to make propaganda films, similar to *Joseon Affairs* and *Japanese Affairs* which aimed at publicising to Koreans and to Japanese the progression of Joseon and increasing mutual understanding, the MPU documented official events and produced instructional materials and newsreels. Yet the subject that the MPU films most frequently dealt with was social edifice, and producing so-called social edifice films (J: *shakai kyōiku eiga*; K: *sahoe gyoyuk yeonghwa*) became the major task for the MPU in the second phase of its activities.[110] This major shift demonstrates that, although the MPU operated independently from the Japanese film world, bureaucrats and educators in Joseon were keenly tuned in to what was going on in Japan where the social discourse of social edifice film was in full development at the time. In accordance with the explosive growth of educational films, the term *educational film* became contested in Japan from the mid-1920s. Critics, led by the noted film exhibitor Komada Kōyō, argued that *educational film* was not an appropriate term to describe propaganda films by governmental entities and thus a new term, which would properly cover the diversity of non-commercial films, should replace it. Yamane Mikihito, a pioneering educational film-maker and theorist, proposed using *public film* (*kōkyō eiga*) as an umbrella term and employing *educational film* to designate films used for truly educational purposes, excluding propaganda films.[111] Eventually, the term *educational film* was replaced by *culture film* (*bunka eiga*) in the 1930s, a translation of the German *Kultur Film*. This movement to separate educational film from the propaganda produced by the authorities testifies to the increasing emphasis on the film's educational possibilities in Japan, which influenced educational film-making in Joseon as well. Tsumura Isamu, for instance, advised the MPU not to limit its activities to producing films that promoted *naisen yūwa* but to be committed to enlightening the people through educational films.[112] In fact, from the mid-1920s until the late 1930s, the MPU directed its major efforts to producing pieces for moral suasion and social edifice.

As I noted, the MPU still left a discernible imprint on the emergent Joseon film culture because it brought the cinema into areas where film culture had not yet arrived despite the fact that MPU's films were fundamentally meant to maintain colonial hegemony and normalise Japan's colonial rule. The most noticeable contact between the MPU and the general film culture began in the late 1920s when the MPU's social edifice business focused on educating people about the film medium itself. At first, the MPU's educational films were targeted mainly at the rural population, as the authorities presupposed that these films would be more effective in educating people in the countryside than urban intellectuals who had 'an ability to choose [educational] materials' other than film.[113] As the MPU's business started taking the form of a film reformist movement, however, the MPU and its advocates strove to find ways to reach larger audiences for educational films. Around this time, an increasing number of Korean and Japanese settler educators and social reformists collectively raised their critical voices against the ill effects of commercial films and repeatedly underscored the educational use of cinema. These figures uniformly suggested that cinema itself was not a bad influence but the problem lay in the misuse of the medium by exhibitors who screened 'lowbrow, entertainment movies'.[114] Educators and reformists maintained that 'although the cinema could have a negative effect on its viewers, if used properly, it has equal power as education',[115] and thus they should find a way to take advantage of the powerful medium for educational purposes.[116] They also added that it was crucial to bring educational films to film fans because these films could be 'a drop of tonic that could clear up people's tired brain messed up by swordfight and chase movies'.[117] The MPU was expected to take a leadership role in this film reformist movement, and it finally took action in collaboration with the supporters of film reform to overhaul and reform the film culture. The MPU tried to release its films for public viewing and, from the late 1920s, screenings of the MPU films at commercial venues steadily increased.[118] The authorities commissioned film-makers to produce, distribute and exhibit educational films and also purchased educational films from them. As a result, the educational film business became privatised with the establishment of film companies specialising in educational films, a significant development in the film culture. In 1929, with sponsorship from the Joseon Public Welfare Corporation, a non-profit organisation, authorities introduced the 'Recommended Film' (J: *suisen eiga*; K:

chucheon yeonghwa) programme officially to endorse 'quality films'[119] produced or distributed by private film firms. To be designated as a recommended film, a film should meet 'an artistic, educational, and also entertainment standard'.[120] This endorsement rendered film-makers some financial benefits because recommended films were exempt from censorship-related fees and expenses. In the midst of the educational film boom, more than half a dozen new film companies started an educational film business. Most of these firms, such as Tokunaga Productions, the prominent educational film company, were owned by Japanese settlers but there was a handful of Korean film-makers committed to the educational film business.

During this film reformist movement, the Joseon Public Welfare Corporation emerged as the main partner of the MPU. In addition to being a major sponsor for the recommended films, the corporation's monthly *Shakai kyōiku jigyō* began its film section in July 1931 to promote wider circulation of films produced by the MPU and film units of the regional governments by offering detailed information about films' formats and content as well as their whereabouts.[121] The reformists' dedication came to fruition with the 1934 film regulation (*The Office of the Governor General Order Number 812*). This new film law is well known in Korean film history because of its notorious screen quota system that restricted screening of foreign films in Joseon.[122] Little known is that this was the first film regulation that entailed clauses which would officially sanction the educational use of cinema. The sixth clause of the regulation mandates that social edifice films as well as other films, such as current affairs films, scenic films, arts and sciences films, and industry-related films, could be exempt from restrictions imposed by the new film law if they were acknowledged by the OGG as non-commercial films.[123] With the film regulation that legislatively fostered educational films and tightly controlled the commercial film business through the screen quota system, limit of screening hours, and more aggressive censoring of the contents, the top-down film reformist movement made great strides, marking the true first step towards total control of film practices by the authorities that would appear a few years later.

MPU's Final Years

In the end, in the late 1930s, the educational, non-commercial film culture took firm root in the colony; in addition to the MPU, all thirteen provinces of Joseon owned their own projectors (twenty-nine in total) and hired film technicians (twenty-two in total), and seven provinces even had their own cameras.[124] Other governmental offices, schools, newspaper companies, and banks ran film units to explore the educational potential of film and produce culture films.[125] With the Second Sino-Japanese War in 1937 which more or less coincided with the end of Cultural Rule, however, the MPU underwent another shift as it was affected by new cultural policies implemented by the colonial government in response to the total war effort. Under the motto of 'offering the cinema to serve the country' (*eiga hōkoku*), the administration took measures, beginning in October 1937, to control tightly film culture as 'its impact on the society continues to grow, and thus filmmakers' roles in enhancing people's awareness of the emergency situation after the China Incident [the Second Sino-Japanese War] are quite extraordinary'.[126] The modifications made in the colonial government's film administration considerably reconfigured the structure and function of the MPU films. In 1937, the MPU produced its first war-related films, so-called wartime films (K: *siguk yeonghwa*; J: *jikyoku eiga*), such as *Joseon at the Home Front*, *Incident News*, and *The Great March of Hinomaru*. (Figure 1.7) From this point on, the colonial administration introduced policies to urge theatres to programme wartime films and, finally in 1940, all movie theatres were compelled to screen culture films. At the threshold of the last stage of the Japanese occupation, the MPU's service seemed to be part of the national policy films (*kokusatsu eiga*) of the empire, as all the films produced in Japan and its colonies had to be war related in one way or another. Like all the other governmental film units in the empire, the MPU, now renamed as the Cinema Unit, was expected to produce more and more wartime films that aimed to mobilise Koreans for the war cause, turn Koreans into imperial subjects of the empire (*kōkoku shinminka*), and uphold the new governing policy of *naisen ittai* or 'Japan and Joseon are One Body'. This new task assigned to the Cinema Unit did not last long, however, as the newly formed state film entities, such as the Joseon Filmmakers' Association (1940, disbanded in 1942), Joseon Film Production Corporation (1942) and Joseon Film Distribution Company (1942), which oversaw and monopolised the entire film business in Joseon, took over this role. In addition, almost immediately after the war with China, newsreels began to dominate Joseon cinema as well but this new development was steered by major Japanese newspapers such as Osaka Mainichi Shimbun, Yomiuri Shimbun, Kyoto Nichinichi Shimbun and Asahi Shimbum which ran Joseon offices. The Cinema Unit returned to its originally intended function, continuing to produce social edifice, educational, and instructional films, along with propaganda films that introduced Joseon affairs to foreigners. These films were screened alongside overtly political propaganda pieces and newsreels.

Through its multi-decade activities, while primarily functioning as the chief promotional and propaganda unit of the administration, the MPU affected the film culture in colonial Korea on multiple levels, as we have seen. The MPU produced more than 250 films which was more than the total number of films produced by commercial film-makers during the colonial period. This statistic is an

Figure 1.7 People seeing off drafted soldiers at the Gyeongseong (Seoul) Station in *Joseon at the Home Front* (*Jūgo no Chōsen*, 1937), one of the wartime films the MPU produced.

indicator which shows the authorities' serious commitment to the employment of the film medium for governance. At the same time, it is suggestive of the very poor film industrial conditions that kept Joseon film-makers from actively pursuing artistic and commercial film productions. As the MPU led the film reformist movement from the mid-1920s when the film culture reached a level of maturity, it even created noticeable enmity between the state-run film sector and the private film business over the interpretation of what the film medium should be and how Joseon film culture should develop. Importantly, the tension between the two sides was also manifested in the different images of Joseon they projected on the silver screen. As a political apparatus, the MPU's films were meant to represent a particular image of Joseon developed by the authorities with little variation. Without being tied to this singular cinematic figuration of Joseon, private film-makers engaged in more diverse efforts (and equally various challenges) to produce Joseon images, as I discuss in the following chapter. In addition to these different representational politics, readers will discover a richer account of the MPU when they situate the MPU's activities in parallel with the broader general film culture I explore in the subsequent chapters.

## Chapter 2
Joseon Cinema, Cinematic Joseon: on some Critical Questions of Joseon Cinema

In Joseon film history, this period was the time when film productions began to form. You could see the signboards of production companies everywhere when strolling down the streets of Gyeogseong [Seoul]. The sentiment for cinema was greatly expanding. However, there were few good movies, and people loaded with money only aspired to become actors or directors, always chanting, 'Production!' 'Production!' This period nonetheless was the time when the foundation for Joseon cinema was laid down.[1]

The popular magazine *Samcheolli*'s account of Joseon cinema of the second half of the 1920s demonstrates the plight of film-making in which hopes and uncertainties coexisted at the nascent stage of commercial film production in colonial Korea. As mentioned in the preceding chapter, two decades after the cinema's arrival, film production for profit finally took off in Joseon, and the immense success of early productions lured aspiring film-makers to pursue film-making professionally. These pioneers, however, found themselves caught in an array of challenges, many of which they could not overcome for many years to come. Owing to lack of financial investment, film production companies were constantly being established only to disband after – or even before – a single project. All film-makers had to share two used film cameras, and it was common for them to film their movies on positive film instead of negative film because of the difficulties of acquiring film stock or securing enough funding and facilities for the post-production.[2] In the absence of film studios, films were shot entirely on location in the daytime and no film-maker could afford a lighting system; underlit scenes in Joseon films became a major source of frustration for film fans, and close-ups were rarely used because of the unavailability of lighting.[3]

Film censorship codes which were systematically implemented in this decade were just one of many hardships early film-makers had to endure. 'I wept for the superhuman efforts of Joseon film-makers who shot fourteen reels of film with only a single 1927 Willard camera and an insufficient lighting system and also hand-washed eighteen thousand feet of film at a storage-like processing lab for a year and a half', a Seoul correspondent for Japanese film magazine *Kinema junpō* reported with empathy.[4]

In spite of appalling production conditions, more and more film-makers succumbed to the glamour of film-making, and more and more spectators flocked to movie houses to marvel at filmic representations of Joseon despite the unsatisfactory quality of the early productions. Oka Shigematsu, a chief censor of the film censorship board, wrote, 'The popularity of film is growing every year, but in Joseon the growth is extraordinary, and cinema has taken the crown of the most popular entertainment.'[5] Oka expressed his amazement at the dramatic evolution of Joseon cinema in the late 1920s by noting that the board had censored 234 more films in 1930 than in the previous year.[6] Slowly but surely, Joseon cinema once again had a growth spurt with the commencement of commercial film-making. By the time Oka was impressed with the unprecedented development of the film business, Joseon cinema certainly had reached a new phase. Importantly, while significantly advancing the film industry, the making of Joseon film yielded rigorous conversations among film-makers, critics and filmgoers concerning how to define characteristics of Joseon film and how best to represent Joseon-ness cinematically. From the film-makers' collective search for the Joseon image emerged germinal cinematic tropes of Joseon cinema which nurtured debates surrounding the visual representation of Joseon-ness.

This chapter explores Joseon cinema's ambivalent nature as a hybrid cinematic entity at the critical intersection of colonial and national cinemas with a focus on how such hybridity was manifested in the cinematic representation and construction of Joseon-ness. Detailing the industrial contexts, cultural forces and historical factors that affected the advancement of the film industry and the creation of the cinematic archetypes of Joseon cinema, the chapter looks into Joseon film-makers' engagement with the cinematic representation of Joseon's distinctiveness, as well as the stakes involved in the representational politics with regard to Joseon's compound modern identity. Postcolonial film scholars typically describe film-makers' struggles to search for Joseon-ness during the colonial period as the embodiment of their fervent nationalist desires to lay the foundation for a Korean national cinema. *Minjok yeonghwa* (ethnic cinema), the Korean term for Korean national cinema, illuminates this historiographical tendency, as it conceptually evokes the nationalist traditions of Korea which date back to the time when the modern concept of Korean nationalism began to form as a way in which to deal with increasing threats from imperial forces. To be more specific, the notion of *minjok yeonghwa* is built fundamentally on Korea's ethnic nationalism that underscores ethnically specific film traditions and discovers the origin of Korean film history from the endeavours of Korean film-makers to create film-aesthetical prototypes for a Korean national cinema under the colonial milieu. Working within the theoretical framework of *minjok yeonghwa*, film scholars' main efforts in recounting colonial film history have been directed at unearthing and underlining elements that contributed to the formation of *minjok yeonghwa* and, at the same time, condemning other factors which they deemed impeded the development of ethnically and nationally specific film conventions. This strategy of screening is inevitable when Korean film scholars try hard to excavate the purely Korean elements from Joseon cinema, essentially a colonial and marginally national cinema, in their attempts to construct a historical account that can seamlessly integrate the colonial film culture into the purview of Korean film traditions. Yet this historical perspective, which considers Joseon cinema simply as the early history of Korean cinema, tends to reduce the task of writing colonial film history to the assessment of whether or not films, practices or individuals made a contribution to the foundation of *minjok yeonghwa*: an assessment to determine if they are qualified enough to deserve a spot in the nation's film history. Anything that deviates from the master historical narrative formulated by this historiographical paradigm is deemed trivial. Furthermore, anyone who seemed to have made a detrimental impact – however minimal – on the development of Korean national cinema is considered unimportant or labelled as *chinilpa*, film-makers who collaborated with the Japanese empire, and thus dismissed.

The actual challenges and issues the film-makers of Joseon had to tackle in their efforts to develop an identity of Joseon film, however, were much more convoluted than what conventional historical accounts tell us because they did not, and could not, construct cinematic Joseon-ness simply with some traits that are associated with Korean identity. The critical definition and historical import of Joseon cinema which the film-makers envisioned, and the image politics they were involved with, developed from their recognition of Joseon cinema as a colonial cinema. In projecting Joseon images on to the silver screen, therefore, film-makers engaged in constant mediation between their attempts to develop cinematic aesthetics that reflected something uniquely Korean and to factor in Joseon's colonial identity. In other words, the film-makers' search for the modern nation-ness and distinctive Korean ethnic identity was inevitably intertwined with Joseon's absence of legislative sovereignty, as well as the imperial discourse of locality that branded Joseon culture as a regional culture of the Japanese Empire. Constantly swaying and switching between the two contradictory, but mutually interlocking identities of Joseon, the film-makers manoeuvred through the process of negotiation between endeavours to assert Korean-ness and struggles – sometimes forced but often voluntary – to contain it within a certain boundary. To track the intricate workings of such negotiations, it is necessary to leave the rubric of the national cinema framework. Challenging the conventional historiography which narrates a historical account along the tensions between Korean film-makers and colonising forces and seeks to identify who was a nationalist or collaborator, my discussion of Joseon filmmaking and its image politics considers Joseon film as a cinematic manifestation of the multifaceted tensions between ethnic and colonial identities. Along a similar line, instead of merely placing individual film-makers and film texts at the centre of my analysis, I focus more on industrial practices, stylistic patterns, recurring themes and ideological questions that characterised Joseon productions. I also examine diverse agents of Joseon cinema, such as film critics, industrial personnel and film spectators, as equally important players who actively participated in the politics of representation.

Nevertheless, my inquiry starts with a single film with which we could concurrently trace the historical and discursive development of colonial filmmaking: *Arirang*. This 1926 modern drama (*hyeondaegeuk*) was undeniably a groundbreaking film, from its unprecedented high production value and phenomenal commercial success to its immense impact on the subsequent development of Joseon film culture and industry. Also importantly, it was credited as the film that first formulated distinctive formal archetypes for Joseon cinema. Owing to its seminal place in the formative years of Joseon film production, *Arirang* is acknowledged as both the pinnacle of colonial film production and the very foundation of Korean *minjok* cinema. In this regard, the film's impact was both instant and historical. While the film gave an immediate boost to commercial film production, much of its historical significance has been accumulating for decades, especially through the politics of postcolonial film historiography. For this reason, examining *Arirang* in the Joseon film context requires the careful task of contrasting and comparing the film's relationship to Joseon cinema and to Korean film history, and thus my discussion begins by critically reviewing the histories and legacies of the film. Probing what has been discussed in the exhaustive studies of *Arirang* will expose what stories have been eclipsed by the *minjok* cinema framework. I then move on to discuss the film's role in the discursive formation of Joseon cinema and the cinematic representation of Joseon. The discussion eventually expands to an exploration of a number of other films in order to inquire further into the cinematic styles and critical discourses they generated for Joseon cinema.

Most of the films I discuss in this chapter, including *Arirang*, are believed to be lost. These films are discursively reconstructed here through a meta-discourse by cross-examining various forms of written texts such as film scripts, literary adaptations of films, trade journals, advertisements, censorship records, and critical descriptions and reflections published in newspapers, magazines and journals. A careful study of the distinctive and diverse qualities of Joseon images conceptualised by colonial film productions that appear from these varied sources will allow us to trace stylistic patterns and critical features of Joseon film.

Desperately Seeking the Joseon Image: *Arirang* (1926) and the Making of Joseon Film Aesthetics

The film *Arirang* narrates the story of Yeong-jin, a student who leaves his school and returns to his home in a rural village when his family goes bankrupt. He becomes mentally ill while going through his family's struggles, and the tension between him and Gi-ho, the agent of tenant farms who plays an instrumental role in Yeong-jin's family's downfall, escalates upon his return. Yeong-jin later murders Gi-ho when Gi-ho tries to rape his sister, taking advantage of Yeong-jin's family's vulnerable situation. At the famous finale where the arrested Yeong-jin is taken by the police, villagers bid a tearful farewell to Yeong-jin to the tune of the folk song *Arirang*, the film's theme song. Through a portrayal of the tragedy of a mentally ill intellectual from a poor tenant farming family, the film inferentially deals with the nihilist atmosphere of the colonial situation and also sheds light on class disparity and destitution in rural Joseon. The representation of contemporary Joseon society in this film strongly resonated with Korean filmgoers. In an article on the history of Joseon cinema published in 1940, *Samcheolli* documented the historical significance of *Arirang* by highlighting the film's unusual appeal to the Korean population, 'Though simple, this work well expressed Joseon people's lives, emotions, ideas, and feelings. People saw something more than the landscape of Joseon, its people or customs from it. They thought something more than material objects were represented in the film'.[7] This passage is intriguing because, instead of unpacking the film-maker's intentions or the aesthetical, technological achievements the film displayed, its discussion of the film's success and significance puts more emphasis on the affective rapport audiences formed with the film. This rather vague but still illuminating statement which seeks the film's legacy from the audience–film relation is illustrative of the critical focus I shall employ in my inquiry into the film *Arirang*. This section concerns *Arirang*'s influence on the development of Joseon cinema on multiple levels, ranging from the film industry to film aesthetics. Nonetheless, its main focus lies in exploring the film's cinematic construction of Joseon-ness which invited film viewers to discover 'something more than material objects' from its representation of Joseon through which the film not only marked a break from previous Joseon productions but earned its historical importance. Before I begin to interrogate the film's seminal position in the development of Joseon film culture, however, I believe it is important to consider first *Arirang*'s historical distinction within the broader Korean film history since, as I will soon elaborate, there are certain discrepancies between the film's relation to Joseon cinema and its historical implication in Korean national cinema.

Arirang and Korean Cinema

In the historical narratives developed in the postcolonial Koreas, the film is valorised as the quintessential cinematic expression of Korea's emerging nationalism and the cornerstone in the formation of a Korean national cinema. Huge amounts of literature claim that the film entails the resistant message encoded by the film's creator Na Un-gyu and his fellow Korean film-makers who intended to 'mobilise ethnic sentiment of Koreans'.[8] The film's importance, therefore, easily goes beyond the field of film history, being deeply integrated into a larger historiographical predisposition that pictures the colonial history with a nationalist perspective. Consequently, much of the historical meaning assigned to *Arirang* is associated more with the politics of the postcolonial Koreas' historiographies than its relation to colonial Joseon cinema. In fact, there are numerous examples that point to how *Arirang* has been historically employed for nationalist discourses in the postcolonial Koreas. According to Lee Yeong-il, a prominent South Korean film scholar who greatly contributed to the development of the *minjok* cinema concept, *Arirang* suggested an ideology of Korean cinema for the first time. He argues, 'I believe Na Un-gyu did not establish a fine film aesthetics nor film theory, but instead Na's instinctive nationalism led him to that path',[9] singling out the film-maker's 'instinctive' nationalist impulses as the primary inspiration for the creation of *Arirang*. The production of *Arirang* is thus deemed as nothing less than an act of nationalist activism because the film-maker's instinctive nationalism, embedded in the film's narrative, strongly inspired Korean audiences to understand properly their nation's challenging situation and proactively look for ways in which to tackle it. As a result, Na Un-gyu is regarded in South Korea as a nationalist hero and anti-Japanese activist. Accordingly, he is buried in the National Cemetery in the city of Chuncheon, South Korea. In 1997 the city of Seoul designated Jeongreung Hill, where the film was shot, as '*Arirang* Hill'. In 2001 the Seongbuk District of Seoul opened

'Film Street' (*yeonghwa geori*) with a newly built, non-profit-making community film theatre – Arirang Cine-Centre – as the centrepiece of the *Arirang* Hill area, and initiated the Arirang Festival to attract tourists.

In the North Korean version of Korean film history, the film has also been an important nationalist signifier as it is in South Korea but North Korea has made much more systematic and well-coordinated efforts to employ *Arirang* for the purpose of historiographical politics. Since the 1960s, the traditional folk song *Arirang* has become one of the most iconic expressions of cultural heritage that designates North Korean nationalism, and it was the film *Arirang*, though already lost, that rekindled interest in this folk song. 'Legend' has it that Kim Il-sung, the first prime minister of North Korea, watched Na's *Arirang* when it came out and was deeply moved by the film's nationalism. The film was credited as the catalyst that inspired him to take a serious interest in the Korean folk song and grasp the nationalist message therein. The 1962 publication of the biography *Na Un-Gyu and His Art* earned Na the distinction of being the first historical figure, other than Kim Il-sung, to become the subject of a biography in North Korea.[10] *Juche* (Self-Reliance), the governing ideology of North Korea developed in the 1960s, aims to rewrite the nation's history by situating Kim Il-sung as the sole historical agent in the founding of New Korea (North Korea) in order to consolidate Kim's monopoly of power. In this nation-founding myth, Kim Il-sung is portrayed as the founder of the nation, and the state of North Korea began in the 1930s when Kim embarked on his political journey as the leader of anti-Japanese military groups. Everything preceding Kim, including traditional cultural heritage, was judged as regressive and counter-revolutionary and thus systematically negated. In this context, the authorities' endorsement and inclusion of the traditional folk song *Arirang*, the film *Arirang*, and Na into the official narration of the nation appear to be exceptional. It is imperative to note, however, that this special treatment of both the song and film *Arirang* does not necessarily digress from the main historiographical strategy of *Juche*. Justifying the cultural and ideological value of this folk song required an unequivocal articulation of its relation to Kim Il-sung, and Na's film *Arirang* created such a bridge. The folk song *Arirang* was sublimated into the ultimate nationalist icon at the very moment when Kim Il-sung viewed the film *Arirang*. In a typical *Juche* manner, Kim is the true protagonist in this story because it was he who bestowed a specific political meaning upon the song. Despite their long contest over how to narrate national history since the division of the nation (1948), the two Koreas seem to chorus their agreement with each other's perspectives on the prominence of *Arirang* in the history of national cinema.

Though the film's historical importance still largely remains intact, there has been an important break in the scholarly study of *Arirang* in South Korea as a handful of scholars began to challenge the general perception of the film as an emblematic nationalist cinematic expression. The first major controversy unfolded in 1995 when Cho Hee-mun, a South Korean film historian, questioned the nationalist discourse built around *Arirang* by highlighting commercial elements of the film in his essay 'Re-evaluation of *Arirang*'. Towards the end of the essay, Cho concludes, 'It is not correct that *Arirang* represents Korean nationalism or symbolises anti-Japanese ideology. *Arirang* was a popular film with exceptional realism.'[11] Not surprisingly, Cho's bold claim shook up *Arirang*'s uncontested image as a nationalist work, generating debates over *Arirang* as well as over Cho's re-examination of the film.[12] Though Cho sparked the major controversy by unearthing *Arirang*'s rarely discussed commercial nature, his position has its own critical lacunae. The main problem with his argument lies in his perception of historical writing as a simple matter of correctness. Thus, he fails to offer an informed theoretical account for the more imperative issue of why and how this 'commercial' film has become a nationalist masterpiece. The superficial treatment of historical materials resulted in the simplified conclusion that the film was not nationalistic because it was mainly intended for entertainment.

Despite its conspicuous limitation, Cho's germinal attempt to question the film's strong association with the discourse of nationalism has left an impact on subsequent studies of the film. Taking cues from Cho's approach, studies of *Arirang* seem to have taken a turn, as more sophisticated historiographical research began to emerge in an attempt to deepen historical understanding of the film. Some trace the nationalist elevation of the film by detailing the varied efforts of postcolonial film scholars,[13] while others intend to uncover the true charms of the film that made it garner filmgoers' enthusiastic responses, such as its imitation of Hollywood genre conventions, the refined narrative device that demarcated the film from earlier Joseon films, or the role of *byeonsa*, the film narrator, in mobilising audiences' nationalist sentiments.[14] What is ironic, however, is that even these revisionist views are still firmly chained to the Korean national cinema paradigm, as they are concerned primarily with determining whether the claim is true that Na is a nationalist or assessing how nationalistic *Arirang* is. Preoccupied with revealing the nationalist curtain thrown over the film and/or how that curtain was fabricated, the recent metahistorical criticism of *Arirang* offers a new critical contemplation of the film's historical significance in Korean national film history but still remains inattentive to the more fundamental question of the film's contributions to Joseon cinema and its overall impact on Joseon culture and society. What made film spectators of the 1920s and 1930s recognise the film as a text of resistance if it were not an overtly nationalist work? What led Joseon film-makers and critics to perceive the film as the greatest masterpiece that best cinematised Joseon identity even in the late 1930s and 1940s when stylistically and narratively more sophisticated films were produced? Was the film's assumed nationalist message the sole contribution to the advancement of Joseon cinema? To answer these questions, to which neither conventional nationalist perspectives nor revisionist approaches provide satisfactory answers, it is necessary to situate the film within the Joseon cinema context, severing its firm attachment to the history and conception of Korean national cinema. Only by doing so is it possible to work out what was that 'something more than' the filmic representation of Joseon people, customs and landscape that Joseon society saw from *Arirang* which turned the film into a crucial turning point in Joseon film history.

Arirang *and Joseon Cinema*

In placing *Arirang* within Joseon cinema context, my inquiry is not prompted by a question of whether or not the film was a nationalist film text. Rather I try to frame this film's legacy in the context of the identity politics Joseon society engaged with in the colonial circumstances. To be specific, I am interested in a critical role the film played in the construction of Koreans' collective identity in the colony Joseon, as the film offered Korean filmgoers an opportunity to participate directly in discovering their shared identity, cultural sentiments and historical destiny. With its strong resonance with Joseon society, therefore, *Arirang* posed an existential question for Joseon cinema for the first time concerning the cinematic expression of Joseon-ness and introduced a set of cinematic archetypes in relation to this question that other film-makers adopted, challenged or experimented with.

Instead of trying to look for answers by constantly going back to the text, the task in understanding the exact nature of this question that *Arirang* raised – how to represent Joseon-ness – should start from an investigation of the film's social reception, paying closer attention to the prolonged effects the film had on subsequent Joseon films as well as on Joseon society in general. To begin with, I foreground the significance of the folk song *Arirang* from which the film's title and theme song came, as the intertwined development of the film and song from the film's premiere in 1926 onwards greatly influenced the social reception of the film. A common perception of *Arirang* as the foremost nationalist film is in large part indebted to the belief in the postcolonial Koreas that the folk song *Arirang* is the cultural artefact that best represents the essential Korean sentiment. In contrast to the popular assumption that the folk song *Arirang* has traditionally been a national icon, however, it was only during the colonial period when people began to recognise it as a national musical tradition. Considered traditionally a vulgar street song or 'indecent song' (*jabyo*)[15] before the colonial period, the song began to acquire a new cultural signifier around the time of colonialisation in close relation to efforts to create modern identities of Korea and Koreans. This process of reconstructing the identity of the folk song as a national tradition finally drew participation from the Korean general public upon the release of the film *Arirang*. Before the film, the song *Arirang* was deemed a regional folk song with a distinct style. A 1924 essay on the Korean folk song defines *Arirang*, 'The most common songs Southern Koreans enjoy singing are *Ryukjabaegi* and *Arirang*. And these songs are a bit cheerful with fast beats, which make them rare upbeat tunes for Korean songs.'[16] What defined the characteristics of the song *Arirang* was the tune and beat with a bit of regional variations; and, as it was a street song, each generation and region freely created lyrics that reflected issues specific to their realities. Importantly, the song often functioned as a counter-hegemonic medium through which commoners poked fun at the authorities, social injustice, class disparity and the strict ethical teachings of Confucianism. In this sense, it is not surprising that *Arirang*'s lyrics began to take on colonialisation as its new subject matter when the nation was occupied. The 1909 Japanese military police's confidential report on public surveillance presents an excellent example. It recorded the latest lyric of *Arirang* in a northern region (Hamheung):

> Let's enjoy, let's enjoy when we are young, because we can't when we become old.
> What kind of world is this? This is the world of the Japanese who make the centre drift around
> What is responsible for the Korea–Japan treaty announced this year? It's our people's uncivilised-ness.
> Drink up, Drink up, until you waste all your money.
> Let's drink and spend. If you become frugal and save up, all your money will fall into the hands of the Japanese.
> Drink, Drink up, why not drink every day, all day long'.[17]

In his study of the genesis of the song *Arirang* as a national oral tradition during the colonial period, South Korean scholar Lee Yong-shik notes that most of *Arirang*'s regional variations were in fact created during the colonial occupation, and these different versions of the song, under the singular title *Arirang*, earned cultural status as the most distinctive traditional song since the late 1920s.[18] According to Lee, in the absence of a national anthem because of colonial status, *Arirang* became the pseudo-national anthem, gaining not only its national meaning but underlying nationalist and resistance connotations, which eventually positioned it to function as a resistance tune. The film *Arirang* was instrumental in this popularisation of the folk song and dissemination of its newly acquired cultural meaning throughout Joseon. The producers of the film *Arirang* arranged a new version of the folk song and wrote a new lyric for the film. This theme song became an instant hit. The proliferation of gramophones and the leisurely activity that emerged around them in the 1930s accelerated the spread of the song. Beginning with the first release of *Arirang*'s theme song sung by the star actress Kim Yeon-sil in 1930, more than a dozen gramophone records came on to the market with various new arrangements of the song throughout the colonial period. The film's significance in the wide circulation of the folk song is evident in that the regional versions before the film were labelled 'old *Arirang*' while those created after the film were dubbed 'new *Arirang*'. Subsequently, old *Arirang* became largely forgotten as the new song composed by the film-makers was deemed a standard song.[19] And 'whether they were in Seoul or the countryside or they were young or old', everyone learned to sing the film's theme song after the film's huge success.[20]

In this way, the folk song and the film jointly took part in culturally forming Korea's new national identity in the colonial context. In the process of constructing a modern national identity, the discovery of history and tradition is crucial in any given national context, as it is instrumental in creating the sense of unity among the members of a nation, and Korea was no exception. Indeed, turn-of-the-twentieth-century Korean historians strove to create a national identity of modern Korea through a construct of historical narrative that positioned modern Korea within its long history. In a manner similar to that of these historians, music scholars brought together different regional versions of the song *Arirang* and elevated it from a local folk song to a national musical tradition that represented the unitary identity of Korea.[21] This process of creating a modern Korean identity was substantially interrupted upon colonisation. Just because Joseon did not have sovereignty, however, Koreans did not stop imagining themselves as a collective entity which shared history, culture, customs and language. Koreans continued to build their common identity after colonisation but they were now forced to shape their modern nation-ness in relation to their nationlessness. Owing to the colonial status of Joseon, the construction of the identity of the colonised nation, in which the song and the film *Arirang* were involved, had to integrate colonial realities into it.

The intermedial effect of the song and the film in infusing the colonial identity of Joseon into the minds of Koreans culminated at the denouement of the film *Arirang* in which Yeong-jin, who is taken into custody by police, stands on the hill and bids farewell to the villagers to the tune of the theme song *Arirang* played by the orchestra. (Figure 2.1) It is a well-recorded fact that, when watching this finale, audiences sang the theme song *Arirang* together, shedding tears. Through the encounter between the film narrative which recounted the madman's tragic life in the destitute contemporary farming village and the sad tune of the folk song whose lyric expressed the emotional state caused by a lost love, the song and

Figure 2.1 Cover art for *Arirang Hill* (*Arirang gogae*, 1933), a script for a play adaptation of the film *Arirang*, that portrays the famous ending of the film in which Yeong-jin's family and the villagers sing the folk song *Arirang* together while bidding a tearful farewell to the arrested Yeong-jin.

film exchanged their meanings. While the film provided a visualised, detailed narrative, and the contemporaneity for the song's lyric, the song granted the film its recognised national identity and alternative cultural nature. The secular song that offered the commoners a cultural forum through which they expressed their feelings about the establishment once again attained new counter-hegemonic subtext but this time the effect was amplified nationally through the mass medium called the cinema. Through the film *Arirang*, therefore, the folk song was transformed into the utmost musical expression of a colonialised nation. In return, the registers of resistance, counter-hegemonic functions and nationalist impulses were instilled into the film. Scholars who, to bolster their case, throw suspicious looks at the film's presumed nationalist nature often use the fact that the film passed through censorship almost unscathed or that its story focused rather on the tensions between Koreans of the different classes with no clear reference to the Japanese occupation of Korea.[22] Though the film itself did not suffer censorship, its promotional pamphlet was severely censored. A day before the film's premiere, about ten thousand copies of the film's promotional pamphlets were confiscated by the police since, according to them, the lyrics of the folk song *Arirang* printed on the pamphlets violated the public security law.[23] In this regard, it was not necessarily the film text or any particular filmic elements that created and imposed a nationalist undertone on its viewers. Rather, the nationalist combustion was ignited quite unexpectedly and spontaneously from the reaction of the film, folk song, and active participation of a massive number of filmgoers. Shin Il-seon, the female lead of the film, recorded her shock when witnessing first hand this 'reaction' in a movie theatre, 'When the film was over, some audiences were moved to cry while others sang *Arirang* together. Even some screamed, "Hurrah for Joseon independence". It was such a feverish excitement.'[24]

Through this reaction, born out of an exceptionally visceral film-viewing experience, a new, combined signifier of Joseon identity was created. From then on, a strong sense of resistance became ingrained in the formation of Joseon's identity as well as in the cinematic articulation of the Joseon image. In his classic *The Colonizer and the Colonized*, Albert Memmi argues that the most serious blow to the colonised is their detachment 'from history and from the community', pointing to the abdication of the chance the colonised could have control over their history, identity and reality.[25] Koreans similarly suffered the loss of control over asserting their national identity. When institutionalised efforts to denounce and disavow Korean-ness and assimilate Joseon into Japan were in place, publicly maintaining a distinctive Korean identity was a challenging task. Therefore, going to Joseon films to consume collectively Joseon images presented local audiences with an extremely rare chance to partake openly in claiming and preserving their new collective identity. Thus, the act of Joseon film-viewing was inevitably perceived and imagined by the colonised as a counter-hegemonic act that could contest and defy the version of national identity and history distorted in the colonial power relationship. In this regard, it is not surprising to see accounts that illustrate the *Arirang* viewing itself as a quasi-nationalist struggle, as in the records by Shin Il-seon or film-maker Lee Gyeong-son who recalled that watching *Arirang* in a movie theatre made him feel like becoming an activist for independence throwing a bomb in broad daylight.[26] Koreans discovered a special venue in the movie theatre where they could perform resistant activities in a public setting 'in broad daylight' by indulging in Joseon images together. The spectacular, performative display of Joseon-ness at the *Arirang* exhibition was strongly imprinted on to people's minds, so much so that Na and exhibitors turned this spontaneously formed spectatorial reaction into a calculated marketing strategy for *Arirang, the Sequel* (*Arirang geuhu iyagi*, 1930). While the newspaper advertisement for the original *Arirang* emphasised the scale of the film, such as the number of extras and the film's budget, in comparison, the language in the ad for the sequel focused on the rhetoric of collective Joseon identity; 'The folk film *Arirang* is the film that tries to make *us* laugh and cry and comfort *us* through the literal reality of Joseon'.[27] Also noticeable is the sequel's epilogue which was used consciously to reconstruct the climax of the original film marked by active audience participation. In the epilogue, which started after the stage curtain rolled down, Na appeared on the stage to make a few introductory remarks, and then female dancers (*gisaeng*) hit the stage, singing and dancing to the tune of the theme song *Arirang* and soliciting the audience's participation. This effort to recreate intentionally the film–viewer interaction, though it frustrated many film critics for its blatant commercial intent,[28] evidences that the discourses of resistance emerged not necessarily from the film text or the film-maker's personal beliefs but from the trilateral interactions among the film, the song and the film spectators.

In this creation of Joseon identity through a popular cultural form which *Arirang* exemplifies, such modern technologies and media as the gramophone, cinema, radio and print were crucial in not only reaching a wider population but also in mass-producing the identity of a modern, colonial Korea under construction. Equally importantly, new technologies and media functioned as a means to homogenise regional variations of the folk song through a consumption of the song (and the film) on a national level. Through these technologies, which collapsed the traditional sense of time and space and facilitated simultaneity across the peninsula, regional differences and local variations were abolished and a universal Joseon identity emerged and spread. Gramophones which repeatedly played the folk song sung by famous actors and singers, and radio shows which aired those songs, in this sense, contributed greatly to the popularisation of the song and also to the creation of a unitary identity of the colonised nation.[29]

The film *Arirang* made similar contributions to this process through the communal consumption the medium offered as well as through its incessant rereleases. The film was rereleased annually in Seoul until the late 1930s.[30] It was also screened across the peninsula for more than a decade after its initial release by Im Su-ho, a Danseongsa-affiliated travelling exhibitor who purchased the rights to the film after the film's premiere in Seoul, reaching the population even in the remotest regions.[31] In addition, the film was published as a novel and adapted into an audio fiction recorded on gramophone record. (Figure 2.2) Through modern technologies and mass media, people watched, or at least came to know about, the film *Arirang* and learned to sing a bar or two of the folk song.[32]

Figure 2.2 Musical score for the song *Arirang* included in the novel adaptation of the film. (Mun Il [ed.], *Yeonghwa soseol* Arirang [Gyeongseong (Seoul): Pakmunseogan, 1930])

Cinematic Archetypes of Joseon Film

As I discussed, the film *Arirang* invited Korean spectators to develop a particular significance regarding the consumption of Joseon images in association with the formation of an identity of their occupied nation. This newly imposed meaning on the act of Joseon film-viewing significantly influenced the image politics of post-*Arirang* Joseon cinema. Overstating the alternative cultural experience that Joseon image consumption offered, conventional film history reached an easy conclusion that all formalistic elements of *Arirang* and many other Joseon productions, ranging from the film-maker's intention to film aesthetics, were intended for this sole purpose. In reality, however, the newly created audience expectation towards Joseon films functioned as a double-edged sword for film-makers. While it helped film-makers to work out how to 'sell' their productions, it became a burden that often limited their creativity. In other words, the narrative trajectories of Joseon films could not digress too far from producing Joseon images for the purpose of constructing a collective identity of Joseon for Korean audiences. Shortly after he had risen to national stardom, Na Un-gyu experienced this dilemma, which his own *Arirang* had created, when he returned to his home town, Hoeryeong, in the far northeast region to screen his two films *Arirang* and *A Hero of the Troubled Times* (*Punguna*) in 1927. The audiences greeted *Arirang* and Na with enthusiastic applause but half of them left in the middle of *A Hero of the Troubled Times*, an action film made in the swashbuckler style.[33] Unlike the urban audiences, who were familiar with the Hollywood genre conventions the film relied on, the audiences in the remotest part of Joseon, where film was not yet established as a regular cultural activity, were not able to take any pleasure in Na's experiment with a foreign genre. As this anecdote demonstrates, the question of how sincerely Joseon films strove for Joseon's cultural and historical specificity became an important marker in consuming, understanding and evaluating those films.

Buried and silenced in the overemphasis on the ideological effect the film had on Korean spectators and Joseon society was the demarcation *Arirang* represented in terms of the development of film aesthetics. The image politics of the film *Arirang* was not just a product of its film-maker's intentions but was indebted to a particular way of representing Joseon-ness. *Arirang*'s impact on Joseon cinema was not only political and industrial but also cinematic. In particular, in the realm of film aesthetics, the question of how to create a Joseon image translated into the issue of film realism. To explore the broad influence *Arirang* had on Joseon cinema, I should like to begin by looking into the common assertion that *Arirang* was the first Korean film to employ film realism.

> In 1926, the Korean film industry began producing/making nationalistic films. In spite of the Japanese occupation, the industry's childish imitations, and old style films, nationalistic films were produced. *Arirang* was the first such film and it's here where the famous film star, Na Un-gyu made his debut ... This film nurtured a fresh, new national spirit in people's minds who were frustrated and full of nihilism by the failure of the March First Independent Movement ... Na Un-gyu was different from other filmmakers in that he depicted real lifestyles of farming villagers with such realism.[34]

> *Arirang* articulates the essential spirit of the Korean people, incorporates anti-Japanese ideology, and also expresses affection toward the poor who suffer under Japanese colonial rule. This silent masterpiece contributed to the nation's patriotic enlightenment movements and was representative of Korean filmmaking in the 1920s and early 1930s. In particular, the film was the first Korean film that explored critical realism.[35]

The above statements display typical views on *Arirang*'s realism from South and North Korea, respectively. While South Korean historians employ the term *national (minjokjeok) realism* to stress the nationalist trait of *Arirang*, North Korean scholars use the term *critical (bipanjeok) realism* to draw a line between the film's realism and their own socialist *juche* realism.[36] Despite their different theoretical orientations, South and North Korean scholars agree that the film's significance lies in formulating cinematic realism for the first time. In fact, audiences ardently responded to the 'realistic' representation of Korean specificity in *Arirang*, which became the main attraction of the film, but this attraction was in many ways indebted to the novelty of the cinematic Joseon image that still captivated Korean filmgoers. A reviewer records:

> As the lights went off and the title *Arirang* emerged, the audience members began to clap hard. This applause is something different from that for Western spectacles. Although they say there is no border in the world of arts, it was much more pleasurable to see a film produced by our own hands. More than that, the audiences that had only seen curvy English letters had greatly missed those Korean words that just appeared on the screen.[37]

This passage illustrates Korean spectators' strong thirst for local films, a rare product made only five or six times a year at the time of *Arirang*'s release. Early film-makers recognised a market that was extremely hungry for the representation of Joseon-ness, regardless of the actual quality of images or visual politics. The Japanese settler exhibitor Hayakawa Koshū (also known as Hayakawa Jōtaro) produced Joseon's first fiction film, *Tale of Chun-hyang* (*Chun-hyang jeon*), with a Korean crew and cast in 1923. Though the film, based on a famous Korean classical story, was more like a crude photoplay that showed still photographs over a *byeonsa*'s narration, it attracted a record-breaking ten thousand spectators for its eight-day release and made huge profits, motivating film-makers to 'greedily seek to produce a profitable movie'.[38] Witnessing its rival theatre's experiment, Danseongsa produced *Tale of Janghwa and Hongryeon* (*Janghwa Hongryeon jeon*) in 1924, and other film-makers began to produce for-profit films, heralding the beginning of commercial film production. All these early productions were commercially successful, as they easily drew in Korean spectators who were anxious to see their fellow Koreans on the silver screen.

Arirang's success seemed to capitalise on Korean spectators' craving for 'films close to their own life feeling'.[39] Yet the film's cinematic representation of Joseon-ness and the aesthetic strategies involved in it were markedly different from those of earlier productions. All the films prior to *Arirang* were based on a literary work and could be grouped into two categories: period dramas based on classical literature and well-known historical tales and events or adaptations of modern Korean or Japanese novels.[40] Unlike these earlier productions, *Arirang* enabled spectators to form a much stronger connection between themselves and the celluloid images, as is well demonstrated in the following passage from the popular magazine *Byeolgeongon*.

> However, here's one epoch-making product, and that is *Arirang* . . . The film shows a collapsing thatched cottage with a sign board that says 'Youth Association' on its pillar. There is the scene where Mr Park, an intellectual residing in a rural village – a college student who is back in his hometown from his study in Seoul – dances and sings together with farmers to the tune of 'It's a bumper crop, it's a bumper crop', wearing a Western suit and traditional peaked hat. This is the film, produced in Joseon, based on all things Joseon. We could see the march of youth association members holding their flags. How much do we miss this kind of scene? The scene does not have dazzling or splendid shots, but instead it exudes deep and solemn agony. Through techniques, Joseon's culture gradually seeps into the film . . . Film is the only device that could record everything in Joseon and show it to us promptly. Everyone is talking about film. We have only one, only one film – *Arirang*. What can you show us next – oh, Joseon film world?[41]

First, the essay, which enthusiastically embraces the film's keen attention to the details of Joseon life and culture, reflects the critic's recognition of what the film medium is capable of in terms of representing Joseon-ness. This realisation of the cinema's representational capacity came to be shared by many others, thanks to *Arirang*'s immense social impact, and this new interest in the film medium per se was one of many contributions *Arirang* made to Joseon film culture. The success of the film resulted in a considerable expansion of the domestic film market as it brought new film patrons to movie theatres. *Arirang*, promoted mainly by word of mouth, became the first film for many Koreans, especially for female and older members of audiences.[42] These new patrons gave a boost to the Joseon film business though many of them did not immediately become regular filmgoers. In addition to the new clientele, *Arirang* also piqued the interest of the intellectuals, artists and writers who had not taken film quite seriously before and encouraged many of them to embark on film production and/or criticism.[43] Two months after the release of *Arirang*, *The Mask Dance* (*Talchum*), the first film novel or *yeonghwa soseol*, a literary genre which combined the features of the novel and film, was published in the newspaper *Donga ilbo*. Na Un-gyu collaborated with renowned novelist Sim Hun, who debuted as a director himself shortly after, as a photographer of the images that accompanied the written text for *The Mask Dance*.[44] The film novel presented film-makers, who struggled to secure financing for their projects, with opportunities at least to 'publish' their film in print media. At the same time, the genre offered novelists a chance to experiment with the film medium, albeit in a limited fashion, by working together with film-makers.

Besides its direct impact on the development of the industry and film culture, *Arirang* substantially altered the representational politics of Joseon film. Written in just a couple of months after the release of *Arirang*, the above-cited *Byeolgeongon* review of the film illustrates the reviewer's zealous reaction to the film's faithful representation of contemporary Joseon culture and society. As the reviewer pointed out, this representation of contemporary Joseon in *Arirang* marked an essential break. Before *Arirang*, early film-makers had tried to exploit the famous stories and literary narratives familiar to Korean spectators to compensate for their insufficient command of film technologies and techniques. This was an inevitable choice for early producers and film-makers because it was nearly impossible for them to master enough creative techniques required to make a story comprehensible to audiences without proper film-making training or filming equipment. Only two years into commercial production, film fans, though still riveted by the filmic representation of Joseon, became frustrated with the technical ineptness of early film-makers and began to express their resentment towards the exploitation by film-makers of filmgoers' fascination with Joseon images without making any noticeable progress in terms of film aesthetics. When Hayakawa released his second film, *A Song of Sad Love* (*Biryeonui gok*, 1924), infuriated fans blatantly voiced their frustration with the poor quality of the film, calling it 'the dirtiest picture I've ever seen',[45] 'rare rubbish you can hardly find these days',[46] though it still attracted film fans and made a solid profit.[47]

Unlike these earlier works, *Arirang* was the first film that represented characters, objects and issues found in contemporary Joseon society, based on an original script written by Na Un-gyu. In this sense, *Arirang* signalled an important departure in terms of the development of film aesthetics. While, before *Arirang*, most films made were historical dramas, after *Arirang*, almost all films were *hyeondaegeuk* or modern drama. Though commercial production began with historical dramas, film-makers seldom produced them for the rest of the colonial period. More important than whether or not Na was the actual director of the film is that Na was the first professional screenwriter who scripted original stories that his contemporary filmgoers could easily relate to. *Arirang*'s main appeal derived from this very fact that Na's original story featured relatable stories and characters that made audiences feel that the film 'reflected contemporary Joseon society like a mirror'.[48] The predominance of contemporary drama was what best characterised Joseon cinema which was even seen as a consequence of Korean filmgoers' penchant for modern drama.[49] Intriguingly, the period drama was briefly revived when sound technology was first introduced in Joseon. Suddenly, film-makers once again adapted classical literature such as *Tale of Chun-hyang* (1935), the first talkie, and *Tale of Janghwa and Hongryeon* (1936), *Tale of Honggildong* (*Hongildong jeon*, 1936) and *Sim Cheong* (1937). The producers of early talkies turned to widely known stories while still trying to work out the new sound technology for the same reason as early film-makers – to fill 'holes' in the storytelling created as a result of their lack of mastery over film technology by relying on the audiences' familiarity with the stories from which the films were adapted.

The Cinematic Construct of Rural Joseon and the Question of Film Realism

Another important trope of Joseon cinema created with *Arirang* was the spatial setting. Rurality became the textual device to construct cinematically 'the reality of Joseon' in Joseon films. As I elaborate in the latter half of the chapter, the cinematised rural landscape would evolve in the mid-1930s from a recurring backdrop in Joseon productions to the very cinematic identity of Joseon, as film-makers at this time consciously crafted this particular image of Joseon with the much more calculated intention to export films to the Japanese market. In this regard, the employment of a rural village as the main stage for *Arirang* created the most archetypal cinematic Joseon-ness that lasted throughout the colonial period.

Given that 80 per cent of the population lived in rural areas, the recurrent rurality in Joseon films does not appear to be peculiar. A discrepancy emerged, however, between filmed rural landscapes on screen and the audiences in theatres, as cinema was the entertainment enjoyed almost exclusively by the urban population in the 1920s and throughout much of the 1930s. 'The urban population makes up entire audiences, whether they are in Seoul or in other cities', wrote Sim Hun in 1928, 'neither farmer nor pure labourer can be found in the audience.'[50] In this essay that critiqued the leftist film-makers' concept of a people's cinema, Sim continued that Joseon's film fans were 'petit bourgeois', and the majority of these audience members were students, and thus a move to make a worker's film was nothing but neglect of the real main audiences for Joseon films. The review of *Arirang* for *Byeolgeongon*, cited earlier, showcases this distance between the rural image and the audience through the reviewer/viewer's identification with the urban intellectual character who comes down to a farming village and works as a teacher to enlighten farmers. For the reviewer, the intellectual's presence in a rural area and his dedication to modernising the backward region are the reality of Joseon, visually coded through the character's awkward fashion that combines a Western suit with a traditional farmer's hat and through his dancing with nameless farmers to the tune of agricultural work songs. In other words, the rural setting in Joseon productions was a reality constructed from film-makers' imaginations rather than the actual reality that the rural population faced. Naturally, the film-makers' attempts cinematically to render rural Joseon for the consumption of their urban audiences drew considerable criticism. Complaints about props, make-up and casting, which poorly represented the details of rural life, were plentiful but even more critiques addressed the more fundamental problems pertaining to Joseon films' over-representation of rural regions. A film critic expressed his discontent with the repeated appearance of rurality in Joseon films and its inaccurate representation, observing, 'lately, films that feature a rural village are produced too often, but these fail to render rural sentiment but instead take us back to urbanity', and there is 'no NAIVETY in its depiction of love affairs', alluding to film-makers' exploitation of the rural landscape for the sake of the romantic plot.[51] Marxist film critic/screenwriter Yun Gi-jeong offered a more in-depth criticism in which he problematised the constant attempts of film-makers to picture rural life just for a story's backdrop.

> Agricultural village!
> How does the film *The Age of Singing* (*Noraehaneun sijeol*, 1930) illustrate rural Joseon of the 1930s? The reality of rural Joseon consisted largely of destitute farmers! What they earn is the interest to their debt, and what they eat is leaves and tree roots. Is at least a piece of their worsening poverty

represented? And are enlightenment movements to tackle the problem of illiteracy that is worse than poverty represented? In case these are not portrayed, then do the farmers' own efforts to survive get represented? Does the film show a conflict developed from a tension between landlords and tenant farmers? Are preparations to organise a farmers' association and tenant farmers' association described?

Films until now principally constructed the beautiful landscape through mountains, fields, trees, rivers, and valleys for a portrayal of love affairs that are unnatural and unrealistic. Evidence of the efforts to romanticise the countryside becomes obvious when no single scene includes rural living.[52]

These critiques reveal that the rural image of Joseon was primarily employed for a romantic backdrop to take advantage of the nostalgia of urban filmgoers. Importantly, the criticism challenges the claim of postcolonial Korean film historians that *Arirang* established a Joseon film realist tradition primarily through its genuine representation of rural Joseon and started a trend for subsequent Joseon productions that repetitively featured rural areas to address critically the bleak realities of colonial Korea. Contrary to postcolonial historians, many film critics of the 1920s and 1930s were frustrated with Joseon film-makers' unrealistic rendering of rural Joseon. Even Na was not free from this sort of criticism. The frequent critique against Na was the lack of realism in his films in which filmed images of Joseon did not establish a realistic relation to it. Overshadowed by the enthusiastic responses to the representation of contemporary Joseon-ness in *Arirang*, critical voices, which point to the film's insufficient realism in representing rural Joseon and its 'pastiche of elements seen from other foreign and domestic films',[53] have been long overlooked. In contrast to Joseon-ness clearly manifested in the story and characters, for instance, many fans and reviewers, along with Na himself, acknowledged *Arirang* was stylistically influenced by Hollywood spectacles as well as by expressionist films. In particular, the themes of madness and the split of the self, which recurrently appeared in Na's works, were obviously influenced by German expressionist films. The first Joseon film that used multiple lightings (*Bell Sound* [*Jongsori*]) was made only in 1929,[54] and Joseon productions did not have an indoor studio in the 1920s so one could easily deduce from these facts that the chiaroscuro, the signature style of film expressionism, was not employed in *Arirang*. Still *Arirang* includes characteristic features of expressionist film: the madman character (Yeong-jin) and his dream sequence. Praised highly by Na's contemporaries and by postcolonial film scholars, Yeong-jin's dream sequence, which exposes his murderous intention in a typical expressionist manner, centres on a brawl among the four characters – who do not appear in the main narrative but are played by actors who also play Yeong-jin and other main characters – in a desert. In this sequence, which makes a critical commentary about class disparity in an allegorical manner, the wanderer, Yeong-jin's alter ego, kills off the merchant character (Gi-ho's alter ego) who refuses to share his water with the wanderer and two other characters who represent Yeong-jin's sister and her lover. Thus, the scene insinuates the violent instinct and inner turmoil of the main character while ominously forewarning of his killing of the antagonist later in the film's climax.

Despite the clear imprint of expressionist style, *Arirang* has been hailed by postcolonial film scholars as the beginning of Korea's realist film tradition. Disregarding the cinematic aesthetics, therefore, the advocates of *Arirang*'s realism tend to understand film realism simply with its plot and story rather than probing it as a film stylistic issue. The gulf between postcolonial film scholars and Na's contemporaries in making sense of Na's films, therefore, emanates from the opposing views towards the film's contact with realist modes. Contrary to the widely assumed belief, shared by film historians, that *Arirang* and Na's other films constituted a film realist tradition for Joseon and Korean cinema, Na's contemporaries' criticism towards the increasing lack of social issues pertinent to Joseon society in Na's works escalated. Indeed, Na found himself busy defending his works from mounting critiques that pointed out his unrealistic depiction of Joseon society, such as the 'exaggerated portrayal of cruel, miserable reality',[55] 'instillation of nihilism and fatalism',[56] and 'reactionary films that ignore Joseon's reality and only pursue commercial gains'.[57] The disdain for Na's inattention to social realism culminated when *The City of Iron Man* (*Cheolindo*, 1930) came out. Employing the conventions of westerns, this silent action film portrays a clash between two adjacent mining towns that have built mutual animosity for generations for unexplained reasons.[58] Reviewers expressed their frustration with the lack of reality in the film, and their criticism revolved chiefly around genre icons and conventions of the western movie. For instance, a critic singled out the unrealistic settings such as a Christian church and bar in the film's rural setting in which major action scenes take place.[59] Another reviewer pointed out a car chase, an action scene on a steamboat, and characters like a bar hostess as too unrealistic in Joseon.[60] These criticisms concerning the lack of realism in Na's work are emblematic of the intolerance towards Joseon film-makers' experimentation with cinematic aesthetics if it digressed from representing the Joseon image. This was a particular problem for Na because the essential nature of Na's cinema had more to do with the language of commercial film genres than the aesthetics of film realism. In the case of *The City of Iron Man*, the film was shot in six different areas/locations without constituting a specific geographic specificity and, indeed, the film simply introduces its spatial setting as 'the two villages located at the upper and lower sides of the mountain had fought for ages'.[61] In this regard, the film's setting is purely a cinematic construct for the director's take on a foreign film genre that required a fictional stage for action scenes shot in a western film style. Such genre icons as the church, bar, duels on a steamboat, and a car chase do not undermine the film's cinematic reality, therefore, because the film-maker's intention was not concerned with representing Joseon or the rural landscape in a realist fashion. Against the escalating criticism, which censured the fallacious portrayal of Joseon and the mechanical inclusion of American film conventions in *The City of Iron Man*, Na defended the film by arguing that his critics missed the point because the film was a parody and, thus, the film's narrative, which did not originate from Joseon society, should be deemed necessary as a cinematic device.[62] Later in the essay, he opined that the criticism denouncing the film as a blind replica of American film conventions was careless because the film's story and expression were not mere copies of those of American films. Na's response indicates that, while admitting the influence of American genre movies, he also asserted that he had intended to localise the filmic conventions of the American western.

Throughout his career, Na endeavoured to adapt and localise Hollywood genre conventions. With his sustained interest in *hwalgeuk* (action) that runs through the entire body of his work, he experimented with the genres of swashbuckler (*A Hero of the Troubled Times*), western (*The City of Iron Man*), monster (*Arirang – The Third Installation*, 1936), and mystery (*Golden Fish*). All these genre films were the first of their kinds in Joseon cinema and, thus, Na can be seen as a pioneering film-maker who explored commercial film genres. Even *Arirang* was Na's attempt to appropriate foreign genre conventions and commercial elements, as demonstrated in his following comments on the production of *Arirang*:

> When I first conceived an idea, I decided to make a film which is not boring or does not make the audience feel dull. To do so, it must also have a sentimental tone and HUMOR. Since viewers' eyes got used to Western spectacles, it must have a huge cast. Thus for the first time in Joseon I cast eight hundred extras for my film. Therefore, quite surprisingly, the film was embraced by the audiences. It was not a boring but a humorous film. Its tempo was speedy and accurate. This film that mimicked foreign films certainly satisfied Korean audiences' taste.[63]

As explained here, Na's chief intention was not only to incorporate foreign styles but to produce a decent spectacle with which he hoped to appeal to Korean audiences who had been spoiled by upmarket spectacles from Hollywood. The language of the *Arirang* advertisement echoes Na's explanation; the newspaper advertisement relies heavily on the rhetoric of spectacle and even that of today's blockbuster, using catchphrases such as 'the grand scale', 'bold camerawork', 'shooting for three months', and 'a budget surpassing fifteen thousand *won*'. (Figure 2.3) In addition, 'casting extras is Mr Na Un-gyu's signature style',[64] wrote a film reviewer, commenting on the great number of extras hired for his movies. As he himself noted, Na was especially keen on the importance of film's scale, the quintessential feature of 'big picture', or what we call a blockbuster today. *Arirang*, which used eight hundred extras, was not the only film that involved the casting of a huge number of extras. The 1927 film *Please Take Care* (*Jal itgeora*) presented three hundred children while *Wild Rat* (*Deuljwi*, 1927) featured five hundred live rats.

Figure 2.3 The newspaper advertisement for *Arirang* that exploits the language of 'blockbusters' such as 'the grand scale', 'bold camerawork', 'shooting for three months', and 'a budget surpassing fifteen thousand *won*'. (*Maeil sinbo*, 3 October 1926)

Inspired by Hollywood

Early Joseon film productions turned to Hollywood cinema, mimicking its genre conventions and styles as well as its emphasis on the film's entertainment value. This stylistic connection between Joseon commercial films and Hollywood productions is the last cinematic convention that *Arirang* established that I will explore in this segment. As they did with Na, corporate entertainment films of Hollywood became a source of inspiration for Joseon film productions in the late 1920s and well past the 1930s. In particular, Joseon films in this period depended primarily on the styles and conventions of action movies. In fact, reading through the scripts, stories, and plots of Joseon films of the 1920s and early 1930s requires a bit of patience, as murder, kidnapping, lynch, rape, scuffles or vengeance were presented in almost all productions; and, regardless of genres and narratives, an action scene seems to be a must, as these violent themes were resolved through vehement confrontations between protagonists and antagonists. Kelly Jeong, in her analysis of Korean colonial literature, illuminates the prevalent themes of moral decadence and violence and posits such recurring thematic concerns of colonial literature as a critique of 'the irrationality and immorality of the system' under disguise due to the censorship that kept novelists from directly portraying the actual violence Japan's colonial rule exercised on the colonial subjects.[65] Whether the pervasive violence in Joseon films was a similar sort of displaced artistic articulation of the violent colonial experience is difficult to determine because of the absence of film texts, making it impossible to analyse in what cinematic ways such gory, violent themes were actually constructed. At least, what is obvious is that such themes provided a plausible cause for a story's climax filled with action, a trend started with *Arirang* whose climax presented an action scene in which Yeong-jin slays sixteen people to rescue his sister from a sexual predator.

In this manner, the language of Hollywood film's commercial entertainment was fully embraced by early Joseon film-makers who tried to cater for Korean filmgoers' penchant for Hollywood genre movies. In interviews and writings, Na repeatedly mentioned that he felt pressurised into making action movies similar to Hollywood spectacles, westerns, and swashbucklers because those films were what the Korean audiences most desired.[66] The censorship records also backed up Na's assertion, pointing out Korean filmgoers' unusual attraction to Hollywood action films.[67] Lee Pil-wu, the multitalented film-maker and film entrepreneur, also confirmed Korean filmgoers' fascination with Hollywood entertainment. Deeply moved by Abel Gance's *La Rue* (1923, released in Joseon in 1927),[68] Lee tried to establish the distribution of European films but, after the first three German films he distributed miserably failed (*Cabinet of Dr. Caligari* [1919], *Faust* [1926], and *Three Penny Opera* [1931]), he focused instead on distributing Hollywood pictures.[69] Similarly, Sim Hun's critique of Na's legacy, which singled out the Hollywood conventions that ran through his work, also demonstrated Hollywood's enormous influence on the form and content of early Joseon films:

> His [Na's] legacy is so huge that it is redundant to introduce him here. But if we objectively assess his legacy, his contribution and fault are equal. He has won the applause of audiences by running, rolling, and chasing, created through the imitation of action films of Douglas [Fairbanks] and [Richard] Talmadge, and shrewdly exploiting a lowbrow taste of common audiences. He is quite good at easily producing a work through weaving and molding, but the content of his film harps always on the theme of pseudo-heroism.[70]

The harsh critique continues, suggesting that Na's success was indebted to these entertainment values often disguised as something serious that alluded to social realities.[71] Many other film-makers were also subjected to similar kinds of criticism that targeted their heavy reliance on the Hollywood entertainment style. Sim Hun deplored it that Joseon films 'should be about Joseon people and expose Joseon people's life' but instead they showed 'a Yankee boy [modern boy] who strolled along the Daedong River, holding a woman in broad daylight' or 'an actor with Douglas [Fairbanks] makeup running over the thatched roofs'.[72] The overriding influence of American cinema in terms of narrative, style, character development and genre led frustrated leftist film-makers to declare that 'all Joseon films are colonised by Americanism'.[73] The popular magazine *Byeolgeongon* also criticised with scepticism, 'Almost all of Joseon's so-called films are the imitation of American cinema.'[74] A similar observation was made by a Japanese settler film critic who fretted that Joseon films were 'suffused with Western sentiment and lacked original technique' and that 'too many scenes are done in Douglas's or Talmadge's lowbrow style', and that there is 'considerable imitation of American film'.[75] It seems reasonable that inexperienced and untrained Joseon film-makers turned to the stories and styles of foreign films for ideas. The influence of Hollywood's filmic conventions was inevitable, in this sense, as the Joseon film market was dominated by Hollywood productions. Owing to the difficulties in securing investments, moreover, film-makers were under pressure to make films that could satisfy audiences and generate revenues. Even Na, the most successful film-maker of Joseon cinema, expressed his irritation with his investors who cared only about making profits,[76] and still urged him to continue to make films 'in a Douglas Fairbanks style' even in the late 1930s, long after the age of Fairbanks's swashbuckling was over.[77] (Figure 2.4) In this sense, it is natural that 'to make audiences laugh and cry was the only thing the filmmakers cared about'[78] in this phase of commercial film production, as the priority for

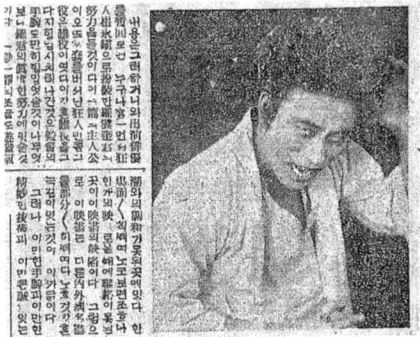 

Figure 2.4 Na Un-gyu as madman Yeong-jin in *Arirang*. (*Maeil sinbo*, 10 October 1926 [left], and *Shinko eiga*, January 1930, p. 131 [right]) Through playing this role, actor Na emerged as an action star, earning the nickname Douglas Fairbanks of Joseon.

the film-makers was to finish their projects at all costs and achieve commercial success in order to survive in the unstable film-making business.

As discussed thus far, there is a considerable gap between Na Un-gyu and his films' historical implications in Joseon cinema and Korean cinema. For the historical narrative of Korean film history, only a single, limited aspect of Na's work is highlighted. Yet Na meant many things to Joseon cinema. Though his fellow film-makers, fans, supporters and critics had varying opinions about his work, everyone agreed that Na laid the foundation for Joseon cinema. Screenwriter Kim Tae-jin, who started his career as actor Namgung Un, a co-star of *Arirang*, published an essay upon the third-year anniversary of Na's death in which he chronicled his decade-long 'love and hate' relationship with Na and his work. In his attempt to define the kernel of Na's film aesthetics in the simplest terms, Kim characterised it as a popular (*tongsokjeok*) form of art.[79] Na and his fellow film-makers during the 1920s to the mid-1930s had to carry out the challenging task of standardising film business practices while exploring ways in which to represent Joseon images. Though they were able to suggest some formal archetypes for Joseon cinema, such efforts were constantly undermined by practical issues which consumed Joseon film-makers, making it difficult for them to engage fully with a more substantial and serious search for the representation of Joseon-ness. Under extremely challenging film-making conditions, Na turned out to be the most prolific film-maker, having been involved in almost half Joseon productions as a producer, director, screenwriter or actor until his death in 1937. After becoming a film-maker himself and parting ways with KAPF around the time of Na's demise, Seo Gwang-je, a pioneering film critic, who was most critical of Na's works, confessed that, when he had critiqued Na as a KAPF member, he had been obsessed with ideological criticism and ignorant of actual film-making conditions but he now understood how challenging it was to make a film.[80] As important as the cinematic archetypes of Joseon cinema he established were, Na also showed his fellow film-makers how they could pursue their profession, surviving waves of challenges that curbed their enthusiasm for the art they loved. These early Joseon film-makers' efforts and passions to keep Joseon film afloat must be what also deserve credit.

Joseon Film Lyricism: Joseon Colour and Joseon Films 'Exported' to Japan

'Directors have done nothing, and the film fails to convey the pleasure the poignant tune of the song *Arirang* offers us', said the *Kinema junpō* review of the 1933 film *The Song of Arirang*, 'but its commercial potential is remarkably high as it uses *The Song of Arirang* as its theme song, and its romance between young lovers and action sequences are enough to please audiences.'[81] Produced and released in 1933 by Takarazuka Kinema, the Japanese musical film *The Song of Arirang*, whose motif came from the mega-hit song of the same title from the previous year, presents us with another angle from which we could look into the issues relating to both the folk song and the film *Arirang*, placing them in a broader imperial context. This reorientation requires me first to bring light to the lesser-known fact that the folk song *Arirang* was the first Korean song that had ever gained immense popularity in modern Japan. Yet it was not Na Un-gyu's film that initiated this cultural phenomenon but the song itself or its rearranged, Japanised version, to be more precise. Around the time Na's *Arirang* was released in Japan (1927), the folk song *Arirang* slowly became known to the Japanese public through gramophone records, and the 1932 song *The Song of Arirang (Ariran no uta)* created *Arirang* fervour in Japan. Arranged by Koga Masao, a celebrity composer, and sung together in Japanese by two top stars, Korean singer Chae Gyu-yeob (known as Hayakawa Ichirō in Japan), and Japanese singer Awaya Noriko, the song became an instant hit, being 'a great fad in every city and town',[82] when the album was published by Columbia Records. With this success, *Arirang* became what the Japanese came to consider one of the cultural artefacts that best embodied Joseon-ness throughout the colonial period and even beyond. Most importantly, *The Song of Arirang* initiated a specific pattern in the way the song *Arirang* was consumed and understood in imperial Japan. Instead of the authentic folk song coming directly from Joseon, Japan embraced *Arirang* mediated by Japanese artists and, thus, the folk song, while becoming recognised as an iconic expression of colony Joseon, was morphed into Japanese popular culture. After *The Song of Arirang*, fifty more gramophone records featuring the folk song were released, and *Arirang* was widely reproduced by Japanese artists in the forms of literature, critical treatise, music and film. Coded through the uneven power relationship between the colonisers and colonised, Japan's appropriation of *Arirang* proved to be a blatant form of cultural exploitation as, in the process of this appropriation, *Arirang*'s original cultural connotation was completely eschewed but Japanese artists' own interpretation of *Arirang*, Koreans, and Korean culture bestowed a new identity on the folk song. The following poem *Willow* (*Yanagi*, 1933) by folk literary writer Shirotori Seigo exhibits how such cultural appropriation took place.[83]

> In tears I parted from the willow in spring
> Now come again
> The smoking rain
> Shrouds my dreams, too, in haze: Neungra Island
> Writing on water with a strand of willow

> What do I reel in
> Birds cry
> The willow is long as the day
> Gently flows the great Daedong River
> Its boats, black boats
> Their masts, too, black
> The willows are green, their blossoms red
> The rain clears
> The rainbow is an illusion
> It soon disappears
> Let us sing *The Song of Arirang* in the willows' shade

In the poem that portrays the idyllic scenery of the Daedong River which runs through Pyongyang city, the encounter between the Japanese poet and pastoral Joseon generates a melancholic sentiment. The imperial gaze of the poet, which depicts Joseon with the language of sentimentalism, is mediated through the popular 'Japanese' song, *The Song of Arirang*. In his journey to the colony, therefore, what Shirotori discovered was not a Joseon sentiment emanating from its natural landscape but, rather, a confirmation of Joseon-ness already constructed in his mind through the Japanese version of the folk song, an emblematic expression of nostalgia, sentimentalism and anguish. Here, the Japanese adaptation of *Arirang* is employed as a lens through which the imperial observer could observe the exotic scenery of the colony and make sense of the sentiments of its people. But that lens is a tainted one which only affirms his superior position that allows him freely to appropriate and mutilate the culture of the colonised for his own artistic imagination. The poet's mobilisation of the emotional poignancy for his portrayal of pastoral Joseon through the folk song echoes Koga Masao's introduction of *Arirang* to his fellow Japanese upon the publication of his *The Song of Arirang*. Koga, who spent his youth in Joseon and credited Korean folk songs as a source of inspiration for his music, presented 'an eerie, overarching pathos' as characteristics of *Arirang* and Korean folk songs as well as Korean ethnic identity.[84] These motions to essentialise melancholy as a unique Korean sentiment demonstrated in both Koga's and Shirotori's appropriation of *Arirang* repudiate the original connotation of the song's melancholy tone. As we saw in the previous section, from the intermedial contact between the song *Arirang* and the film *Arirang*, a new, modern and contemporary definition of Joseon-ness was created, and the rhetoric of melancholy came to be a direct reflection of colonial reality and an expression of Korean resistance. While erasing *Arirang*'s historically specific connotations born out of the present situation of Joseon, Japanese artists connected the melancholy, sentimentalism and fatalism to the past history of the colony. Through the commodification which disavowed the original cultural signifier that could potentially pose a threat to the empire, therefore, the folk song *Arirang* was turned into a 'safe' ingredient that could be used to spice up Japanese popular culture.

The process of cultural appropriation which clouded the original implications of the song *Arirang* was anticipated even before *The Song of Arirang*. The advertisement for the film *Arirang*'s release in Japan exploited the identical politics of cultural disavowal and essentialism. Created by the distributor Yamani Trading Company, the catchphrase for the film's *Kinema junpō* ad was, 'a melancholy song created from ingenuous ethnic sentiment of Joseon', and the ad further introduces the film as the story of farmers 'who learn the evanescence of time and sing to the sad and heart-aching tune'.[85] Quite different from the language found in the ads for the film and its sequel in Joseon, this description of the film for Japanese filmgoers put overt emphasis on the rhetoric of melancholy, rurality and simplicity, framing them as inherent characteristics of Koreans while offering no hint of the story's contemporariness. In doing so, Koreans' misery and sadness, along with their will to survive, became what characterised the essential identity of Korea, having nothing to do with the present political status. In this sense, as opposed to the original cultural import of *Arirang* emerging from present-day Joseon, Japan's configuration of Joseon-ness went back to the mythical past.

Melancholy, pastoralism and simplicity – this set of cinematic tropes which appeared with the 1926 *Arirang* had gained a persistent currency in the cinematic rendering of Joseon well into the 1930s, as I have noted. In the wake of moves to industrialise the film business through co-productions with Japanese major studios and the 'exportation' of Joseon films to the Japanese film market in the mid-1930s, these elements were more consciously employed to increase the marketability of Joseon films in Japan. Consequently, the cinematic tropes created and employed by Joseon film-makers to represent Joseon images became entangled in a process of negotiation with the imperialist reconfiguration of Joseon culture. As demonstrated in the appropriation of *Arirang*, however, original connotations of cinematic Joseon-ness, along with heterogeneous perceptions of, and intense debates over how to conceptualise cinematically Joseon identity, evaporated into thin air in this negotiation but, instead, a homogeneous meaning was assigned to Joseon. In particular, initially conceived by the Japanese to designate the distinctive culture of their colony, the discourse of local colour (K: *jibangsaek*; J: *chihōiro*) or Joseon colour was picked up by Joseon film-makers in their efforts to elevate Joseon cinema aesthetically and industrially. The filmmakers' constant oscillation between Joseon identity and the orientalist notion of local colour in representing Joseon images became a defining component that redirected aesthetical development and representational politics of Joseon cinema in the second phase of Joseon film-making.

Discussions about the local colour discourse in relation to Joseon cinema appeared in the early 1930s when Joseon cinema suffered a setback created by the global economic downturn and Japan's invasion of Manchuria. In 1934, Joseon cinema had 'a deplorable year',[86] in that it produced only two films, marking the least productive year since the beginning of film production. The Joseon film world also recognised that film-makers held responsibility for Joseon cinema's stagnation as they could not make any substantial progress in terms of aesthetics. The poor quality of Joseon films became more noticeable with the arrival of sound film technology, making Joseon talkies look 'miserable' to Korean audiences that regularly appreciated 'the quality films of Will Frost, René Clair, Julien Duvivier, and Jacques Feyder'.[87] Catalysed by the crisis caused by multiple factors, rigorous discussions, which attempted to fathom the problems of Joseon film production and seek solutions, soon swept across Joseon cinema. Ten years into film production, therefore, Joseon film-makers started searching collectively for a new direction, engaging in more in-depth and mature deliberations about the present and future of Joseon cinema.

In 1936, the tail end of the sluggish years of Joseon productions, *Samcheolli* gathered a group of noted producers, directors, actors, magazine editors and critics, including such big names as Na Un-gyu, Lee Myeong-wu, Park Gi-chae, Kim Yu-yeong, Mun Ye-bong and Kim Yeon-sil, to discuss the possibility of Joseon film exports.[88] This round-table discussion showcased Joseon film-makers' efforts to place Joseon cinema within the global context both industrially and culturally. Towards the end of the discussion, in which the discussants were asked about the future direction of Joseon cinema, they all agreed that Joseon cinema's industrial growth lay in looking beyond the small Joseon market and exploring overseas markets, starting with Japan, Manchuria and China, and eventually Europe and North America. When asked how to achieve this challenging task, the discussants collectively suggested a conscious effort to take advantage of Joseon culture and the customs international film viewers might find exotic. Several participants, however, including Na Un-gyu, opposed the idea of blatantly exploiting Korean traditions but, instead, proposed finding a way to carry out such efforts through the aesthetic elevation of Joseon films, modelled particularly after the art cinemas of French and Czech film-makers. This discussion demonstrated a widely shared belief at that time that Joseon cinema could not move ahead unless it evolved from the independent production phase to a studio system; and, in order to industrialise Joseon cinema, the need to make films for foreign markets was inevitable. Also, there was a realisation that the cultivation of international markets involved a development of film aesthetical strategies that could better 'sell' Joseon productions globally. The participants in the *Samcheolli* round-table discussion did not have to wait long to see their ideas realised. The 1937 melodrama *The Wayfarer* (*Nageune*) finally delivered a long-awaited breakthrough for Joseon film-making.

The Wayfarer and the Practice of Film Co-production

When *The Wayfarer* was premiered in April 1937, the film became a phenomenal success; and film-makers, critics and fans alike were not hesitant in acclaiming the film as a masterpiece. The film was compared with *Arirang* because of its cinematic and film-technological achievement as well as its impact on Joseon film-making. Significantly, *The Wayfarer* was the first Joseon film that had made a notable impact on the Japanese film world. Co-produced between Seongbong Yeonghwawon of Joseon and Shinko Kinema of Japan, which released the film nationwide in Japan in May, *The Wayfarer* or *Tabiji* (*The Journey*, the title for the Japanese release)[89] also garnered considerable attention from the Japanese film circuit for the unprecedented practice of co-production as well as its aesthetic sophistication. The film ranked in twelfth place on the *Kinema junpō*'s famous annual film rankings.[90] Japanese film critics hailed the film: 'Thanks to *The Wayfarer*, Joseon cinema is now visible in the Japanese film world'[91] and *The Wayfarer* is 'the only decent film Joseon has produced'.[92] After the film's success, collaborations between Joseon film-makers and Japanese studios became a trend, and the Japanese film market was finally opened up for Joseon films. In succession, a number of Joseon films were released in Japan and gained both commercial success and critical attention; co-productions, such as *Military Train* (*Gunyong yeolcha*, 1938), *Han River* (*Hangang*, 1938), *Fishing Fires* (*Eohwa*, 1938) and *Miles Away from Happiness* (*Bokjimanli*, 1941),[93] along with Joseon productions distributed by Japanese distributors, such as *Heartless* (*Mujeong*, 1938), *Dosaengrok* (1938), *A Village Shrine* (*Seonghwangdang*, 1939) and *The Border* (*Gukgyeong*, 1940), enticed Japanese filmgoers. The success of *The Wayfarer* and other so-called export films was deemed instrumental in Joseon cinema's major strides towards the industrialisation of the film business.

Though the films 'exported' to Japan and the investment and commerce they generated uplifted Joseon cinema industrially, technologically, and aesthetically, not everyone in the Joseon film circuit was supportive of the collaboration with Japanese studios. In fact, the Joseon film world was torn between excitement for the technological and aesthetical leaps and anxiety about the possible negative consequences of the partnership with powerful Japanese studios. Nevertheless, witnessing the remarkable success of *The Wayfarer*, Joseon film-makers decided to take the risk, though they were aware of the potential dangers involved in luring support and investment from Japanese studios. Both the concerns and the hopes were soon realised. While the gamble paid off handsomely, as commercial and critical interest in Joseon films in Japan continued to grow, Japanese studios, through the collaboration with Joseon film-makers, quickly expanded their influence over the frail Joseon film business. The major Japanese studios competitively searched for theatres to build their direct distribution and exhibition networks in Joseon. According to the standard film historical accounts, Joseon cinema became subsumed into Japanese imperial cinema because of the changes in the political climate and film regulations with the advent of the Second Sino-Japanese War which put Joseon cinema under direct control of the authorities. This view is only partially true, however, because this perspective, attributing every change that took place in Joseon cinema from the late 1930s onwards to wartime imperial policies, overlooks that the series of events which ensued within the film world clearly signalled the Japanese film industry's takeover of Joseon cinema. It was Japanese film capital that first transformed and threatened Joseon film culture even before the authorities took official measures to obliterate the autonomy of Joseon cinema at all levels. The reasons for this increasing interest of the Japanese studios in Joseon cinema were multifaceted. Fierce competition among Japanese studios at the advent of sound technology led them to explore new business models and aggressively cultivate overseas markets, resulting in mergers, nationwide upgrades of movie theatres, co-productions with Joseon, Chinese and Manchurian film-makers, and so on. In addition, the introduction of a screen quota for foreign films in 1934 which limited the screening of foreign films at movie theatres in Joseon, a decision made independently from Japan by the colonial authorities of Joseon, created an opportunity for the Japanese film industry to increase its market share in the colony. In return, the growing interest of Japanese industry in the Joseon film market helped Joseon films be consistently released in Japan and helped Joseon film-makers find partners in Japan. With the exception of Osaka, the city that boasted the largest Korean community, where Joseon films found regular audiences, Joseon films had not been distributed nationally. With the nationwide release of *The Wayfarer*, which 'made the general Japanese public discover that Joseon produces movies',[94] Joseon cinema began to receive serious industrial and critical attention for the first time.

The transformation of industrial and production practices was not the only effect the emerging industrial collaboration between Joseon and Japanese cinemas brought to Joseon cinema. Equally importantly, this change prompted intense debates surrounding the question of how to define Joseon cinema. Upon its release, *The Wayfarer* immediately generated a debate on whether or not this film could be labelled as a Joseon film. The practice of co-production introduced by this film drew a mixed response. Praise for the film – 'It is an undeniable fact that the film certainly laid a solid foundation for Joseon talkies'[95] and 'It is an absolute truth that no Joseon film produced after the advent of the talkie era could surpass the extraordinary quality of *Wayfarer*'[96] – was coupled with an uneasiness with the co-production – 'From which part to which part of this film can be called a (Joseon) film'[97] and 'The question of how much support this work received from the Japanese is an issue'.[98] By the time *The Wayfarer* was co-produced, Japanese studios already directly managed a significant number of theatres in Joseon, pushing local exhibitors out of business and/ or making them mere agents for the Japanese film industry. Therefore, Joseon film-makers feared that co-production might further facilitate the Japanese film industry's active pursuit of their film market and ultimately destroy Joseon cinema's autonomy.

In opposition to the view concerning the detrimental effects of co-production, some tried to defend it by explaining the collaboration as a matter of creative exchange. Seo Gwang-je presented a fine example:

> It is very imprudent to be concerned that the film [*The Wayfarer*] would damage Joseon culture just because it was co-directed by Mr Suzuki and Mr Lee Gyu-hwan ... partnering up with Mr Suzuki or a Chinese director – it is a technical issue of the film, and it will become a cultural question to be seen only after the film is complete. That is, it is the original work of the film that truly determines every social and cultural feature [of the film]. In this sense, I believe technical cooperation is a must, as it would only help the lagging Joseon cinema to mature and develop technically and culturally.[99]

Seo argued that *The Wayfarer* was essentially a Joseon film because Lee, as the original writer and director of the film, was still able to instil Joseon-ness into it. Thus, he viewed the role of Japanese film-makers as mere technical support. In fact, Lee and other film-makers, including Seo himself who debuted as a director of *Military Train*, a co-production with Toho studio in the following year, primarily turned to Japanese studios for technical support. Typically, Joseon film-makers were in charge of the original story, screenwriting and directing, and thus the majority of shooting was done in Joseon on location, with some interior scenes filmed in studio lots in Japan, and most of the cast were Korean actors. Meanwhile, almost all the post-production, such as editing, sound, post sync, dubbing and even music, was done in Japan. This arrangement was set up by Lee and Suzuki Shigeyoshi, the director affiliated with Shinko who had trained Lee when they worked together at Teikoku Kinema in the late 1920s. When working on the pre-production for the film, Lee visited Suzuki to seek support in finding solutions to the poor sound technology of Joseon film and also to pursue possible investment.[100] The deal between the film companies, however, did not simply involve the division of labour and technological support but also the split of distribution rights and revenue. In the case of *The Wayfarer*, Seongbong was given the rights to the distribution of the film in Joseon while Shinko was in charge of the film's distribution in Japan and overseas. Joining up with a major studio such as Shinko, Toho or Shochiku was crucial because it guaranteed a national release in Japan through their theatre chains and contracted theatres. Considering this arrangement of the Joseon–Japan co-production, which relied heavily on Japanese studios' financial investment, technical support, post-production facilities, distribution network, and publicity system, Seo's claim sounds quite naive because it was unlikely that Joseon film-makers could limit Japanese support only to the technical part. In the end, as many feared, the issue concerning Joseon film's Joseon-ness was taken to a more serious level when film-makers began consciously to produce Joseon images to entertain Japanese audiences, which fuelled another debate regarding the representational strategies of Joseon films exported to Japan.

As noted earlier, *The Wayfarer* achieved both commercial and critical success in Japan, especially attracting serious interest from 'the intellectuals',[101] including film critics. The number of Joseon films released in Japan beginning in 1937 offered Japanese film critics and journalists, including such veteran critics as Iijima Tadashi and Hazumi Tsuneo, enough film texts with which they could conceptualise their theories about Joseon cinema. Almost immediately after the release of *The Wayfarer*, they brought the notion of local colour into their attempts to explicate the charm of Joseon cinema by attributing the enthusiastic responses to *The Wayfarer* in Japan to 'its locality, the unusual representation of Joseon customs'.[102] Indeed, Japanese critics frequently employed this discourse of Joseon colour when discussing *The Wayfarer* and its success in Japan, commenting on the film's exceptional representation of Joseon's locality and local colour and noting how skilfully it incorporated 'Joseon's customs, habits, and natural scenery' into its narrative and visual portrayal of Joseon.[103]

What is, then, Joseon's distinctive local colour as represented in *The Wayfarer* and subsequent Joseon films released in Japan, and how is it represented? According to critical descriptions by Japanese writers, Joseon colour represented in films consisted of an emphasis on natural scenery, a penchant for tragedy and melancholic sentiments. These characteristics of Joseon-ness, summarised by Japanese critics, evoke the conventional features of Joseon film established prior to the exported Joseon films, as discussed in the earlier section. In fact, the stories of *The Wayfarer* and other exported films sound quite similar to *Arirang* and earlier Joseon productions. Set in a remote fishing village in Gyeongsang

Province, *The Wayfarer*, for instance, narrates a melodramatic story of a poor family. The story centres on Bok-ryong, a fisherman who occasionally leaves his home town to work at a fish market to make extra money for his family. While he is away, tragedy befalls his family: his father meets a mysterious death and his wife Ok-hui, who is left alone with a baby boy and broke, finds herself in a desperate situation when her child becomes ill. Sam-su, the barber who is attracted to Ok-hui, tries to take advantage of her vulnerable condition by consoling her and paying for her son's medicine. In the climax, in which Sam-su finally makes a move and kidnaps Ok-hui to violate her, Bok-ryong, who arrives in his home town and finds out what is about to happen to his wife, rushes to Sam-su's residence where he slays Sam-su who also turns out later to be the one who had murdered his father. Bok-ryong is taken into custody for his crime and sent to the city for interrogation, and Ok-hui sees him off in tears.

The film's story, which is strikingly similar to that of *Arirang*, exploits the conventions of Joseon films, such as the rural setting, struggles of the poor and the tragic, sentimental ending. The film even includes Joseon cinema's typical action sequence in which 'some characters suddenly get mad and try to kill each other' and turns the film abruptly into 'a mediocre action drama',[104] along with the violent themes of vengeance, rape and murder that provide a narrative plausibility for the sequence. It seems obvious that *The Wayfarer* did not entirely deviate from the tropes of mainstream Joseon films in terms of the subject matter and storytelling. The archetypal Joseon film narrative employed by *The Wayfarer* and subsequent Joseon productions released in Japan did not enjoy favourable reviews there. Sloppy storytelling, the deep-seated problem of Joseon film, originating from the absence of a professional screenwriter, was noticed by Japanese critics who were all underwhelmed by the 'overly simple story' and 'primitive narrative structure'[105] that ran through Joseon films. Japanese critics uniformly pointed out Joseon film's 'sub-standard screenwriting'[106] that produced the appalling storytelling but, still, most of them were quite forgiving because the stunning visual exposure of Joseon colour compensated for the problems in the narrative structure. What truly fascinated Japanese filmgoers and critics, in other words, was not the story or narrative of Joseon films but the visual aesthetics persistently employed by film-makers effectively to exhibit Joseon's local colour while veiling an unattractive plot and poor narrative.

According to Japanese film theorists, the slow tempo, long takes and minimal editing and dialogue were cinematic devices used repeatedly in Joseon films. Importantly, these techniques were employed to construct visually the Joseon image in a picturesque manner and to allow Japanese viewers fully to appreciate the exotic landscape of Joseon and take pleasure in discovering the objects, culture and customs which comprised Joseon's local colour that they had conceptualised. Iida Shimbi wrote, 'This film (*The Wayfarer*) is a fictional drama, but more than half of the film represents the real scenery of Joseon as it is. It is a work filmed in so-called pseudo-documentary style, which exudes distinctive attraction.'[107] Iida further suggested that, like travelogues, *The Wayfarer* and *Han River* brought out the local colour from the landscape by taking shots of it in a 'postcard' style.[108] A Korean film critic made a similar comment on the visual aesthetics of *Han River* but with a critical tone, 'For one hour a scroll of landscape painting runs by on the screen', and concluded that the film just put the image of the Han River to the forefront with intermittent dialogue and music that emanated Joseon sentiment.[109] (Figure 2.5)

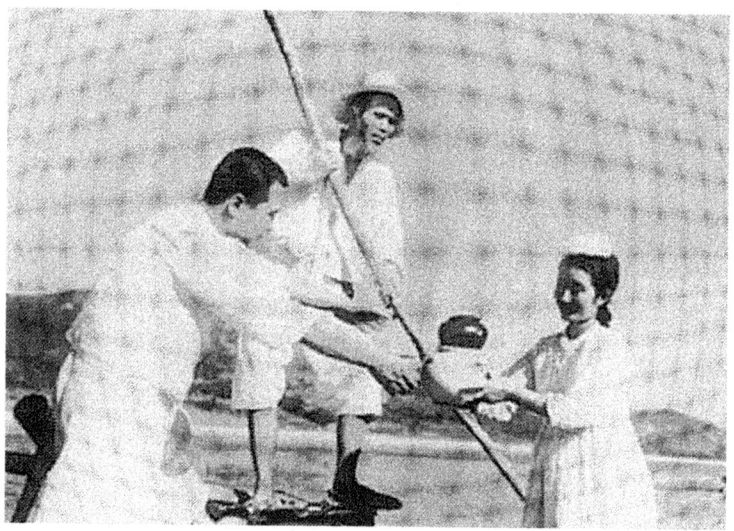

Figure 2.5 A promotional still for *Han River* (1938) that features three main characters in white *hanbok*, a traditional Korean attire. (*Nihon eiga*, 1 August 1939, p. 123) The Japanese saw the white *hanbok* as an object that best represented Joseon-ness at the time. A Korean film reviewer sceptically branded the characters wearing white *hanbok* in Joseon films set in fishing villages such as *Han River* and *Fishing Fires* as a 'bleached rarity', referring to the unlikely unsullied state of the farmer or fisherman characters' attire in films targeted for the Japanese market. (Nangchoin, 'Geukgwang yeonghwa *Oehwa*reul bogo', *Joseon ilbo*, 9 October 1938)

For Japanese critics, the representation of unique local colour became the sole standard that determined the quality of a Joseon film. In this regard, it seems inevitable that they singled out co-production as a potential weakness that might undermine the authenticity of Joseon film. Iijima Tadashi, a noted pioneer of Japanese film criticism, opened his extensive examination of Joseon cinema published in *Shin eiga* with a discussion of this problem:

> *Military Train* is a work co-produced with Toho Studio, so it cannot be a pure Joseon film. Yet the director is a Korean, and the majority of staff is from Korea, so it should be OK to label this film a Joseon film. Also *Fishing Fires* was supervised by Shimazu Yasujiro, and its music was done here. But this considerable intervention of Japanese elements is inevitable for the film's release in Japan proper, so it should be fine to take this one as a Joseon film as well. The same issue can be raised with *The Wayfarer* released last year. Personally, I am more interested in Joseon films purely produced by filmmakers of Joseon, but for now I should feel gratified to meet Joseon cinema through this sort of film.[110]

The concern expressed by Iijima about the issue of authenticity seems to be legitimate because some parts of *The Wayfarer* were shot in Shinko's Tokyo studio lot located in Ōizumi[111] (Toei's Tokyo Studio today) and featured a cast of Japanese actors in minor roles.[112] In contrast to Iijima's unease, however, it was actually through the collaboration with Japanese film-makers that Joseon film-makers could produce more effectively the image of Joseon which better catered for Japanese viewers. Indeed, producing Joseon films with the notion of local colour was not entirely the burden of Joseon film-makers. Rather, Joseon and Japanese film-makers collaborated in trying to find filmic devices that could increase Joseon films' appeal in the Japanese market. *Fishing Fires*, one of the only two films that survive today among the co-productions made at that time, nicely demonstrates how Joseon and Japanese film-makers collectively worked to produce cinematically the distinctive Joseon colour.

Fishing Fires, a co-production between Geukgwang Yeonghwasa and Shochiku, makes it obvious from the opening scene that the film's main purpose is to expose every bit of the remote village and depict its scenic beauty as much as possible. After the title sequence that superimposes the film credits over a series of paintings which portray traditional Korean customs and culture with a traditional Korean musical tune, the film opens with rhythmic montage shots of a group of villagers dancing to the tune of a folk song. The sequence undergoes a transition to a long shot that films the two main characters/lovers from afar against the beautiful landscape of the seaside and then cuts to the characters who start up a conversation. As the story progresses, the film frequently employs long shots and long takes to capture the scenery of the fishing village and often includes insert shots that exhibit the natural splendours. Though effective in exposing the serene atmosphere of a fishing village, these insert shots often disrupt the narrative flow and make it difficult for a viewer to build an emotional connection with the characters because they have little to do with the story. In other words, the frequent use of long shots, long takes, and inserts is intended to display the rural landscape, the quintessential component of Joseon's identity.

In tailoring Joseon images for Japanese viewers, Joseon and Japanese film-makers combined their efforts. The original story was written by Joseon film-makers and the film was shot in Joseon under Korean film-maker An Cheol-yeong's direction. The initial version of the film was re-edited by Shimazu Yasujiro, a famed Shochiku director who supervised the production of *Fishing Fires* before it was released at Shochiku theatres in August 1938.[113] In addition, the theme music, which employs a traditional Korean tune, was composed and played by Japanese musicians. Therefore, many of the key formal elements that were used to construct a Joseon image were designed by Japanese film-makers. The collaborative work between film-makers of Japan and Joseon went much deeper than the level of financial and technical support, even influencing the image politics of the film.

Though the film faithfully employs typical cinematic techniques and representational tactics that were used by exported Joseon films to maximise Joseon's exoticness, *Fishing Fires* was deemed a failure by Japanese film critics. It was critiqued not because the film's representation of Joseon was compromised by the intervention of Japanese film-makers but because its representation of Joseon was not exotic enough for the eyes of Japanese viewers. The film narrates a story of downfall and redemption of In-sun, an innocent fisherman's daughter who moves to Seoul to escape a forced marriage with a landlord to whom her family owes debts but ends up working as a *gisaeng* (professional female entertainer) until her lover rescues her from her misery and takes her back to their home village. Thus, much of the film's story takes place in Seoul where the unfortunate chapter of In-sun's story unfolds. Japanese film critics were not pleased with the second half of the film which was set in the metropolis because, they argued, the film's urban setting damaged the film's representation of Joseon-ness. A *Kinema junpō* reviewer remarked, 'The setting is changed to Seoul in the second half of the film . . . the landscape of the fishing village at the beginning of the film amused us, but the writer failed to take advantage of the natural landscape, as he was preoccupied with advancing the cheap storyline.'[114] To rephrase the reviewer's comment, the film's failed attempt to showcase 'authentic' Joseon-ness originates from the film's story which takes viewers to an urban setting that does not correspond to the Japanese perception of a Joseon image. The unfavourable reception of *Fishing Fires* clearly shows that, to appeal to Japanese audiences, the way in which Joseon film represented Joseon images could not betray the conception of local colour envisioned by the coloniser with regard to their colony. In other words, whether or not films were produced by Joseon film-makers or co-produced was not a decisive matter for Japanese viewers provided the films effectively rendered the image of Joseon they desired to see. As a result, finding the representational strategies which could create a Joseon image that responded to the preconstructed version of Joseon in Japan emerged as an important task for Joseon film-makers. Being anxious to export their films to Japan, Joseon film-makers not only took up this challenge but often willingly participated in cinematically affirming the imperial notion of Joseon colour.

Cinematic Lyricism: from Czechoslovakia to Joseon

The conscious construct of a Joseon image for the sake of distant observers was what fundamentally demarcated the exported films from previous Joseon productions. Most importantly, the presentation of Joseon images in those films was done through stylistic aestheticisation that relied on art cinema practices in selling Joseon films overseas. As evidenced in the above-discussed *Samcheolli* round-table discussion, the art cinema discourse was strategically put forth by Joseon film-makers who switched the major source of inspiration from Hollywood entertainment to European art cinema in an effort to export Joseon films. Even a film censor took notice of this shift in Joseon cinema. Complimenting Joseon film-makers' dedication to art, Okada Jun'ichi wrote, 'Films produced in Joseon these days show drastic improvement; different from the past, they [film-makers] abandoned an erroneous notion that Joseon film should contain a certain bias, and it's great that they instead stride toward the improvement of film.'[115] This orientation towards the art cinema discourse took a toll on the counter-hegemonic, political undertone of Joseon films, a legacy built from *Arirang*, and even censors were pleased by the depoliticisation of Joseon productions. Joseon film-makers' intentional suppression of the resistant component of Joseon cinema in favour of art cinema aesthetics was evident in the change in the source of inspiration for their pursuit of a new film style. For those seeking to maximise Joseon film's appeal to Japanese spectators, the art cinema of Czechoslovakia became an important point of reference. This Joseon–Czech connection has not received any scholarly attention but it was a frequently discussed topic in both Joseon and Japan in association with the discourse of local colour. In particular, as a Korean writer noted, 'These days everyone talks about lyricism or poesy.'[116] Czech cinema's lyricism was commonly likened to the new visual trend of Joseon film, starting with *The Wayfarer*. Accordingly, a parallel comparison was made by film critics in Japan who saw that Joseon film 'seems to be concerned about a slice of life in nature just like Czechoslovakian film',[117] and '[is] an idyllic cinema in a Czechoslovakian style'.[118] Hazumi Tsuneo, who thought the lyricism was Joseon film's main charm,[119] grouped together the films that employed local colour and analysed their relationship to Czech cinema, commenting, 'People tend to associate them [*The Wayfarer*, *Han River* and *The Border*] to Czech films such as *The River* (*Reka*, 1933), and it seems that Joseon's local colour, characterised as anguish and tenderness, is similar to that of Czech cinema.'[120]

Czech cinema's lyricism first enticed international audiences at the 1934 Venice film festival where four Czech films won awards. The cinematographer, Jan Stallich, who shot two of these films, *Ecstasy* (*Ectase*, 1932) and *The River*, was credited as the one who had developed these cinematic aesthetics. The essential elements of Czech lyricism comprise the poetic visual style, the use of natural landscape and a representation of the countryside as a homeland.[121] The 1933 film *The River*, the film most frequently discussed by critics in Joseon and Japan to describe the Joseon version of lyricism and 'scenic poetry',[122] exhibits the core features of Czech lyricism. (Figure 2.6) As *Variety* analysed, the story of this globally successful film is 'an extremely simple one' that narrates the love of two poor young couples who live in a fishing village by the river but the simple love story is compensated by the 'genuinely fine' cinematography that stunningly portrays the beautiful landscape of Czechoslovakia.[123] The film's opening sequence most tellingly displays its endeavours to expose cinematically the idyllic beauty of Czechoslovakia. The establishing shot consists of a series of images that discovers the natural beauties of the country. Shot and edited in a rhythmic montage style, the scene invites viewers to experience visually the pastoral landscape of the new nation through documentary-like images of rivers, valleys, lakes and other natural objects until it takes them to the fishing village where the story finally begins to unfold.

This visual rendering of Czechoslovakia was closely related to the new nation state's effort to create and assert its national identity. Founded in 1918, the Czechoslovak Republic gained its statehood when the two ethnic groups, the Czechs and Slovaks, joined efforts to become an independent nation state after the Austro-Hungarian Empire (1867–1918) dissolved at the end of World War I. As Abby Innes's description, 'a marriage of convenience', indicates, however, the merger between the considerably different ethnic groups with distinctive histories and cultures immediately created friction between the two.[124] Czech lyricism was an artistic endeavour to cope with this challenge, trying to create a unified identity for the new republic established on the tension between the two ethnic groups. Czech cinema's lyricism was a highly political cinematic language that displayed the emerging nationalism of Czechoslovakia and, as a matter of fact, the lyricism continued to influence

Figure 2.6 A newspaper advertisement for *The River* (1933). (*Joseon ilbo*, 14 January 1935)

Czechoslovakian art, including cinema, even after World War II. Thus, it is quite ironic that Joseon film-makers discovered Czech lyricism, an artistic expression inspired by the ideals of nationalism, when attempting to find a way to create a particular image of Joseon for the viewing pleasure of Japanese viewers. It should be noted, however, that the artistic manifestation of nationalism in Czech films was completely abandoned when the concept of cinematic lyricism migrated to Joseon because Joseon film-makers embraced only the exotic appeal Czech lyricism had on international audiences. In Joseon films, visual articulation of the nationalism of Czech lyricism was replaced by the poetic rendering of Joseon colour. In other words, Joseon film lyricism, like the original Czech lyricism, was employed to assert cinematically an identity of a national culture but it was used only to reaffirm the identity imposed on the colony by the colonisers, that is, the local colour of Joseon. The major difference between the two lyricisms becomes obvious when comparing their primary intended audiences. Unlike the Czech lyricism, which primarily aimed to solicit participation from domestic audiences in its attempt to discover the nation's cohesive identity, Joseon lyricism was intended to satisfy foreign (Japanese) audiences' pre-constituted perceptions of Joseon culture. In this manner, Joseon film-makers and Japanese film critics alike disregarded the nationalist impulses embedded in Czech cinema's lyricism because they paid attention only to the effectiveness of lyricism in visually representing Joseon-ness in association with the discourse of Joseon colour.

Joseon Colour and the Dilemma of Joseon Film-makers

For advocates of local colour, it was necessary to capitalise on Joseon colour to uplift Joseon film production. *Donga ilbo* argued that the future of Joseon cinema was dependent on how well Joseon films would represent Joseon colour.[125] The Joseon lyricism that was designed to satisfy the imperial gaze, however, drew considerable criticism in Joseon because, contrary to the Japanese, Korean critics found it 'difficult to relate to the reality represented in the film'.[126] The essence of the criticisms against Joseon images created through Joseon lyricism was most succinctly summed up in the writer Lee Tae-jun's perceptive assessment:

> The gourd, the tobacco pipe, spitting on the street, and the totem pole, which is supposed to be on the street, on a top of a mountain – this is just deplorable. There are so many people out there who interpret the so-called Joseon mood and sentiment as *miyage* [a souvenir] at a department store.[127]

To rephrase Lee's words, for critics of Joseon colour, film-makers simply packaged the exotic Joseon-ness for the pleasure of foreign audiences and offered them a superficial cinematic tour to Joseon. (Figure 2.7) Novelist An Dong-su offered a similar but more straightforward criticism, 'When portraying rural villages and the rural population, they [Joseon films] unnecessarily include many exotic scenes in order to appeal to the Japanese market, which makes (Korean) spectators frown.'[128] Kim Tae-jin warned his fellow Korean film-makers and critics, 'Japanese film critics and intellectuals seem to show much sympathy toward Joseon films, but we should not take seriously that kind of film criticism that tries to get something (out of Joseon films)', because the Japanese film circuit exaggerated Joseon colour to make a profit.[129] To Japanese film critics, film critic Ju Yeong-seob tried to relay this concern in his *Kinema junpō* essay, 'Japanese film critics' view toward Joseon cinema is as simple as Joseon film. As portraying Mount Fuji and *geisha* does not represent modern Japan, Mount Geumgang, *gisaeng* or *Arirang* are not about contemporary Joseon.'[130]

Figure 2.7 A promotional still for *The Wayfarer*. (*Asahi Graph*, 28.20, 12 May 1937, p. 23) Helpless Ok-hui (played by Mun Ye-bong) is on the hilltop, leaning against a totem pole, waiting for her husband's return. The Japanese popular magazine *Asahi Graph* described the image, 'It is the moment when Mun Ye-bong's beauty is at its best.' In contrast, Korean novelist Lee Tae-jun singled out the totem pole in this very scene, which was located on a hilltop instead of on the street where it should be, in his critique of Joseon film-makers' misrepresentation of Joseon culture in their attempts to increase the marketability of their films in Japan. ('Lee Tae-jun, Park Gi-chae yangsidaedam [ha]', *Donga ilbo*, 14 December 1938)

At the height of Joseon film's increasing visibility in cinemas in Japan in 1938, Murayama Tomoyoshi, a renowned Japanese avant-garde artist and playwright, sought the reason for this trend in the economic conditions of Joseon cinema by noting that it was generally difficult for Joseon films to break even in the Joseon market, and that led Joseon film-makers to try eagerly to open up the Japanese market and seek an opportunity to work with Japanese studios.[131] The self-orientalist use of local colour in an attempt to facilitate collaboration with the Japanese film industry and to cultivate the Japanese market turned out to be the most enabling but, at the same time, limiting condition for Joseon cinema at an important juncture. In her critical observation of a mainstream culture's appropriation of the culture of the marginalised and colonised, bell hooks comments on this very dilemma raised for the Otherised culture, 'Marginalized groups, deemed Other, who have been ignored, rendered invisible, can be seduced by the emphasis on Otherness, by its commodification, because it offers the promise of recognition and reconciliation ... The acknowledged Other must assume recognizable forms.'[132] To make Joseon cinema noticed by the imperialist culture, Joseon film-makers willingly took the assigned role of the producer of local, marginalised film aesthetics, satisfying the imaginary image of Joseon developed by the Japanese. While films such as *The Wayfarer* or *Han River* successfully wrapped Joseon colour as a cinematic 'souvenir' for Japanese patrons and achieved considerable advances for Joseon cinema, Joseon film's autonomous nature was significantly compromised. As I discussed concerning the cultural appropriation of *Arirang* earlier in the section, the intrinsic problem of the local colour discourse developed from the coloniser's essentialist view towards Joseon culture which tied the colonial culture to the mythic past. Indeed, through repeated encounters with the pastoral landscape of Joseon, Japanese spectators were convinced that Joseon films represented a Joseon that 'preserves the appearance of a few centuries ago, because the blade of culture does not permeate so easily, unlike Japan'.[133] Emphasising Joseon's backwardness and underdevelopment, in the end, the cinematic enunciation of Joseon colour consolidated the colonial hierarchy and thus implicitly endorsed Japan's colonial domination of Joseon.

The End of Joseon Colour

The Joseon film boom in Japan triggered by *The Wayfarer* did not last long because it was soon thwarted when more aggressive assimilation efforts were implemented in Joseon by the empire that tried to mobilise colonial subjects for its total war efforts. In making the colonised recognise the war as their own, it was crucial to eliminate any hint of difference between the empire and its colonies. Accordingly, the local-colour discourse on Joseon film, which floated around until around 1940, began to dissipate. Mizui Reiko, a Seoul-based settler film critic, offered the most critical voice against Joseon film's local specificity in her essay published in 1942. While admitting that *The Wayfarer* had improved the overall quality of Joseon cinema, Mizui undermined the film's appeal and influence by arguing that the film was successful only because it had a characteristic that could be completed by a 'Japanese perspective',[134] something Koreans were never able to create. She continued:

> For many reasons, I have been strongly asserting that Joseon cinema must be supported by Japanese [film-makers], and *The Wayfarer* proved my point. That's because tiny Joseon does not need to independently establish a separate character. Recognising Joseon cinema's specificity out of empathy is to ruin the bigger picture . . . There were opinions that Joseon cinema should produce bucolic films similar to the Czech film style, independently from Japanese cinema, but I opposed that opinion. A comparison to Czech cinema must sound sweet to the filmmakers of Joseon, but I believe we should avoid shallow ideas.[135]

Mizui argued *The Wayfarer* was essentially Japanese because of Japanese intervention, and Japanese elements instilled into the film were what truly improved the quality of *The Wayfarer* and overall Joseon cinema. Mizui's strong opposition to the separatist view on Joseon cinema, in fact, echoed the political climate or so-called New Order in which the assimilation of Joseon into Japan and the conversion of Koreans into imperial subjects were essential to the empire. When she said that the widely spread idea of maintaining Joseon cinema's distinctive identity would ruin 'the big picture', the message here was quite obvious. It was a warning to her fellow critics and film-makers, discouraging them from arguing for Joseon cinema's uniqueness and thus vouching for the local specificity of Joseon. It is intriguing, contrary to Japanese critics who had hailed the film's distinctive Joseon colour upon its release by trying to minimise the Japanese contribution, that Mizui claimed that the components in *The Wayfarer* which appealed to her had nothing to do with Joseon's locality or elements exotic to Japanese observers but, instead, the attraction of the film originated from the Japanese elements implanted into the film. Mizui even maintained that it was not Lee but Suzuki who actually directed the film. Importantly, in her other essay about Joseon cinema, written three years earlier, Mizui argued that the only glimpse of hope for Joseon film production depended on how well it could represent Joseon's distinctive nature and its local colour.[136] Mizui, as a settler film critic, was also highly critical of Japanese film capital's intrusion into the Joseon film industry when Japanese studios began directly to run movie theatres beginning in 1935.[137] Mizui's dramatically changed position on Joseon cinema in just three years proves that her negation of Joseon cinema's specificity and locality was, in fact, politically motivated. Between her two essays on the triangular associations among the Joseon film industry, the practice of co-production, and the discourse of local colour, both the Joseon and Japanese film industries were placed under the firm control of the authorities, and the cinema's essential function became a mobilisation of the masses for war. Any suggestion to create a demarcation between Koreans and the Japanese in carrying out 'the holy war' to liberate Asia from the Western invasion was nothing but an obstacle that hindered the unity of all imperial subjects. To this end, it was an argument, like that of Mizui, that was acceptable only in the last phase of the Japanese Empire when Joseon-ness was systematically and belligerently negated and eradicated. The discourse of Joseon colour became unnecessary and even irrelevant.

Not only in Joseon but in Japan, artistic representation of Joseon-ness began to be dealt with more seriously as the war progressed. Obliteration of any hint of distinctive Joseon-ness became the basis for a new wartime cultural policy and, thus, Joseon locality was not tolerated. Even the mere use of the Korean language in arts was discouraged and banned in Japan. In July 1940, for instance, the Society for the Study of Joseon Music and Dance of Seoul was warned by the city of Osaka when its show, held in that city, included the use of Korean, and thus the troupe took out the part that featured the Korean language for its next show in Kyoto.[138] Nevertheless, even at this last stage, the ambivalence of assimilation continued to exist. Use of the Korean language in propaganda films produced in Joseon was allowed as a way to educate better the Korean population that had not mastered Japanese. Yet this was not tolerated in Japan, as Japanese authorities, in a manner similar to the strict monitoring of Joseon songs and stage performances, tried to ban these propaganda films because of the use of the Korean language. This frustrated the colonial administration of Joseon which tried to publicise its war efforts through the release of its propaganda films in Japan. In addition, even though the authorities put pressure on the industry to get rid of Joseon cinema's distinctive traits, in reality, industrial professionals and film policymakers continued to imagine Joseon cinema as a separate entity. As illustrated in Japanese film critic Uchida Kimio's *Eiga hyōron* essay, the Japanese film world had a hard time erasing the demarcations between Japanese cinema and its colonial cinemas and seeing them as one national cinema.[139] When reviewing propaganda films co-produced by Joseon and Japanese film-makers which aimed cinematically to validate the collaborative war efforts, Japanese film critics still complained that they were not 'pure Joseon' films.[140] Despite its persistent inconsistency and unfeasibility, the empire-wide effort to eliminate the local specificity of the colony and assimilate colonial subjects into the empire still destroyed any lingering autonomous elements in Joseon cinema. With Joseon cinema's integration into the imperial cinema, Joseon film-makers' brief experiment with Joseon colour and 'export film' saw its abrupt end.

Chapter 3
Migrating with the Movies: Japanese Settler Film Culture

In 1933, the Association of Gyeongseong (Seoul) Exhibitors (AGE), formed a year earlier collectively to tackle the economic slump triggered by the Great Repression,[1] was faced with an unprecedented scandal that infuriated many of its members and accordingly received considerable media attention.[2] At the centre of the scandal was Tokunaga Kumaichirō, a veteran Japanese settler film distributor and exhibitor who, allegedly, approached Shochiku Studio of Japan to acquire the rights to distribute its films in Seoul.[3] According to media reports, Shochiku was displeased with the aging facilities of Taishōkan Theatre, its long-standing partner. The rift between these two old partners had opened when Kido Shiro, the head of Shochiku's Kamata studio, visited Taishōkan earlier that year to promote the studio's talkie spectacle *Chushingura* (1932) but became frustrated with the theatre's poor sound system which could not take full advantage of Shochiku's advanced film sound technology. The studio found this unacceptable because, after a fierce, decade-long competition, Shochiku had become the most dominant film studio in Japan, supported by its swift, aggressive conversion to talkies through its sound-on-film Tsuchihashi system.[4] Shochiku started to look for a venue with more up-to-date equipment that would be suitable to show off its technological advances and maintain its reputation as the producer of the finest Japanese talkies. Soon a rumour became widespread that Tokunaga and Shochiku had almost reached an agreement which would give Tokunaga exclusive rights to Shochiku studio films on the condition that he would build a brand new Shochiku-affiliated movie theatre in Seoul. Taishōkan and other members of AGE openly criticised Tokunaga's unethical business practices and put pressure on him to give up the partnership with the studio. As the two parties failed to resolve the matter, Wakejima Shujirō, the president of AGE, and the Hon-machi police chief intervened to settle the matter, calling for a series of meetings. At the meetings, Tokunaga claimed that he had been approached by Shochiku when he travelled to Osaka and agreed to visit the studio to work out this issue. Upon AGE's request, Shochiku arranged a meeting with Tokunaga and other members of the association at the Shimonoseki harbour in Japan. At the meeting, Tokunaga and his colleagues explained their situation to the studio. Yet Shochiku was adamant about changing its partnership and even refused an exhibitors' proposition that Taishōkan serve as a second Shochiku theatre in Seoul. As the studio handed over exclusive distribution and exhibition rights to Tokunaga, the partnership between Taishōkan and Shochiku was finally terminated in the summer of 1933. This was a huge blow to Taishōkan which was not at all prepared for the cancellation of the partnership. Taishōkan was not able to find a new partner studio and instead had to continue on a film-by-film basis contract with a range of film distributors, a practice dubbed as the *kakusha* (all companies) deal. In the end, the theatre shut down entirely near the end of that year, ending its twenty-year business as one of the four major Japanese movie theatres in Seoul. This scandal shocked settler exhibitors as they witnessed the degree of influence the Japanese film studios could exert on the Joseon film business if they were determined so to do. As they feared, Tokunaga's partnership with Shochiku turned out to be an emblematic event that signalled the increasing intrusion of Japanese film capital into the Joseon film business in the final decade of the Japanese occupation, eventually pushing the majority of Japanese settler and Korean film professionals to the margins of (and often out of) the Joseon film business. Even Tokunaga was 'abandoned' only a year later by Shochiku who had found a new partner. The Japanese version of ruthless film capitalism had finally arrived in Joseon.

Figure 3.1 Young Tokunaga Kumaichirō. (*Katsudō shashin meikan: zenpen* [Tokyo: Katsudō Shimbunsha, 1922])

The rise of Tokunaga and the infamy surrounding it in the middle of the 1930s were among the decisive events which anticipated the key changes that were about to take place in Joseon cinema in the following years, ranging from changes in film censorship, modifications in the film distribution and exhibition systems, and the influx of Japanese film capital into the Joseon film market. All these changes will be further elaborated in later sections and chapters but here let me devote a bit more attention to Tokunaga Kumaichirō to elucidate the focus of this chapter. Born in the city of Fukuoka of Kyūshū Prefecture in 1887, Tokunaga migrated to colonial Korea in 1920 at the age of thirty-four.[5] Leaving his journalist career in his home town, Tokunaga arrived in the city of Daegu where he was hired as a manager for a Japanese movie theatre.[6] He did not stay in Daegu long, and he left for Seoul with his family to open his shop, the Tokunaga Moving Picture Shop (J: Tokunaga Katsudō Shashin Shōkai) which specialised in the sale of film strips and film equipment rentals. Tokunaga soon began to distribute Warner Brothers' and FBO's movies as well as films of Japanese studios such as Tōa and Tōgatsu.[7] His business was in partnership with Danseongsa, the premier theatre for Koreans located in Seoul.[8] When the production of Joseon film attracted players in the Joseon film business in the mid-1920s, Tokunaga established a production wing (Tokunaga Productions) which produced *The Song of the Unforgettable* (*Bulmanggok*) and *The Plaintive Song of Crimson Love* (*Hongryeon biga*) in 1927. But, after these two films, Tokunaga Productions stopped producing commercial films. Instead, the production company switched to producing and distributing educational films, becoming the leading educational film company in Joseon.[9]

Time after time, Tokunaga proved to be an exceptionally gifted film entrepreneur. In 1928 Tokunaga began to run his own theatre which earned him greater recognition. Tokunaga acquired ownership of Koganekan, which had struggled for years,[10] and changed its name to the Tōa Club, honouring its new partnership with Tōa Kinema, one of many Japanese film companies established in the 1920s (1923). Upon acquisition of the theatre, Tokunaga resorted to a drastic business strategy in the midst of the economic recess in 1930, reducing its admission fee to just 10 cents and changing its programme every three days instead of the standard five to seven days.[11] Tokunaga's move turned out to be successful, as the Tōa Club was packed every day with film patrons looking for cheap entertainment. As 'a new rising star of the Seoul exhibition world',[12] Tokunaga's reputation reached Japan, and many Japanese film journals and trade magazines reported on his business activities. *Kokusai eiga shimbun*, for instance, introduced in detail the 'unprecedented tactics' that Tokunaga used to promote Charlie Chaplin's much-awaited *City Lights* (1931) for its release at his Tōa Club (and simultaneously distributed for Joseon Geukjang, a Korean theatre) on 1 June 1934;[13] according to the trade journal, the film's success was record-breaking, noting that it was the first time ever for a foreign film to be shown for ten days in a row at a Japanese theatre in Joseon. Also importantly, Tokunaga was instrumental in the conversion to sound at cinemas. When sound systems were still incomplete, and thus only dialogues were played at movie theatres that lacked a full film sound technology installation, he acquired the distribution rights to Warner Brothers/First National's Vitaphone talkies for Joseon and Manchuria and screened them at his Tōa Club beginning in May 1932. He also installed the Japanese-made Nipton sound system in his theatre in order to take full advantage of the Vitaphone talkies he acquired.[14] Tokunaga's pursuit of the contract with Shochiku would be his next move to secure further his position in the film exhibition world. At the same time, he was also desperately in need of this new partnership, not only because his old partner Tōa Kinema had permanently closed down in 1932 but because Takarazuka Kinema, a new partner he had found, had been running a shaky business from the outset in 1932 as a result of its labour conflicts. Once he had successfully won the rights to Shochiku's films, his theatre's name was changed again to Shochikuza in July 1933. Around this time, he added another theatre, located near Seoul, to his company, Keiryūkan in Yongsan.[15] Though his business was primarily based in Seoul, Tokunaga also operated another movie theatre, Yūaikan, in the city of Chuncheon in Gangwon Province. Tokunaga seemed almost unstoppable at this point but the decade-long expansion of his business finally stalled when the partnership with Shochiku did not last beyond the first term of the contract. Shochiku did not renew the contract with Tokunaga, as he struggled to build a new theatre that would replace his twenty-year-old one, a part of the deal he had made with Shochiku. Instead, the studio made a new contract with Ishibashi Ryōsuke, a famed land developer and entrepreneur, who guaranteed the studio a brand new upmarket modern theatre. Ishibashi's Meijiza opened as a Shochiku-affiliated theatre in 1936. Despite this setback, Tokunaga continued to play an important role as the new president of AGE. He somehow managed to deliver his promise to Shochiku rather belatedly, when he significantly upgraded his theatre in 1936.[16] This newly renovated Koganeza, now showing Makino films, was one of only a few theatre buildings at the time built with concrete and steel. The theatre survived for the next six decades, despite the eventful postcolonial South Korean history, under different names and ownerships until it was permanently shut down in 1999 upon the advent of the multiplex era.

Tokunaga migrated to Joseon a decade after Japan's colonisation of Korea and almost fifty years after the first Japanese migration began in the late 1870s and thus benefited from earlier Japanese settlers' decades-long efforts to build up their businesses in Korea/Joseon. Still, it took Tokunaga nearly two decades to reach the top of the Joseon film industry. Not all Japanese migrants were as successful as Tokunaga. In fact, Tokunaga's film career presents one of the greater success stories because many Japanese migrants failed to establish themselves in Joseon and continued to meander across the empire seeking new opportunities. Though he was one of the most successful film businessmen, however, Tokunaga was not the only Japanese emigrant who firmly established himself in the Joseon film world. In this sense, Tokunaga's life and career present a model account of those settler film professionals who became an integral part of Joseon cinema. Yet the film culture of Japanese migrants, their contribution to Joseon cinema, and their place in Japan's imperial cinema remain significantly studied. In fact, Tokunaga and other Japanese settlers were quickly thrown into oblivion around the time the Japanese Empire began to dissolve, and it is nearly impossible to track their life stories after the end of the colonial occupation.

Reconstructing Tokunaga's career over the twenty years took a bit of work, piecing together fragments I gleaned from archives located in Korea, Japan and the United States, but it was not entirely impossible. My effort to recount Tokunaga's story sums up the kind of research I engage with in this chapter. Between the years 1876 to 1945, tens of thousands of Japanese migrated to Korea/Joseon to find a new home. This chapter is an attempt to shed light on the film culture of these settlers, ranging from film entrepreneurs, film-makers, and theatres, to film critics, fans, and their film tastes, yet another forgotten but essential facet of Joseon cinema. Historiographically speaking, this particular contact zone turns out to be rather a grey area between Japanese and Korean national film histories because Japanese settler film culture, despite its critical importance in bridging the film cultures of the empire and the colony, has faded away both in Korea and Japan. Figures such as Tokunaga have been, at best, located on the peripheries of two national histories and largely ignored because they do not fit neatly into the master narratives of Japanese or Korean national cinemas. As discussed in the Introduction, after about a dozen films from the colonial period were discovered in the first decade of the twenty-first century, the past few years have seen increasing numbers of scholarly works that look into the intertwined natures of Japanese and Joseon cinema at the last stage of the empire, when Korean and Japanese film-makers were mobilised to collaborate for propaganda purposes. These collaborative efforts are generally seen as the primary point of convergence between imperial Japanese and colonial Korean cinemas and thus accordingly receive considerable public and scholarly attention. The overemphasis on this most obvious and intense form of interaction between the cinemas of the empire and the colony, however, obscures much of the complex entwining nature of Joseon and Japanese cinema throughout the colonial period. In particular, the fixation on the later years of collaborative film-making practices does not quite illuminate the important figures who played more instrumental, but often ambiguous, roles in linking the Japanese and Joseon film cultures. Equally problematical, the narrow focus on film-makers and film texts in the 1940s obfuscates the evolution of the settler film culture from around the turn of the twentieth century, including Japanese migrant film entrepreneurs, such as Tokunaga, film critics, and film spectators. These individuals, who assumed a major presence in the first forty years of development of Joseon cinema, also helped the Japanese film industry to go beyond Japan proper and cultivate one of its first 'foreign' markets during the Japanese film industry's growth in the 1920s and 1930s.

Settlers do appear occasionally in Korean film history but mostly as some sort of side note to Korea's national film history. A common image of Japanese settler producers, exhibitors and film-makers has it that they were shrewd business persons and/or even blatant exploiters whose sole purpose was to take advantage of the poor condition of the Joseon film world and thus 'occupied' or delayed the development of 'Korean' cinema.[17] They are seen merely as the extended arm of the empire that facilitated imperial causes and exploitations in the colony. Over fifty or sixty years of residence on foreign soil, however, Japanese emigrants developed their own unique identities. Japanese settlers engaged in a kind of negotiation between their ethnic identity as Japanese (and colonisers) and cultural identity as emigrants. In terms of numbers, the settlers were a minority group but their influence, power, financial capacity and other benefits they were entitled to as Japanese made them superior to the locals in every respect. At the same time, while life in the colony opened up a new opportunity for many settlers, their physical dislocation from Japan proper placed them somewhere between the colonised Koreans and coloniser Japanese in the imperial hierarchy. Also importantly, Japanese film entrepreneurs' interest was not always in accordance with that of the empire. In *Brokers of Empire* (2011), a landmark study of Japanese settlers in colonial Korea, Uchida Jun shows that Japanese emigrants' primary interest lay in commercial opportunities and thus their pursuit of economic gain did not always match the empire's master plan and the colonial government's governing strategies; rather they formed a stronger political alliance with Korean elites to represent better their interest in the colony which made their relationship with the authorities more ambiguous.[18]

In standard Korean film history, the multiple relationships of Japanese settlers with the colony and empire disappear; instead, Japanese emigrants are put into the same category 'Japanese' as are film-makers of Japan, merely in terms of their ethnic identity, and are described as an equally oppressive force. Indeed, despite renewed interest in colonial cinema for the past decade, there have been minimal efforts to expand the historical perspective, as those efforts are not focused on questioning the very problem of film historiography that still forsakes any endeavour to narrate other possible stories embedded in Joseon cinema. The recent studies of colonial cinema prove how resilient the framework of national cinema, as well as nationalist film historiography, is and how difficult it is for film historians to embrace an idea of looking beyond an oppressor–oppressed dichotomy in exploring Joseon cinema. Merely picturing the film culture of the Japanese settlers as one of the major obstacles Korean film-makers had to overcome, historians not only denounce that very culture because 'the quintessence to the formation of Joseon/Korean cinema is the process of negotiation and competition that ensued in Joseon cinema field caused by Japanese capitalists' but also reaffirm that it is fine to disregard settler film-makers because 'it was not Japanese migrants, who looked for a new opportunity in Joseon cinema, but Korean filmmakers who remained in postcolonial Korea and became the foundation for North and South Korean cinemas'.[19] Evoking the importance of placing Korean film-makers at the centre of the historical narrative trajectory, this view presents readers and fellow historians a guideline in dealing with a taboo subject: Japanese settlers should be negated as they did not make any significant contribution to Korean national cinema. Japanese settlers, just like the censors, Japanese studios and the authorities, were simply obstructive and even damaging elements that were essentially the 'Other' of Joseon cinema who 'observed Joseon cinema mainly from their superior position'.[20] Portraying settlers as the destructive other of Joseon cinema exploits a general assumption that inflexibly attaches a negative label to the settler film culture and disavows the formative aspect of Joseon cinema.

To understand Japanese settler film culture more impartially requires an effort to take a leap and accept the fact that Joseon cinema was a colonial cinema, that settler film culture embodied a fundamental identity of Joseon cinema. In addition, to map settler film culture properly, I argue for a clearer demarcation between the film cultures of the Japanese and the Japanese settlers; wedged between the two film cultures, Japanese settlers developed their own film-cultural identity quite distinct from the Japanese film culture. After all, they were constituents of Joseon cinema rather than Japanese cinema. Their presence in Joseon cinema, in this regard, was not an exogenous force that automatically impeded the development of colonial film culture but a very vital part of it. Narrating a colonial film history through marginalising and villainising these figures might be useful in adorning an unfortunate chapter of Korean film history but that could be accomplished only at the sacrifice of history. As I unravel in the rest of this chapter, the compound relationships of the settlers to both the film culture of the Koreans and the film culture of their homeland were among the core components that directed the formation of the film industry, practice and culture in Joseon. Therefore, it is crucial to bring these figures back from historical obscurity and reassess their place in Joseon and Japanese cinemas in order to understand the complex functions of Joseon cinema. Each of the following two sections interrogates the relationship of the settlers with the two separate film cultures. The first section looks into the formation of the film culture of the Japanese migrants, detailing the distinctive traits of the settler film culture in comparison to the film practices in Japan, while the second half of the chapter scrutinises the ways in which the interactions between the settler film culture and local Korean film culture influenced the construction of the colony Joseon's film culture.

The Formation and Characteristics of Settler Film Culture

When it comes to the earliest moments of Korean film history, many questions still remain unanswered. As I noted in Chapter 1, the issue of when the first movie screening happened – or when film arrived in Korea – is the most challenging question with which film historians have been taxed. Hanseong Electric Company's promotional film screening event is now widely recognised as the first public and commercial film screening in Korea (1903) but there is no consensus on the very first film screening. The problem of pinpointing where the first film screening was held is not an issue unique to Korea. Many national cinemas struggle properly to record their early film histories largely because of the deficiency of historical materials and evidence which often generates contested historical views and speculation. In Korean film history this issue is even more difficult to tackle because Korea had no indoor theatre tradition or established venues for film exhibition which significantly delayed the implementation of public film screenings. In many cases, movie screenings occurred in private settings which makes it even more challenging to find any form of documentation that could definitively establish the details of these film screenings. The most commonly accepted assumption is that films were first screened privately in various foreign residential areas and hotels by and for foreign visitors and residents of turn-of-the-century Korea. Among many possibilities, a theory that the first screening in Korea happened in 1897 at a Japanese private household or community centre in Hon-machi, a Japanese residential area in Seoul – the Chungmuro area today – has recently gained some support. Unfortunately, there is no single document that directly confirms this screening, and only varied versions of stories concerning this screening have been passed down by word of mouth. Several film essays from the 1920s and 1930s, which attempt to reconstruct the earliest encounter with cinema in Korea, claim that the first film screening was done in a Japanese residential area but offer no concrete evidence.[21] Incorporating this theory in his

The Creation and Construction of Asian Cinema (1941), an attempt to film-theorise imperial Japan's ideal of 'Greater East Asia Co-Prosperity', Ichikawa Sai, president of the Japanese film trade journal *Kokusai eiga shimbun* and film theorist, writes that the first film screening took place in a Japanese residential area but he also makes a note that there is no actual documentation regarding this screening.[22] Whether or not that private film screening at a Japanese residence was indeed the earliest film screening in Korea seems quite difficult to determine unless more solid information come to light but the fact that a film screening in a Japanese residential area is deemed as one of the possible first film screenings in Korea is certainly intriguing for many reasons. First of all, it reveals how deeply the Japanese film culture had penetrated Korean film culture long before the Japanese colonial occupation officially began. Another overriding issue here is the very presence of Japanese settlers in the heart of the nation's capital in the late 1890s and their pivotal roles in the formation and development of film culture in Korea. In addition, it is intriguing that films quickly became part of the cultural lives of Japanese migrants, just a few years after the invention of the medium.

Japan's 'great migration' to Korea started in 1876 when Japan used military threats to force the Joseon Dynasty to sign the Ganghwa Island Treaty (February 1876). This unequal trade treaty heralded the Japanese imperial march towards Korea, which had maintained a strict policy of isolation, *swaeguk* (shutting off the nation), as a means to repel the trade demands from various imperial forces. Importantly, the treaty included the granting of residential rights for the Japanese in Korea, which designated special areas for Japanese migrants where Korean local law did not apply. Migration was slow at first but a breakthrough occurred in 1905 when Korea became the protectorate of Japan. The migration accelerated once again in 1910 when many of the restrictions related to Japanese emigration to Korea were lifted and, upon Japan's official colonisation, the peninsula became a safer place for Japanese migrants to reside. From there, the numbers of Japanese migrants rose sharply throughout the 1910s, and the growth of the Japanese population continued to accelerate through the 1920s; at the end of the war in 1945, seven hundred thousand Japanese civilians, along with three hundred thousand military personnel, resided in Joseon. So-called Japanese residence areas began to develop around the early 1900s, and Japan's settler colonialism particularly affected the cultural landscape of urban areas where the majority of Japanese settlers took up residence. In Seoul, for instance, in the 1910s, one quarter of the city's population was Japanese settlers and, in port cities developed during the colonial period, the number of migrants made up a large proportion of the total population. Along with other types of show business, cinema came to Korea to entertain Japanese migrants as early as the 1900s. Unlike Korea, Japan had a long tradition of performing arts enjoyed by commoners, and almost all types of Japanese performing arts came with the settlers to Korea. Owing to the absence of indoor theatres, however, Japanese entrepreneurs had first to construct a venue where they could put on their shows even before Japan officially occupied Korea. It is unclear when exactly the first Japanese theatres were built, as early theatres were mostly makeshift and did not leave concrete records. According to the existing documentation, the first theatres for Japanese migrants began to appear around 1907 in Seoul and in port cities such as Incheon and Busan which had a large number of Japanese migrants.[23] With the exception of the High Entertainment Theatre (1910), the first theatre solely dedicated to film screening, these early theatres did not focus particularly on any single performing art or entertainment. At first, film was screened as part of theatre programmes that featured a number of different kinds of shows, a practice that lasted until the mid-1910s. Sometimes the theatres devoted a few days exclusively to screen films. This kind of early film programming was not unique, as films were first included as a part of other entertainment such as vaudeville shows in many other countries. Nevertheless, what is distinctive about this programming in early Japanese settlers' theatres is, as Hong Seon-yeong insightfully points out, the smudged boundaries between highbrow theatre, such as kabuki, Noh, *bunraku* and *shimpa*, and lowbrow, popular entertainment, such as *kodan*, circus, magic shows, street performance, magic lantern, and film.[24] Owing to the extreme scarcity of venues, films were featured not just as part of *yose* (Japanese vaudeville) but sometimes along with traditional Japanese performing arts such as kabuki and Noh at the same venue, which was not a common practice in Japan where theatres typically specialised in a single performing art or genre. The exhibition practice which bundled together all kinds of theatre arts stemmed from multilayered absences, such as the limited numbers of theatres, audiences and performers in colonial Korea. This unfavourable situation for the traditional performing arts, on the contrary, led to the advance of cinema as the most popular entertainment from the mid-1910s onwards.

The majority of theatres newly built in the 1910s and 1920s were movie theatres or theatres primarily dedicated to film screening, and many early theatres built from the mid-1900s to the early 1910s for traditional performing arts and stage dramas were closed down or switched to movie theatres in this period. In 1916 a Japanese settler wrote:

> Between the end of 1914 and the summer of last year, moving pictures became predominant in Seoul's entertainment world but their heated popularity seemed to cool down a little bit. Still when looking at the overall development of the entertainment business throughout this year, you would realise that the moving picture's influence is amazing, particularly compared to other entertainment.[25]

Similarly, the Japanese language newspaper *Busan nippō* reported on 'the recent prosperity of the motion picture' that two-thirds of total entertainment revenues was generated from movie theatres in 1916 in Busan, the port city located at the south-eastern tip of the Korean peninsula that functioned as a gateway into Joseon from Japan.[26] Out of 350,000 attendants to all kinds of entertainment (kabuki, *shingeki*, *naniwabushi*, *joruri*, sumo, magic shows, *rakugo* and moving pictures), the newspaper continued, 240,000 spectators (over 68 per cent of theatre patrons) went to the movies. This steep rise of film in the entertainment world for Japanese migrants can be understood in relation to the structure of the early theatre programme. As the entertainment business was a small market, it was almost impossible regularly to produce performing arts programmes that featured local performers, staff and producers. Entertainers did not make up a significant part of the Japanese migration to Joseon during the pre-colonial period. In fact, almanacs and name books (*meikan*) that list Japanese immigrants and their businesses published before the 1910s, such as *Zaikan jinshi meikan* (1905), *Nikkan shōkōjin meiroku* (1908), *Chōsen shinshiroku* (1909), and *Keijō to naichijin* (1910), do not even contain a section for any form of entertainment business and thus include no entertainers, performers or exhibitors. Typically, theatres had to invite performance troupes from Japan but it was never easy, financially and logistically, constantly to bring in theatre groups and performers from the homeland. In addition, the poor condition of the theatres was yet another obstacle that kept Japanese performers from performing for their fellow Japanese in Joseon. In 1908 Kawakami Otojiro, the dramaturge/exhibitor who is now deemed the father of *shimpa*, was invited by Seoul exhibitors to put his show on stage at theatres in Seoul. After he visited the city to check on the stage conditions at theatres, however, he turned down the invitation because, according to Kawakami, his drama troupe would not give their best performance because theatres lacked proper lighting.[27] This was an embarrassing incident not just to people in the entertainment business but to settler community leaders; and it made them realise that there was a dire need for a decent theatre, leading some ashamed settlers to propose publicly to raise the funds to build a major theatre.[28] This anecdote reveals the hardship of early settler exhibitors who had to start their business by constructing a theatre and bringing in performers from their homeland.

Considering these cultural and industrial backgrounds, the rise of the cinema seemed inevitable. Film emerged as the most popular form of mass entertainment, not just because it was cheap, accessible entertainment for patrons but also because it was a cheap show business for exhibitors. Unlike other performing arts or entertainment, film did not involve professionally trained performers, staff members, producers and so on. After all, to run a film business, they just needed a projector, a screen, film prints and a small group of experts such as *benshi*, musicians and projectionists. In addition, when it came to programming, compared to other forms of entertainment, it was a lot easier to change the programmes for films which must have been perfect for exhibitors in Joseon who had constantly to provide new programmes (typically every three to seven days) for their highly restricted consumer base. Importantly, this relatively simple film business practice explains the discrepancy in colonial Korea between the quick advancement of cinema and the much slower development of other modern mass culture that required theatre space, such as stage drama and the revue. Stage drama, ballet and modern dance began to offer competition to the film business only in the 1930s, though they never really posed any meaningful challenge to cinema. Dongyang Guekjang, the very first theatre for stage drama, was established in 1935 but suffered its first bankruptcy just four years later. Lamenting the absence of venues for kabuki and *shimpa*, in an essay published in the settler magazine *Chōsen oyobi Manshū* in 1935, Nitta Ryujiro explained that, as kabuki and *shimpa* exhibitors had to bring in troupes from Japan, and Koreans had no interest in the performing arts, it was almost impossible for the stage drama business to succeed financially and, as a result, movie theatres were the only available entertainment, even for a big city like Seoul.[29]

The correlation between this specific attribute of Joseon entertainment and the dominance of film can be further illuminated by the popularity of *naniwabushi* (traditional Japanese narrative singing), one of the two major forms of entertainment, along with the cinema, in the 1910s. Commenting on the growing popularity of film and *naniwabushi* within the migrants' entertainment world, lacking in traditional performing arts such as Noh and kabuki, Japanese intellectuals who had just moved to Joseon after colonisation expressed their frustration with the dowdy cultural scene they encountered upon arrival. A contributor to *Chōsen kōron*, who had just arrived in Seoul, commented on how dismal the Japanese migrants' culture was, 'Seoul used to be the capital of Joseon, so I assumed it must have an advanced entertainment business, but this thought quickly disappeared. When comparing it to Japan, the taste for art here is almost a century behind.'[30] The author concludes 'Generally they [Japanese settlers] have almost no taste for art. Vulgar moving pictures and *naniwabushiko* are the most popular arts, and this fact clearly showcases the level of their artistic taste.'[31] Another writer expresses similar disappointment in his essay entitled 'Naniwabushi and Moving Pictures in Joseon', in which the author commented that the popularity of *naniwabushi* and the moving picture was indicative of the vulgar nature of Seoul entertainment. The author maintained:

> When you look at the pamphlets that introduce Seoul's entertainment, it is always either *naniwabushi* or moving pictures. Or a new theatre (*shingeki*) that just charges ten cents for every seat. This fact quite clearly epitomises how miserable Seoul's entertainment institution is and how vulgar people's taste is here. Such taste is embarrassing not only to foreigners but also to Koreans.[32]

These authors were hasty to judge the Seoul entertainment business by grounding their perception on their uneasiness with the two popular arts which, quite interestingly, also grew into the most popular forms of entertainment in Japan. Both authors scoffed at Japanese immigrants' penchant for lowbrow popular culture by insinuating that *naniwabushi* and motion pictures were the culture of the lower class or for those who had poorer cultural taste. In other words, critiques which ultimately related the unique nature of Seoul entertainment to the deficiency in cultural capital of the Japanese settlers were nothing but reflections of the stereotypical view on Japanese migrants, the majority of whom were businessmen, as they failed to consider the preconditions that limited the ways in which the entertainment business was developed and run in Joseon at the time. It should be noted here that *naniwabushi* did not involve a large group of performers. It was a simple narrative art that required only a narrator and *shamisen* player. Like cinema, the simple format of *naniwabushi* offered a solution to exhibitors' issues stemming from the lack of entertainment, performance art and theatrical tradition in Joseon. Unsurprisingly, *naniwabushi* continued to thrive as a cheap entertainment.[33]

As film gained more and more favour from exhibitors and theatre-goers alike, exhibitors who specialised in the distribution and exhibition of film began to appear, along with movie theatres, which thereby initiated a germinal move to institutionalise the film business. The majority of film entrepreneurs in Joseon were opportunists, meaning they had not had any film-related careers while they were in Japan but manoeuvred themselves into the film business after they had established themselves in other business fields in Joseon. Hayakawa Jōtaro, the pioneer of Joseon entertainment, for instance, came to Korea in 1905 as an army official and was invited by the Korean government as a financial adviser.[34] In 1909, he started his own business offering a delivery service and soon was engaged in another business in land surveying. In 1913, he stepped into the moving picture business as manager of the Koganekan[35] and formed Hayakawa Entertainment Company (Hayakawa *engeibu*) that became the most influential film exhibition company in the 1910s. He later moved to the newly opened Kirakukan in 1919 and joined Joseon Geukjang, a Korean theatre, in 1922. Most notably, in the mainstream version of colonial film history, he is known as Hayakawa Koshū, a name he used for his director credits for the film *Tale of Janghwa and Hongryeon*, one of the first Joseon films. He was well regarded in the settler community and even known to the Japanese film industry as a pioneering exhibitor and film-maker of Joseon cinema. Hayakawa made a couple more films and left Joseon Guekjang to manage the Koganekan again until he rather abruptly resigned from the theatre and returned to Japan for reasons which are unclear.[36]

Hayakawa's rivals soon began to emerge[37] and, like Hayakawa, after having established themselves in other business sectors, they became intrigued by film's commercial potential. Nitta Kōichi, the patriarch of the Nitta family which ran a number of movie theatres in five different cities in the early 1920s, quit his job at Mitsui Butsusan (Mitsui & Co.) in 1910 and moved to the new colony Joseon to 'make it big'.[38] Arriving in Seoul, Nitta quickly realised that land values were on a steep rise and jumped into real estate development which made him a fortune 'in the blink of an eye'.[39] In 1912, he moved into the film business with an intense passion to create a 'cultural space for families in Joseon'[40] by building a brand new theatre, Taishōkan. Since Seoul Stock and Spot Trading Office had opened in 1920, which initiated stock trading in Joseon, Nitta Kōichi continued to flourish as a financier, running his stock brokerage and spot transaction firm, Nitta Shōten, affiliated with Takehara Shōten of Osaka,[41] expanding his business into insurance, investment trust and so on. As his business continued to grow at a dizzying pace, Nitta handed over the entertainment sector that ran the theatre business in Seoul, Pusan, Incheon, Daegu, and Wonsan to his older brother, Hideyoshi.[42] He also brought in Byōhei, the youngest of the Nitta brothers, who was the sole member of the family who had pursued a career in the film business as a *benshi*, from Japan and put him in charge of their newly acquired cinema (Hisagokan) in Incheon.[43] (Figure 3.2) The Nitta brothers had powerful influence because of their financial capacity and network in Joseon.[44]

Hayakawa Entertainment Company and Nitta Entertainment Company developed a rivalry by joining up with Japan's Tenkatsu studio and Nikkatsu studio, respectively, and together dominated the film scene of the 1910s. Another important early exhibitor, who deserves to be mentioned here, is Wakejima Shujirō who eventually became the most powerful figure in the Joseon film industry and remained influential until the empire took complete control of the film culture in Joseon. Wakejima had a most conspicuous career because he was a known member of a Japanese yakuza gang based in Kyūshū. He moved to Manchuria after he married the daughter of the leader of Okayama Yakuza and created his own Wakejima family (*Wakejima-gumi*) in Dailian, China.[45] Wakejima settled in Seoul in 1915, initially working as a sumo promoter. With the acquisition of Gyeongseong Theatre in 1919, Wakejima entered into the film and

Figure 3.2 Hisagokan Theatre located in Incheon, one of the theatres managed by Nitta Entertainment that distributed Nikkatsu films. (*Chōsen no jijō* [Keijō (Seoul): Chōsen Kōronsha, 1922], p. 121)

theatre business. He soon became the representative of the Joseon branch of Dai-Nippōn Kokusuikai established in 1919, a right-wing yakuza organisation that still exists today and which many suspected was the financial supporter for Wakejima's business in Joseon.[46] He is today best known as the owner and executive producer of Gyeongseong Film Productions (Gyeongseong Yeonghwa Chwalyeongso) opened in 1934.[47] Wakejima served as the first president of the Association of Seoul Exhibitors established in 1932. Despite his influence, however, many film-makers expressed their unease about his yakuza background and even despised him. As a matter of fact, the feud between his yakuza group and a rival gang,[48] and his leadership role in the right-wing yakuza organisation which used violence and fear to attack liberal social groups in Seoul, often made newspaper headlines.[49]

These early Japanese film entrepreneurs were certainly instrumental in establishing the Joseon film industry from the mid-1910s to its maturation in the 1920s and 1930s. The fact that these figures were flung into the film business only after they migrated to Korea, and most of them did so only after they had established themselves in other business areas, is worth noting because it indicates that their film business was more locally based. Eventually, these early entrepreneurs were joined by a new generation of exhibitors, such as Tokunaga Kumaichirō and Sakuraba Fujio[50] (Figure 3.3) who all learned to run film businesses in Joseon. Addressing the issues and problems derived from the unique Joseon cultural circumstances proved to be quite important when running a film business. Soon after commercial film-making began in Joseon, some established entrepreneurs from Japan attempted to venture into the Joseon film business. For example, established film-makers such as Toyama Mitsuru,[51] a renowned *kengeki* (sword-fighting drama) actor, and the founders of Daeryuk Kinema (1928), came to Joseon in the late 1920s to take root in Joseon cinema through producing and directing films. Failing to establish themselves in the film business, however, they ended up returning to Japan after their short stint with Joseon cinema. Naturally, Japanese settlers in the Joseon film industry, from the officers and censors of the Office of the Governor General to film fans, were convinced that Joseon cinema was unique and different from the Japanese film industry. This emphasis on Joseon cinema's difference suggested by the Japanese settlers, moreover, became one of the critical factors that influenced the formation of the entire Joseon film culture, ranging from film policies and censorship to movie fans' film-going practices, as I will elaborate with more concrete examples in the following sections. Indeed, Japanese settlers tirelessly tried to educate cultural policymakers, people in the Japanese film industry, and even the authorities in Japan with regard to this distinctiveness, and frequently critiqued their inattention to Joseon cinema's unique nature.

This prevalent rhetoric of uniqueness illuminates the ambivalent relationship between the film culture of the settlers and the Japanese film industry and practices, as Japanese film practices provided the core foundation for the institutionalisation of not only the migrants' film businesses but the entire Joseon film culture. Theatres of Joseon, for instance, were almost identical in every respect to movie theatres in Japan. Until the mid-1930s, when the construction of upmarket, 'modern' movie theatres became a fad both in Japan and Joseon, movie theatres were modelled after Japan's traditional *yose* theatre. Cinemas were typically two-storey buildings with the second floor designated as the best seats. Spectators had to take off their shoes to sit on the *tatami* mats in these seats, and, having received their orders, *ōchako* or tea ladies brought tea to these spectators. About a quarter of the first-floor seating was designated as seats for women, though, as in Japan, gender segregation was not vigorously enforced; if escorted by male companions, female spectators were allowed to sit in the men's sections with them. Influenced by the film exhibition practice of Japan, both Korean and Japanese movie theatres in Joseon changed film programmes every five to seven days, according to newspaper theatre listings from the 1920s and 1930s. Again in the same manner as in Japan, each programme consisted of several films, even after the end of one-reelers and the advent of feature-length

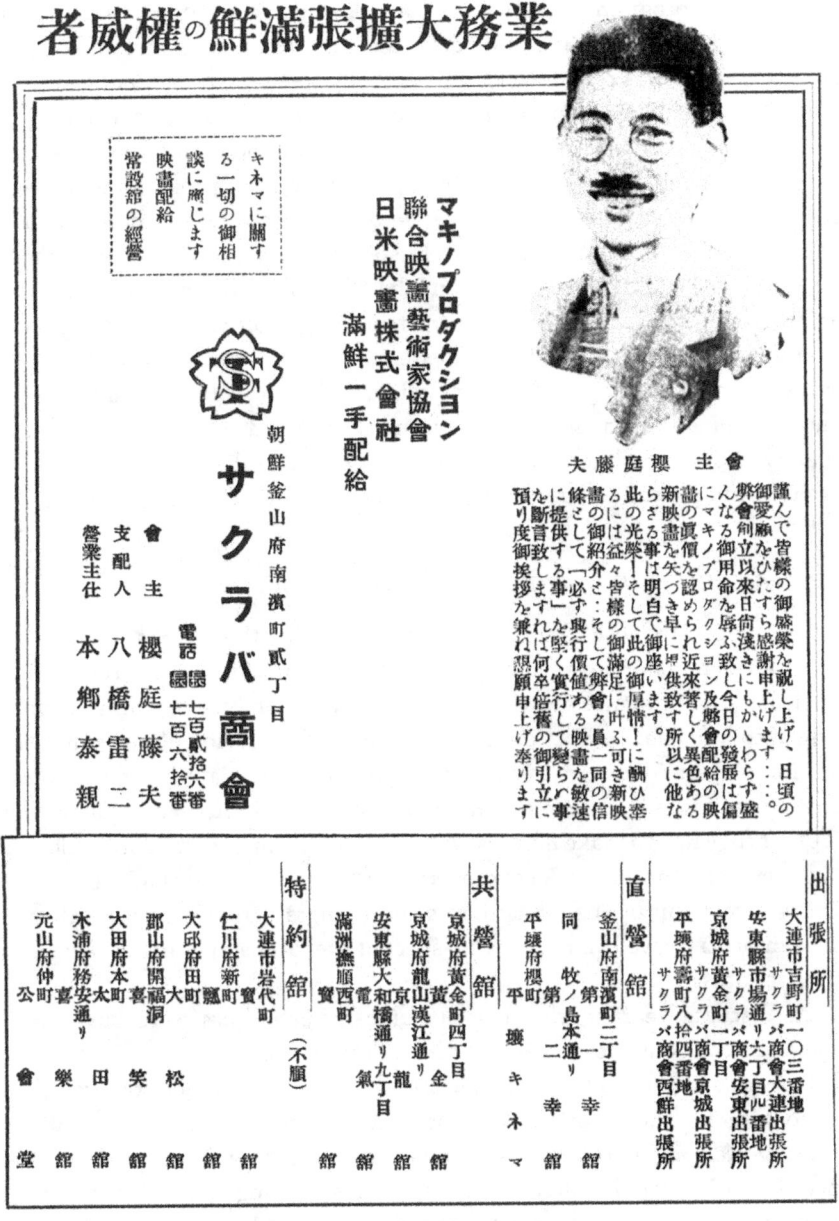

Figure 3.3 Advertisement for Sakuraba Shōkai published in a Makino studio's fan magazine, featuring the owner Sakuraba Fujio. (*Makino eiga*, 27, June 1926) Based in Busan, Sakuraba Shōkai was the largest film distribution company in Joseon and Manchuria, distributing Paramount Pictures, Makino and Nichibei films.

films, so one programme lasted quite a long time, sometimes continuing for more than three hours. The number of films did not matter but the length of one programme was restricted by the number of reels (*kan*); in other words, one programme should not have more than twenty reels of prints, as in Japan.[52] As one reel was approximately 10 minutes long, one programme could last more than three or four hours so, typically, theatres ran their programme only once or twice a day, and they often offered discounts to spectators who came in one or two hours after screenings began. Despite this apparent influence from the Japanese film industry, ranging from the theatre's building structure to film programming, Joseon cinema's infrastructure underwent some significant localisation. For the remainder of this section, I shall elucidate this localisation process of migrated Japanese film practices in Joseon, focusing particularly on the development of the settler film culture that embodies the obvious influence of Japanese cinema but, at the same time, exudes its distinctiveness resulting from the unique cultural and social contexts of colonial Korea.

The Localisation of Japanese Film Practices

The influx of Japanese film practices accelerated as the Joseon film business went through major advancements from the late 1910s to the early 1920s. In particular, the immense growth in the film exhibition business and the beginning of commercial productions invited a massive migration of film professionals from Japan. The newly arrived film professionals played seminal roles in this critical phase in Joseon film history. Upon arrival, these individuals found out that they had to make necessary changes to the film practices to which they had been accustomed, as Joseon presented them with new challenges. Therefore, a discussion of the adjustments these migrant film professionals made will demonstrate well an important aspect of the localising process of Japanese film practices.

As discussed earlier, the majority of early exhibitors were businessmen who had not had any career in the film industry when they were in Japan but there were several groups of people who pursued film careers before migrating to Joseon – most noticeable among them were the *benshi*. Quite different from investors, exhibitors, theatre managers, and early film-makers, *benshi* were specialists who were required to have extensive training and had to go through years of apprenticeship to master the skills required to become a *benshi*. In Joseon, it was difficult systematically to train *benshi* and thus they were continually recruited from Japan. Among all the film workers working in the Japanese Empire and its colonies, *benshi* seemed to be the ones who most actively travelled across the colonial territories during the silent era, long before the empire acquired Manchuria, the south-east part of China, and other south-east Asian countries where the motto of the *Greater East Asian Sphere* was faithfully practised by the Japanese film industry in the last decade of the empire. This was possible because, as in Joseon, in other parts of Japan's early colonies, such as Manchuria, Taiwan and Karafuto, there were more theatres aimed at Japanese migrants than ones for the local population. Owing to the geographical proximity to Japan, many of those *benshi* who worked in the colonies first moved to Joseon from Japan before moving on elsewhere, though it was not entirely uncommon for *benshi* who worked in Manchuria or Taiwan to come to Joseon to find their new home. In the 1910s, movie theatres employed just a few *benshi* but soon the number of *benshi* each theatre hired increased as the film business flourished towards the end of the decade. Theatres typically hired three or four main *benshi* who hosted screenings while being in charge of the main narration and performing the main characters, along with around ten *benshi* who provided voices for other minor roles. In Seoul, where five theatres, including Keiryūkan, a movie theatre located on the border between Seoul and Yongsan (Ryūzan),[53] began to compete with one another; after the opening of the Chūokan in 1921, the competition for employing star *benshi* was quite fierce and intensified as more and more movie theatres began to appear throughout Joseon from the mid-1920s. The most successful *benshi*, who first established himself in Joseon and then continued to thrive after returning to Japan, was Ishida Akika. When Ishida was hired as the chief *benshi* for Kirakukan in Seoul in 1917, he quickly became the most sought-after *benshi* in Joseon. He left Joseon a few years later, however, when he was recruited by Teikoku Gekijō of Osaka where he eventually became the manager.[54] Ishida's success was quite exceptional as not many *benshi* were able to return to Japan and resume their careers there as *benshi*. In fact, recruiting and keeping *benshi* turned out to be the most challenging task for theatres and, as a result, Japanese filmgoers in Joseon were not very pleased with the overall quality of *benshi*.

For the most part, Japan's *benshi* culture was practised similarly in Joseon. The notorious *benshi* apprentice system also migrated with *benshi*, and, as a matter of fact, there were many *benshi* aspirants among the settlers but few seemed actually to complete the training. Noting that he received anything from five to twenty enquiries about *benshi* apprentices in any given month, Momoyama Long, a popular *benshi* who moved from Fukuoka, wrote an essay in which he detailed what to expect during the apprenticeship and pointed out to *benshi* hopefuls all the hardship they would have to endure.[55] As in Japan, *benshi* was a popular film star much admired by film fans which certainly explains why theatres were so eager to bring in top-notch *benshi* from Japan. Indeed, the most frequently discussed topic in the film sections of *Chōsen kōron*, a Japanese-language monthly that regularly ran film-related articles and reviews in Joseon, was none other than *benshi*. The content of those writings about this silent movie star varied, ranging from performance analysis of each different *benshi* and introduction of newly arrived *benshi* to their scandals and miscellaneous reports on their personal lives. Many articles on *benshi* featured in *Chōsen kōron* and other Japanese settler press, however, lamented that there was only a handful of quality *benshi* in Joseon, which adversely affected their film-viewing experiences.[56] Some *benshi* were promoted or moved up to other positions at movie theatres in Joseon. Theatre manager was a common option for a *benshi*'s next career stop but some quickly became chief executive of theatres. This rather steep, rapid promotion for *benshi* was possible in Joseon only because of the lack of reliable film professionals in the Joseon film industry.

Directors of photography (DP) were another group of experts who left their profession in Japan to find a new opportunity in the emerging Joseon cinema. The DP who left the most noticeable imprint on the earliest productions of Joseon cinema was Miyagawa Hayanosuke.[57] Miyagawa is best known in Korean film history as the DP for *Loyal Vengeance* (1919), the chain drama that is often credited as being the first Korean film. Except for the fact that he was a DP affiliated with Tenkatsu when recruited by Danseongsa's Park Seung-pil to film *Loyal Vengeance*, nothing specific was known about him until recently.[58] Miyagawa is recorded in Korean film history as the DP for *Loyal Vengeance* and two other chain dramas produced almost simultaneously but he actually worked on more than a dozen films and chain dramas. After his initial contract with Danseongsa, Miyagawa returned to Japan but then migrated to Joseon shortly after. Following his return, he became an executive of Mansen Motion Picture Trading Company, an educational film firm,[59] and continued to film commissioned documentaries for regional governments.[60] His name is last seen in a newspaper report in 1930,[61] and there is no record of his career or life after that. Nishikawa Hidehiro, the DP for such films as *Tale of Unyeong* (1925, *Unyeong jeon*), *Tale of Sim Cheong* (1925, *Sim Cheong jeon*), *The Pioneer* (1925, *Gaecheokja*), *Janghanmong* (1926), and *The Secret of Chinese Street* (1928, *Jinagaui bimil*), was another settler DP who made an impact on Joseon films. There were other Japanese DPs active in Joseon but not all the Japanese DPs settled into the colony like Miyagawa or Nishikawa.[62] Many of them were hired on a single-project basis and returned to Japan. Importantly, the DP was the one position that consistently went to Japanese film-makers because local film-makers had hardly had the chance to be properly trained to be in charge of a film camera. A newspaper article series on burgeoning local film production, published in 1927, reported that almost all the DPs, regardless of their ethnicity, were trained in Japan and that even directors could not control these specialists because they were the sole masters of film technology among the crews. The article sceptically concluded that this empowerment of the cinematographer was 'a rare phenomenon unique to Joseon'.[63] It was only in the mid-1930s that Korean DPs began to take over the camera from Japanese DPs but Japanese DPs did not entirely disappear until the very end of the colonial occupation. Even the best Korean DPs of the 1930s and 1940s, such as Lee Pil-wu (trained in Teikoku Kinema and Shochiku), Yang Se-ung (Tōa Kinema), Lee Chang-yong (Shinko Kinema),[64] and Lee Byeong-wu (Tokyo Geijutsu Eigasha), were all trained in Japanese studios. Lee Pil-wu was the first Korean professional DP who started his career early in the 1920s but he also trained for several months in Teikoku Kinema. Lee, Miyagawa, and Nishikawa filmed almost all the films and chain dramas produced before 1926. Lee, who circulated among a number of different positions in production and exhibition throughout his career, confessed that 'the cameraman in Joseon is the most miserable one in the world' because of the poor film technology, lack of lighting staff and equipment, and no available assistant, which forced cinematographers to assume multiple roles in the shooting.[65]

The fact that *benshi* and cinematographers were constantly imported from Japan is a good indication of the slow development and feeble status of the Joseon film industry. The absence of a studio system, the project-by-project investment, and the small domestic film market made it challenging systematically to train these professionals who needed to acquire in-depth knowledge about film technology. Even projecting films, which also required mastery of technology, was primarily done by foreigners, including the Japanese, in the 1910s. The chief projectionist for the first movie theatre, High Entertainment Theatre, for instance, was Nakamura Shōtaro, a Japanese projectionist who worked for Yoshizawa Trading Company and M. Pathé as a projectionist and technical trainer; his recruitment was one of the five promotional attractions featured in the newspaper advertisement for its opening.[66] Eventually Koreans took over this role but, even in the late 1920s, one third of the projectionists in Joseon were Japanese.[67]

Japanese Movie Theatres and Film Fans

The institutionalisation of film exhibition was prompted by the rise of two entertainment companies, Hayakawa Entertainment Company and Nitta Entertainment Company. Instead of purchasing movies print by print, often through intermediaries, these two companies made exclusive distribution and exhibition contracts directly with major Japanese film studios. While Nitta joined Nikkatsu and Nikkatsu Mukojima Studios, Hayakawa exclusively distributed Tenkatsu movies as well as foreign films.[68] High Entertainment Theatre was not able to compete with the theatres these two new companies worked with, and, as described in Chapter 1, after years of struggle, it was turned into a movie theatre for Koreans, and eventually shut down. The film line-ups in the 1910s consisted of Japanese films (mostly Nikkatsu films), French Pathé films, and Hollywood movies, particularly Universal films and Bluebird photodramas, Universal's in-house studio. Universal serials enjoyed an enormous popularity from the mid-1910s, a trend initiated with the phenomenal success of *The Broken Coin* (1915) released in 1916. This twenty-two episode Universal serial was even serialised as a newspaper novel for the Japanese language newspaper *Chōsen shibō* from July to August 1916, a promotional event for the film's premiere in the city of Busan (Saiwaikan). (Figure 3.4) The film attracted Korean filmgoers as well. Korean film-makers reminisced that this serial was the film that truly initiated the first film boom in Joseon and gave birth to Joseon's first Hollywood star, Eddie Polo, the star of the serial.[69] Film serial's popularity in Joseon persisted even throughout the 1920s when most of the production firms stopped producing serials, leaving only Pathé and Universal, the two most prominent producers of serials since the success of the genre, in this once-profitable field.[70] This popularity was shared with Korean audiences who also enjoyed the serials even into the late 1920s. Owing to the prolonged popularity of serials, serious Japanese film fans based in Joseon, who considered themselves 'high class (*kōkyū*) fans', expressed their discontent about film bills that still programmed serials as the main attraction, critiquing exhibitors' tasteless chase for profit.[71]

Japanese migrants' film culture underwent a major transformation triggered by the changes that took place in the Japanese film industry in the first half of the 1920s. Though a number of movie theatres began to appear throughout Joseon in the mid-1910s, the real evolution began to unfold several years later. When Yūrakukan, Seoul's new Japanese movie house opened in 1916 – the name was changed to Kirakukan in 1919 – the theatre had a difficult time getting full houses.[72] Accordingly, film fans and reviewers expressed concern about the future of this new movie theatre, wondering whether Seoul had enough customers for five movie houses (six including Keiryūkan) catering for Japanese migrants.[73] In fact, because of the sudden increase in theatres, the over-rapid growth of the film business seemed to hit a brick wall, leading to the closure of two theatres, Kotobukiza and Sekaikan (the new name for the High Entertainment Theatre). This proved to be only a momentary setback for the growing film business, as film's popularity soon picked up the pace again, resulting in more and more movie theatres being built across the peninsula. A more imminent problem posed for film exhibitors was the lack of variety in their film programmes. Even though the demands for new films began to increase, film programmes were not diverse enough. As Nikkatsu studio became

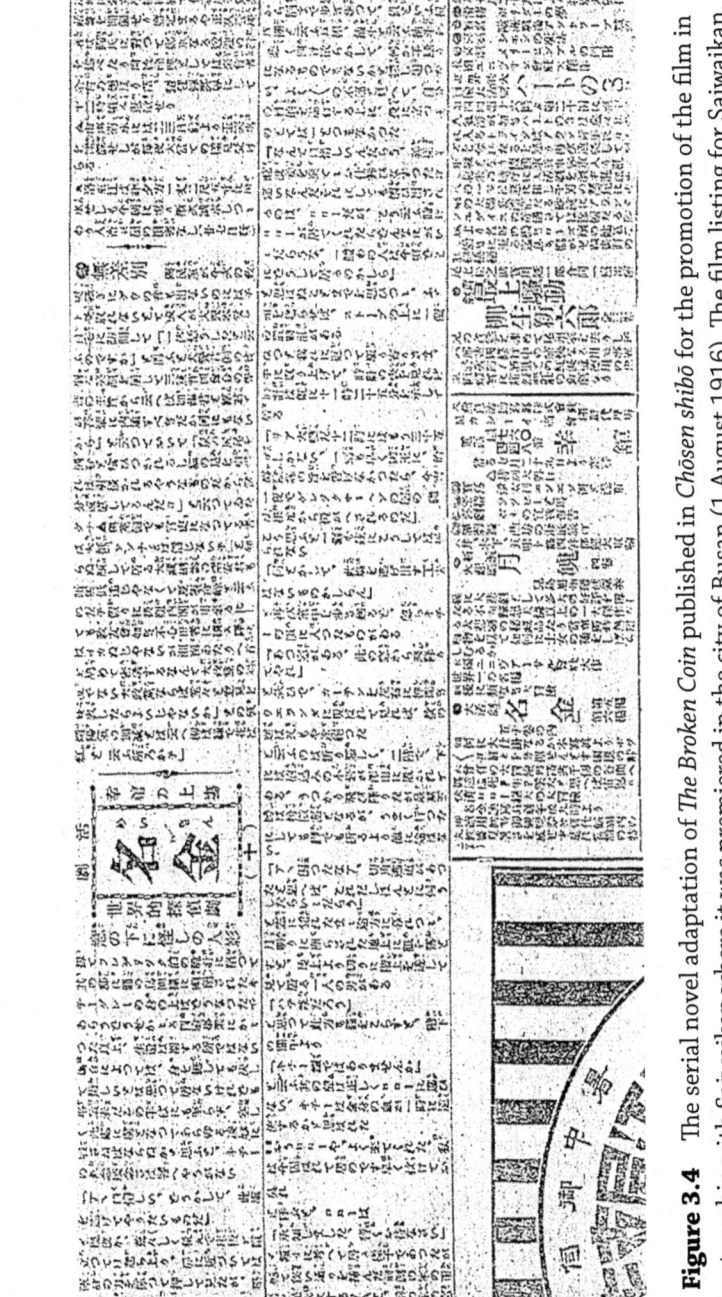

Figure 3.4 The serial novel adaptation of *The Broken Coin* published in *Chōsen shibō* for the promotion of the film in partnership with Saiwaikan where it was premiered in the city of Busan (1 August 1916). The film listing for Saiwaikan, featuring *The Broken Coin* (*Meikin*), is shown at the bottom of the image.

the dominant force in the Japanese film industry, exhibitors competed to distribute Nikkatsu films. In 1921, all the Japanese theatres in Seoul established contracts with Nikkatsu, causing filmgoers to be extremely frustrated about the lack of choice;[74] and Nikkatsu films, along with Hollywood productions, prevailed at Japanese theatres across Joseon. But this situation turned around in just a couple of years.

The drastic change of Japanese migrants' film culture in the early 1920s was prompted by the rapid growth of the Japanese film industry at the time. According to film censorship records, assembled by the National Police Agency (*keishichō*) of Japan in 1923, while the number of American films censored grew from 1,295 in 1920 to 2,502, censored Japanese films increased even more dramatically, from 519 to 2,279.[75] This statistic suggests not only the expansion in scope of the Japanese film culture but also the rapid rise of local film production. Teikoku Kinema or Tei-kine and Shochiku, the entertainment company, began film production in 1920, and the emergence of these two studios signalled the end of Nikkatsu studio's domination of the domestic film market. Following these two studios, a number of new studios was formed, giving the Japanese film industry the sort of fierce competition it had never seen before. The word *competition* seems to be an understatement, as Japanese film studios, during the five or six years after 1920, indulged in frenzied struggles, including mergers, acquisitions, partner changes, and the stealing of actors, directors, and theatres. The intense competition found its way to Joseon where Nikkatsu's monopoly was challenged as exhibitors now sought to join up with the new studios. The settler film-exhibition world was soon thrown into chaos – which cannot be adequately described in a full account here – as theatres and exhibitors frantically changed their partner studios over a number of years. Beginning in 1924, the situation began to improve as the exhibition system finally stabilised. The years 1924 and 1925 were commonly referred to by settler film fans as 'the golden age'[76] of the Joseon film world which indicates how much the advancement of film culture was indebted to the overall growth of the Japanese film industry. Nikkatsu's dominance was still felt at this time as many theatres in regions other than Seoul and Busan remained loyal to the studio. Nikkatsu, however, eventually lost its influence over the settler film culture. In 1926, the films of four studios (Shochiku, Makino, Nikkatsu, and Tei-kine) collectively dominated the settler film market.[77] The changing state of the Japanese film studios was well illustrated in the settler film fans' responses to their productions. Labelled sceptically as old drama (*kyūgeki*), Nikkatsu's stubborn adherence to period drama lost the favour of fans but Shochiku and Makino attracted loyal fans who called themselves 'the Shochiku group (*tō*)' or 'the Makino group'. Shochiku films were applauded by film fans for their artistic value and modern drama while Makino, the studio run by Makino Shōzō, the revered film-maker who is often credited as the father of Japanese cinema, captured the attention of fans with its genre films, such as mystery and revisionist period dramas. Makino was known for its highly dedicated fans in Japan, evidenced in the recently reprinted fan magazines *Makino* and *Tōjiin*. These fanzines featured many fan letters sent from Joseon fans.[78] In addition to the films of the four studios, another notable film genre that gained popularity was the so-called sword drama (*kengeki*) of Bandō Tsumasaburō who rose to stardom in Japan at this time.

Typically, Japanese films came to entertain settlers two to three months after their initial release in Japan,[79] but film fans in Joseon appeared to be content with the theatres' Japanese film programmes because competition in Japan meant that the studios' best films were sent to Joseon. Japanese studios even occasionally sent their actors to Joseon to do *butai aisatsu* or 'stage greeting' before the audience at theatres, which enthralled film fans. Bandō Tsumasaburō, Makino Teruko, Nakane Ryūtaro, Matsuura Tsukie, Marata Masao, Yamamoto Kaichi, Koizumi Yoshisuke, and Sakai Yoneko were among the stars who travelled to Joseon to meet their fans. (Figure 3.5) Even Onoe Matsunosuke, the first superstar of Japanese cinema, planned to visit Joseon but the plan was thwarted by his sudden death in 1926. The overall growth of Joseon film culture was, in this regard, tied to the major advances in the Japanese film industry. Yet the significant changes in film programmes caused by the film industry's transformation in Japan brought about a radically different characteristic of settler film culture. The influx of a sizeable number of Japanese films superseded Hollywood and European movies in theatre listings. 'Strangely', settler film critic Mizui Reiko noted with frustration that 'Japanese theatres did not play foreign films'.[80] As the 1920s went on, fewer and fewer Hollywood and European films were screened at Japanese theatres. In the late 1920s, Japanese films constituted almost 70 per cent of film programmes and, in the early 1930s, it was not uncommon for Japanese theatres not to include any Hollywood productions for a couple of weeks or to project movies a few years old. Unlike Japan, which had theatres that specialised in foreign films (*yōga gekijō*), there was no such venue in Joseon for Japanese settlers. Naniwakan, the single *yōga gekijō* for Japanese settlers, opened in Seoul only in 1933. This imbalance between Japanese films and foreign imports in film line-ups at Japanese movie theatres was even worse outside Seoul, as it was common for theatres in other cities and small towns to screen foreign movies only sporadically, 'as if they were a spice',[81] or not to hire any foreign films at all, forcing disappointed fans to 'pay for an expensive train ticket to travel to Seoul just to watch foreign movies'.[82] Japanese settler fans became almost constantly irritated with the film programmes of their cinemas that were considerably lacking in foreign films.

128 Eclipsed Cinema

Figure 3.5 Japanese settler movie fans came out to welcome Bandō Tsumasaburō and Makino Teruko at the *Keijō nippō* building in Seoul during their tour to Joseon for the promotion of Makino films. (*Keijō nippō*, 11 June 1925)

This unique programming format, characterised by the stark contrast between an excessive number of Japanese films and a diminishing number of Hollywood productions, was accentuated even more when compared to the theatres for Koreans whose film programmes looked radically different. Unlike the Japanese theatres, the so-called *Joseonin* (Korean) theatres presented Hollywood productions as their main attractions, intermittently complemented by Joseon films and European pictures, while not playing any Japanese films. The co-existence of these two sorts of theatres, serving separate ethnic groups, and their differing film programmes were key factors directing the structural development of the Joseon film business. Therefore, examining only Koreans' film culture and Korean film-makers cannot properly describe the Joseon cinema culture and, at the same time, analysing the settler film culture separately generates a similar kind of historiographical problem. One of the most crucial characteristics of Joseon film culture can be revealed only through scrutinising the interplay between the two ethnic film cultures and interrogating the complex implications of both the connection and division between the ethnically segregated film cultures.

'A Film Practice Distinctly Joseon': the Ethnic Segregation of Movie Theatres

The first report from the national film censorship board, newly formed in 1926, which offers comprehensive information, data and analysis of the Joseon film culture documents the uniqueness of the film-exhibition and film-reviewing practices in Joseon as follows:

> Compared to Japan proper, the number of theatres is small, but there are some differences about Joseon moving picture theatres from those in Japan in terms of exhibition. That is, the audiences are divided into the two groups according to the two different kinds of films screened respectively for Japanese and Korean spectators for the sake of business. While theatres for the Japanese are almost entirely managed by Japanese, Korean theatres mostly involve Korean management, but it is not uncommon for the Japanese to run Korean theatres.[83]

In a similar manner, *Kinema junpō* reported, 'Japanese films are absolutely unpopular among Korean filmgoers. Korean theatres are like another world where only foreign films are screened with an explanation given in the Korean language.'[84] Apparently, the ethnically specific and segregated exhibition practice was perceived as the unique aspect of Joseon film culture. One of the most visible changes, appearing during the major expansion of the Joseon film industry in the mid-1910s to mid-1920, was the emergence of theatres catering for the Korean population. Indeed, as mentioned earlier, going to the movies became the most popular leisure activity for both settlers and Koreans alike, without any major challenges from other forms of entertainment. In spite of being the foremost mass entertainment throughout the colonial period, beginning in the mid-1910s, however, cinema's growth was often slowed for a number of reasons. The scarcity of movie theatres was one of the major obstacles I have noted which affected the film culture of the Korean population more adversely. Most movie theatres were geared primarily to Japanese immigrants.

As of 1926, of thirty-two permanent movie theatres, only seven were listed as Korean theatres[85] and, as a settler journalist wrote, 'Koreans do not enjoy the benefit of the movie theatre. It is because there is not enough financing to run a cinema, but even though one finds enough investment to open a theatre, there is no guarantee that a theatre would generate profit.'[86] Even up to the late 1930s, when the ethnically specific film exhibition practice began to disappear, movie theatres existed mainly for the pleasure of Japanese audiences. In other words, in many cities and towns which had only one or two movie theatres, there was no permanent venue for Korean audiences.

In fact, movie theatres were first built in those cities that had larger Japanese populations. For the majority of Koreans, especially those who lived in small cities, towns or rural areas, movie-going was not part of their everyday cultural activities. The lack of a permanent venue was one thing but many Koreans were not able to afford entrance fees; for them, film-going was still not cheap entertainment. The average daily wage for Korean urban male factory workers in 1930, one of the better paid jobs, for instance, was about 90 cents (*jeon*), and female workers made even less than that, around 60 cents.[87] The average cinema ticket price at the time was 55 cents for a standard seat[88] which was even higher than that charged at theatres in Tokyo or Osaka, and not falling until the end of the 1930s.[89] Given that Koreans in rural regions earned a lot less than urban workers, it was natural that only Japanese migrants were able to enjoy movies regularly in those areas. In her article on film exhibition in Gunsan, the port city located in Jeolla Province which was developed by Japanese settler merchants around 1900, Wi Gyeong-hae points out that, during the colonial period, class divisions in the city formed more or less along ethnic lines, as Koreans migrated to this newly built city from adjacent farming villages in search of manual labour in the port. According to Wi, Gunsan's theatres initially catered for Japanese settlers as it was simply impossible for Korean labourers to enjoy movie-going as a regular leisure activity. It was only in the early 1930s, after the increasing influx of Korean migrant workers beginning in the late 1920s, that the city saw its first Korean movie theatre but, even then, most port manual labourers could not afford its admission fee, and thus movie-going never really became their regular leisure activity.[90] The owners and managers of theatres in small cities often found it quite difficult to manage their business with only the limited Japanese clientele. Thus, letting these theatres became a core business, and some of the main patrons who leased theatres were travelling film exhibitors who screened films (mostly Joseon and Hollywood films) for Korean spectators. For these Korean spectators, therefore, film-viewing per se was still a special, occasional cultural event rather than a regular evening's entertainment. In this sense, the ethnically segregated film-viewing practice in these locations was not entirely along ethnic and/or cultural lines but was more economically motivated. Japanese theatre owners in smaller cities and towns, which had a much smaller Japanese clientele compared to bigger cities such as Seoul, Busan, Incheon or Pyongyang, were troubled with constant financial problems, so much so that they even had to find a way in which to lure Korean audiences. The open correspondence between two managers of cinemas in mid-sized cities, published in *Kokusai eiga shimbun*, showed the difficulties in running theatres in smaller cities. Located in the city of Shinuiju, Joseon, and Kōriyama of Fukushima Prefecture, Japan, the owners of these two theatres exchanged their thoughts about the challenges in attracting enough filmgoers and maintaining their daily programmes. The owner of Sekaikan in Shinuiju wrote that he changed his film programmes every three days instead of the standard five days and lowered the admission to attract more patrons. He added that, to keep his theatre afloat, he found it necessary to cater for Koreans as well because of the small Japanese population in his city, but expressed his concern that the majority of Korean filmgoers who started coming to his theatre were 'lower class'.[91] Obviously, the major challenge to both owners was insufficient numbers of potential patrons because the cities' Japanese populations were not enough to sustain their businesses. To deal with this problem, exhibitors in smaller cities and towns had to schedule special screenings for Korean spectators and/or let out their theatres to travelling screening troupes who showed films for Korean audiences. Japanese theatres in this case were turned into Korean theatres for a short period (typically from several days to a week). Kokusaikan, a Japanese theatre in Busan, for example, was transformed into a Korean theatre in June 1927 for just a few days in which Danseongsa's travelling exhibition team screened six Joseon films for Korean viewers.[92] In the meantime, recognising the inconvenience for Korean patrons who could not understand Japanese *benshi*, Mansegwan of Hamheung City screened films alternately for Korean and Japanese filmgoers every three days.[93] Using these two exhibition strategies to incorporate Korean patrons into the Japanese theatres' business, theatres tried to find a way to serve both ethnic groups which resulted in limiting, and even eliminating, the chance for the two ethnically different patrons to mingle, even though they shared the same theatre space.

Seoul was the only city in which Korean and Japanese movie theatres developed concurrently from the early 1910s, and therefore the most serious and more complex form of ethnic segregation began to take shape from early movie theatre years. Owing to the rapid urbanisation during the colonial period, the cultural industry, including the film business in Joseon, was disproportionately concentrated in Seoul. As the colonial capital of the Korean peninsula, and a crucial gateway for Japanese imperial expansion to continental Asia, Seoul functioned not only as the centre of Japanese colonial rule in Korea but also as one of the most significant cities in the Japanese imperial territories, accommodating all the major imperial, political and economic institutions. Accordingly, Seoul had the largest Japanese population outside Japan and thus boasted highly developed 'Japanese' urban and film cultures. As a result, ethnic segregation became a defining component of the urban cultural scene in Seoul and played a decisive role in shaping urban modernity. The ensuing discussion of this segregation, therefore, will most obviously demonstrate the ways in which the film cultures of the coloniser and colonised interacted with one another.

Active segregation at movie theatres began in Seoul from the early 1920s when Danseongsa, Joseon Geukjang, and Umigwan were in business together with five Japanese theatres. A practical reason for this was the language barrier. Even ten years into colonial rule, only a fraction of the Korean population could understand Japanese (ten thousand, 0.5 per cent of the entire population),[94] thereby ethnic segregation was necessary to cater for the increasing Korean film patronage. As more Korean spectators began to visit theatres, exhibitors saw a need to build a theatre that could better serve this particular clientele. A more substantial reason for the ethnic segregation, however, was closely associated with the Japanese settlers' overall isolation from the local Korean communities. Following the signing of the Japan–Korea Trading Treaty in 1885, which allowed Japanese immigrants to purchase real estate legally in Seoul,[95] most Japanese settled in Seoul, and thus so-called Japanese streets began to appear around the Japanese Embassy located near the Namsan and South Gate areas. At about the time film took off as mass entertainment, Seoul was fully transformed into an ethnically divided colonial – or hybrid – city where ordinary Japanese cultures and customs had migrated, blended, and clashed with Korean ways of life. After colonisation, Seoul lost its position as the nation's capital and, in October 1910, became a city belonging to Gyeonggi Province, with its name mandatorily changed from Hanseong to Gyeongseong (Keijō in Japanese pronunciation).[96] In spite of these changes, Seoul continued to function as the colonial capital. The rapidly modernising metropolis witnessed a sharp growth in its population throughout the colonial period, in large part because it attracted not only Koreans from across the peninsula but also Japanese people. Japanese immigrants in Seoul accounted for about 20 to 25 per cent of the total population of the city beginning in the mid-1910s onward. In 1915, about sixty thousand out of Seoul's 250,000 residents were Japanese and, in 1925, when the city's population reached four hundred thousand, approximately one hundred thousand were Japanese immigrants.[97]

By the 1920s, Seoul had become one of the largest cities in the Japanese imperial territories. Throughout Japan's imperial reign, Seoul was the colonised city that had the largest Japanese population outside Japan itself. The Cheonggye Stream (Cheonggyecheon) served as a symbolic border between the

Korean-populated *Bukchon* or North Village (today's Jongno district) and the Japanese-dominated *Namchon* or South Village (today's Chungmuro and South Gate areas). (Figure 3.6) The ethnically segregated city engendered distinct cultural forms. Unlike other Korean cities, where only one or two movie theatres were in business, Seoul functioned as the cultural centre and, in the 1920s, boasted a total of eight movie theatres. Among those theatres, Taishōkan, Keiryūkan, Kirakukan, Chūokan, and Koganekan, located in South Village, exclusively served Japanese film patrons. Joseon Geukjang, Danseongsa, and Umigwan in North Village, on the other hand, catered for Korean spectators. From the mid-1910s to the mid-1930s, these ethnically specific film exhibition practices created little opportunity or need for Japanese and Korean film patrons to come together at the cinema. Of course, this segregation of film exhibition did not entirely block the flow of film fans. In fact, in the 1910s, when movie theatres were scarce and patrons were too few even to fill those small numbers of movie theatres, cinemas were eager to reach out to different ethnic groups. For instance, in 1917, when two epics by Italian Ambrosio Film became the talk of film fans in Joseon, Koganekan ran ads in Korean newspapers to attract Korean filmgoers.[98] After the emergence of Korean cinemas in the early 1920s, theatres discontinued their efforts to attract different ethnic film patrons.

Figure 3.6   Hon-machi (today's Chungmuro), one of the so-called 'Japanese streets' in South Village.

The only people who still tried to contest the ethnic separation were avid Japanese film fans who were frustrated by the decreasing number of Hollywood films at their theatres and so went to Korean cinemas where there were better Hollywood film line-ups.[99] The passion for the cinema led Japanese film enthusiasts to go to Korean cinemas to catch up with the latest Hollywood production, but the trip was a rather reluctant one as the segregated film exhibition practice created inconvenient and uncomfortable film-viewing experiences for them. In fact, only dedicated, hard-core movie fans were brave enough to walk into Korean-filled theatres and overcome the cultural differences and language barriers there. A fan noted:

> The [byeonsa's] explanation at the Korean theatre, though its script is printed in Japanese, is done in Korean. So I don't understand it at all. I try hard with my English knowledge I learn from schools and [Korean] subtitles. It nonetheless would not pose too much trouble if you had considerable prior information.

The fan continued, 'The reason we are fond of Korean theatres is they screen high-quality foreign movies' and 'typically foreign movies come to Joseon about six months after they arrive in Japan'.[100] Another fan even claimed that the best theatre in Seoul was the Joseon Geukjang because it was the only high-end theatre specialising in foreign films and complained that, in Seoul, Koreans enjoyed a much better film-viewing environment than Japanese settlers did.[101] Matsumoto Teruka, a long-standing film reviewer for *Chōsen kōron*, also reported it was typical that 'the majority of the films with high quality are being returned to Japan proper as soon as they have been played at Korean theatres', without even being screened at Japanese settlers' theatres.[102]

Many settler film fans and critics saw this practice as a major issue created by exhibitors who were trying to save expense by choosing not to screen Hollywood and European films. This seems to be a probable assessment of the film programming at Japanese cinemas because exhibitors and fans alike in Joseon constantly complained about the astonishing commission fees exhibitors had to pay for foreign films. In fact, every individual in the film business, regardless of ethnicity, expressed anger and frustration about the costs of bringing in foreign films. It was the custom for exhibitors to pay extra money for delivery and other related fees, as film prints generally made their way through the subsidiaries and distributors of studios in Japan (generally after being screened there), and exhibitors in Joseon typically paid triple the fees their counterparts in Japan did for the same film prints.[103] For Korean exhibitors, this was a serious problem because Korean cinemas had to programme Hollywood films as their main attractions because they could screen domestic films only intermittently.

Quite ironically, the segregated film practice made Japanese immigrants look on Korean film fans as being more erudite film spectators or 'high-class' (J: *kōkyū*; K: *gogeub*) fans who had developed better taste in film. A *Chōsen kōron* reporter observed, 'The Korean public has a relatively good eye for film appreciation, and I believe it is because they have grown accustomed to foreign movies instead of Japanese films, which enables them to analyse the essentials of film.'[104] Maeda Muro also asserted, 'Unlike Japanese settler fans who are ignorant, Korean spectators have a truly high-end taste for film.'[105] Similarly, a film censor who worked on the film censorship board in Joseon wrote in his contribution to *Kokusai eiga shimbun* that Korean audiences must have a more discerning eye for foreign movies than even Japanese film fans in Japan itself because they had had a lot more opportunities to appreciate them.[106] Another censor made a similar observation, 'Japanese [settlers] are intoxicated by sword drama, cheap sentimental film, and feel-good stories without substance. Meanwhile, it is Koreans that have an eye for films, because they are trained by Western movies.'[107] This widespread perception of Korean filmgoers as *kōkyū* fans who could better appreciate films than general Japanese immigrant film fans and even filmgoers in Japan was actually related more to the Japanese film fans' perception of Hollywood films than to Korean filmgoers' cultural capital or taste, as shown in the citations above. Though Japanese cinema had made tremendous strides aesthetically and industrially since the early 1920s, Japanese films were still deemed to be inferior to Hollywood productions. As almost all the films Korean film spectators enjoyed were Hollywood films, Japanese immigrants believed that this had helped Korean fans develop over time a much better taste in film. In fact, there was little evidence to substantiate the Japanese immigrants' view of Korean spectators but was based just on Korean filmgoers' excessive exposure to Hollywood productions. In the meantime, Japanese immigrants saw their own film culture as problematic and even flawed primarily mainly because their limited opportunity to appreciate films of better quality, namely Hollywood pictures. Thus, Japanese film reviewers and fans in Joseon frequently linked the poor line-up of films at Japanese cinemas to the exhibitors' lack of taste and knowledge about film, and/or their blind pursuit of money.[108] In particular, fans and reviewers pointed out that the problem lay in the fact that exhibitors were not fully committed to the film business because they had other businesses to run and therefore took their film business lightly. Some even suggested that the domestic film-centred programme reflected the poor taste of settler fans who preferred action films, and drove intellectuals away from the cinema.[109]

That which more vividly exposes the disconnection between the two ethnic film cultures is the absence of Japanese films at Korean theatres and Joseon films at Japanese theatres. A Japanese settler fan noted that it made him feel uncomfortable to find out that Korean cinemas never screened Japanese films.[110] Finally, in 1934, the administration recognised this as a significant problem which led it to introduce a screen quota that required every cinema to screen domestic films while controlling the number of Hollywood productions at theatres. This authoritative action, which mainly targeted the Korean cinemas, exposes the intrinsically biased and flawed nature of the ideals of *naisen yūwa* (ethnic harmony), mutual understanding, and assimilation. An equally, if not more, unnatural aspect of the segregated film exhibition was the total absence of Joseon films at Japanese theatres. In fact, unlike film-makers, exhibitors, distributors, critics and censors, regular settler patrons remained almost completely indifferent to the development of Joseon film production. Newspapers and magazines sporadically ran items on the status of Joseon film productions but the films were never released for Japanese filmgoers. Given that some of the Joseon productions were released in Japan, this absence appears even more striking. The film *Arirang*, for instance, was released to theatres in Japan through the Yamani Trading Company, a foreign film distributor but Japanese movie theatres in Joseon did not play *Arirang* at all. In other words, *Arirang*, the film that elevated Joseon film-making to a new level, did not mean much to a large proportion of film fans in Joseon as they did not even have an opportunity to appreciate it; no Japanese movie theatre screened the film and no Japanese-language newspaper published in Joseon wrote a single article on *Arirang* at the time of its release. More than half of the cinemas in Seoul and more than two-thirds of all movie theatres in Joseon did not even play the film *Arirang*.

Ethnically Segregated Film Practices and the Policy of Assimilation

This rather baffling historical fact concerning the *Arirang* screening illustrates how the settler film culture functioned somewhat autonomously both from the film culture of the homeland and from the Korean film culture. The critical question I intend to raise here concerns the ethnically segregated film practice's problematic relation to the empire's assimilation policy. Indeed, it is important to interrogate the very nature of the Japanese Empire – its emigration and assimilation policies, in particular –adequately to understand the social and cultural implications of its ethnic segregation at theatres. As discussed earlier, the vigorous flow of imperial and colonial subjects across Japan's colonial territories and in Japan proper stemmed from Japanese imperialism's fundamental ideological and political scheme which stressed the ideals of assimilation that aimed to have colonial subjects become Japanese. With the exception of Russia, Japan was the sole modern imperialist country only to colonise its adjacent countries. Quite different from the British or American imperialist models, Japanese imperialism encouraged, and often forced, the Japanese and colonial subjects to intermingle and migrate to other colonial territories. Migration across the Japanese Empire also exposes a unique characteristic of the Japanese imperial project, what Leo Ching calls 'imperialism without capital',[111] indicating that Japan itself was in dire need of industrialisation and modernisation, just like its colonies. Consequently, Japan's migration policies were tied to the modernisation efforts across the Japanese colonial territories which constantly demanded labour forces. The active migration and connectivity between Japan and its colonies, in conjunction with the assimilation efforts, formed the central agenda of Japanese imperialism. There was a serious imbalance, however, between the ideal of assimilation and its actual application. Tessa Morris-Suzuki argues that as Japan 'attempted to juggle two essentially contradictory principles – the principle of the nation-state on the one hand and the principle of colonialism on the other – official definitions of nationality and national identity in the Taishō period were almost inevitably fraught with insoluble paradoxes', and 'one of the most important of these paradoxes was that the colonial order needed to produce both similarity and difference in its subjects'.[112] Thus, as Morris-Suzuki points out, assimilation and discrimination, and Japanisation and exoticisation, were different sides of the same colonial coin.[113] After all, the colonial project was, in essence, hardly in accordance with the ideology of equality.

It is erroneous, nevertheless, to presume that this paradoxical ideology was at its core a vain political manifesto. Indeed, Japanese imperialism ardently produced its imperial system and structure by firmly grounding them in this very paradox. Regarding how this ideology took effect in reality, Leo Ching writes:

> *Doka* [Assimilation] and *kominka* [Imperialisation], by urging and then insisting that the colonized become Japanese, conceal the inequality between the 'natural' Japanese, whose political and economic privileges as citizens are guaranteed, and those 'naturalized' Japanese, whose cultural identities as Japanese are required, but whose political and economic rights as citizens are continuously denied. In short, it was to conceal the fundamental problem of the citizenship of the non-Japanese within the empire that the categories of 'Japanese' and 'imperial subjects' were constructed and mobilized.[114]

What is particularly intriguing in his analysis of the intrinsic problems of the assimilation efforts is the distinction Ching draws between cultural identities and political or economic identities. The word *culture*, or *bunka* in Japanese, as used here, is in fact a tricky term to define because this term signified more than just culture. As discussed in Chapter 1, in August 1919, a few months after the most serious and widespread nationalist movements swept across the Korean peninsula, the Office of the Governor General introduced Cultural Rule, which replaced the previous Militant Rule, as a means of soothing escalating Korean nationalism. Under the slogan of *naisen yūwa* (The Harmonious Relationship between Japan and Joseon), Cultural Rule showed a certain degree of tolerance. In this regard, the word *cultural* in Cultural Rule, or *bunka* in *bunka tōchi*, here was employed as opposed to 'militant' and thus connoted placatory, peaceful, lenient and civilised. What is more striking about Cultural Rule are the ways in which the words *culture* or *cultural* are associated with assimilation. *Yūwa* could be roughly translated as *harmony*; but *wa* means *harmony* and *yū* actually means 'to melt down' or 'to integrate'. So *yūwa* as a whole connotes to 'melt down together to become harmonious'. On the surface, Cultural Rule purported to pledge a certain degree of autonomy for Koreans, modelling itself after Britain's colonial rule of Ireland. But it actually aimed at gradually turning Koreans into Japanese by more sophisticated or cultural ways of governing colonial Korea and controlling colonial subjects through its focus on assimilation. Cultural Rule was based on the contradicting notions of differentiation and assimilation of the colonised population, reflecting the general politics of Japanese imperialism and translating its paradoxes into the practice of colonial rule in Joseon. The internal discord of assimilation ideology remained an unresolved dilemma for Japanese imperialism until its very end, even after the late 1930s when the empire administered more thorough and organised assimilation policies. This incompatibility was clearly inscribed upon every social sphere in Japan's colonies, as in Joseon.

The symbiosis of the Japanese migrants' film culture and the Korean film culture and the segregation between the two in Joseon, especially in the colonial capital of Seoul, is indicative of the inherent problems and limits of Cultural Rule and Japan's general colonial politics, as well as the limitation and complexity of the empire's assimilation endeavours. Importantly, I would argue that this paradoxical nature of the assimilation ideology was not incarnated in the Joseon film culture in random form but manifested its own specific patterns. In terms of film exhibition, the law of segregation prevailed while, at the level of film production and distribution, assimilation or integration between the colonisers and the colonised was much more apparent. Until the early 1940s, however, when the empire put the entire film industry under its firm control, so that the collaboration between Japanese and Korean film-makers was not only encouraged but coercively enforced, integrative film-making practices relied on commercial markets rather than on the political struggles of the empire for assimilation. The collaborations among Koreans, Japanese settlers and Japanese film-makers in the field of film production before the final stage of colonial rule were done for commercial purposes; there were no governmental efforts to encourage or discourage such collaborative film-making activities. What is worse, these collaborative efforts were underplayed, often actively, by the very people who initiated and carried them out. Take Joseon Kinema, the first film company in Joseon, for example: the founders of Joseon Kinema were Japanese business people based in Busan who raised the money to establish the first film corporation in Joseon in 1924. The founding members of the firm, located in the port city of Busan, consisted of Nade Otoichi (a company executive), Kato Seichi (the director of a hospital), Watanabe Tatsuchiru (a painter), Kuboda Orō (a lawyer), and Takasa Kanjo (a Buddhist monk).[115] Joseon Kinema established a contract with the Korean Literary Arts Association (Joseon Munye Hyeobhoe), a *sinpa* group whose members were mostly dramatists and actors. The majority of the staff for *A Plaintive Melody of Sea*, its first project, including the producer and director, were Japanese settlers but the firm also brought in a cinematographer from Japan while the actors were mostly Koreans. Apparently, this first film corporation was created to take advantage of Korean spectators' growing desire for Joseon films but its first project was geared not only towards Korean viewers; the company aimed to 'practice harmony between Japan and Joseon (*naisen shinwa*) through filmmaking and introduce the Korean situation to the Japanese'.[116] Thus, the company successfully 'exported' its first film to Japan through Nikkatsu studio, which premiered it at Sanyukan and Nihonbashi Gekijō of Tokyo in December 1924.[117] Commercially, the film was quite successful, clearing a 3,000 *won* profit from the Japanese and Joseon markets combined.[118] Joseon Kinema's next two projects were also released in Japan through Nikkatsu, which purchased these three films together and released them over a three-month span.[119] What is intriguing about Joseon Kinema's attempt to develop the film market is that the company did not even try to reach Japanese settlers, another potential market inside the colony, despite its financial struggles. It would have been reasonably easy for the company to consider expanding its target audience through appeals to Japanese audiences within Joseon but the company was too preoccupied with developing the film market for Koreans by disguising the company's Japanese involvement which eventually resulted in its total failure. Takasa Kanjo, one of the founders who directed three films for the company, used the Korean name Wang Pil-yeol for his film credit as a means to evade the Korean audience's possible anti-Japanese sentiments. This manoeuvre to confuse Korean audiences seemed to be successful because even some Korean film critics at the time assumed that Takasa/Wang was a Korean director when they expressed their disappointment in the last two films Takasa/Wang directed for Joseon Kinema.[120] Ju Sam-son, an actor who worked for Joseon Kinema, was known to be Japanese but his real Japanese name remains unknown because he used only his Korean name for his film credits. After Takasa and Ju, other migrant film-makers often followed this ruse in order to assimilate better into the Joseon film industry. The way Joseon Kinema limited its audience to Koreans once again proves the fact that the two film cultures in colonial Korea – Japanese migrant film culture and Korean film culture – were basically seen as two separate entities. The Japanese settler-owned film productions in Joseon seemed faithfully to practise the assimilation principle of the empire but they mainly pursued a covert form of collaboration in the disguise of their Japanese origins and catered only for Korean spectators which meant that their collaborative efforts were actually built on the segregated film culture.

The exhibition of two Paramount productions, *The Four Feathers* (1929) and *Fast Company* (1929), the first talkie films theatrically released in Joseon, in the meantime, demonstrates how segregation and differentiation worked in the realm of film exhibition in Joseon while testifying to the connections between the settler film culture and the local Korean film culture in the area of film distribution. In Korean film history, the films' premiere on 27 January 1930, at Joseon Geukjang, a Korean cinema, is recorded as the very first screening of a talkie in Joseon. Yet it is less known that the films were also released on the same day at Chūokan, a Japanese cinema, for Japanese film viewers.[121] Therefore, the talkie era in Joseon began with the same films screened at two separate theatres geared towards two different ethnic audiences. (Figures 3.7 and 3.8) These double screenings of *The Four Feathers* and *Fast Company* elucidate the structural segregation of film audiences between the Japanese and Koreans. This ethnically segregated film exhibition and consumption did not correspond with and, if anything, undermined, Japanese imperialism's assimilation policies and efforts. In fact, radical differences in film programmes at cinemas engendered two very different film cultures even in the same urban space. At the same time, however, the fact that Japanese and Korean film patrons watched the same films and experienced talkies for the first time on the same day reveals that both audiences were still somehow interconnected without realising it, as Korean and Japanese film distribution systems in Joseon shared the same commercial interests and, thus, often worked together.

To conclude this chapter, I should like to present a compelling example that physically represents the interrelated but, at the same time, segregated film cultures between the two ethnic audiences and validates the interplay between them: the bicycle boy. Because only a single film print was available for films screened separately at Korean and Japanese cinemas – unless illegally copied

Migrating with the Movies 141

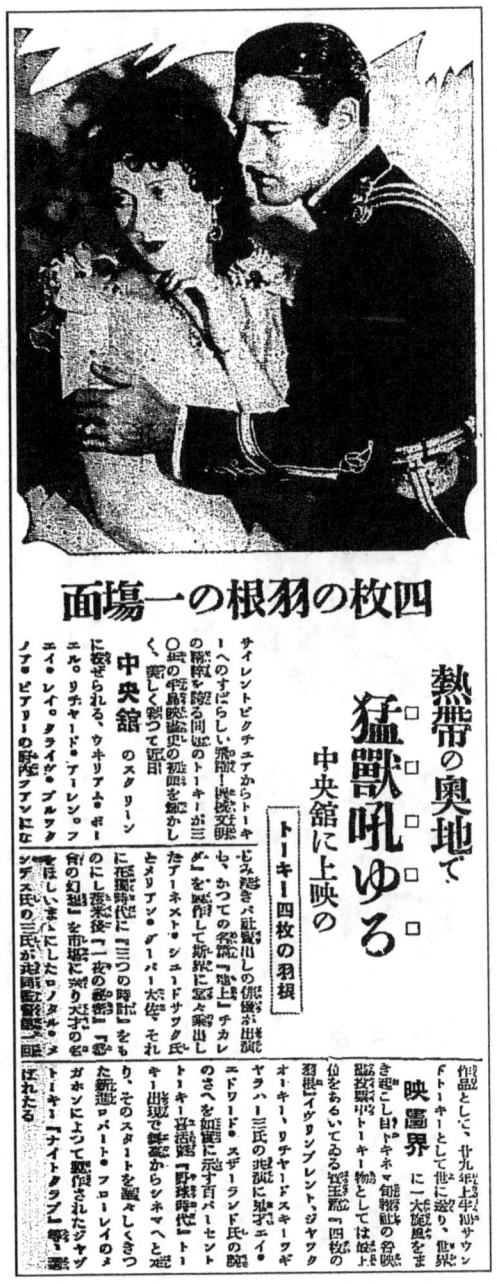

Figure 3.7 A Japanese-language film preview of *The Four Feathers* published in *Keijō nippō*. (25 January 1930)

Figure 3.8 Advertisement published in the Korean-language newspaper *Donga ilbo* for *The Four Feathers* and *Fast Company* (Korean and Japanese title: *The Age of Baseball*). (*Donga ilbo*, 28 January 1930)

prints were in circulation – to screen the film for their respective film patrons, movie theatres located on either side of Cheonggye Stream in Seoul had to schedule the same film at different time slots so that a film print could be shuttled from one theatre to another. For example, if Joseon Geukjang, a Korean cinema, programmed *The Four Feathers* from 7 to 9 p.m., Chūokan, a Japanese theatre, scheduled it from 10 p.m. until midnight to allow a bicycle boy to deliver the film's print, riding his bike from Joseon Geukjang to Chūokan during the interval between the two screenings. In more extreme cases, in which two cinemas' screenings in North and South Village could not avoid overlapping, bicycle boys delivered the films reel by reel; as soon as they finished being projected at one theatre they would be shuttled to the other.[122] This practice epitomises both the segregation and connectivity between the two ethnic film cultures.

As I have shown, the settler film culture, including settler film-makers, distributors, exhibitors, *benshi*, movie theatres, critics and audiences, was an integral part of Joseon cinema. Settler film culture's place in postcolonial Japanese film history or Korean film history, however, is so obscure that it has become an apparition of history whose presence everyone refuses to admit. Indeed, a critical study of Korean and Japanese national cinemas suggests that it does not belong to either. On the one hand, Korean film history, which is still firmly grounded in a nationalist historiography, easily dismisses this symbiosis as yet another concession made for imperial exploitation, as discussed earlier in the chapter. On the other hand, the overwhelming silence in Japanese film history over Japan's decisive and distinctive presence in its former colonies' film cultures remains largely intact. Though settler film culture and its complex relation to the film culture of the locals were what fundamentally characterised the essential nature of film culture in colonial Korea, the suppression and avoidance of historical realities and materials in the postcolonial Koreas and Japan have erased this decisive aspect of Joseon cinema. To illuminate further this and other related historiographical issues, I direct my attention to Korean movie theatres in the following chapters to observe Joseon cinema from the perspective of another important member of Joseon cinema who has been marginalised: the film spectator.

Chapter 4
Colonial Film Spectatorship: Nationalist Enough?

In his article 'A Trajectory of Joseon Cinema I' (1946), which reflects on the colonial film culture with a focus on Hollywood's dominance in the Joseon film scene of the 1920s, film critic Kang So-cheon states that the popularity of Hollywood films among Korean film spectators is indicative of the essentially nationalist nature of colonial spectatorship. According to Kang, Korean filmgoers ignored Japanese films in favour of Hollywood productions – Universal studio pictures, in particular – as a way in which to express their anti-Japanese imperialism sentiments. The author further asserts that Japanese films were only consumed by Japanese settlers at Japanese movie houses while Korean filmgoers went to foreign films, and this ethnically distinctive movie-going pattern eventually turned Japanese movie theatres into second-rate ones, compared to the theatres geared towards Korean spectators.[1] As I discussed in the preceding chapter, most of the films Korean filmgoers enjoyed were the products of Hollywood owing to the considerable lack of commercial Joseon films. In employing this historical fact, however, Kang's account of colonial film spectatorship, written only months after Korea's liberation from the colonial occupation, shows us how quickly postcolonial film historians engaged with an effort to redeem Korea's colonial history through the lens of nationalism. The author's problematic manipulation of historical facts in his attempt to overstate Korean film spectators' nationalism, therefore, deserves more critical attention. Laced with an overtly nationalist historiographical approach, the critic considers Korean spectators' assumed collective political disposition as the sole reason for the popularity of Hollywood productions, without taking industrial, institutional or cultural context into his assessment. In contradiction of the author's claim that Japanese theatres for Japanese migrants were inferior to Korean theatres and financially struggling, they were stable businesses and hugely outnumbered Korean theatres, as discussed in detail in the previous chapter. As we have seen, moreover, Japanese films were hardly ever shown in Korean movie theatres because of the ethnically segregated film exhibition practice that resulted from cultural and language barriers. Korean spectators had no need to visit Japanese theatres that programmed films exclusively for the taste of Japanese settlers, and thus Korean patrons had no means with which they could intentionally decide the fate of the Japanese theatre business. It is simply erroneous to maintain that a nationalist impulse was what led Korean filmgoers to develop their penchant for Hollywood films and that their taste pushed Japanese movie theatres out of the competition. The film-viewing tendency of Korean filmgoers as described in Kang's essay, therefore, predicts a master agenda of postcolonial Korean film historiography that seeks to frame colonial film culture fundamentally as a constant struggle between the occupying forces and nationalist desires.

Though exploiting a partial truth for the sake of nationalist film historiography, Kang's essay still evokes the importance of approaching film history as something more than just the mode of production and thus presents us with another significant yet rarely discussed area of Joseon cinema to consider. Kang's detailed account of Korean spectators' film-viewing patterns in delineating colonial film culture suggests that film-viewing might be an intricate cultural activity informed by various social, political and historical factors that shaped Joseon film culture. In the final two chapters, I turn my focus to the problematics of film spectatorship and reception in order to extend further the topography of Joseon cinema. In particular, I approach movie-going practices as part of a cultural sphere in which various forms of political and social tensions in Joseon society were represented and mediated. For my attempt to reconstruct critically movie-going practices in relation to modern experiences of Joseon, Kang's essay presents a point of departure. Traditionally, studies of colonial film spectatorship are mostly fixated on Joseon films that conjured obvious political, ideological and cultural questions for Korean filmgoers. Kang's essay allows us a rare glimpse into an often-neglected aspect of Joseon film culture: the predominance of Hollywood and its impact on Korean filmgoers' film-viewing. According to Kang, Korean film spectators tried to find a way to express their cultural and social ethos, mainly through the appropriation of foreign texts, owing to the dearth of local film productions they could regularly enjoy. As I elaborate in the following sections, much evidence documents that Korean filmgoers did, indeed, contemplate their own social and political issues while watching foreign films in movie houses. Contrary to the common assumption that the reception by Korean film fans of local productions was what raised the main concern for authorities, more frequent and intense tensions between the authorities and Korean film fans actually involved Hollywood productions. The relationship between Korean spectators and foreign images, however, was a lot more heterogeneous and complex than Kang's description in his essay. To delineate a more vibrant relationship between the images on screen and the audience in the cinema, as well as to explore the equally colourful social responses and reactions to film culture and film patrons, I argue, it is necessary to liberate colonial spectatorship from the confines of local productions. According to the police bureau's documentation that records film censorship, for instance, among 2,422 submissions the censorship board censored between August 1926 and February 1927, only eighteen films could be labelled as 'pure Joseon films',[2] while 876 American films were censored.[3] As these figures evidently show, given the perennial shortage of local films in film programmes, Korean filmgoers were inevitably bound to consume an overwhelming number of foreign-origin films. Considering this context, any attempt to relate Korean spectators' movie-going and film-viewing patterns exclusively to Joseon films is essentially limited and myopic. In an endeavour to overcome such limitations, therefore, I purposefully observe the issues in colonial film spectatorship in relation not only to local but also to imported films.

In her insightful study of African American spectatorship and its manifestation of American racial politics in the segregated American urban space of the early twentieth century, Jacqueline Stewart illuminates the ways in which African Americans negotiated confrontations with cinema as a major feature of modern American culture. Expanding the discussions of the politics of racial representations, Stewart introduces the notion of 'reconstructive film spectatorship' which refers to 'a formulation that seeks to account for the range of ways in which Black viewers attempted to reconstitute and assert themselves in relation to the cinema's racist social and textual operations'.[4] According to Stewart, this reconstructive spectatorship illustrates how the public dimension of spectatorship persisted for Black viewers, complicating the presumed pleasures and limitations of classical absorption and distraction designed for the idealised spectator. At the beginning of the classical Hollywood era, Black audiences were not meant to be fully integrated into the developing narratives on screen nor into American theatre audiences because 'the conspicuousness of Black bodies did not disappear in darkened theatres'.[5] Encountering derogatory descriptions of their race that reflected American racial politics, African Americans were led to deconstruct and then reconstruct the racial representations embedded in the film narratives.

Korean spectators' film-viewing experiences under the colonial milieu resonate in many ways with Stewart's study of the constitutive relationships between early film spectatorship and internal colonialism and also with her notion of reconstructive Black spectatorship. Colonial realities, film censorship, active surveillance at the site of film exhibitions in the form of the police force present at film screenings, and political slogans and posters that surrounded the screen – all contribute to the impossibility of Korean spectators' thorough immersion into the images on the silver screen without constantly being reminded of their colonial situation. What fundamentally demarcates Korean colonial film spectatorship from that of the African Americans described in Stewart's research, however, is that most of the films Korean audiences engaged with at the cinema did not directly concern them in terms of subject matter, narratives and representational politics because the films were foreign in origin. Korean spectators' 'reconstructive spectatorship', therefore, had to begin from proactively constructing a certain connection between foreign images and their lives, societies, and the historical moments in which they lived so that they could project back on to the screen those newly assembled meanings that might keenly address their reality.

By interrogating Korean spectators' reception of imported films, which involved multiple processes of decoding and recoding, the present chapter aims to constitute film spectators as one of the key agents in the image politics of Joseon film culture. In particular, detailed accounts of cultural receptions and interpretations of Hollywood films and social reactions to their dominance in the Joseon film scene will show us how the engagement of Korean spectators with American films emerged as a main subject of political confrontation and hegemonic struggle with regard to the colonial situation. The first section of the chapter maps out in broad strokes, the diverse perceptions of Hollywood films as well as the social and cultural conditions that affected them, leading to the more vivid picture of film–spectator relationships I shall draw up in the second half of the chapter.

Korean Spectators, or How they Learned to Stop Worrying and Love Hollywood

One day in 1917 Colonel Jasper E. Brady, a manager of the script department of Universal Pictures, and his staff stopped their work to work out the content of a script they had received from an aspiring screenwriter. Written in a language they could not comprehend at all, this six-page treatment led them to look for a colleague who could decipher its mysterious writing. After a studio-wide search, they were able to locate a staff member, a Korean native, who interpreted this treatment as written in Korean and sent from a fan in Joseon. According to *Motography*, a trade journal that reported this event, the script even included the list of actors the writer preferred to work with if his script were given the green light. 'He has selected a cast composed of about a dozen Bluebird and Universal stars', *Motography* recounted, 'but he proved that his acquaintance with the personnel of the two lists of the film actors was wide, for he mentioned Dorothy Phillips, Lon Chaney, Ella Hall, Herbert Rawlinson, Jack Mulhall and Gretchen Lederer.'[6] *The Moving Picture World*, which also ran an item on this occasion, concluded its report by noting 'another proof that all climes and nations are represented in the aggregation of the Big U Company'.[7] The writer turned out to be a hard-core Korean movie enthusiast or *aehwalga* (a film lover) as they were called in Joseon at the time. This anecdote displays the deep affection for Universal that led this film fan to send his script to the studio. It also demonstrates his extensive knowledge about the studio, including the Bluebird Photoplays, Universal's in-house studio which enjoyed unusual popularity in Joseon and Japan, and newly contracted actors such as Lon Chaney who, a few years later, would rise to global stardom with such hit movies as *The Hunchback of Notre Dame* (1923) and *The Phantom of the Opera* (1925). Intriguingly, this episode vividly exposes Korean film fans' fascination with the novelty of cinema and the pleasure of film-viewing, another seldom-explored issue in colonial film history. As I unpack this subject in detail in the next chapter, the most immediate attention will be given to the object of the fandom: Universal films and Hollywood productions in general.

Sent in 1917, in the wake of Joseon cinema's major breakthrough, this hard-core Universal fan's treatment encapsulates Hollywood cinema's dominant place in the development of Joseon film culture. Joseon's first film magazine *Nokseong*, which was published in the same year, presents a clue with which we could further contextualise the Korean fan's serious fan activity. In the complete absence of locally produced films, *Nokseong*'s first issue consisted almost entirely of items on Hollywood, including reports on stars such as Charlie Chaplin, Eddie Polo and Pearl White, and reviews of Hollywood films. In addition, the magazine featured half a dozen so-called films-in-a-magazine (K: *jisang yeonghwa*; J: *shijō eiga*: a film preview format that introduced films as short stories)[8] of Universal and Bluebird films, which filled up nearly half of the issue. (Figure 4.1) From an industrial standpoint, both the aspiring screenwriter's script submitted to Universal and Joseon's first film magazine, as the American trade press boastfully reported, were good indications of Universal's pioneering role in Hollywood's aggressive cultivation of the global market in its first decade. The flow of Hollywood films into Joseon accelerated in tandem with the rapid growth of Joseon cinema in the 1920s and, thus, despite slow development and poor industrial conditions, film fans in Joseon were not left out of the global film culture in this golden decade of silent film.

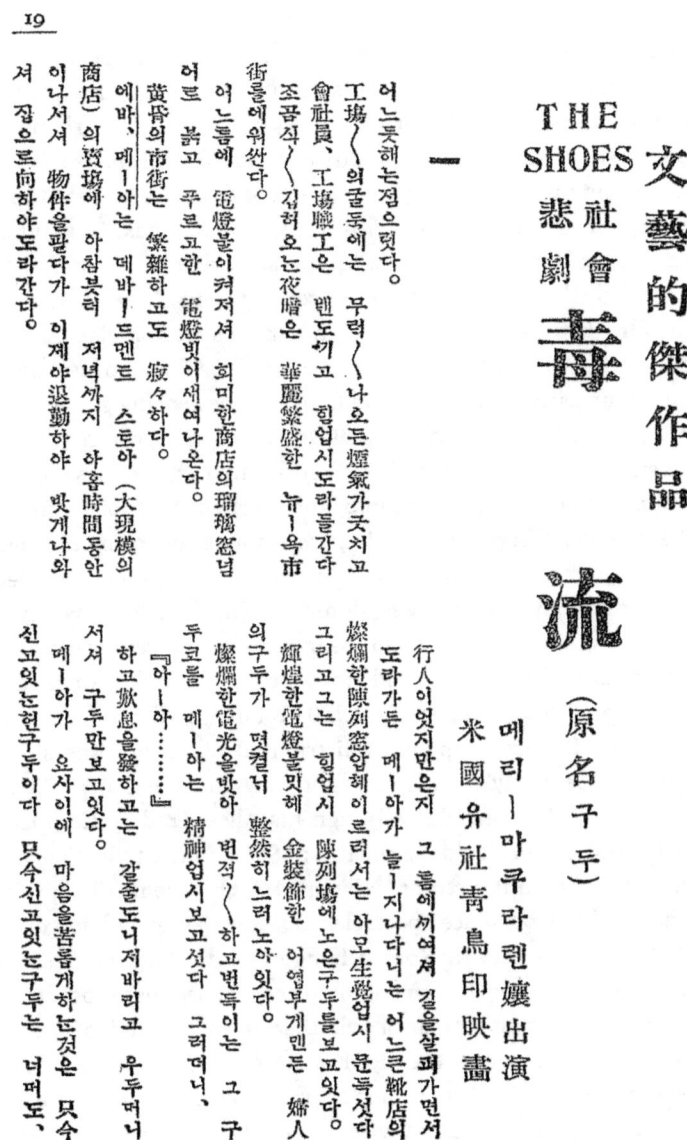

Figure 4.1 *Jisang yeonghwa* or 'film-in-a-magazine' featuring the Bluebird film *Shoes* (1916, directed by Lois Weber) published in the first issue of *Nokseong*, Joseon's first film magazine. (*Nokseong*, November 1917, p. 19) Though considered minor productions in the United States, Universal's Bluebird films enjoyed enormous popularity in Joseon and Japan alike. *Shoes*, for instance, was remade twice by Shochiku Kamata studio in 1922.

In the mid-1910s, when only a few movie theatres and playhouses had just started seriously exploring the film business, Hollywood films were not particularly popular in Joseon. Universal's film serials quickly gained public recognition, however, as they were more regularly imported than any other Hollywood movies through American businessman G. H. Morris who served as the Universal agent while running his car sales and service centre, Morris Trading Company, which opened in Seoul in 1915. Like Japanese migrants, Korean spectators also could not resist the sensational world of Universal serials with their signature cliffhangers and attractive serial queens. Towards the end of the decade, the film distribution system began to be institutionalised, and the evolution from a print-by-print contract to the rise of distribution agencies was fostered by the competition for Hollywood films. The newspaper advertisement for Umigwan, a Korean movie theatre, on 19 December 1919, for instance, claimed that it had signed a contract with Universal through its Japanese branch office to receive films directly from the studio, and boasted that, for the first time in Joseon, it employed a direct distribution system without the involvement of an agency.[9] The ad further explained that this contract was inevitable because of the American film industry's growing dominance in the world market after the war in Europe. As the ad suggests, European films were rarely available in Japan and Joseon towards the end of World War I, and this allowed American movies to flood the region. Subsequently, in 1920, Tokunaga Kumaichirō opened his Tokunaga Motion Picture Shop which distributed Warner Brothers' and FBO's movies (and later Germany's Ufa films),[10] and the American George Allen opened Paramount's Seoul office in 1922 through his Allen Trading Company which engaged with the Joseon Geukjang theatre of Seoul in the following year exclusively to screen Paramount pictures.[11] (Figure 4.2) Opened in 1922 primarily for stage dramas and performance spectacles, Joseon Geukjang had converted to a movie theatre mainly serving Korean filmgoers with its new 'special contract (K: *teukyak*)' with Paramount, which ignited the Danseongsa–Joseon Geukjang rivalry for the title of best Korean movie theatre that would last for the next fifteen years. Gisin Yanghaeng, the first Korean-owned distribution firm, joined the competition in 1927 by distributing films of Metro-Goldwyn-Mayer (MGM) and United Artists,[12] while Fox movies joined the competition a bit later, in 1928, through a Japanese settler's trading company (Fujii Shōten).[13] Among these distributors, Gisin Yanghaeng turned out to be a game-changer owing to its aggressive business practices. Generally, Hollywood movies arrived in Joseon at least several months after they had been first released in Japan but Gisin expedited that process, bringing in Hollywood films within a month or two of their premiere in Japan.[14] In addition, Gisin newly negotiated the distribution rights to Paramount just months after its establishment which allowed the

Colonial Film Spectatorship 151

Figure 4.2 A Hollywood trade journal's report on Paramount's exclusive 1923 deal with Joseon Geukjang, a new upmarket three-storey cinema opened in 1922. The photo shows the Paramount logo, along with billboard images from its films, displayed on the facade of the cinema. ('Theater Tourists at Korea', *Exhibitors Herald*, 16.22, 26 May 1923, p. 51)

firm to distribute about fifteen Hollywood features a month.[15] Gisin's business, which later included the distribution of European films as well as Paramount pictures, continued to grow enough to be able to purchase the Aegwan theatre of Incheon (1927) and Joseon Geukjang (1934).[16] The company later formed its own film production wing that produced *Tale of Sim Cheong* (*Sim Cheong jeon*, 1937),[17] becoming Joseon's first vertically integrated film company. (Figure 4.3)

By the time its golden age began, Hollywood dominated the Joseon market in the same manner as it did in the rest of the world through its systematic distribution network and overseas agencies. By 1926, 90 per cent of imported films in Joseon were American.[18] European films could not compete with Hollywood

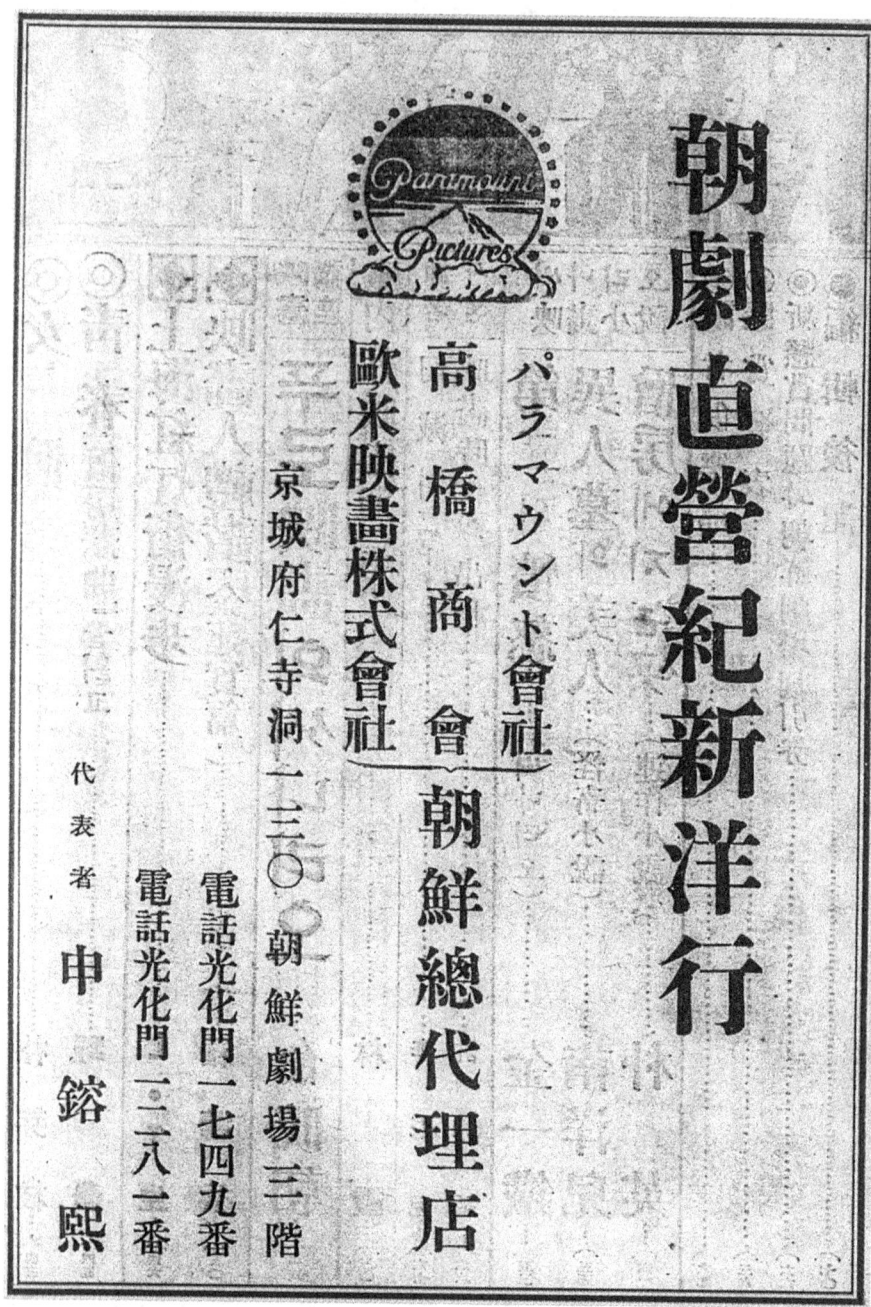

Figure 4.3 Advertisement for Gisin Yanghaeng, the first Korean-owned film distribution company. (*Yeonghwa sidae*, 1.3, May 1931)

in the Joseon film market primarily because of this inequitable global distribution network. Several distributors sought to distribute regularly European films after the phenomenal success of Abel Gance's *La Rue* (1923) in Joseon (released in 1927) but they had to travel to Japan to make arrangements with the Japanese film companies which resold the rights only to old films.[19] As a result, Hollywood prevailed without much competition; Universal, in particular, one of the minor studios (Little Three), which had already established a strong distribution network in East Asia with its offices in Shanghai, Tokyo, and then Seoul, became dominant in Joseon. To compete with the Umigwan, Danseongsa brought in other Hollywood movies soon after its reopening in 1918 but it could not sway the loyalty of Korean moviegoers for Universal, a devotion that had been formed over almost six years.[20] After years of competition, Danseongsa finally took over the distribution rights to Universal pictures from Umigwan in 1923,[21] allowing the studio to continue to dominate the Joseon film market. By 1927, among Hollywood studios, Universal sent the most films (213) to Joseon followed by Paramount (136) and First National (42).[22] Universal's dominance waned gradually as more and more films from other Hollywood studios began entertaining Joseon film fans; and, in the mid-1930s, Paramount's movies overtook Universal films. Still, Universal, together with Paramount, remained the two Hollywood studios that sent the most films to Joseon.[23]

The Political Mobilisation of Hollywood Film-viewing

The reign of Hollywood continued well beyond the 1930s. Film censor Okada Jun'ichi noted in 1936 that almost all of the foreign films censored in Joseon were Hollywood films, and European films were extremely rare.[24] It is important to point out here that Hollywood's growth was partly indebted to the tendency of the censorship board to be more lenient with 'pure entertainment films' from the beginning while strictly restricting films from socialist countries, such as Russia, and banning films that dealt with nationalist movements of European countries such as Ireland, Poland and Finland.[25] According to a censor, this political consideration was intended to make Korean spectators perceive film primarily as a form of entertainment and, indeed, it influenced Korean filmgoers to develop their penchant for westerns, melodramas and action movies.[26] This initial view towards the apolitical nature of Hollywood's entertainment movies held by the authorities, however, became considerably modified over time and the seemingly unstoppable popularity of Hollywood was abruptly ended by none other than the censorship entity. In 1934 the Office of the Governor General approved a proposal from the censorship board for a new film regulation that entailed a screen quota system limiting the screening of foreign movies in movie theatres.²⁷ What led the authorities to change their view towards American cinema so drastically over the course of a decade and turn to such an extreme measure that explicitly targeted Hollywood productions?

In tracing the authorities' changed perceptions of the relationship between the Korean spectator and Hollywood, I should like to quote a fan response to a Hollywood film that displays the most overt form of political connotations appearing from the encounters of Korean filmgoers with Hollywood productions. *Joseon ilbo*, one of the major Korean-language newspapers, launched its fan review section, 'Impression of a Film', on 9 May 1925, with *Peter Pan* (1924, filmed for Famous Players-Lasky and distributed by Paramount Pictures, Figure 4.4). The reviewer/fan, 'Mr H', writes about this heavily promoted Paramount 'money picture':

> The country that produced a movie as dreamy and beautiful as *Peter Pan* must be a happy place. A spectator who listens to and sees this beautiful story is also happy . . . the scene where the children fight the pirates on the pirate ship made me wonder, 'How free is their world? Oh, how happy their country must be!' When the children sang, 'My country is your country. Oh, land of freedom, a great country', while replacing the pirate flag with the American national flag, I burst into tears. My heart had a dull pain from too much joy. Miss Betty Bronson and the others also acted freely.²⁸

This fan review, which starts with the word 'free' and ends with 'free', is the first of many subsequent reviews on Hollywood films submitted for the fan review section. This particular reflection of *Peter Pan*, which interprets an undisguised Americanism embedded in a Hollywood fantasy as a liberating force and thus inferentially comments on the unfree status of Koreans under colonial rule, obviously demonstrates that the popularity of Hollywood films often went much deeper than just the filmic level. As the above review exemplifies, when watching foreign images, Korean spectators engaged with a process of decoding through which they granted a set of new meanings to those images, actively creating a brand new relationship between spectators and films of foreign origin. This new meaning emerging between the silver screen and the fans in the audience was largely informed by Joseon society's particular perception of 'the country that produced' films.

The deep affection for American cinema expressed in this particular case, in other words, was related to Joseon's colonial state which made Koreans consider the United States a potential ally or even a rescuer who could possibly help Joseon liberate itself from Japanese colonial occupation. The publicly built image of the United States was that it was the ultimate democratic society, especially in the light of President Woodrow Wilson's vital role in founding the League of Nations and shaping the Treaty of Versailles which denounced all kinds of imperialism from the

Figure 4.4 Advertisement that showcases Paramount's heavy promotional campaign of its globally successful 1924 'money picture', or blockbuster, *Peter Pan*. (*The Film Daily*, 23 November 1924)

previous century. It is important to note that this makeover of the United States as a guardian of humanity was, in fact, a systematic political manoeuvre by Washington, especially under Woodrow Wilson's presidency in the late 1910s. Wilson's administration emphasised universalising the individual's rights and extending them to colonised people. What this commitment to the right of independence for colonised nations did, in turn, was to allow the United States to become deeply involved in world politics, spread the American way of democracy and, more importantly, develop the economic interests of the United States.[29] As Maria Josefina Saldaña-Portillo explains, disseminating its ideas of democracy and freedom was closely entwined with 'expanding the network of trade for the United States'.[30] Whereas the United States certainly broke away from the old form of imperialism, it also moved towards a new kind of hegemony that was based primarily on capitalist expansion and economic exploitation articulated to the rhetoric of freedom, liberation and democracy. This awkward marriage between political benevolence and economic expansion has been the sustaining theme in American foreign affairs from the late 1910s to the present.

Still, the Wilsonian foreign policy of the United States offered Koreans a tremendous sense of hope. It is a well-known historical fact that President Wilson's call for global democracy and national self-determination, proclaimed in 1918, was one of the ideological inspirations for the 1919 Independence Movement. Koreans sincerely hoped that Washington would take diplomatic action to support their movement for independence; and, whenever there was a chance, Koreans tried hard to relay their strong desire for independence to the country they thought of as a resilient fighter against imperial forces. An editorial published in *Donga ilbo* on the occasion of a visit by a delegation of American congressmen in 1920, for instance, opined: 'In the name of twenty million Koreans we extend our heartiest welcome to the congressmen who are just entering our land' and the piece continues:

> Coming as they do from a great country, a country that Nature has endowed with the awe-inspiring Rockies, with mighty rivers and opulent prairies; a country that has produced men like Lincoln and Washington; a country that has for its foundation liberty of conscience for all its people; a country which is in the vanguard of humanity as regards freedom and justice.[31]

The United States as a land of freedom and justice, or utopia, picturesquely portrayed in this editorial writing, even written in English for the benefit of visitors from the United States, echoes the film fan's heartfelt longing for America that he discovered while watching the blockbuster *Peter Pan*. Thus, the positive reaction to Hollywood cinema was not just indebted to Hollywood's sophisticated cinematic achievement, entertainment value or advanced global distribution network but it was one of many reflections that mirrored Korea's strong sense of connection to, and anticipation for, the country that produced these films which were again grounded in Koreans' aspirations for their own nation's independence. For the colonial authorities, the efforts of Koreans to seek out support from the United States by making contact with representatives of the American Congress was a growing concern, in addition to the American missionaries' support for the Korean nationalist movement discussed in Chapter 1; and they tried to undermine such efforts in the name of 'Korean' flunkeyism (K: *sadae juui*)',[32] a typical Korean trait, according to the colonial authorities' definition, that attempts to resolve issues through the involvement of the powerful. The tension between the administration and the Korean people over the US delegates was, in fact, quite intense; the welcoming reception for the 1920 visit of the congressmen led several thousands to a street demonstration in Seoul, a desperate gesture to notify American visitors of their yearning for independence.

As one of few available windows through which Koreans were able to peep into American society, Hollywood was viewed as a visual articulation of Americanism. In an article which examines the national characteristics represented in film, for example, a Korean film critic defined 'colourfulness', 'gorgeous brilliance', and 'jazz's rapturous tune' as the American cinema's embodiment of American-ness, in quite a similar manner to the aforementioned editorial writing.[33] He particularly urged readers to take seriously the recently produced Hollywood war epics, which had gained popularity among Korean filmgoers, as those films contained the elements that conceptualise American national sentiment. Likewise, the wave of film reviews on Hollywood productions linked the overt representations of sexuality, free love and individualism to the American values of freedom and democracy. Importantly, this politically charged reading of Hollywood productions was not just done by film critics and fans on an individual level but by more concerted efforts to build a connection between American images and local politics. In Chapter 1, I traced the activities of the Moving Picture Unit (MPU) of the Office of the Governor General as the first film production entity in the wake of the empire-wide interest in the educational function of film. The government offices or other organisations which supported colonial hegemony, however, did not monopolise the educational and enlightening use of film. As part of its efforts to reform colonial governance, the Saitō administration lifted many controlling regulations with regard to freedom of speech, public gatherings and association. Consequently, diverse Korean social, religious and reformist groups and associations were able to arrange events for a variety of public causes. And, almost immediately after the MPU's establishment, social associations began to incorporate film screenings into their public events to attract participants and better promote their agendas. Though their definition of, and approach to, enlightenment and social edifice would differ significantly from that of the colonial authorities, these groups employed film as the main educational and promotional tool in an identical manner to the MPU to educate and enlighten fellow Koreans but with very different political intentions. Intriguingly, Hollywood films, regardless of the nature of their content, were often used as a main feature for political or public events arranged by Koreans.

It was the Tongyeong Youth Association (Tongyeong Cheongnyeonhoe) of Tongyeong County that initiated the practice of including a film screening in a political event. After the success of the first film screening event it held in the county,[34] the association purchased a film projector and organised a Moving Picture Band (K: *hwaldong sajindae* or *hwaldong sajindan*) in 1921 to hold mobile film-screening events across the peninsula to 'advance Joseon culture and propagate the expansion of educational institutions'.[35] (Figure 4.5) This groundbreaking event, along with two other travelling film exhibition tours held in the subsequent years (1922 and 1923), was detailed in Korean-language newspapers. Hailed as 'a model film unit that uplifts culture'[36] and an 'immeasurable contribution to the education of the Korean people',[37] the Moving Picture Band screened films for Korean populations in many towns and cities. With the complete absence of locally produced films at the time, the delegates travelled with foreign films consisting of American educational films, American and Gaumont newsreels and Hollywood westerns, melodramas and comedies. Following the exhibition conventions of the silent era, their screenings opened with a one-reel comedy and then featured a couple of short newsreels and educational films. After an intermission, which presented singing or dancing performances by the locals, the event concluded with a feature-length film.[38] Though the Band guaranteed that all its films were suitable for educational purposes,[39] a programme consisting of a slapstick comedy, tragic love story, or western still seems to be rather irrelevant to their endeavours for education and to the undercurrent nationalist impulse to enlighten their fellow Koreans. At that time, youth associations were dedicated to the improvement of their communities and often functioned as local hubs of nationalist movements. The Tongyeong Youth Association was especially well known for its uncompromising nationalist activities, resulting in frequent run-ins with the police force and even arrests of its members.[40]

What created the bridge between Hollywood movies and a noble intention to enlighten the Korean people was not necessarily the content of the Hollywood film but the event itself. In other words, Hollywood pictures were screened as a main attraction to lure more participants to those events. In fact, the organisers charged admission fees and donated them to schools and other educational institutions which was the main purpose of the event.[41] In a manner similar to commercial screenings, in this regard, they needed to draw in as many viewers as possible to raise more donations. On the screening night, they even hired a

Figure 4.5 *Donga ilbo*'s report on the arrival of the Moving Picture Band of the Tongyeong Youth Association in Seoul. (9 September 1921)

brass band to play music to entice passers-by while members from the association were promoting the event outside.[42] Hollywood films were chosen for the same end. Newspaper reports on the Moving Picture Band's arrival in respective cities, for example, encouraged readers to attend the events by stressing that the screening would feature 'rare films that we will never be able to see again'.[43] The Tongyeong Youth Association's method was quickly adopted by many other social associations and, soon, this practice, now labelled the Moving Picture Event (K: *hwaldong sajin daehoe*), became a staple of social movements in Joseon. Films screened for such events varied from Hollywood products, newsreels and educational pictures to commercial Joseon films that became available a few years later. A religious group hosting a special three-day screening of the entire twenty-two episodes of *The Broken Coin*[44] or the screening of *Monte Cristo* (1922, Fox) by a newspaper company for its subscribers exemplified typical cases of moving picture events.[45] Hollywood films, in this manner, were brought into social events and counter-hegemonic activities of the colonised.

Hollywood at the Centre of Colonial Hegemonic Struggles

When it came to politically overt films, it was fairly easy for the censorship body to monitor them, ban them and/or cut out scenes it found unacceptable. Joseon films were subject to the most severe form of censorship; as a Japanese settler critic put it, no single *Joseon* film was completed without some scenes being chopped off.[46] About one-third of the 1926 film *A Hero of the Troubled Times*'s initial version was cut by the censorship board, for instance, making it nearly impossible for film-makers to come up with an understandable final cut, thus necessitating a reshooting. Soviet films comprised another group of films that suffered equally severe censorship, as the empire was paranoid about socialist movements, and any politically sensitive films underwent closer scrutiny from the film censorship board. Hollywood films did suffer a form of censorship but for different reasons, that is, for their representations of sexuality and violence. The censors saw Hollywood films as a threat to the traditional mores and ethical values of Joseon and Japan but not as a menace to the political hegemony. Despite the authorities' endeavours to control and regulate explicitly political films, however, Korean spectators still managed to engage with an oppositional reading of Hollywood films that even lacked an element which might threaten the colonial hegemony or to employ those movies to benefit their political agendas. Korean viewers' act of 'textual poaching',[47] which actively analysed and reinterpreted film images for their political causes, was something neither a censor nor even a producer of a text could have any control over. The only way to prevent this was to strip Koreans of any chance to watch Hollywood films. Over time, therefore, colonial authorities began to view Korean fans' film-viewing patterns as the true cause of the problem. In other words, the particular film tastes of Korean spectators became a growing concern for the administration. Having observed the persistent popularity of Hollywood films and film programme patterns at Korean movie theatres, which programmed too many Hollywood films without screening a single Japanese film over the years, the censors on the film censorship board began openly to express their aggravation. Subsequently, attention of the authorities was directed to that particular movie-going practice that continued to nurture Koreans' fascination with Hollywood. Thus, eventually, the practice of ethnically segregated film screenings itself began to occupy the centre of the tension with regard to Hollywood productions.

Importantly, discussions and critiques of the overwhelming quantity of Hollywood films screened at Korean theatres primarily addressed the issue of ethnic assimilation. An article from the Japanese film magazine *Eiga junpō* (July 1943), which chronicles a history of film censorship in Joseon, particularises:

> In fact Korean filmgoers were inclined to love foreign films from the outset, and the film industry cared only for making profits, which led foreign films with great entertainment value to flood into [Joseon]. As a result, the influences of the frivolous and low-brow cultures and customs contained in American films became gradually apparent ... In the meantime the fundamental policy of *naisen ittai* ['Japan and Joseon are One Body'] in governing Joseon must be firmly rooted, and thus it is urgent to spread Japan's good customs and cultures inherent in domestic [Japanese] films. In this context, in August, the 9th year of Shōwa [1934], Motion Picture Film Censorship (*Government Order No. 82*) that limited the screenings of foreign films went into effect ... It would give Korean people more opportunities to appreciate domestic films by reducing the screening ratio of foreign films and allowing domestic films to easily reach Joseon.[48]

This article perceived Korean spectators' film taste as an obstacle to the Japanese Empire's assimilation policy. As it indicates, the literal annexation and assimilation of colonial subjects into the empire was the fundamental principle of the Japanese imperial structure. The Japanese imperial enterprise's ideological justification, from the beginning, was grounded on its 'Pan-Asianism' that aimed at solidifying Asian countries under Japan's leadership in order to fend off the Western imperial expansion into the region. This assimilation effort had accelerated since the Cultural Rule era in Joseon and, thus, even before *naisen ittai*, the blatant assimilation policy mentioned in the above film magazine, was proclaimed in 1937 by then Governor General Minami Jirō, the Japanese Empire had always been serious about assimilation. *Eiga junpō* rebuked the profit-driven film industry in service of the popular taste as the primary reason for not only spoiling Korean spectators but impeding Japan's assimilation efforts. Yet, as a matter of fact, colonial authorities had addressed the same concern associating the popularity of Hollywood films with the issue of 'Japanising' Koreans long before the empire began to take notice, almost ten years before the publication of the special Joseon cinema issue of *Eiga junpō*. Oka Shigematsu, a chief film censor, for example, expressed his unease about the popularity of Hollywood films and framed this issue in a manner similar to *Eiga junpō* in his essay, 'Miscellaneous Feelings about Film Censorship', published in 1934. Oka wrote:

> What makes me angry is the prevalence of foreign films and the audience's attitude. From early on, Joseon cinema has had a strange custom: movie theatres have been clearly divided between Japanese and Korean theatres. Of course Japanese theatres screen domestic films, but Korean theatres only screen foreign and Joseon films. These days they completely boycott Japanese films. Since they produce only one or two Joseon films, according to our survey, twenty million Koreans only have contact with foreign movies . . . What kind of consequence would it generate if twenty million Koreans ignored the films of our homeland and only admired foreign movies?[49]

Oka went on to single out American cinema and discussed how the 'Yankeeism' represented in American films had threatened traditional values of Joseon and Japanese society, deploring the fact that more and more people had succumbed to the 'devilish attraction' of Hollywood entertainment.[50] Both Oka and *Eiga junpō* called for the authorities' devotion to upholding the assimilation policy in the fields of film-making and film exhibition but, paradoxically, this demand only discloses that Japan's assimilation campaigns did not proceed smoothly. As I discussed in detail in the earlier chapter, assimilation always coexisted with discrimination as a means to maintain the colonial order. The exclusive Japanese communities formed across the Korean peninsula are among the many indicators that testify to the imbalance between the ideal of assimilation and its actual application, which also resulted in ethnically segregated film cultures. In other words, the paradox of the Japanese imperial project which engendered both assimilation and discrimination – or similarity and difference – for its imperial and colonial subjects was certainly inscribed upon the segregated symbiosis of the film cultures of the colonisers and colonised. What essentially obstructed the assimilation endeavour was the inherent limitation of the assimilation policy itself, not Hollywood movies, not the profit-driven film industry, nor Korean film spectators' particular tastes.

In fact, when the ethnically segregated film exhibition practice was first formed, the authorities took it for granted. The 1927 censorship record acknowledges this practice and expounds it as inevitable because of cultural differences.[51] Over time, however, the anxieties towards the ever-increasing popularity of Hollywood films, in contrast to the absence of Japanese films in the programmes at Korean movie houses, grew and the authorities finally decided to take action. To get rid of the decade-long segregated film-exhibition practice that, the authorities now believed, allowed Koreans to develop their distinctive film taste and become the source of problems for assimilation efforts, in 1934 the Office of the Governor General introduced a new film regulation that required all movie theatres to screen a certain number of Japanese films.[52] As such, this new film regulation was introduced mainly to implement a screen quota; it did not specify, however, the details of the screen quota but left them in the hands of regional governments.[53] Though there were slight variations across regions, typically, in 1935 25 per cent of the footage of the total number of films screened had to be Japanese films. The proportion of domestic films increased to one-third in the following year and, from 1937 onwards, Japanese films had to comprise at least 50 per cent of the films screened at all cinemas.[54] This screen quota was the very first of its kind in the entire empire, even preceding the Film Law, introduced in Japan in 1939, which limited the screening of foreign films. As the most regulatory film censorship ever to emerge from the empire, it offered the authorities a means effectively to control the flow of foreign films into Korea.

In the end, what perturbed the colonial authorities was not only the dominance of Hollywood films but the absence of Japanese films at Korean theatres.[55] In introducing the 1934 Joseon film law, *Kinema junpō* conveyed the authorities' concerns that only 62 per cent of the films screened in Joseon were Japanese films and that no Korean theatres presented a Japanese movie, quite a difference from the Japanese market where domestic films comprised 85 per cent of film bills.[56] The authorities' attempts to control Hollywood and its ill effects on the Korean (and Japanese) population were also based on acknowledgement of film's power to influence spectators and, thus, the move to control foreign films was related in many ways to the authorities' film-reformist activities. In his contribution to *Kokusai eiga shimbun*, which introduces the main purpose of this screen quota to Japanese readers, Ikeda Kunio, the film censor of the Office of the Governor General, alleged that, in addition to an effort to correspond to the assimilation policy, the regulation resulted from 'culture-educational considerations'.[57] In the eyes of the authorities, permitting Koreans to develop a taste for Hollywood films was an improper use of this powerful medium, and Japanese films should, thus, replace Hollywood films to capitalise best on the educational capacities of cinema and to assist the authorities' struggles in assimilating the Koreans. Indeed, as discussed in Chapter 1, another important characteristic of the 1934 regulation was the inclusion of clauses that aimed to support the educational use of cinema. In addition, the regulation also contained clauses that offered the authorities an unprecedented authority over commercial film exhibitions, making it possible for regional governments to order any theatre to halt film screening, whenever they deemed a screening inappropriate, without having to specify the infractions leading to such action.[58]

This unequivocal move by the administration to regulate tightly commercial film screening was not welcomed by exhibitors and fans alike. Japanese settlers were more critical about the regulation and overall censorship issue, perhaps simply because they were able to be so, as Koreans could not openly criticise the authorities. While acknowledging the need to monitor the influx of Western customs and culture through films, the settler film reviewer Yamaguchi Torao warned that censors should be careful when censoring films in order not to ruin the pleasure that films offer or to have a negative impact the film industry.[59] Pointing out the flawed censorship system, another reviewer argued that exhibitors should step up to protect their films from 'getting chopped by an ignorant censor's scissors'.[60] In this regard, the authorities' endeavour to restrict Hollywood productions should not be seen merely as another stand-off between the authorities and Korean film-makers and fans because it represents the decade-long effort to reform the entire Joseon film culture. In both political and economic senses, the 1934 film law was the most radical measure taken by the colonial administration that tried to shape film culture as it deemed appropriate. The film regulation designed to control the commercial film culture, however, seriously threatened the local film business. Though it brought an end to the ethnic segregation as the authorities intended, Joseon film fans still chose not to go to Japanese films, especially period dramas, because they took no pleasure in watching culture that was 'foreign' to them.[61] In the end, the regulation significantly damaged the entire film business.

The potential impact the new Joseon film law might have also attracted attention from across the Pacific. Hollywood took notice of this drastic measure with regard to their products, and trade journals began to run items on the introduction of the screen quota.[62] Hollywood noticed what happened in Joseon because the latter had imported a sizeable number of films from it. A larger concern posed for Hollywood might have been the potential influence the Joseon screen quota could have on the much larger Japanese market in which growing concerns about Hollywood's dominance led many openly to raise their critical voices. In its detailed article on Joseon's screen quota, for instance, *Motion Picture Herald* reported with a concerned tone that a similar proposal to protect the Japanese motion picture industry was made in Japan though it was unlikely that such a proposal would be realised any time soon.[63] In contrast, the screen quota opened up an opportunity for the Japanese film industry as it was now able to develop new film patronage among Korean filmgoers. The timing could not have been better because film's popularity was on a steep rise in both Joseon and Japan. Still this quota was a more politically charged decision than an economic consideration aiming to support the growing Japanese film industry. It is important to note here that the introduction of foreign film regulation ironically offered the Joseon film industry 'a golden opportunity'[64] for growth because all films produced in Joseon were to be categorised officially as 'domestic' (Japanese) films. Given that Joseon films, regardless of their quality, still drew in Korean filmgoers who had strong desires for local films, it was apparent that Korean movie theatres intended to screen as many 'Joseon' films as possible to fill the 'Japanese' film quota, as reported by *Kokusai eiga shimbun*.[65] *Donga ilbo* optimistically anticipated that the quota would render Joseon cinema 'an unprecedented opportunity', coupled with the entering of 'big players' into the film business, and concluded that it was the only industry that seemed to flourish in the midst of the economic slump created by the Sino-Japanese war.[66] As explored fully in the earlier chapters, Joseon cinema did see extraordinary growth from the mid-1930s until it was rather abruptly thwarted by wartime film policies and practices.

As I have discussed, Korean spectators frequently attempted to interpret those foreign texts and appropriate them to ponder over and address their colonial situation, while the authorities saw the popularity of these films as a potential threat to the colonial order and their political endeavour to create and develop 'an imperial identity' for Koreans. This contested interpretation of Hollywood film, which mediates the colonial realities, shows how the consumption and reception of foreign cultures could become a cultural domain where political tension surrounding the colonial situation, especially the formations of ethnic and imperial identities, surfaces. In this sense, it is important to recognise that Hollywood was not seen simply as an oppressive force. Some scholars deem Hollywood a force equally as oppressive as Japanese cinema that obstructed the Joseon film industry, grounding their analysis primarily in the industrial context.[67] As we have seen, however, the manner in which Hollywood was received in the colony Joseon cannot be explained as a simple matter of figures, statistics or economic gains, since the Korean audience willingly embraced Hollywood films, rather than seeing them as a 'threat', despite the fact that Hollywood movies monopolised the film market for Koreans. The economic dominance of Hollywood productions in the Joseon film industry did not mechanically determine their social reception. Instead of merely turning to an assumed adverse role of Hollywood in the formation of the local film culture, therefore, we need to take a more nuanced approach.

Indeed, the Korean spectator–Hollywood relationship and the social debates about it also represent colonial Korea's ambivalent relationship with imperial forces and thus reveal the relative nature of imperialism and nationalism. Nick Deocampo shows that in the Philippines, where cinema was first introduced in 1896, only one year before Spanish imperialism was almost immediately replaced by American imperialism, the indigenous film culture suddenly valued and embraced Spanish elements in its attempt to counter the new form of imperialism in the early twentieth century.[68] Similarly, the immediate presence of Japanese imperialism led Korean spectators to embrace and adopt another form of 'imperialism' – Hollywood, which embodied the growing dominance of American culture across the globe and the rise of Americanism as a neo-imperialist force after World War I – without much resistance. This suggests that not all imperial forms were considered equally oppressive but, depending on a specific colonial context, some imperialism could be interpreted or 'disguised' as a positive and even liberating force for the colonised in contrast to the presence of a more oppressive imperial power. What happened at movie theatres in colonial Korea invites us to reconsider and re-evaluate the function of Hollywood as a powerful cultural imperialism in the construction of a local film culture. In a national cinema-building process, Hollywood usually takes the role of antithesis, constantly situated in antagonistic dialogue with a national cinema under consideration and often directing the shaping and reshaping of the concept and boundaries of a national cinema. Andrew Higson, in his influential essays 'The Concept of National Cinema' (1989) and 'Limiting Imagination of National Cinema' (2000), underscores the crucial part that the audience reception – especially the reception of Hollywood cinema and the way it is morphed into a national cinema – plays in the formation of a national cinema. His argument shows us that the conversation between local cinema and Hollywood cinema cannot be characterised merely as a hostile one. Highlighting the transnational movements of films across borders and the diversity of audience reception in the debates about national cinema, Higson categorises the local film culture's responses to cultural imperialism into three distinctive modes. According to Higson, the first response is an anxious concern about the effects of cultural imperialism that might possibly infect the local culture or even destroy it. The next response is that the introduction of exotic elements may have a liberating/democratising effect on the local culture. And a third possibility is that the foreign cultural products are not treated as exotic by the local spectators but, instead, are interpreted according to a local frame of reference.[69]

The reception of Hollywood films in Joseon demonstrates all of the three responses Higson describes, as I illustrated above. But what complicates even more the ways in which the reception and consumption of Hollywood movies had forged into Joseon cinema is that Joseon cinema is a marginally national cinema. Joseon cinema is a more compound entity than a national cinema because its members had more contrasting views towards its assumed identity. Intriguingly, by examining the various players' different takes on the dominance of Hollywood films, we could learn and identify each different perception of Joseon cinema. For the authorities, Hollywood was a major obstacle to its colonial governance and struggles to control Joseon film culture; for Korean film fans, Hollywood film functioned as a liberating force; for traditionalists and film reformists, Hollywood embodied the worst example that illustrated the misuse of the medium and functioned as a conduit of decadent Western cultures, duping the public and destroying local customs; for industry professionals, it was a vital commodity essential to their business. Hollywood, as the primary presence in Joseon cinema, was caught in the nexus of varied perceptions of what Joseon cinema was and should be, and thus the heterogeneity of Joseon cinema was most discernibly exhibited through conflicting, but mutually influencing, perceptions of this powerful global film enterprise.

Performing Colonial Identity: the Transcolonial Practice of *Byeonsa/Benshi*

> Back then Seo Sang-ho was the finest *byeonsa* in Joseon and he even spoke Japanese fluently. As a main *byeonsa* at the Seoul High Entertainment Theatre, he danced better than anyone and was very amusing. One day when I went to the movies, a film featuring a duel between a Western boxer and a Japanese *Judo* player was screened. Seo narrated the film more passionately than usual. Suddenly the tension escalated between the Korean and Japanese audiences. I myself clenched my fists and impatiently waited for the result of the duel. When the boxer won the first match, the Korean audience celebrated, while the Japanese audience cursed at the screen. Then in the next match the *Judo* player won which brought the praises of the Japanese and the disappointment of the Koreans. At one point, Seo cheered for the *Judo* player. The Koreans shouted at him, 'You bastard, you are also a Korean! Which side are you on!?' The film finished with the victory of the *Judo* player. In the dark, a fight erupted – the Japanese and Koreans hurled floor cushions and mandarins at one another. The screening ended in chaos. Even the Japanese police could not control the situation. I will never forget this incident.[70]

As we have seen, varied receptions of Hollywood in colonial Korea were marked by societal issues and changing politics, and the particular movie-going patterns and tastes of the Korean filmgoers eventually became the subject for hegemonic struggles. The above quotation, which recounts a first-hand film-viewing experience by a movie patron in Joseon, vibrantly illustrates how the political ferment of colonial Korea gave dramatic impact to Korean film spectators' appropriation of the film texts that seemingly had little to do with their realities. This seems to validate, as well, the colonial authorities' perceived concern about Korean filmgoers' encounters with foreign texts. Significantly, this film-viewing experience was mediated by an extradiegetic element that played a crucial role in film exhibition and film–spectator relationships in colonial Korea: the practice of *byeonsa*. This section interrogates *byeonsa*, which designates a practice from the silent cinema era where a film narrator or voice performer narrated and commented on events that occurred on-screen, and its critical function in shaping colonial film spectatorship. A study of *byeonsa* and their part in the development of Joseon film culture would further elucidate historiographical questions raised in the earlier sections. The extremely visceral and violent film-viewing experience depicted in the opening quote allows us to reconsider and challenge the exhaustive attempts to associate the concepts of colonial and national cinemas mainly with various aspects of film production – film-makers' intentions, productions of national and/or nationalist films – or the consumption of locally produced films. Through the discussion of this filmic practice, which originated in Japan, this section continues to explore the ways in which modes of exhibition were inextricably tied to the construction of the colonial identity of Joseon cinema. By investigating Korean film spectators' attempts to decode and resignify the meanings of imported images and the *byeonsa*'s role as a mediator between those texts and Korean audiences, I further illuminate the physical and discursive formations of Joseon cinema at the sites of film exhibitions and consumption. Instead of simply picturing *byeonsa* as an icon of Korean nationalism in the way that standard nationalist historical accounts do, however, I aim to shed light on the complex manner in which the practice of *byeonsa* embodied the tensions and negotiations between the cultures of the coloniser and colonised. By juxtaposing *byeonsa* with its original *benshi* practice in Japan and tracing its localisation process, I address a set of questions to consider in historicising this yet another contact zone between Korean and Japanese cinema.

From Benshi to Byeonsa: the Migration of the Benshi Practice

As the opening quote clearly demonstrates, the *byeonsa*'s presence at the cinema was decisive in forming the early film–audience relationship and film culture in general in Joseon. The *byeonsa*, who usually sat on the left side of the screen and narrated and/or interpreted the images, served more than just an explanatory function. Commenting on the crucial role of *byeonsa*, an anonymous film reviewer notes:

> A motion picture is a sort of pantomime that expresses its beauty just with its form. Hence only after a *byeonsa*'s explanation, a spectator understands it [its beauty] in detail. Also through the *byeonsa*'s explanation, the artistic

value of a picture could be exposed. Therefore a *byeonsa* must completely understand the facts and nature of a picture and explain it properly according to the actors' expressions in a picture. Only then can its artistic value be fully revealed. Thus, a moving picture *byeonsa* must possess more knowledge than stage actors and even analyse the progression of human knowledge in order to satisfy audience's needs.[71]

As this quote suggests, the *byeonsa* was regarded as the final touch that would, after carefully examining a film's every aspect, complete a [silent] film by delivering its innermost 'beauty' to the audience. In other words, the *byeonsa* was not just a component of a film's screening or exhibition but was an integral part of the very film itself. Thus, only after a *byeonsa*'s interpretation and transference of a filmic text could film spectators fully appreciate its final form. For these reasons, filmgoers' expectations of *byeonsa* were incredibly high. Being a *byeonsa* was never an easy job because she or he was expected to possess extensive knowledge of the film language and style, actors, and even the cultural and historical background of the countries from which the films came. Even worse, a *byeonsa* had to face ferocious film fans who did not restrain their strong desire for a qualified *byeonsa* nor their contempt for a poor performance. It was quite common for spectators to express openly their anger at a *byeonsa*'s poor performance during a screening. Many devoted fans also sent fan letters to newspapers and magazines to analyse and criticise a *byeonsa*'s routines and even to denounce some *byeonsa*'s ethically inappropriate lifestyles. One of the most notorious incidents involving a *byeonsa* happened at Umigwan when a spectator, enraged by a *byeonsa*'s meagre explanation, threw burning charcoal at him in the middle of the screening.[72]

All these point to the importance of the *byeonsa*'s function in film exhibition in Joseon during the silent-film era. In this regard, it is not surprising that the Korean *byeonsa* was a pivotal figure in shaping early film–spectator relationships. Though the films that *byeonsa* explained were almost entirely foreign films, mostly from Hollywood, it did not matter because the *byeonsa* constantly linked images on the screen to Korea's colonial reality during the performance. Despite its nationalist public image, however, the Korean *byeonsa* was a direct import of the Japanese *benshi*, a well-known Japanese silent-film practice. Thus, the paradoxical nature of *byeonsa* stems from the localisation process of its Japanese counterpart. In addition, there was a significant number of Japanese *benshi* in Joseon who performed for Japanese audiences in Japanese movie theatres. Japanese *benshi* and Korean *byeonsa* had very different audiences and political constituencies but, at the same time, they shared a certain fate. Owing to their stardom, immense influence over the audience and, most of all, their

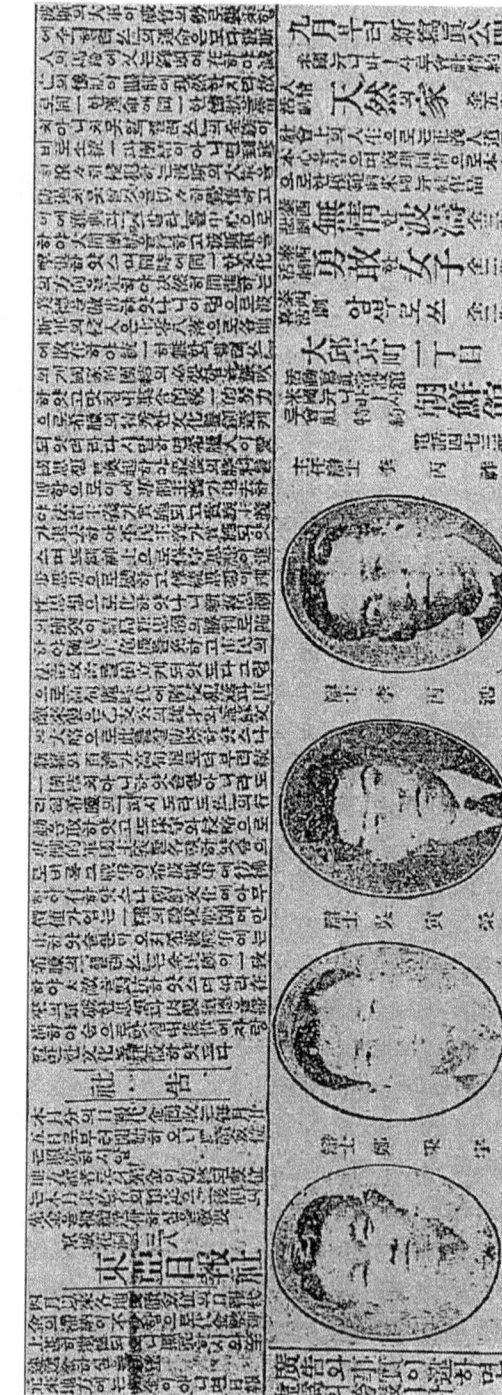

Figure 4.6 A theatre listing in a newspaper with the photos of *byeonsa*, evidence of the significance of the *byeonsa* practice in early film culture and business in Joseon. (*Donga ilbo*, 30 August 1920)

improvisational performance style, *benshi* and *byeonsa* were under the constant scrutiny of authorities and policed by the same censorship and regulations. Most importantly, the active movement of this unique Japanese film practice across 'borders', insofar as it was not contained within the 'border' of its original nation, suggests a prevailing influence of Japanese cinematic practices over Korea as well as the rest of the East Asian region. Specifically, *byeonsa* is indicative of colonial cinema's ambivalent relationship with imperial cinema, which reflects both the tensions and negotiations between the cultures of the empire and the colony. I use the word *border* in an ironic way because 'borderless' East Asia was the imperial agenda of Japanese imperialism and was often manifested in its various imperial slogans, such as '*Ni-Man* (Japanese–Manchuria) bloc' (1931), '*Ni-Man-Shi* (Japan–Manchuria–China) Bloc' (1933), '*Tōa Shinchitsujo* (New Order in East Asia)' (1938) and '*Dai Tōa Kyōeiken* (Greater East Asia Co-Prosperity Sphere)' (1940), which sought to justify ideologically Japan's colonisation of other Asian countries. But, in reality, there were many distinctive borders and hierarchies wedged between and among the colonisers and colonised. Therefore, whereas Japanese *benshi* and its influence over the cinemas of Japan's colonies cinematically embody the Japanese Empire's pan-Asianist ideal – an imperial transnationalisation of the region – the Korean *byeonsa* reflect the emerging nationalism of colonial Korea which defied the spread of the empire's transnational ideal. The very culture of the coloniser was thereby transformed into an effective cultural means of engaging in hegemonic struggle with the empire. This conflict was also noticeably visible within the Korean peninsula because *benshi* and *byeonsa* coexisted in the same urban spaces, often competing with each other and sometimes struggling together under the film censorship and oppressive film regulations.

Benshi has been one of the most researched cinematic subjects ever since Joseph L. Anderson and Donald Richie's influential and comprehensive study of Japanese national cinema, *The Japanese Film* (1959), boosted scholarly interest in Japanese cinema in the anglophone world, primarily because it has been deemed a unique Japanese tradition that clearly distinguishes its cinematic idiom from that of the West. While *benshi* is a Japanese film tradition in origin, however, it was not practised only in Japan; *benshi* was widely practised in Joseon, Taiwan, Thailand, and also among Japanese communities in Hawaii and on the west coast of the United States.[73] Despite its rigorous regional movement, there are few scholarly works that deal extensively with the practice of *benshi* in a wider Asian or transnational context. This omission could be traced to a historiographical tendency in studies of imperial Japanese cinema which strives to find Japanese cinema's internationality or uniqueness from its film style rather than from its historical presence in its former colonies. Early Japanese cinema – and Japanese cinema in general – is one of the most prolifically studied non-Western national cinemas in the West and it is often considered an alternative form of national cinema, compared to Western film practices, aesthetics, and styles. In a similar manner, Japanese national cinema is almost always examined as one under continual foreign influences, especially those of Hollywood or European cinemas, rather than as a national cinema that influences other national cinemas. In other words, Japanese cinema's international position during the empire tends to be determined in its relationship with the West, the United States and Hollywood. It is problematic to employ Japanese cinema as the prime example of a non-Western or 'alternative' cinema. Certainly, in terms of film aesthetics, Japanese cinema displays unique and different features from American and European film. But, on a historical level, early Japanese film history is more aligned to Western film histories than it is to other non-Western or colonial cinemas, as the early development of Japanese cinema was intertwined with the Japan's imperial project. These types of historiographical approaches obfuscate, sometimes actively, the presence and influence of Japanese (imperial) cinema over its surrounding region. In this sense, the conspicuous lack of discussion on the circulation of *benshi* outside Japan is symptomatic of this specific historiographical problem in studies of Japanese imperial cinema.

In the meantime, since Korea has had a prolific *byeonsa* tradition second only to Japan, Korean film historians have casually embraced *byeonsa* as a Korean film tradition without ruminating much on its origin. Interestingly, studies of *byeonsa* in both North and South Korea have been mostly confined to the Korean context; *byeonsa* has been regarded as 'an amalgam of media developed in the arts of conversation of the Orient',[74] 'a prominent artist in [Korean] silent cinema',[75] and 'a figure who is so crucial in discussing [Korean] national cinema'[76] rather than as another example of an imperial culture imposed upon colonial Korea. This naturalised acceptance of *byeonsa* as a 'unique' or 'traditional' Korean film practice generates the same historiographical problematic that arises when studies of *benshi* remain geographically confined to Japan, because both paradigms neglect the vigorous exchanges between the film cultures of Japan and its former colonies, such as Korea.

Byeonsa was, in fact, so promptly localised and integrated into Joseon film culture without any resistance from either Korean exhibitors or Korean spectators that it is difficult to pinpoint accurately how and when *benshi* was Koreanised as *byeonsa*. The primary reason for the smooth localisation of the Japanese *benshi* practice in Joseon is related to the absence of a theatrical tradition – as stage drama. Owing to this absence, the so-called New School (K: *sinpa*; J: *shimpa*) groups, which performed Western-style modern stage dramas with contemporary subjects, had to study modern Japanese dramas because modern Western culture was primarily channelled through Japan from the late 1900s. Thus, many *sinpa* performers went to Japan to pursue modern dramaturgy. They did not necessarily have to go to Japan because they could study at any number of the early theatres which had been built in Joseon by the Japanese as a place to house Japanese stage dramas for the Japanese immigrant audiences. The key figures who adopted the Western-style drama circa 1910 learned the very basics of the modern stage drama from these Japanese theatres located in Seoul, such as Keijōza, Kotobukiza and Kabukiza.[77] As a result, Korean *sinpa* groups learned and picked up many of Japanese drama's unique traits, such as *onnagata* (a male actor impersonating female characters), *rensageki* (chain drama), and the use of a narrator which would later become the inspiration for Japanese *benshi*. Korean theatres' and theatre groups' names followed Japanese styles, and performance styles used in the earliest of stage productions were heavily influenced by the modern Japanese stage drama. From production to reception, the institutionalisation of theatre as a new cultural venue in Korea/Joseon was closely tethered to the modernisation of the Japanese theatre system. As Carter J. Eckert points out, much of what the Koreans came to consider 'modern' during, and even prior to, the Japanese occupation was actually to a large extent Japanese in origin; Western civilisation was largely 'filtered through a Meiji or Taishō prism'.[78] In other words, it was 'modern' culture that Korean stage and film professionals aspired to learn, not necessarily Japanese culture. *Byeonsa* was part of this process of importing Western or 'modern' theatrical and cinematic institutions from or through Japan. *Byeonsa/benshi* was seen as one component of a cultural institution called 'moving picture' that originated from the West, and thus the fact that this was invented in Japan went largely unnoticed.

In this manner, *benshi* (*katsudō shashin benshi* in full) was, without much resistance, incorporated into Joseon film practices. The term did not even change, except that it was transliterated as *byeonsa* (*hwaldong sajin byeonsa*) in Korean.[79] Korean *byeonsa* began to appear around 1910, much later than when the *benshi* appeared in Japan; the first Japanese *benshi* performance dates back to 1899.[80] The precursors to *byeonsa*, however, existed in the form of lecturers, translators or commentators.[81] The term *byeonsa* began to be used around 1908 but it did not disseminate widely straight away because lecturers or translators were more commonly used as late as the early 1910s.[82] It was in the 1910s when *byeonsa* was standardised as part of the film-exhibition practice and became a chief attraction in the movie-going experience. A 1914 newspaper article reads:

> It [the moving picture] has been a mere part of various shows, but it has developed quickly for the last two, three years, and naturally five, six movie theatres have opened in Gyeongseong [Seoul], and even *byeonsa* who explain the pictures began to appear . . . Now we have several Korean *byeonsa*, and many more will follow soon, but Kim Deok-gyeong has a promising future and will be considered the best of the bunch.[83]

This newspaper article demonstrates that the rise of *byeonsa* was indebted to the advent of movie theatres and also attests to film's rapidly growing popularity from the early 1910s on. The influence of *benshi* over Korean *byeonsa* continued throughout the silent film era as the development and changes in the *benshi*'s performance constantly informed those of *byeonsa*. Typically, the *benshi* performance consisted of two parts: *maesetsu*, introductory remarks prior to film screenings, and *nakasetsu*, explanation accompanying events that occurred on-screen throughout the screening. Until the late 1910s, *benshi* devoted a large portion of their performance, twenty to thirty minutes, to *maesetsu* because of the short length of films but, as films became longer, *benshi* eventually shortened their *maesetsu* to five or six minutes and instead focused more on providing live comments.[84] Korean *byeonsa* not only employed such performance terms as *maesetsu* and *nakasetsu* (K: *jeonseol* and *jungseol*) but followed the major shift in the narration style of *benshi*,[85] which indicates that it was not just the *benshi* practice but the *byeonsa*'s performance styles that were initially imported from Japan. Wu Jeong-sik, an aristocrat from a renowned family and avid movie fan who frequented the Gwangmudae Theatre, a makeshift theatre evolved from East Gate Motion Picture Site, is generally considered Korea's first professional *byeonsa*. Wu was recruited by the manager of Gwangmudae, Park Seung-pil, who realised that a commentator was in demand because films' narratives had become increasingly sophisticated and complicated. Wu's first performance consisted solely of *maesetsu* as he appeared on stage before screenings and just offered a summary of stories and some background information about the films.[86] Because of his weak voice and slow pace, Wu failed to rise to stardom but was still revered as a pioneer and remained as a practising *byeonsa* at Danseongsa.[87] The first star *byeonsa* was Seo Sang-ho who served as the chief *byeonsa* for the Gyeongseong High Entertainment Theatre, the very first movie theatre in Joseon. Before he became a *byeonsa*, Seo worked as a Japanese interpreter so he was fluent in both Korean and Japanese which made him a perfect choice for the High Entertainment Theatre's mixed Korean and Japanese attendance in its early days. Seo turned out to be a great performer; his eloquent voice acting and his signature dance prior to each screening made him a favourite with film fans, catapulting him to stardom.[88] Despite his popularity, Seo eventually became less and less popular with exhibitors because he was constantly changing his employers, moving from one theatre to another, and had a drug problem. In the meantime, rivals to Seo soon began to appear. Kim Deok-gyeong, who would later become the chief *byeonsa* for the Second Taishōkan Theatre in 1914 and then for Danseongsa in the 1920s, joined Seo at the High Entertainment Theatre a year after Seo's debut. Lee Hangyeong, another *byeonsa* on the rise, debuted at the Umigwan, a movie theatre built in 1912 which catered for Korean audiences. (Figure 4.7) Many other *byeonsa* stars would emerge after these three early celebrities made their mark.

Figure 4.7 Lee Han-gyeong (left) and Seo Sang-ho (right), early *byeonsa* stars featured as two of the hundred most influential individuals in Joseon entertainment in *Maeil sinbo*. (11 June 1914)

The *byeonsa* performance in front of both Japanese and Korean audiences as described in the opening quote for this section disappeared as the ethnic segregation of film cultures took place towards the mid-1910s. As movie theatres began to serve Japanese and Korean spectators separately, more and more Japanese *benshi* appeared in Joseon, as discussed in the previous chapter, and immediately outnumbered Korean *byeonsa*. This preponderance would continue throughout the entire silent-film period. Taishōkan (1912) and Koganekan (1913), the first two Japanese movie theatres erected immediately after the High Entertainment Theatre, had many *benshi* and had the luxury of each *benshi* playing a film character or two. Thanks to the ethnically segregated urban space, different target audiences of each theatre and the language barrier, *benshi* and *byeonsa* did not necessarily compete against each other. When a movie theatre decided to change its nature, however, in other words, its intended spectatorship, it implied imminent trouble for one party. The Second Taishōkan Theatre, which changed its name from High Entertainment Theatre after the Taishōkan Theatre acquired it in 1914, initially catered for Japanese viewers, and thus hired a number of Japanese *benshi*. Yet, when it became a theatre for Korean patrons in June 1914, it dismissed all the Japanese *benshi* and hired Kim Deok-ryong and Choi Byeong-ryong, two Korean *byeonsa*.[89] The theatre shifted its target audience once again after the notorious Umigwan/Taishōkan deal which allowed Umigwan to monopolise the market for Korean moviegoers. This time, Korean *byeonsa* were released and replaced by newly hired Japanese *benshi*.[90] Sometimes, Japanese *benshi*, who performed in Japan, travelled with films to Korea. When D. W. Griffith's *Way Down East* (1920), one of the most popular silent movies ever screened in Joseon – released to theatres five times in Seoul and countless times in other major cities and towns throughout the 1920s – was imported for the second time in 1923, its distributor, Lee Pil-wu, bought the distribution rights to the film in Joseon from a Japanese agency and contracted two top-rated *benshi* affiliated with the Shochiku studio. These Japanese *benshi* became a major marketing point in the promotion of the film for Japanese migrants. Even in the 1920s, Japanese *benshi* far outnumbered the Korean *byeonsa*. In 1922, when the *byeonsa*/*benshi* permit system was introduced, records show that, in Joseon, fifty-four *byeonsa*/*benshi* applied for the qualification test and only thirteen were Korean *byeonsa*.[91] The introduction of the permit system in both Japan and Joseon in 1921, though the first annual test was offered in 1922, signals that Korean *byeonsa* and Japanese *benshi* became the subjects of active film censorship in the empire and demonstrates their social influence. They were considered potentially 'dangerous' public figures, particularly because of their improvisational performance style and their stardom. The following incident, involving an overtly political gesture made by a *byeonsa* during his performance, portrays how unexpectedly a *byeonsa* could utilise his position and his influence over the audience for his own political ends:

> Around 9.30 p.m. on 5 July Jeong Han-seol (22), who has worked diligently as a *byeonsa* at Umigwan for the past three years, suddenly appeared on stage during the ten-minute intermission, faced the audience with a tense look and excited voice, and shouted with his fists firmly clenched, 'Today is the day we are shouting out freedom and today is the day we are waiting for action. Let's spill our pure and boiling red blood all over the world to draw the world's attention to us and make all the countries in the world realise

our existence and struggles.' Since he made inappropriate comments which had nothing to do with the moving picture, he was immediately arrested by a police officer present at the screening and is under custody at the Jongno police station as of now. This is the first speech-related arrest involving a *byeonsa*.[92]

This incident, occurring before any specific film law was in place, certainly evinces the potentially threatening nature of the *byeonsa/benshi* performance, explaining why the permit system needed to be instituted. At the same time, film censorship and regulations of the silent-film period illuminate the various ways in which film exhibition practices, especially in relation to *byeonsa/benshi*, were censored and controlled. It was not until 1918 that the Japanese government became serious about film censorship. The local police took charge of film censorship and eventually initiated a pre-censorship screening process as its main method of surveillance in Joseon and Japan alike. Two major film regulations were finally introduced in colonial Korea in 1922 and 1926. The 1922 Exhibition and Exhibition Sites Regulation, which sought to monitor entertainment including film, stage and dance performances, drew all kinds of other public spaces – schools, factories, hospitals, and so on. – under its watchful eye. Initially, however, this regulation was not implemented nationally but, instead, was limited to the Gyeonggi Province, which included Seoul, and only over time was taken up by each different local government which incorporated locally specific issues into its own version of the regulation. The first official, colony-wide film-censorship law, the Motion Picture Film Censorship Regulation, was announced in Joseon on 5 July 1926, became effective from August and was one part of a larger censorship movement being crafted by the Japanese Empire, not only in its colonies but also in Japan. While Japan's censorship regulation, in effect a year earlier, was managed by the Ministry of Home Affairs, under the 1926 Joseon film regulation, the Office of the Governor General (Department of Documentation and Publication, *toshōka*) took direct charge of film censorship in Joseon. What is most compelling about this regulation is that it focuses mostly on film exhibition, including the submission of the *benshi/byeonsa*'s performance scripts prior to screening, without including any specific clause on the production side.[93] It suggests that film censors were just as interested in how films were screened as they were in what was being screened. Naturally, their attention was concentrated on *benshi/byeonsa* performances. The Office of the Governor General tried to censor *byeonsa* performances by way of carefully examining their scripts along with the film text in advance but there was never an absolute guarantee that *byeonsa* would adhere to the approved scripts. In addition, the police officers present at each screening could only censor a *byeonsa*'s action after the performance was done. As in Japan, therefore, the regulation of *byeonsa* by the censorship authority focused primarily on verifying personal backgrounds and credentials of *byeonsa*. According to Aaron Gerow, a *benshi*'s qualification in Japan was dependent not on his or her 'oratorical skills or entertainment value' but on his or her 'character standard' because authorities hoped to transform the *benshi* into a public figure or even a potential censor whose role was not simply to explain what was projected on screen to the viewers but to lead them to comprehend a socially more appropriate meaning.[94] Licensing *byeonsa* in Joseon was administered in a very similar fashion as the *byeonsa/benshi* test consisted of quizzing applicants on 'common sense' and police officers interviewed them to examine whether or not they were persons of 'good conduct'.[95] The 1929 *byeonsa* test, for instance, asked aspiring *byeonsa* and *benshi* to define such terms as 'proletariat', 'guidance of ideology (K: *sasang seondo*; J: *shijō zendō*)' and 'socially conscious film (K: *sahoemul*; J: *shakaimono*)'.[96] The main effort, that is, was placed more on weeding out early those *byeonsa* who were inappropriate to the ideal *byeonsa* performance envisioned by the censorship entity rather than on regulating the *byeonsa*'s live performances at cinemas. Gerow notes that the regulation of *benshi* in this manner seemed eventually to become effective in Japan, especially after the nationalisation of film censorship in 1925, because censorship previews and the *benshi* licensing policy, along with various efforts to reform *benshi* both within and outside the film industry, had left little margin for *benshi*'s intervention at film exhibitions and, finally, *benshi* were no longer considered a major problem.[97]

In contrast, *byeonsa* continued to pose some serious problems for film-regulation efforts in colonial Korea, mainly because Korean *byeonsa*'s 'unruliness' was not only socially acceptable but even actively encouraged and expected. A *Jungoi ilbo* film reviewer, for example, boldly asserted that the *byeonsa*'s responsibility lay in influencing the general public positively and that they should take advantage of the rare opportunity for freedom of speech that film screening presented by way of 'throwing hints to audiences whenever film scenes resemble our situation'.[98] Indeed, many reported incidents disclosed the logistical holes in the censorship system as well as the difficulties in regulating *byeonsa* performances. This problem raised for the censorship entity also derived partially from the fact that, unlike in Japan, the *byeonsa* practice was never properly institutionalised in Joseon. Mastering the art of *benshi* customarily required years of training and apprenticeship, and the standardised practice migrated to colonial Korea with Japanese *benshi* who emigrated to work for Japanese theatres in Joseon. This traditional practice, however, was not firmly upheld by Korean *byeonsa*, and the lack of a proper training system contributed to the locally specific development of *byeonsa* performances. Though the apprentice system did exist, it was not as strict as for Japanese *benshi*. According to the famed *byeonsa* Seong Dong-ho, he was pushed on to the stage after a mere two weeks' training owing to the shortage of practising *byeonsa*.[99] Similarly, the *byeonsa* Park Eung-myeon confessed that he studied the art of *byeonsa* on his own, and he couldn't finish his debut performance because he was booed by the dissatisfied audience.[100] With no systematic training in place, *byeonsa* could only train themselves and learn techniques through actual on-stage performances. Though a basic format of the *benshi* performance, such as *maesetsu* and *nakasetsu*, formed the basis for Korean *byeonsa* performances, *byeonsa* still had to fill in some gaps on their own owing to the lack of systematic training which, consequently, brought about stylistic digression. I noted earlier that Seo Sang-ho, the first star *byeonsa*, gained his reputation thanks to his buffoonery dance called 'the fart dance' during intermissions and between screenings.[101] This kind of performance was undesirable for the Japanese *benshi* who tried relentlessly to uplift the *benshi*'s cultural status and elevate its performance as a legitimate art form. In other words, though the fundamental style of *benshi* was learned by Korean *byeonsa*, stylistic localisation began almost as soon as the first professional *byeonsa* began to put on their performances. The absence of a standardised performance style was what characterised the performance of *byeonsa*. Thus, when in Japan improvisation was dismissed as inappropriate and thereby actively discouraged, it still prevailed in a Korean *byeonsa* performance because its evolution was not completely in tune with how *benshi* performance had developed in Japan. Acknowledging the shift in Japanese *benshi* performance style in the 1920s, *byeonsa* Lee Seung-wu complained that Korean *byeonsa* had failed to improve their performance styles, and *byeonsa*'s non-stop 'mumbling' was not what *byeonsa* art was truly about.[102] Similarly, the critic Kim Il-yeong critiqued the *byeonsa*'s outdated improvisational style: 'Film narrators should focus on explaining the intertitles, but our Joseon film narrators still are more concerned with a creative performance than being truthful to the intertitles.'[103] Fans also expressed their frustration with the long *maesetsu* before the screening still practised by many *byeonsa* that made them feel like they were 'attending a lecture'.[104] In contrast, Kim Yeong-hwan, a highly regarded *byeonsa*, still advocated the improvisational style by arguing that *byeonsa* should 'freely make commentaries' on images on-screen based on their different styles and interpretations without 'fixed restrictions' because a *byeonsa* is a film's 'fourth creator' after the original writer, screenwriter, and director.[105]

One of the most famous cases involving a direct confrontation between a *byeonsa* and the censorship authority occurred at a screening of the MGM spectacle *Ben-Hur: A Tale of the Christ* (1925) at Danseongsa in 1929 and the tension started from the *byeonsa*'s improvisation. In particular, the scandal surrounding the screening of *Ben-Hur* bears witness to the conflicted relationship between film censorship policies and the abilities of the *byeonsa* to portray their assigned function, to generate alternative meanings. Yun Chi-ho (1865–1945), a progressive political activist and renowned English interpreter, who for more than twenty years kept journals, mostly in English, that vividly recorded his colonial experiences, jotted down his impression of the *Ben-Hur* screening in his journal. Yun remarked:

> I went with Jang and Ki to Danseongsa to see *Ben-Hur* screened. The *byeonsa* or the interpreter used the word *gamsa* (a governor) instead of *chongdok* (a governor general) to designate the Roman Governor of Palestine. Strange the police had permitted the films in Joseon at all.[106]

As Yun's thoughts astutely points out, it was indeed quite odd for a film such as *Ben-Hur* to be permitted, given the biblical epic's narrative implications – the film's portrayal of the Jewish people's struggle for liberation from the oppression of the Roman Empire inferentially evoked the colonial condition of Korea. Lee Gu-yeong, a film-maker who began working as the head of the Public Relations department for Danseongsa in 1925, told the story concerning *Ben-Hur*'s release in his extensive interview.[107] Upon previewing *Ben-Hur*, Lee realised that the film had the potential to become a hit, as its subject matter could potentially appeal to Korean spectators. He thus came up with an idea for how best to evade the censorship problem. Lee learned that Detective Yoshida had been assigned as the censor for the screening of *Ben-Hur*. He then researched Detective Yoshida's background and learned that he had just published a haiku poem in a magazine. When Lee screened the film for Yoshida for his approval, he began to praise Yoshida's haiku skills just as the film approached the most politically charged scene. Both distracted and pleased by Lee's praise, Yoshida approved the film. Lee, aware that the film could be still banned after its release, instructed his *byeonsa*, Seo Sang-pil, to read the carefully prepared script and not to improvise lest the audience becomes too excited. Despite Lee's instruction, Seo got carried away and became very vocal and enthusiastic during his performance, at one point proclaiming, 'You Roman's one hour is equivalent to a hundred years for us Jews', thus invoking the hardship of the Korean people. A policeman who attended the screening came up to Lee immediately after and asked for the *byeonsa*'s explanatory script. The next day, Lee was ordered by the police to resubmit the film which subsequently was temporarily banned. At the time, Yoshida, the elite policeman who was newly appointed to the film censorship board in Joseon, had inside political rivalries with other censors who had been in the colony for more than a decade, and thus refused to admit his oversight and ardently deflected any challenge to his authority. As a result, *Ben-Hur* was rereleased after only a three-day suspension and was the enormous success that Lee Gu-yeong had anticipated.

The controversies surrounding the showing of *Ben-Hur* demonstrate some of the core features of film spectatorship in colonial Korea. Most significantly, the enthusiastic response to this MGM epic suggests that Korean viewers felt strong connections to this foreign text because of their political realities which formed a key facet of Koreans' film spectatorship. This particular connection which Korean filmgoers tried to make with Hollywood productions was obvious not only to the exhibitors who tried to take advantage of it but to the censors who strove actively to regulate it. In spite of the film's remote relationship to Joseon's actual political situation, Korean film spectators partook in a paradoxically cross-national and cross-racial identificatory practice through their decodification and reconstruction of this text's alternative meanings. The reception of foreign films in colonial Korea, exemplified by *Ben-Hur*'s success, again illustrates how, within the historically, culturally, and institutionally conditioned local context where the exhibition of foreign films massively outnumbered that of locally produced ones, the reception and consumption of foreign films became one of the critical determinants in the construction of Joseon cinema. Bridging imported images and local audiences, *byeonsa* incessantly and directly influenced, shaped and intervened in the ways in which the audiences received, appropriated and recreated the meanings of the films they enjoyed.

The Koreanisation of Benshi *and Question of Film Historiography*

In 1938, Seo Sang-ho was found dead in the Umigwan Theatre from a drug overdose. Seo's drug problem prematurely put an end to his career in the mid-1920s when he was repeatedly sent to prison for opium use and, near the end of his life, was spotted on the city-centre Jongno streets begging for change. The infamous death of Seo was seen by his contemporaries as an emblematic event that suggested the dusk of the *byeonsa* era. One of the many magazine and newspaper articles that chronicled the rise and fall of Seo after his death paralleled his career with the fate of *byeonsa* in general:

> Now the time has changed, we live in a talkie era, and the trace of *byeonsa* can only be found at third- or fourth-rate theatres outside the city or in the countryside. But only seventeen or eighteen years ago, when the silent movie reached its peak, the quality of *byeonsa* was so crucial that it literally determined the fate of movie theatres. Every theatre was more serious about getting a good *byeonsa* than good movies and invested its effort and money

into bringing in a topnotch *byeonsa*. Among all those *byeonsa*, Seo Sang-ho was without question the best in all of Joseon . . . His death and difficult life make us ponder over the vagaries of life once again.[108]

The report corroborates how quickly the practice of *byeonsa* declined, suggesting that it was nearing extinction only three years after the release of the first Korean talkie, *Tale of Chun-hyang* (1935), and noting that *byeonsa* was then only practised in culturally underdeveloped areas. The author makes *byeonsa*'s practice in rural areas sound like an indication of *byeonsa*'s demise but many Korean filmgoers did not 'live in a talkie era' even in the late 1930s. According to a comprehensive list of movie theatres in Japan and its colonies, compiled by *Kinema junpō* in 1936, forty-three theatres out of fifty-two in Joseon had installed sound systems, and all twelve cinemas in Seoul had finished the conversion to sound.[109] Just a few years later, all theatres in Joseon were equipped with sound systems.[110] The conversion to sound, however, happened only at established movie theatres. In rural regions, where films were screened by travelling exhibitors at makeshift theatres or in tents set up to project films, *byeonsa* was not only in practice but continued to function as a major attraction for spectators. Consequently, Korean *byeonsa* did linger on even after the colonial period. Wi Gyeong-hae's *A Cultural History of Theatre in Honam* (*Honamui geukjang munhwasa*), an extraordinary study of the regional film culture of Honam in the south-western region of the Korean peninsula, demonstrates with ample archival research materials and interviews that the legacy of the *byeonsa* lived on even into the 1960s as an integral part of film exhibition in this predominantly rural region where the overall cultural development was significantly later than in other parts of the nation.[111] According to Wi, the high rate of illiteracy, scarcity of movie theatres, and slower installation of sound systems in newly built cinemas, all contributed to the extended survival of the *byeonsa* practice. In this way *byeonsa* remained an important aspect of regional film culture as late as the early 1960s when movie-going finally became an everyday cultural and leisure activity. Wi further explains, however, the *byeonsa* practice in postcolonial South Korea was quite different from that of the silent era because it became so localised. Traditional *byeonsa*'s performances came to merge with national and regional oral performance art traditions such as *chang*, *pansori* and *madanggeuk* which effectively purged its origin as a Japanese film-art form and completely altered its original performance style. I argue that the astonishing longevity of *byeonsa* cannot be attributed solely to film technological or institutional issues but is also indebted to the film cultural condition. Newly emerging filmgoers in rural Korea of the 1950s, when Hollywood films, once banned in colonial Korea during the last years of colonial occupation, began to flood into

South Korea and dominate the postcolonial film culture once again, were in need of 'translators' of the foreign cultures projected on the silver screen. This need of film spectators was, in fact, strikingly similar to that of early film spectators in Korean or Japanese urban areas of the 1900s and 1910s who viewed *byeonsa* not merely as entertainers or translators but as experts in foreign cultures who could provide them with much-needed information about the exotic images unfolding on the screen.

This late thriving of *byeonsa* raises some important critical questions with regard to film history as well. The *byeonsa*'s prolonged life in Korea is clear proof of the slow development of film culture and the considerable unevenness embedded in that development. At the same time, the practice of *byeonsa* reveals yet another example of the compound nature of the interwoven histories of Korean and Japanese cinemas that persists well beyond the colonial period. The migration and localisation processes of the Japanese *benshi* practice in Joseon/Korea disclose not only the influence Japanese film practices held over the construction of colonial cinema in Japan's former colony but the ways in which the colonial culture adapted to, and proactively transformed, an imperial film practice into its own. The essentially transnational nature of the *benshi* practice that spread across the empire, the coexistence of Japanese *benshi* and Korean *byeonsa* in the same, but often segregated, urban space, and the continued localisation of this film art form after the end of colonial occupation urge us to question the conventional concepts of both Japanese and Korean national cinemas.

Chapter 5
Film Spectatorship and the Tensions of Modernity

After buying tickets, we headed directly towards the main exhibit. When we passed by four or five people coming out from the exhibition, we heard them telling a joke aloud, 'Those two Korean animals displayed at the main hall were utterly funny', and then they walked on. When we reached a certain spot where a dim daylight was falling, we saw a Korean man with a traditional hairdo and outfit, sitting on a chair in one corner. In the other corner, a lady was sitting on a chair, and she wore a long Korean skirt with which she completely covered her head leaving only eyes exposed. A friend of mine immediately turned pale, sighed, and deplored, 'They are the two Korean animals those Japanese talked about'. Oh . . . alas![1]

This chapter opens with this rather peculiar anecdote recorded by a group of Korean college students in Tokyo after their visit to the Tokyo Industrial Exposition (1907) because the unusual encounter between two different groups of Koreans on the opposite sides of a gaze emblematically exposes the essentially conflicting nature of Korea's overall experience of modernity. Since The Great Exhibition (1851), the first international-scale exposition held in London, the world's fairs and expositions were among the most popular cultural features in the latter half of the nineteenth century and throughout the early twentieth century in the West. They served primarily to celebrate the great achievements of Western modernisation and imperialism by way of exhibiting its technological and scientific achievements, as well as the actual bodies of 'Others' from the 'uncharted' territories it had conquered. Imperial Japan not only participated in the fairs and expositions of the West in order to 'demonstrate its place among the powers of the world'[2] but borrowed the imperialist politics of the world's fairs and expositions from the West to hold its own versions of them.

Japan's expositions functioned similarly to its Western counterparts, aiming to commemorate Japan's imperial expansions and also to display its differences from other Asian countries. By casting an imperial gaze upon Japan's 'uncivilised', 'underdeveloped' and 'not-yet-Westernised' neighbours, Japanese expositions sought to validate the nation's imperial project and consolidate its role as a regional leader that aspired to modernise the region and protect its neighbouring countries against threats from Western imperial forces. The Ainu, Okinawans, Taiwanese and Koreans were put on display at Japan's expositions for this very purpose. The 1907 Tokyo Industrial Exposition, for instance, was held to offer the country a chance to celebrate its victory in the Russo-Japanese war (1905), to demonstrate the country's ongoing progress and, most importantly, to declare its transformation into a world power. The display of Koreans was particularly meant to boast about another of Japan's accomplishments and its march towards being a major imperial force: the 1905 Korea–Japan Treaty (also known as the Eulsa Restriction Treaty), an unequal treaty that turned the Korean Empire into a protectorate of Japan and laid the essential foundation for Japan's complete colonisation of Korea in 1910.

Creating a distance between Japan and its colonies was particularly important for the Japanese Empire, as the distance from its colonies in geographical, economic, cultural and ethnic senses was often not great enough. The exposition was one of many cultural institutions Imperial Japan appropriated as a way to reshuffle the regional hierarchies and demonstrate that it had become the new leader in a new order premised upon the modernisation of the region. In addition to the empire's constructed sense of distance from its colonies, the Tokyo exposition also illustrated another intriguing sense of distance. In most cases, the distance between the observers and observed in terms of geography, race and culture at the world's fairs and expositions was the primary precondition for the former to fetishise and 'otherise' the latter. There is, however, a striking lack of distance between the subject and object in the case of the Koreans at the exposition of the Japanese, their soon-to-be coloniser. The world exposition, an invention of Western modernity and product of Western imperial powers, therefore, came with considerably different meanings for Korean students in Tokyo who came to enjoy the up-to-date urban culture only to find themselves shocked and angered when witnessing their own people on display, as filtered through Japan's own version of orientalism and reproduced according to Japanese imperialist needs and logic.

At first glance, there appears to be a complete lack of distance between the two different groups of Koreans here – the lack of ethnic difference – but suggestions of proximity between them give way to the rift of immense economic, social and cultural differences. At one side of the gaze, there is a

Korean couple who are so poor that they sell themselves to be part of a public display which marks visually the clear distance between Korea and Japan. At the other side of the gaze, we have Korean college students who have the rare privilege of enjoying a modern life, education and culture in the imperial metropole; and their distance from Japan is virtually non-existent except for the ethnic difference, as they are physically present in Japan, studying abroad in this most advanced and Westernised country in the region. What makes this discomforting exchange of looks at this particular exhibit of Koreans both fascinating and poignant is the mixed sense of distance. Korea's modernity was composed of nothing but this mixed, complex sense of distance. While being modern connoted excitement, transformation, development, and the new, modernisation and modernity at the same time signified colonial occupation and exploitation for the Koreans. Thus, modern Korea could not have, and should not have, looked away from its colonial reality despite its relative proximity to its colonisers. Just like looking at the displayed Korean bodies at the exposition, modern Korea was constantly reminded gaze at the fact that its modernisation was grounded primarily on the aggression of colonial occupation. The Koreans on both sides of the 'look' all stood for the essentially contradictory modern experiences that Korea was subject to. Colonialism and modernisation were not mutually antithetical; the colonial experience was an integral part of Korea's version of modernity. And it was this colonial modernity that yielded the mixed sense of distance between the two groups of Koreans at the exposition and also defined the incongruous nature of Korea's modern experience.

This chapter explores how this compound nature of modern experiences of the colony Joseon was manifested through the film culture. The preceding chapters have approached Joseon film culture by attempting to broaden the historical views on colonial cinema. The present chapter continues to undertake the same endeavour of expanding the historiographical approach as it looks into aspects of Joseon film culture that have been overlooked and overshadowed because of the limited ways in which film histories are written. Yet, in this final chapter, I am principally interested in moving beyond the discourses of ethnicity and nation which have been the major focus of previous chapters. By moving beyond, however, I do not mean to disregard the magnitude of the national and ethnic in interrogating Joseon film culture but, rather, I should like to underscore the significance of efforts to unearth the issues that have been left out as a result of the often myopic emphasis on such questions as nation, nationalism and colonialism. In the light of the fundamentally violent nature of colonial rule and its detrimental effects on Koreans' lives for a number of decades, it is unsurprising that modern experiences in the colony Joseon are almost always synonymous with a history of exploitation. The period of colonial occupation has commonly been pictured as a cultural dark age, tainted by colonialism, economic exploitation, physical violence, policing and political oppression. Though this view unquestionably contains truth, it has been often overlooked that this pessimistic or nationalistic account was only one side of Korea's modern experience. Most importantly, becoming modern also stood for new, liberating, pleasurable and exciting occasions. Such popular terms as *new woman* (*sinyeoseong*), *new humankind* (*sinillyu*), and *new age* (*sinsegye*) heralded the arrival of a modern era. Advanced sciences, technologies, knowledge and cultures from the West were a source of awe and shock for many Koreans. As Shin Myeong-jik points out, in his study of modern cultural life in Seoul under colonial occupation, the coexistence of colourful neon lights in South Village and dirty water gushing out from sewers in North Village symbolically represent the double nature of Korea's colonial modernity.[3]

The same historiographical predisposition dominates the study of colonial film history. To highlight the baleful influence of imperial aggression on film culture, few scholars explored Korean filmgoers' fascination with the novelty the cinema offered. It is therefore necessary to reveal this aspect of film culture suppressed in the excessive politicisation of Joseon cinema in order to track the more diverse forms of modern experiences that Joseon cinema embodied and mediated as the most dominant and popular form of modern cultural institutions. To emphasise the importance of unearthing the pleasure of film-viewing and its historical implications, I should like to turn to the record of the very first encounter between a Korean and the cinematic medium which predates any existing documentation that records early film screenings in Korea. Intriguingly, this historic occasion took place not in Korea but in Russia. Sir Min Yeong-hwan, a high-ranking official of the Joseon dynasty, was sent by King Gojong as a special envoy to Russia to celebrate the reign of the new Russian tsar, Nicholas II (Nikolai Aleksandrovich Romanov) in 1896 and, during his visit, he attended a film screening. He recorded his film-viewing experience in Russia in his travelogue as follows:

> At 7 p.m. we entered into a dark cave house located inside the botanical garden. Suddenly the glass on the front wall turned bright, and shadows were thrown on it. People walked and a horse galloped. And a man and woman flirted. And they drank and danced. All sorts of forms and figures. Moving verisimilitude. Everyone who saw it said it was mysterious and strange. The method is to light up the picture screen and shake the objects with electricity. It is not possible to fathom its exquisiteness.[4]

Written only six months after the Lumière brothers' public screening at the Grand Café in Paris, Sir Min's reflection of film-viewing vividly illustrates the unfiltered sense of wonder the film-viewing experience offered for early spectators. Sir Min did not even have proper Korean words to describe this new technological marvel. He described the theatre as 'a cave house', the screen as 'the glass', and even came up with his own term *hwaldong pibjin*, which can be roughly translated as 'moving verisimilitude', instead of *hwaldong sajin* (moving picture), the term used later in colonial Korea to designate this new medium. This first encounter even affected the course of film development in Korea. Sir Min, who attended moving pictures, ballets and other performing spectacles during his visit to Russia and subsequent trips to the United States, United Kingdom, Germany, France, Hungary and Austria as Korea's minister plenipotentiary, became a rare advocate for a theatre, unlike most intellectuals who condemned theatres as a decadent cultural form from the West. Upon his return, he argued for a need to build a theatre, as a way to showcase Korea's modernisation, and became instrumental in the establishment of Hyeobryulsa, Korea's first indoor theatre. Sir Min's encounter with the cinema ended abruptly, even before it was fully developed, when he committed suicide in 1905 as a form of protest against the protectorate agreement made between Korea and Japan. The anecdote of Sir Min's involvement with early film history, which ends with his tragic death, is yet another instance that demonstrates the double nature of Korea's modern experience.

As this, the oldest Korean record of a film-viewing experience exemplifies, the cinema was, more than anything else, an irresistible attraction for Korean filmgoers. The novelty of the cinema lingered on longer in Joseon because most of the population did not experience the medium until into the 1920s and even 1930s. Importantly, the images projected on to the screen, together with cinema technology, were equal sources of awe for film spectators in Joseon. Films were the main channels through which Western cultures and customs flooded into Korea/Joseon. Detailing the specific cultural conditions in Joseon, settler film critic Mizui Reiko documented that the film had an unusually intense impact on the way in which Koreans formed their perceptions of the Western world:

> Joseon did not really have any entertainment. The old palace had court music, but the general public had no entertainment but melancholic folk songs. In this context, it was inevitable that the attraction of imported foreign films spread and expanded at an astonishingly fast pace. This attraction, coupled with Western customs, saturated into the life of liberal people ... foreign movies offered entertainment beyond imagination.[5]

As the most dominant modern cultural institution, cinema exercised a considerable influence on the ways in which people perceived and understood the concept of modernity. In a similar manner to the world's fair attendees, filmgoers at movie theatres formed and developed a locally specific sense of what modern meant through their encounter with the medium originating from the West and their engagement with the foreign images unfolding on the silver screen.

Though the modern technologies, Western lifestyles and cultures of foreign films in themselves fascinated many, these same wonders were also always subject to society's suspicious scrutiny because many other Koreans feared the destructive effects they might bring to Korean customs and traditions, and even to the nationalist efforts and aspirations for the nation's independence. Consequently, cinema was caught in heated social debates surrounding modern life and culture and, thus, major tension arose between those who embraced the liberating effects the film-viewing experience granted and others who deemed it as a threat to traditional customs and social mores. In this decades-long conflict, not only the content of films but also filmgoers and movie theatres had become the very subjects of social debates and even condemnation. Besides colonial occupation, therefore, the collision between pre-existing cultural traditions and emerging modern cultures played an equally crucial role in shaping film-going experiences throughout the colonial period. The clash between the modern and the traditional, however, was not something completely separated from colonial realities. Many traditionalists, social reformists and nationalists even viewed the kinds of pleasure the cinema and other modern cultural products offered Koreans as irrelevant and problematic when the nation was suffering under colonial occupation. These critics lamented that the younger generation's consumption of foreign images and cultures at movie theatres, and the imitation of the modern way of life they learned there was nothing but an indication of their indifference to the dire situation of their colonised nation.

In this manner, the movie theatre became a major discursive site in which the tensions surrounding what connoted the modern in Joseon were manifested. The following sections look into how these tensions were represented through the film culture by interrogating the ways in which they underwrote varied social perceptions of movie theatres, acts of movie-going and specific groups of film patrons. The significance of film-going as a cultural practice which constituted the concept of the modern becomes more apparent when we consider its influence and relation to other emerging popular entertainments and media at the time. As an attempt to situate film culture within a broader popular cultural landscape, I shall explore an array of popular media, cultural outlets and leisure activities, such as literature, popular magazines, cartoons, fashion, shopping and urban strolling. While this endeavour will enable me to develop a richer account of the articulations of the tensions of modernity in the cultural terrain, it will also reveal how pervasive the influence of cinema was across the range of popular entertainment as the most seminal form of mass culture in the colony of Joseon.

Modern Girls and Boys go to the Movies: Cinema, Modernity and the Colonised Nation

In the last several decades of the nineteenth century, many Korean intellectuals and high-ranking officials were eager to learn from the West and employ Western systems in their efforts to modernise Korea. Such figures were labelled *gaehwapa*, which can be translated as the Enlightenment Sect. Many *gaehwapa* members travelled to and/or studied in Japan, Europe or the United States, and they tried to incorporate what they learned from those modernising countries in their struggles to reform Korean society. In the 1880s, *Gaehwapa* became a powerful political force and their political hegemony culminated with *Gabsin Jeongbyeon* (1884, Political Unrest in the Year of Gabsin) and *Gabo Gyeongjang* (1894–96, Reformation in the Year of Gabo). *Gabsin Jeongbyeon*, led by Kim Ok-gyun and his fellow radical *gaehwapa*, was a coup, aimed at overthrowing the government, which lasted only three days, while *Gabo Gyeongjang* was a top-down approach to reform Korean society led by the cabinet members of Kim Hong-jib, a moderate *gaehwapa*. The two reformist movements failed miserably and both Kim Ok-gyun and Kim Hong-jib were later assassinated in the midst of the chaotic political turmoil that plagued Korean society at the time. Prior to Japan's occupation, the modernisation efforts in Korea were largely attributable to political rivalries and tensions among various political groups and partisans, such as the moderate *gaehwapa*, radical *gaehwapa*, royal family members and the so-called *sugupa* (Traditionalist Sect).

At first, the term *gaehwapa* designated this particular group of people who shared the same political ideals and eagerly tried to adopt Western modern political and social systems but, over time, it was widely used for anyone who vigorously embraced Western civilisations and cultures. While *gaehwapa* referred to a group of people, an individual who belonged to *gaehwapa* was called *gaehwakkun*. 'Kkun' means a person but it is a degrading term that generally denotes a person whose ethics are in question – *noreumkkun* (a gambler) and *sachaekkun* (a loan shark), for instance – which implies that *gaehwapa* and *gaehwakkun* were not socially respected. There was another term, *eolgaehwakkun*, which was used to denigrate people who blindly adopted Western culture and lifestyle. The affix *eol* signifies incomplete or flawed, and *eolgaehwakkun* was specifically employed to describe people who pursued the modern thoughts, cultures and lifestyles imported from Japan and the West for personal motives only, not for political reasons or for the purpose of national enlightenment. The newspaper caricature entitled 'Mimicry of Others' portrays a group of *eolgaehawkkun* as monkeys wearing Western suits with top hats and canes, mocking their pursuit of Western or modern style. (Figure 5.1)

Film Spectatorship and the Tensions of Modernity 191

Figure 5.1 'Mimicry of Others'. (*Daehan minbo*, 17 June 1909)

Compare these 'monkeys in Western suits' to 'things that crawl out when the autumn leaves are falling' in Figure 5.2. The overtly demeaning tone of this 1927 illustration from *Byeolgeongon* dehumanises so-called modern girls and boys by labelling them 'things that crawl out when the autumn leaves are falling'. It is

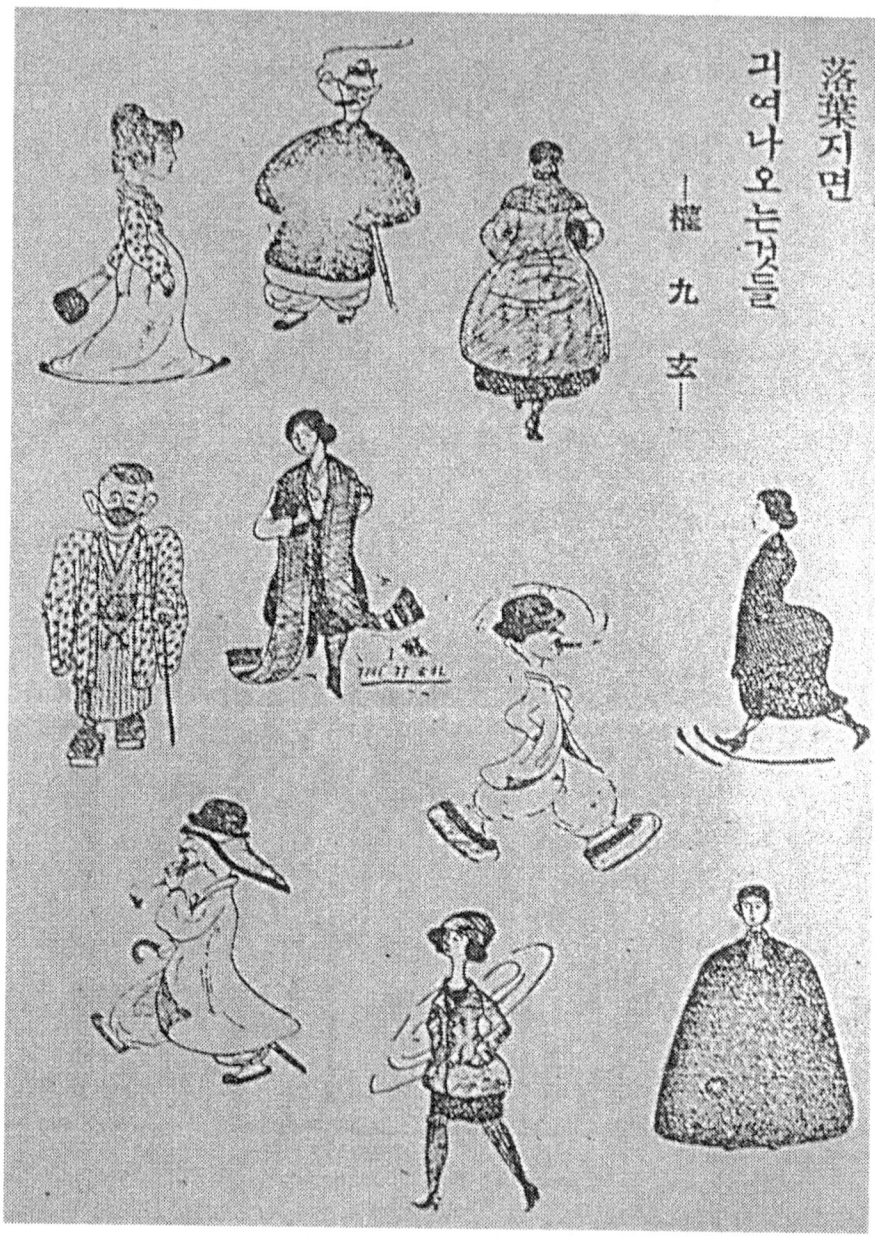

Figure 5.2 Modern boys and modern girls or 'Things that crawl out when the autumn leaves are falling'. (*Byeolgeongon*, December 1927)

in many ways quite similar to the portrayal of the *eolgaehwakkun* or 'monkeys' in a newspaper from 1909. The illustration from *Byeolgeongon* shows a certain association made between *eolgaehwakkun* around the turn of the last century and modern figures of the 1920s. *Gaehwapa, gaehwakkun* and *eolgaehwakkun* were the prototypical figures of modern boys and girls who appeared in the late 1920s. The demarcation between *gaehwakkun* and *eolgaehwakkun* is particularly intriguing because it not only illuminates how those who pursued the modern lifestyle and enjoyed modern cultures were socially perceived at the time but anticipates the similar social accusation of the next generation of *eolgaehwakkun* in the 1920s. In his study on the development of nationalist thought in the colonial world, Partha Chatterjee notes that the figure of the new woman in colonial India was to be modern but she would also have to display signs of national traditions and thus would be essentially different from a Western woman.[6] To extend Chatterjee's argument, in colonial Korea, being modern was only selectively acceptable if it was meant to make certain contributions to the nation's modernisation efforts and benefit the nation in one way or another. If one had embraced Western modern culture only for personal interest, that person was considered decadent, unpatriotic and not nationalist enough. The supposedly liberating force of being modern aimed to dismantle the rigid social system. Like *eolgaehwakkun*, however, modern boys and girls frequently faced severe social condemnation that targeted them as both the reason for, and the result of, the nation's decline.

Another important parallel between the two periods' portrayals of modern figures can be found in the fixation on their fashion and style: the 'surface' of being modern. *Byeolgeongon*'s image depicts modern girls and boys in outfits combining Western, Japanese and Korean styles, making them look rather unorthodox and even ridiculous. In this sense, they look little different from the 'monkeys' in Western suits. Indeed, popular discourses, critical of the modern girls and boys from the 1920s and 1930s, cast aspersions mainly at their modern, consumerist lifestyle, especially fashion. Subsequently, the pursuit of modern culture by these modern figures was simply reduced to a matter of style and consumerist activity.

The terms *modern boy* and *modern girl* came into popular use during the mid-1920s and quickly became two of the most socially debated terms. *Byeolgeongon*, a major popular culture magazine at the time, published a special issue on modern boys and girls from which the above illustration came, and the editor of the issue wrote, 'We should not reckon that a woman who has short hair and wears Western attire is more of a MODERN GIRL than a woman who wears traditional attire. We should look at their social consciousness.'[7] Here the editor clearly warned against society's fixation on surface attributes in discussing the modern girl and modern boy. The contributors seemed to differ, however, as their writings categorised and criticised these figures solely on the basis of their looks. One of the writers noted:

> She has her hair cut short as if she were a traditional artist and wears high heels. Nothing she wears is cheap. The red lipstick she wears – that blood-like colour makes people who look at her feel agitated. People around me call her MODERN GIRL . . . Summarising their [modern boys' and modern girls'] traits, they are lewd, extravagant, and decadent. Even though these young people could not earn their livelihood by themselves, they continue to pursue a luxurious, wasteful, and lavish lifestyle . . . The majority of MODERN GIRLS are harlots and prostitutes, and MODERN BOYS are sons of capitalists and bourgeois.[8]

This emphasis on fashion and vogue in relation to the figures of the modern girl and boy was closely related to society's uneasiness with the emerging discourse of the new woman. Imported from Japan in the 1910s, the term *sinyeoseong* or *new woman* became a symbol of challenge against the rigid patriarchal order of Joseon society in the 1920s.[9] Threatened by the advent of the new woman, along with other forms of liberalism, traditionalists sought to counter increasing attacks against conventional values and social mores, which resulted in aggressive backlash against the germinal women's movements and, towards the end of the 1920s, Joseon society turned in a more conservative direction.[10] The neology *modern girl*, which was imported from Japan around this time, could be understood in relation to this sociocultural shift. The overemphasis on fashion or surface attributes of the modern and/or new women in popular media and discourse thus represents the attempt to undermine their political nature and simply render them as mere caricatures which were nothing but unfortunate by-products of Joseon's modernisation. In 1927, when the terms *modern girl* and *modern boy* began to grasp the public's attention, *Jungoi ilbo*, for instance, explained the term *modern girl*, 'It refers to an undereducated flippant woman who enjoys a beastly pleasure'.[11] In the 1930s, those who engaged in the women's rights movement and other social activities employed the newly coined term *intelli-woman*, a shortened form of the English words *intellectual woman*, when designating themselves, to distance themselves from the negative social connotation of modern girls.

The traditionalists' take on style, fashion and looks as the main sources of criticism against modern figures intriguingly reveals that they were significantly perturbed by modern figures' outer appearances and their potentially subversive cultural function. In her study of the Japanese modern girl (*mo-ga*), Sarah Chaplin argues that modern Japanese women tackled gender problems by aligning themselves with the West in order to move outside the fixed gender categories assigned to women.[12] Similarly, in Joseon, modern figures sought to defy the repressive social system and customs by making an alliance with an outside force – the West – and the adoption of Western style or fashion was the most important aspect of this manoeuvre. Indeed, as an important visual signifier, one's Westernised style and fashion delivered a powerful message in the context of Korea's early modernisation. The photograph of Emperor Gojong, taken circa 1900, for instance, displays his strong aspiration to modernise his country. (Figure 5.3) His official move concurrently to end five hundred years of the Joseon dynasty and promulgate the

Figure 5.3 Emperor Gojong (circa 1900). (Source: *Hanguk Sajin Yeonguso*)

Korean Empire in 1897 was the culmination of the government-led modernisation efforts and, at the same time, a rather desperate attempt to protect its sovereignty from the increasing threats from imperial forces. The official photo, taken after the establishment of the Korean Empire, presents Emperor Gojong with a short haircut and wearing a Prussian military uniform. This Westernised, militaristic appearance of the emperor visually encodes not only his determination to cope with any form of militant threat to his empire but also his strong commitment to the nation's modernisation. The messages embedded in the representation of the emperor's dignity, armed with Western attire, short hair and military gear, were obviously intended for imperial powers that were looking to control Korea, messages which were also sent to his fellow Koreans who vehemently opposed the emperor's modernisation drives that inevitably dismantled traditional values and mores.

Among these new, modern appearances, the short haircut turned out to be the subject of the most intense social debates and criticism. The Confucian ideology of Joseon society taught its people to value one's body as if belonged not to them but to their parents and, thus, cutting hair was considered to show complete disrespect for, and lack of filial piety towards, one's parents. In 1895, the reformist Kim Hong-jib's administration enforced the 'Short Cut Order' (*Danbalryeong*) which obliged people to cut their traditional long hairstyles. The order met with fierce resistance and even revolt. In the Short Cut Order's wake, a wave of articles in magazines, newspapers and books presented seemingly endless debates on the policy. The controversy surrounding short-cut hair continued to pervade popular media in the following decades. The social discussion was elevated to a whole new level in the 1920s after the pioneering women's rights activist Heo Jeong-suk (1902–91) publicly cut her hair short in 1920, igniting the so-called bobbed-hair movement led by female intellectuals who aimed to convey their dedication to proto-feminist politics through body politics. As bobbed hair became associated with the women's movement, as well as with the figures of the new woman and the modern girl, it turned out to be one of the topics most frequently featured in social debates on gender politics.

Criticism against modern figures' fashions and styles keenly reflected the tension between the traditional and modern. Kim Ki-rim, the renowned male poet, who was empathetic towards the women's movement, noted, 'A short cut is still seen as a vulgar custom in Joseon', but 'the *bob* haircut is the best symbol of the women's movement and liberation, as represented by Nora [from *A Doll's House*]'.[13] 'However,' Kim continued, 'I despise the so-called modern girl, an apparition that walks around streets during broad daylight, who stores thousand-year-old rotten, outdated spirits inside her bobbed head.'[14] Even though the poet endorsed women's short cuts in his support for the women's rights movement, he made it clear that this hairstyle was acceptable only when it clearly served a political function. The general public was even more unforgiving, commonly associating this haircut with 'modern girls that disgust me'.[15] In this manner, the short haircuts of modern women became one of the most controversial subjects for popular debate in regard to modern culture in Joseon society.

Cinema and Sexuality

Quite interestingly, it was the bobbed haircut that constituted an important connection in the public's imagination between cinema and the figures of modern girls, boys and new women. Entitled '*Modan* (modern) Girl's View on Marriage', a 1927 newspaper item about 'the typical flapper', Clara Bow, presents an interview with one of the most popular silent Hollywood stars in colonial Korea.[16] The word *modan* in the title is a word play that combines Chinese words *mo* (hair) and *dan* (cut), and this portmanteau was popularly used instead of the English word *modern*, which sounds similar to *modan* to Koreans, when describing modern girls in Joseon. Dubbed 'Lady It'[17] or the 'It Girl', Clara Bow was an iconic figure of the so-called roaring '20s and particularly enjoyed her

Figure 5.4 Clara Bow with her signature bob hairstyle featured in a review of *It* (1927), a so-called flapper movie that led her to global stardom and earned her the nickname the 'It Girl'. (*Donga ilbo*, 23 December 1928)

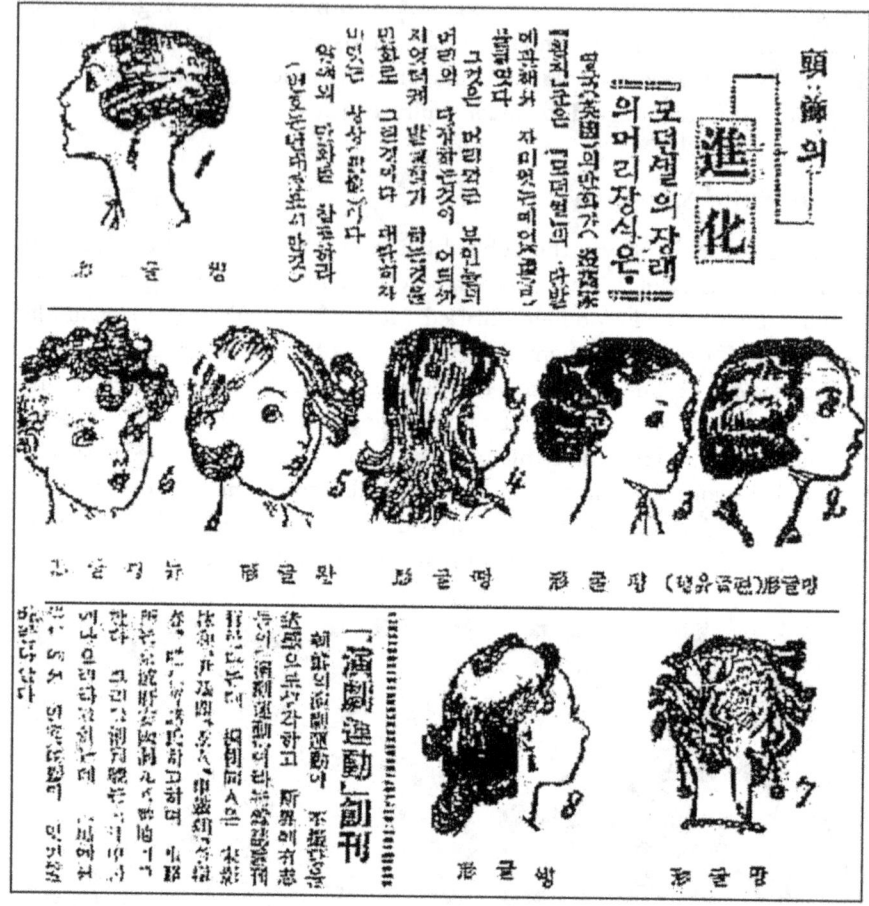

Figure 5.5 *Donga ilbo*'s report on the trends in modern girls' hairstyles (6 March 1932).

global fame through her screen persona as a flapper, though her celebrity rather quickly waned because of a series of scandals. Hollywood actresses were often brought into the social discussions about modern girls but it was Clara Bow who was discussed most in relation to the modern girl and boy in Joseon, mainly because her global popularity, which reached Joseon, coincided with the advent of the notions of modern boy and girl. In fact, with the release of the Paramount film *It* (1927, released in Joseon in 1928), Clara Bow's flapper image was integrated into the emergent discourse on the modern girl in Joseon. Signifying a woman with 'sexual appeal',[18] the phrase *It Girl* gained global recognition with the success of the film *It*, and similarly entered into the popular vocabulary in Joseon. Clara Bow was known to the Joseon masses as 'the epitome of the erotic'[19] and 'the originator of the modern girl',[20] a figure that best personified the key traits of the modern girl, ranging from her short haircut, lavish lifestyle and overt sexuality. Clara Bow's personal scandals further fostered the Joseon popular press's construction of her image as an emblematic figure of the modern girl/flapper. The spate of media reports on her off-screen married life, love affairs and scandals contributed to reinforcing the public imagination that the actress herself was leading such a life as the symbol of the modern girl. Thus, the actress and her screen persona collectively played an influential role in the social formation of the modern girl character when the term was introduced and spread in Joseon.

Inserting a Hollywood star into the escalating social tensions surrounding the figure of the modern girl was not a far-fetched move because film-going was one of the most common cultural activities associated with the modern girls and boys of Joseon. In fact, in the construction of the modern figures' styles or 'surfaces', films were immensely influential, and Hollywood films, in particular, became a major inspiration for modern boys and girls. Originating in Japan in the 1910s,[21] the essay cartoon (J: *manbun manga*; K: *manmun manhwa*), which combined a cartoon with a short essay explaining the content of a cartoon, was an influential visual medium of the 1920s and 1930s in Joseon, and modern boys and girls were a regular feature of these essay cartoons. Essay cartoons' representation of the modern figures often focused on the fashion and hairstyle they were sporting.

> The various fads of the modern era, especially in Joseon, are indebted to the powerful influence of moving pictures. The flickering shadow on screen has more power than a school's curriculum, a pastor's sermon or a father's switch. Fashion affects people much more than the spiritual. Harold Lloyd's horn-rimmed glasses became a fad among the Joseon youth, Valentino's sideburns brought 'goat hairs' to the cheeks of young Joseon men, Buster Keaton's derby hat put 'cattle dung' on the heads of Joseon youth, and the cowboy's leather pants from American westerns led the Joseon youth to put on bell-bottomed trousers.[22]

As this essay cartoon illustrates (Figure 5.6), Hollywood cinema became an integral part of the cultural lives of modern boys and girls. Accordingly, the movie theatre came to be the main pilgrimage locale for them. For this reason, the movie theatre was constantly critiqued along with modern boys and girls, and

Figure 5.6 'Modern Boy's Stroll' portrays the association between Hollywood movies, fashion and modern boys. (*Joseon ilbo*, 7 February 1928)

specifically it was viewed as a location that facilitated sexual misbehaviour of modern girls and boys. In the essay cartoon presented in Figure 5.7, modern boys gather around two modern girls on the second floor of a cinema and look to flirt with them while they are sitting there. The modern boys' eyes are all fixed on these two modern girls, not on the silver screen. The caption reads, 'Even in an empty theatre, once a woman appears, guys move to the corner close to the women's section, leaving their seats.'[23] Another essay cartoon entitled 'A Love Patient by the Silver Screen' tells a story of a modern boy who went to cinemas to enjoy watching the women's section during the intermission. The story goes that after he was conned out of money by a woman he had met at a cinema, he never went to the pictures again.[24]

By shedding light on the unethical conduct of modern boys and girls in cinemas, these illustrations underscore the extent to which films were associated

Figure 5.7 In 'The Scenery of Late Autumn', modern boys are watching modern girls, not films, in a movie theatre.
(*Joseon ilbo*, 26 October 1930)

with another controversial modern phenomenon: free love. The cinema was thought to instigate modern boys' and girls' quest for free love which was deemed a significant social problem because it completely disrupted the gender and sexuality traditions of Joseon society. The 1929 article from the art magazine *Joseon munye* elucidates the typical way in which the connection among cinema, sexuality and modern figures was constructed:

> In the darkened movie theatre, when young people's mouths, shoulders, and waists get close to one another, a GIRL takes out her powder puff and puts it on her face while looking at a coin-size mirror. The smell of the powder makes the heart of the boy in the bell-bottomed pants and moon-shaped derby hat run faster ... On Saturday afternoons, those who wear artificial stockings, modern shoes, and frock coats flock to movie theatres. When the love scene appears on the screen, they enjoy the strong stimulation while slightly trembling and leaning on their friends' shoulders. They hang the posters of John Gilbert, Ronald Colman, and Ramon Navarro on the walls in their dorm room and smile at them.[25]

Through its meticulous description of the filmgoers' fashion, the passage reiterates the emphasis on appearances in making sense of these figures, and its cynical account of their obsession with modern looks rhythmically alternates with the pseudo-pornographic depiction of sexually mischievous acts they indulge in while attending a film screening. Even further, by interpreting the content of the film and film fandom as an issue of sexuality, the critic bemoaned the fact that the entire film culture of young filmgoers was nothing but an alternative sexual experience. It is interesting to note that the plethora of essays, which critiqued the promiscuity of modern figures at cinemas, in fact, almost always foregrounded the sensational portrayals of their sexual acts there. There is no question that, while raising a concerned voice, the popular press took advantage of sexual motifs in order to sell more copies. Modern figures, therefore, were made deviant for the public angst and, at the same time, for popular consumption.

In fact, this kind of criticism against film-going, which links it to the issue of sexuality, appeared long before the discourse of modern girls and boys emerged in the late 1920s. Many studies of early film culture demonstrate well that it was a universal phenomenon that cinemas were often socially criticised by conservatives, social reformists and religious groups in many countries when they became the major venues for popular entertainment. In Korea, the situation was all the more serious because the theatre was a brand-new cultural institution and, thus, its nature, characteristics and social functions were not clearly defined. From the very beginning, the theatre was considered to be an import of

Western culture and thus was believed to be a threat to traditional customs. The negative view was also concerned with the fact that theatres were initially linked to the performing arts and dances which, in the Joseon dynasty, were considered to be indecent forms of art for the lower classes. Thus, they were deemed to be places that prompted immoral activities and lewd conduct that would ultimately corrupt the social standard of ethics. Among others, critics were appalled that theatres allowed men and women to intermingle in a confined space and thus became convinced that they challenged one of the most important cultural customs, that is, the gender segregation based on Confucian ethics.

Indeed, Hyeobryulsa, the first indoor theatre in Korea, and its rival East Gate Moving Picture Site spawned social debates as soon as they opened. *Hwangseong sunbo* reported in 1906:

> These days they hold moving picture exhibitions and various performing arts at the electricity company inside East Gate. According to the attendees, they show a lewd act between a man and woman, and this agitates vigorous men and women to indulge in adultery . . . Ignorant young people are filling up the theatre, and the situation in Hyeobryulsa is not any different. The police have the responsibility to protect people, and thus they should prohibit theatres.[26]

In a similar manner, in his official petition to Emperor Gojong submitted in 1906, Lee Pil-wha, a high-ranking official, who was in charge of public education, singled out Hyeobryulsa as one of the main problems obstructing the government's devotion to education:

> Thirdly, I would like to point out the depraved practices at Hyeobryulsa. Confucius once told his disciple Yan Hui that dispelling Cheng's music was a virtue required for ruling a nation. I do not know who is in charge of this place called Hyeobryulsa, but they offer amusement all night long, and men and women blend together and do lewd conduct. Isn't this Cheng's music or what? I am gravely worried about the nation and people as this place misleads people's minds and destroys our good customs. We must have the police department get rid of this origin of lewdness.[27]

Lee concluded his petition by claiming that, once people were properly educated, they would no longer be interested at all in the lewd acts happening at Hyeobryulsa and, for this reason, the most urgent issue the emperor must take care of was education.[28] Lee's petition, and his call for public education as a potential solution, are particularly intriguing in the sense that they reflect the anxiety of

Confucian scholars, upholders of traditional values in Joseon who were losing their voice in the midst of rapid social changes. The danger of theatres, to Lee's Confucian eyes, lay exactly in their subversive social function in harbouring all kinds of sensory amusements and experiences for the general public which fundamentally endangered the Confucian principle of keeping a stoical state of mind, separated from earthly pleasures. In this line of criticism, film-going was seen as more than just a visual entertainment but, instead, it was perceived as a bodily experience that was designed to stimulate all the senses. Emphasising all the different kinds of stimuli film spectators were presumed to be given, critics of film culture voiced that even non-filmic elements at the sites of film screenings, as well as the images on the screen, were sources of the problem because they were meant to maximise bodily pleasures for filmgoers, making film-viewing experiences almost the same as sexual arousal.

Gojong accepted Lee's proposal and closed down Hyeobryulsa that year. It is also noteworthy here that, in addition to the critiques of Hyeobryulsa as a den of vice, Lee linked the problems of the theatre to the nation's dismal destiny. As the emergence of theatres coincided more or less with Japan's colonisation of Korea, the social concerns surrounding the spread of theatre culture were often entwined with the national crises.

> Today so-called stage theatres such as Danseongsa, Hyeobryulsa, and Eumaksa have been established, and dancers, entertainers, and actors gather together and perform shows like *Tale of Chun-hyang* and *Tale of Sim Cheong* every night. The audience members are young debauchees and what happens there is nothing but lewd conduct . . . Theatres are hurling general society into chaos and damaging the national economy as young people use up their money there. Also theatres mislead our people and even threaten people's lives due to their unsanitary environments. Unchaste women and female dancers gain wealth from their performances, which influence other women very negatively. For these reasons, it is not exaggerating to say that the nation's demise originates from these theatres. The people running these places must reflect on their behaviour.[29]

The author spoke as if the theatre single-handedly brought about the nation's downfall. Despite its highly hyperbolic tone, this article handsomely summarises the chief rhetoric of social condemnation against the theatre space by connecting it to the discourses of sexuality, nation and modern culture. This view persisted into the 1910s when theatres began to appear across the peninsula,[30] and even into the 1920s. The criticism against the theatre for being a haven for 'lewd' modern girls and boys, therefore, is an extension of this earlier view.

Cinema and Colonial Flânerie

The bleak realities under the colonial occupation fuelled the social criticism of the modern girls and boys for their indulgence in modern consumerist culture and accompanying lifestyles. They were deprecated as good-for-nothings, the negative by-products of the burgeoning capitalist society, immersing themselves into extravagant lifestyles while paying no attention to the nation's dismal state. Many essay cartoons often juxtaposed modern girls and boys with hard-working labourers in order to highlight the idle lives that modern boys and girls were pursuing. In a similar vein, these modern figures were constantly described as people who did nothing but walk around the streets, showing off their fashion sense and looking for a date, which accentuated their apparent non-contribution to society and selfish dissipation. An Seok-yeong, the foremost essay cartoon artist, who was also a film-maker, noted in his essay cartoon, 'When they [modern boys] stroll across the streets of Joseon which only have collapsing thatched cottages, they might still feel as if they were walking in a foreign landscape. I have no idea why you people walk around without anything to do.'[31] In contrasting modern boys with the destitute situation of Joseon society, this essay cartoon stresses another cultural activity that was frequently associated with modern girls and boys: a stroll. Along with movies, fashion and sexual freedom, *sanbo*, leisurely streetwalking or strolling in the street and driving around in a car emerged as new cultural activities in the late 1920s and they were conceived as modern cultural traits that best represented the slack lifestyles of modern boys and girls.

Quite interestingly, however, leisurely streetwalking was even enjoyed by those who most criticised that of modern boys and girls. Like An Seok-yeong, most essay cartoonists were highly critical of the lifestyles of modern boys and girls, including their idle strolling. Ironically, essay cartoonists often came with titles that demonstrated that the essay cartoonists themselves engaged in strolling through the streets while observing modern society as the following examples evince: 'My Opinion on the Street', 'Strange View on the Street', 'Scenery on the Street', and 'Parade in Seoul'. In this sense, *sanbo* or *flânerie* was not a cultural activity monopolised by modern girls and boys but, instead, it was a prevalent cultural phenomenon resulting from urban modernisation. As Walter Benjamin explains in *Charles Baudelaire: A Lyric Poet in the Era of High Capitalism*, the figure of a *flâneur*, the nineteenth-century stroller on the city streets, was the ur-form of a modern intellectual. The *flâneur*'s object of inquiry was modernity itself; *flânerie* became one of the significant methods of scrutinising the rapid modernisation and urbanisation in turn-of-the-century Europe. According to Benjamin, by strolling across the urban space, a *flâneur* – a person who performs *flânerie* – took on the role of a silent observer whose inner life could be enriched by the city landscape only to the extent that he remained physically distanced from it. *Flânerie* does not, however, signify a passive urban experience. Importantly, as his book title explicitly suggests, Benjamin stresses the link between *flânerie* and the modern capitalist society. Benjamin's notion of the *flâneur* (for which Baudelaire provided the prototype), immersed in the flux of high capitalism and urban modernity, strolled through boulevards, arcades, department stores and the urban crowd, observing the city 'passively' and trying to distance himself from social reality even though he was always ready to 'sell out' and fling himself into the torrent of capitalism.[32]

Benjamin perceives *flânerie* as an intellectual device with which to interrogate modern society. Like Benjamin, essay cartoonists in the Joseon of the 1920s and 1930s critically observed the urban scenery and vividly captured it in their essay cartoons. The *flânerie* of these artists, however, is vastly different from that of Benjamin or other European intellectuals, as the subject of their critical examination was colonised urban life. Colonial urban modernity was also well illustrated in literary works from the 1920s and 1930s, when the modern urban landscape, consumerist culture and colonial Seoul had become legitimate literary subjects, and many writers incorporated colonial modern urbanity into their works. Among those writers, Lee Sang is a particularly important figure not only because he is the pioneer of modernist literature in Korea but also because his works venture deep into the conflicting aspects of colonial modernity and urban visual culture. In his short travelogue 'Remaining Feelings for A Mountain Village' (*Sanchon yeojeong*, 1935), Lee employs cinematic techniques for describing his trip to rural areas:

> The simple nihility that I taste after watching a moving picture – Zhuang Zi's 'Dream of Butterfly' must be like this. My round but rectangular head just becomes a CAMERA, and how many times with my weary LENS I have taken shots of and projected the landscape of early autumn when the corn is getting ripe – melancholia floating as a FLASHBACK – these are some STILLS of my heartbreaking grief I am sending to a few lonely FANS still left behind in the city.[33]

As the quote shows, in this travelogue Lee Sang used his eyes like a camera; he freely changed points of view (from a long shot to an extreme close-up, for instance) to create a vivid portrayal of rural landscapes, employed abrupt 'editing', and inserted flashbacks when he brought up his urban experiences – Hollywood movies, actresses, department stores, modern boys, female factory workers, sales clerks, and the new woman – to depict and contemplate the objects and people he observed during his travels. Lee's use of Zhuang Zi's 'Dream of Butterfly' story is also intriguing in the same vein because it reveals his take on cinema's illusionism. 'Dream of Butterfly' refers to a dream of Zhuang Zi, one of the founders of Taoism, from China, in the fourth century BC. One day Zhuang Zi dreamt that he became a butterfly flying happily. When he woke up, he wondered how he could possibly determine whether he was Zhuang Zi, who had just woken up from a dream in which he was a butterfly, or a butterfly that had just begun to dream he was Zhuang Zi. With this famous Taoist metaphor, Lee Sang illuminates the cinema's powerful reality effect.

Lee Sang's renowned essay, 'Boredom' (*Gwontae*, 1937), demonstrates a more compound presentation of colonial *flânerie*. In the conclusion of his essay, in which he portrayed his aimless drifting on the streets of Seoul and his retreat to the inner world, Lee Sang wrote:

> I come back to my room and look into myself. My life detached from everything – my life from which I can't find a single clue even for suicide is the extreme of boredom itself. A moth flies into a candle flame. It must be dead or burnt. Yet even a moth knows how to live – it can jump into fire. Is there passion to look for fire or is there a flame? No, nothing. I have nothing, I see nothing. I can't anticipate a thing.[34]

Benjamin considers boredom as the very characteristic of *flânerie* when he writes, '*Flânerie* is the rhythmics of this slumber'.[35] He further defines boredom and explains its relation to *flânerie* by noting, 'Boredom is a warm gray fabric lined on the inside with the most lustrous and colourful of silks . . . One can well imagine the elegant set mimicking the pace of this creature more easily in the arcades than on the boulevards.'[36] Siegfried Kracauer similarly identifies boredom as 'the only proper occupation, since it provides a kind of guarantee that one is, so to speak, still in control of one's own existence'[37] and argues that, in a state of boredom, one can keep one's subjectivity intact against the drudgery demanded by capitalist society. Simply put, for European white male intellectuals, boredom was a self-controlling and self-empowering intellectual apparatus. In contrast, Lee Sang's boredom and *flânerie* represent the absolute frustration of a colonised male intellectual. In his other famous short story 'The Wings' (*Nalgae*, 1936), Lee recounts a story of a male intellectual who, deprived of a professional opportunity, relies financially on his wife's prostitution which symbolises the de-masculinisation of the colonial male subject. Lee Sang's excessive withdrawal to the internal world stands for the social status of a colonial male subject whose political and economic power has been forcefully stripped away by the colonial occupation. Though Lee Sang, a colonial *flâneur*, could wander around the city, delve into his inner world, and observe the colonised nation, unlike the European *flâneur*, he could not 'fling into the torrent of reality'; instead, he hopelessly continued to dream about the day he could get himself his own 'wings'.

In *Migration to the Movies*, Jacqueline Stewart re-examines the European male-oriented notion of *flânerie/flâneur* through her studies on black urban modernity and film spectatorship. According to Stewart, the concepts of *flânerie* and boredom can normally be attributed to bourgeois, white male subjects who enjoy a freedom of physical movement and anonymity in public space which is unavailable to most African Americans in racially segregated urban America:

> Black spectatorship is elaborated within the contradictions of the modernist promise of urban mobility, and the persistence of racial hierarchies and restrictions impeding smooth transitions into and through urban modernity. African American spectators share with the *flâneur*, the surrealist, and [Giuliana] Bruno's female streetwalker a kind of cultivated distance from the immobile spectator-in-the-dark position imposed by the classical cinematic apparatus and its attendant theories of the gaze. But for Black viewers this distance can prove unpleasantly isolating; it is not always voluntary; and it risks the consequences of challenging mainstream cinema's racial and sexual economies of desire and identification.[38]

The immobility and inaccessibility of the colonial *flânerie* exemplified by Lee Sang and African Americans in colonised urban spaces demarcate the fundamental differences from its European (or imperial) counterparts. In other words, free roaming across urban space was intrinsically impossible for those colonial subjects. Most importantly, ethnically segregated Seoul largely limited the mobility of Koreans because Koreans could not freely walk into Japanese residential areas without being subjected to the watchful eyes of their colonisers, just as the racially segregated American urban space substantially constrained the movement of African Americans. In addition, the presence of Japanese police was crucial in defining the modern sense of mobility and movement in colonised urban spaces in Joseon because the police was used as the main controlling mechanism in Japan's colonies.[39] The Cultural Rule that replaced the Militant Rule in 1919 changed the main law-enforcement authorities from the military and military police to the regular police in order to tone down the oppressive image of colonial occupation. Yet the police-based colonial system did not mean that the authorities had become more lenient with regard to controlling Koreans. Instead, it was meant to devise a more thorough surveillance system through its rapidly growing numbers in the police force. Before 1918, the total number of policemen in

Korea did not exceed five thousand but, in 1919, the year when Cultural Rule was introduced, the numbers tripled (15,392) compared with the previous year (5,402), and it reached its highest point in 1921 with 20,753 policemen.[40] The number of police stations also drastically increased from 751 (1918) to 2,761 (1919).[41] Throughout the 1920s and 1930s, the number of policemen was sustained at eighteen to nineteen thousand but, when World War II began, the number increased sharply. By 1941, here were about sixty thousand policemen – one policeman to every four hundred people – in Joseon.[42]

Cinemas were not free from this police surveillance; it was local police stations that were in charge of film censorship before the film law was implemented in 1926, and policemen attended every film screening at theatres. It was not uncommon for film screenings to be disrupted by the police present in movie theatres. Sometimes, even military police stopped the screening by force and chased film patrons out of cinemas. One of the most notorious incidents involving the military police transpired at the screening of Pudovkin's *Storm of Asia* (1928), the first Soviet film ever shown in Joseon. When the film, which deals with the independence movement in Mongolia, played at the Joseon Geukjang in October 1931, the military police raided the theatre and coercively ended the screening. The authorities belatedly realised that Pudovkin's film was apparently double trouble because the film entailed a lethal combination of their two most feared ideologies: socialism and nationalism.

As discussed in Chapter 4, with the examples of the ways in which Korean film spectators appropriated Hollywood films to make sense of and address their colonial situation, movie theatres often offered Korean filmgoers a cultural domain in which they could express their colonial experiences through culturally and socially specific forms of film reception. The potential function of movie theatres as alternative public spaces, however, was greatly discouraged and undermined by the colonial network of dominance and surveillance. When the audiences were keenly aware of the presence of surveillants (for example, Japanese policemen) and that their specific spectatorial behaviours of receiving and reacting to a film text might get them into serious trouble, movie theatres could not fully function as alternative public spaces.

In the end, those who pursued modern life and enjoyed modern urban culture had to confront and deal with multilayered social condemnation. Colonial realities, rigid societal norms, the call for urgent modernisation and nationalist aspirations collectively drove society to label the figures of modern girls and boys as nothing but social nuisances who purposely neglected and even obstructed the collective efforts to improve the nation's situation. As the colonial *flânerie* of Lee Sang exemplifies, however, idle strolling, mindless visits to movie theatres, and the boredom of modern girls and boys symbolically reflected a colonial reality that stripped them of any opportunities to engage in socially acknowledged productive activities and thus echoed the nihilistic social atmosphere. At least intellectual *flâneurs*, such as essay cartoonists and writers, fulfilled their social 'functions' as they turned their walking the streets into works of art. Most of the modern girls and boys, however, could not find a venue where they could express their inner worlds. Or perhaps they were so unmotivated as even to initiate such acts. After all, they were judged only by their 'surfaces'.

Mobility, Movie Theatres and Female Film Spectatorship

In his contribution to *Donga ilbo* entitled 'A Tendency in Women's Liberation' (1921), Frederick Starr, an American anthropologist who visited colonial Korea many times and published several books and essays on Korean traditions and religions, opened his reflection on the changed social status of women in Joseon with what he had observed at a cinema a few nights before.[43] According to Starr, what grabbed his attention was the number of female film spectators who were present for the film screening. He added that he also spotted female attendees at his public lecture. About this observation, Starr wrote:

> As far as I remember, the custom that confined Joseon ladies to their residences was abolished not long ago. When ladies went out, they had to cover their faces, and they were not allowed in the public space. And common women could not act freely in public. Yet it is now clear that these customs have been changed.[44]

In the previous section, I looked into a range of social and cultural conditions that discouraged and even restricted filmgoers' total immersion into the pleasure of film-viewing. In addition to those factors, female filmgoers in Joseon were subject to another serious social constraint that kept them from freely going to a film: the conventional gender norms which considerably limited their mobility in the public sphere. As Starr's observation illustrates, women in Joseon were finally able to venture out of their private domain in the early twentieth century but their presence in a public space was still not welcomed and, thus, they were placed under the watchful eyes of the men who once monopolised that space. Cinema, as the prominent mass entertainment institution, repeatedly provoked social anxieties about women's newly acquired mobility and its potentially adverse effect on traditional values. Coming into the 1920s, therefore, when more and more female filmgoers began to attend movie theatres, female film spectatorship became a constitutive element of Joseon film culture in both the physical and discursive senses. Indeed, cinemas were seen as rather singular public spaces in which the presence of female film patrons was institutionally tolerated and industrially promoted. Paying concerned attention to the increasing visibility of female spectators in movie theatres, a cultural institution that seemed further to nurture women's mobility, social criticisms of film culture often took a gendered form by foregrounding female spectators' presence as a primary reason for, and consequence of, the social ill-effects of movie-going. In an effort to expand the discussion of the tensions of modernity manifested through film culture, the final section of this book explores the place of women in the Joseon film scene as well as the ways in which their roles in the formation of film culture were tied into the changing gender politics of Joseon society.

Social Paranoia about Female Spectators in Movie Theatres

In Starr's essay, the anthropologist described in detail the female spectators he had witnessed at movie theatres: 'Their behaviours were gracious and virtuous, and thus they did not cause any inconvenience or disturbance for general audiences'.[45] Joseon society's general illustration of female spectatorship at movie theatres, however, was radically different from the way in which Starr portrayed it. As an example, note the 1927 *Byeolgeongon* report on female spectators' behaviour at a cinema when the number of female spectators noticeably increased:

> You could witness how movie spectators have changed lately when you go to movie theatres – especially the quietness therein during the screening. Also there are fewer under-aged spectators because the admission fee is pretty expensive ... In addition, one more conspicuous change is that the women's section, which used to be almost half-empty, is as packed as the men's section every night. Old ladies, middle-class young maidens, *gisaeng* [female entertainers], female students are those who occupy the section, and the rare sight is that half of the female spectators are young female students who have just had their eyes opened to sexuality. The more shocking thing is that at 'kiss' scenes, there are always gasping shrieks coming from the women's section – surprisingly from the seats where young married women sit together. Go ask people who frequent movie theatres whether or not it is true. Anyway, the world has changed. For sure.[46]

Most obviously, this widely shared observation of the surge in the numbers of female film patrons as a major change in movie theatres indicates that, by the late 1920s, the cinema had become an important part of the cultural life of many women, regardless of their social backgrounds. It details female film spectatorship, focusing particularly on how the issue of female sexuality is played out at the movie theatre, which again attests to the prevalent associations made among movie theatres, modern girls (and boys) and sexuality that I discussed earlier in the chapter. By reporting on female filmgoers, a once-rare sight, and their indulgence in the act of film-viewing, the popular magazine lamented how much 'the world has changed'. As this report shows, it was not until the late 1920s that cinemas began to be patronised by female filmgoers. The 1930s saw the gradual integration of female spectators into film culture, and the number of female spectators continued to grow throughout the decade. In the 1940s, finally, female spectators surpassed male viewership because they accounted for about 60 per cent of the total film clientele.[47]

It took almost four decades for women to be able regularly to enjoy films in Joseon society, and this extremely slow inclusion of female patrons into film culture resulted from Joseon society's rigid gender segregation that systematically disallowed women's presence in public spaces. Prior to the 1920s, women rarely went to the cinema as the so-called 'Law of the Avoidance between Man and Woman' (*Naeoebeob*) from Joseon society still influenced the everyday gender politics of colonial Korea. This customary gender segregation law was one of the core Confucian principles which provided the fundamental architecture of the cultural mores of the Joseon dynasty. The word '*nae*' from '*Naeoebeob*' means the interior, and '*oe*' signifies the exterior, and eventually '*naeoe*' came to mean 'woman and man' or 'wife and husband'. Even today, this phrase is widely in use; '*naeoe*' denotes 'man and wife' and a verb '*naeoehada*' means 'intentionally to avoid each other'. *Naeoebeob* concerned practices of gender division and segregation and, according to this law, man and woman were not allowed to share the same space unless they were immediate family members, and women's outdoor activities were especially rigorously controlled. Gender segregation even influenced the arrangement of domestic spaces, informing the architecture of the private houses of aristocrats on whom the most severe gender segregation was practised. The typical house of an aristocrat was divided into two areas, *anchae* (the interior building) and *sarangchae* (the exterior building), which were designed to 'protect' women from being seen by visitors because women were to stay only in the *anchae*. This gender division was also practised in public. Frederick Arthur McKenzie, in his travelogue *The Tragedy of Korea* (1908), recorded how this segregation worked in Korea at the turn of the twentieth century:

> As darkness came on, signal fires were lit high up on the great hills, Namsan and the others, four lights on four hills, telling watching signalers in distant provinces that all was well, and that Korea was at peace. An hour after sunset all men retired within doors, and the women came out. This was the women's

hour, when they could parade the streets with freedom. Woe be to the unhappy male who found himself among them! Then the great bell in the centre of the city boomed forth its warning. It was curfew, and Seoul was at rest.[48]

Considering this strict spatial gender segregation, observed circa 1895, it is not difficult to imagine the considerable social shock when women began leaving their traditional private domain, strolling down the busy streets and exploring public spaces. One of the main causes of anxiety about the emergence of theatre, from the first decade of the twentieth century throughout the 1930s, was the co-presence of the opposite sexes in the same space, as mentioned in the previous section. Owing to ceaseless censure against this social integration and space sharing between men and women, in 1916 movie theatres introduced the women's section.[49] Theatres designated a quarter of the seats on the first floor as the women's section but, if escorted by men, women were allowed to sit in the family section or the first-class seating on the second floor. More often than not, theatres did not strictly adhere to this gender segregation so that they could accommodate as many customers as possible.[50] The enforcement of gender segregation in movie theatres did not dampen the social criticism against women's movie-going. Even in the late 1920s, when women's attendance at movie theatres had become more socially tolerated, women spectators were still seen in a negative light. In a report which offered an admonition about 'dangers' and 'vices' that young female students might confront in the big city, a *Byeolgeongon* writer documented what he observed in a movie theatre where this kind of danger most commonly ensued.[51] While researching the licentious conduct of young female students and modern boys, the reporter went to a cinema, wherein he spotted several groups of female students and watched their behaviours closely, 'As soon as I entered into a theatre, I looked at the women's section. I noticed two, three groups of women who had short bangs, wore makeup, mingled with the bunch of *gisaeng*, and continually glanced at the men's section.'[52] The reporter followed a group of female students, and the modern boys they met after the screening, and reported on the sexual misconduct he witnessed. According to the reporter, all this immoral behaviour began at the cinema, a claim that is strikingly similar to that of the aforementioned Lee Pil-wha's petition to the emperor in which he criticised Hyeobyulsa for providing a space where men and women mingled in a manner that gravely threatened the moral standard of society. The true anxiety underlying the *Byeolgeongon* story, which so adversely depicted female spectators, was that society and the state were no longer able to control women's sexuality. Modern woman's sexuality was now out of control. It was one of the most visible impacts of modernisation on

Joseon society – allowing women to go to places where they were not traditionally permitted and to spend a considerable time there with men. Not surprisingly, the cinema was an easy target because it was a rare public venue in which women were regularly to be found. In his essay, 'Women and Cinema: Its Influences on Joseon Women', film critic Seo Gwang-je asserted that cinema was quite an erotic art for women because women were more easily influenced by films in which female characters played dominant roles in sexual relations and, grounded on this claim, he dismissed female patrons' film-viewing experiences as a blind, uncritical addiction to the modern concepts of love and sex represented in Hollywood pictures:

> You cut your hair short like Louise Brooks, expose your body like Billie Dove, draw on your eyebrows like Clara Bow, put on your lipstick like Pola Negri, smile like Alice White, and flirt like Janet Gaynor. You swiftly walk around on the asphalt with your handbags and parasols in your high heels and seduce sex-hungry loafers with a flagrance of your body. You modern girls – except for makeup skills and techniques of love affairs, what else did you learn from American cinema?[53]

Seo further scorned female filmgoers' cinematic illiteracy by asserting that their admiration of Hollywood stars, with their lavish styles and the romantic relationships they portrayed in films, kept female audiences from critically engaging with the cinematic images and thus they failed to be informed viewers. Juxtaposing Joseon female filmgoers with famous vamp and flapper characters from Hollywood films, Seo devalued female film spectatorship as a mindless consumption of, and superficial pursuit of, the modern way of life. Lee Tae-jun's 1929 short story 'Modern Girl's Feast' (*Modern girlui manchan*) similarly portrayed that a modern girl's ulterior motive for movie-going, in fact, lay in something else: a sexual adventure. The story features Kkotbun, a modern girl who is approached and invited on a date by a stranger at a cinema. She goes to meet him the next day with high expectations. She soon finds out that she is being mocked, as the address she is given turns out to be that of a correctional facility, an interesting metaphor that appears to be a fitting place for this modern girl full of vanity. Kkotbun returns home with a bitter mind and eats burnt rice for dinner instead of the fine dining at an American restaurant she had wished for.[54] It is obvious that Lee's description of the modern girl echoes the above-discussed popular interpretations of modern girls' film-going as sexual adventures. At the same time, the short story, which pokes fun at a modern girl's vanity, also presents another popular tendency in portraying modern girls at that time: taking pleasure in witnessing women in distress in the public sphere.

Film Spectatorship and the Tensions of Modernity   215

Indeed, across the range of media outlets in the 1920s and the 1930s, countless reports, stories, anecdotes and cartoons portrayed the embarrassment women faced in the public sphere which was almost always caused by women's ignorance of appropriate behaviour in public spaces and/or their carelessness. For example, a cartoon published in a woman's magazine, *Singajeong*, features a woman who hires a photographer while going out for a stroll but slips into a pond by mistake while posing for the picture. (Figure 5.8, left) Another cartoon 'This Is How I Lost My Leg', from the same magazine, takes this sort of joke to a vicious level by describing a story of a young woman who hurts her ankle while trying on high heels for the first time and ends up having her entire leg amputated at a hospital. (Figure 5.8, right) Mocking women who undergo

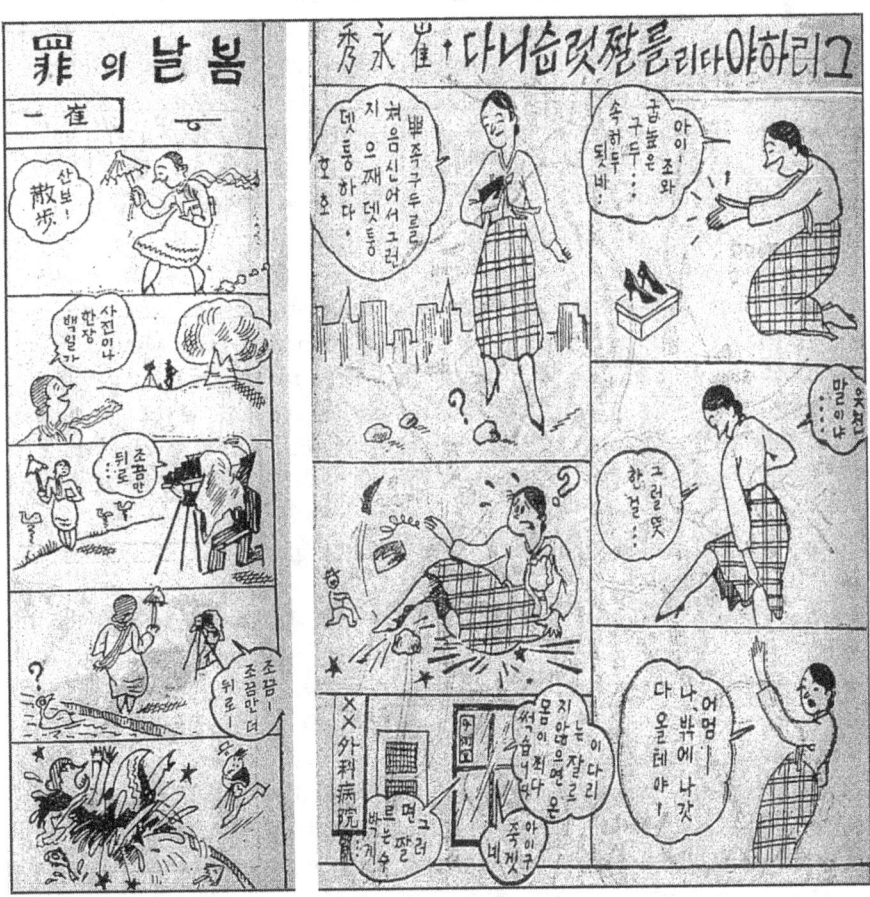

Figure 5.8 (*left*) 'The Sin of Spring Day'. (*Singajeong*, 1.4, April 1933) (*right*) 'This Is How I Lost My Leg'. (*Singajeong*, 1.4, April 1933)

embarrassment and puzzlement in open, public spheres, as captured in both Lee Tae-jun's short story and the cartoons, implies that women do not quite grasp how to behave properly in such public spaces, as they are new to these spaces. This cynical, and even malicious, representation of women's presence in a public place was ultimately employed by concerned traditionalists to reaffirm their point that women were unfit to be in the spaces once available only to men. Like those women who look lost in the public space, female filmgoers were similarly perceived as spectators who came to films for inappropriate reasons and thus paid no heed to the more profound social and cultural functions of film-viewing. In this manner, while expressing anxiety towards women's increased mobility and visibility in the public sphere, society cast sceptical looks at those women who ventured out into the streets and public venues.

Despite the social denunciation, however, cinema continued to attract female filmgoers who comprised a considerable portion of the film clientele in the 1930s. From the early 1930s women's magazines began to feature the 'film-in-a-magazine' (*jisang yeonghwa*) section as a staple in their issues which reflected the increasing interest in movies by female readers. As the decade progressed, women's magazines even presented more serious types of film articles that introduced how to analyse films critically, such as 'How to Appreciate a Film'[55] and 'The Cinema and Our Life'.[56] Round-table discussions and interviews printed in women's magazines at this time often broke the ice by asking a casual question about participants' favourite films and stars which indicates that film was deeply ingrained into women's everyday cultural life. Around 1940 housewives started going to the movies regularly[57] and thus film finally entertained the whole range of the female population in Joseon. Even when movie theatres saw half their clientele in women, however, and their presence in cinemas and other public spaces was more socially accepted, the social uneasiness towards that presence did not entirely vanish. The 1936 film *Sweet Dream* (*Mimong*) offered the quite resilient social suspicion towards women's mobility through its negative portrayal of modern woman's exploration of urban culture. One of the few surviving Joseon films, *Sweet Dream* narrates the mischievous adventures of Ae-sun, a married woman. Frustrated with her conservative husband, Ae-sun leaves him and her daughter, Jeong-hee, and enjoys her freedom, indulging herself in the earthly pleasures the streets of Seoul offer. She stays at a hotel with a man who had stolen her purse at a department store only to return it to her in order to pose as a good Samaritan and win her trust. After Ae-sun discovers the man's true identity, she realises the danger involved in her new lifestyle, regrets her irresponsible act and decides to return to her daughter. On her way home, the taxi Ae-sun is riding in accidentally hits her daughter and seriously injures her. The guilt-ridden Ae-sun loses her sanity and commits suicide next to her daughter's hospital bed.

This cautionary tale, recounted by *Sweet Dream*, is a blatant cinematic embodiment of the public angst about the peril brought to the traditional gender hierarchy as well as the social aversions cast on modern women. Considering the film's explicit depiction of the modern woman's morally questionable lifestyle, and its tragic and highly sentimental ending, it is quite surprising that the film was actually a propaganda film commissioned by the Gyeonggi Province. In fact, *Sweet Dream* was a so-called traffic film financed by the Security Department of the Gyeonggi Province which was in charge of transport and was supposed to increase the public awareness of traffic safety.[58] According to the title sequence of the film, screenings were also arranged by the newspaper *Manchuria and Korean Traffic Times*. The film is not a typical propaganda film because it integrates its didactic message seamlessly into the film narrative instead of overtly promoting traffic safety. For instance, Jeong-hee's tragic car accident is foreshadowed on several occasions earlier in the film. In her first appearance, the camera captures her walking past the showroom of Ford Automobile's Seoul branch on her way home. Later in the film, spectators are taken to Jeong-hee's classroom where a traffic-safety lecture is in progress. On the other side, the film turned out to be an ineffective propaganda piece, because it failed clearly to convey its intended message. The Security Department seemed to be displeased with this project and they expressed their wish that the next traffic film they planned to sponsor would be 'more cheerful and artistic'.[59]

It is, indeed, difficult to see this film as a propaganda film without having the piece of information about the film's production, so it seems obvious that it failed as a propaganda film. Yet, the fact that it was a traffic-safety film is what makes its representation of a modern girl even more intriguing because the car was a modern technology which was often associated with the characters of modern girls and boys. As noted earlier, 'going for a drive' was a leisure activity which had emerged in the late 1920s, and it drew severe social criticism in a similar manner to walking and strolling the streets because driving cars for pleasure was seen as a 'meaningless behaviour' and 'lousy taste'.[60] This new leisure activity was often pinpointed for negative representation of modern boys and girls. Professional drivers who participated in a *Joseon ilbo* round-table discussion, for example, angrily shared their frustrating experiences of modern girls and boys, who had hired them for a drive, by exposing the modern girls' and boys' sexual engagement in the back seat of their cars.[61] It is intriguing that Ae-sun's tragic ending is triggered by the car, which is considered to be an important part of a modern girl's careless cultural life. It is the taxi she rides in that causes Jeong-hee's accident and, thus, the car accident serves in the narrative as an appropriate punishment for Ae-sun's irresponsibility. (Figure 5.9) Importantly, the motor car is also a symbol of Ae-sun's mobility that ultimately results in her family tragedy.

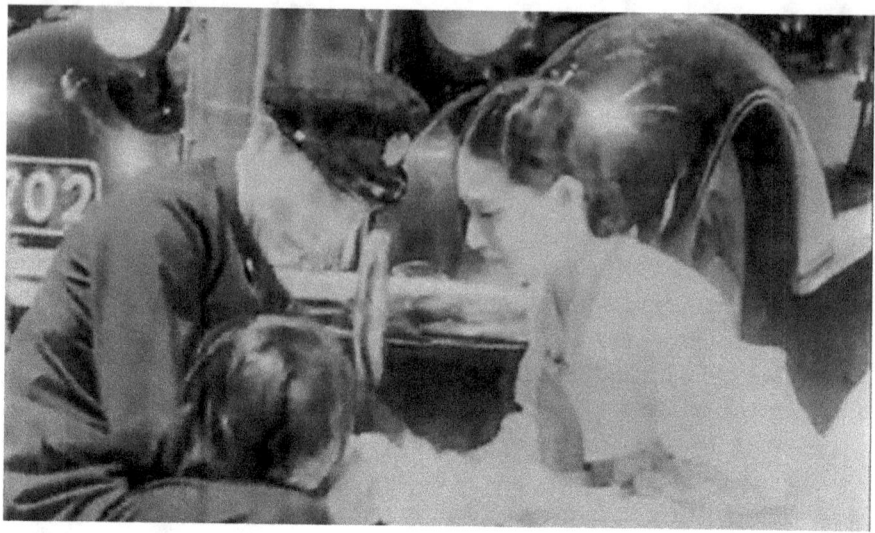

Figure 5.9 Ae-sun is shocked to find out that the victim hit by the taxi she was riding in is her daughter Jeong-hee. (*Sweet Dream*, 1936)

In fact, the film's narrative is firmly grounded on the negative social connotations attached to the woman on the move. The car, the most apparent modern and technological representation of the sense of mobility, is not the only new product associated with Ae-sun's mobility. The film opens with the close-up shot of a bird in a cage – a popular metaphor for women's chaining to the domestic sphere at the time – and then cuts to Ae-sun's bedroom where, while putting on her make-up, she starts an argument with her husband who angrily speaks ill of another shopping spree at a department store she is about to embark on. Her first line goes, 'I am going to a department store to buy a Western dress.' The couple's quarrel is yet another example that shows the ways in which Joseon society used the issue of consumerism in its criticism of modern girls. Subsequently, in the very next sequence, viewers find Ae-sun browsing through the store. It is in this department store where her misadventure begins because, there, she develops a relationship with a conman with whom she ends up living at a hotel after leaving her family. Socially, the store was seen as a hangout for modern girls who 'stop by the department store after their leisurely drive or stroll'.[62] The department store was therefore deemed to be an emblematic space that stood for modern girls' ostentatious lifestyle and rampant consumerism. The theatre is another public venue where Ae-sun's moral debauchery is highlighted. When she visits a dance performance with her new lover, she becomes fascinated by the lead dancer (played by Cho Taek-won

[1907–76], a noted modern dance performer) and tries to court him backstage by showering flowers and gifts on him, only to be scorned by the dancer. All the public spaces, such as the department store, hotel, cafe and theatre, where the major events in the film's narrative take place, serve as backdrops to display Ae-sun's moral decadence, and the film delivers the message that it is her newly acquired access to these spaces that brings about her self-destruction.

In this way, *Sweet Dream* exploits a pervasive social anxiety about the consequences of women's attainment of unprecedented mobility. All the disasters which occur in the film are caused by Ae-sun's mobility, in both the social and physical senses, from her irresponsible decision to leave the place where she is supposed to be (her home) and her careless ventures into the public environment to her taxi ride that claims the lives of her daughter and, ultimately, herself. The representation of Ae-sun's ill-fated attempt to escape from 'the bird cage' in the film, in this regard, reveals the society-wide paranoia about women's emancipated mobility and independence. As *Sweet Dream* demonstrates, the modern woman's entry into the public domain was simply equated to, and censured, as a selfish, decadent pursuit of worldly pleasures which posed serious threats to traditional values, social mores and even to Joseon society itself.

Gisaeng: Challenging the New Woman Discourse

Despite the stringent gender segregation that undermined women's mobility, including the act of film-going, there was one group of women for whom this social stigma was hardly an issue. Here, let me return to the 1927 *Byeolgeongon* essay cited earlier in which the essayist described groups of women 'who had short bangs, wore makeup, mingled with the bunch of *gisaeng*'[63] and claimed that they came to films to seduce male patrons. While closely observing the conduct of the female patrons, quite intriguingly, the author did not pay any attention to the *gisaeng*, or professional female entertainers, who sat right next to the young girls and female students, as if the *gisaeng*'s cinema patronage was not something worth discussing in his report on the lewd sexual behaviour of female viewers. This contrasting perspective the *Byeolgeongon* essay projects towards the *gisaeng* and other 'general' female spectators alludes to the fact that Joseon society, in fact, had two disparate standards for female film spectatorship. In other words, in contrast to all other women, the figure of the *gisaeng* was not chained by the spatial gender segregation upheld by colonial Joseon society. Consequently, *gisaeng* comprised the only group of women who freely enjoyed film and modern popular culture without being socially denounced.

This last section of the chapter unpacks the place of *gisaeng* within the Joseon film scene by highlighting their mobility that enabled *gisaeng* not only to become main patrons of the film business but also to be a major agent in the development of film and other entertainment industries. To begin with, the uniqueness of *gisaeng* in regard to Joseon's gender politics derived not only from their physical mobility but also their ambiguous relationship to the multiple senses of social mobility. Mapping the figure of *gisaeng* within the contexts of film culture, female film spectatorship and the new woman discourse brings to light another lacuna in the study of Joseon cinema. As I will elaborate, *gisaeng* played a seminal role in the development of early film culture but the fact that it has not been fully acknowledged unveils how the conventional film historiography marginalises women's places in film history for the sake of privileging the masculine subject of the nation and national history. The excavation of the *gisaeng*'s forgotten contributions to the institutionalisation of cinema will show how nationalist Korean film historiography is essentially gendered. An examination of the unique but ambivalent social status of the *gisaeng* both as a traditional and 'new woman' figure in Korean society, which allowed *gisaeng* to become an integral part of the emerging film culture, will also expand the study of urban culture and the new woman's role and place therein that frequently foregrounds new forms of commodification, consumption and leisure. In fact, the modern woman discourses of cultural studies tend to confine the position of women in modern cultures to the realm of consumption, such as department stores, arcades, cafes and theatres, and thus seek to valorise modern women's empowerment from their consumerist activities. Despite the significance of this approach in revealing the gendered formation of the modern urban space and re-evaluating female mobility in relation to modern capitalism, which required the mobilisation of women both as cheap labourers and consumers, it can be limiting because it often puts aside other potential activities of modern women in the urban cultural scene. In addition, it is important to note that access to the public spaces was, by and large, the privilege of the educated, affluent and middle-class women, which raises the question concerning the class identity of the new woman. By investigating the multifaceted contributions *gisaeng* made to all aspects of film culture, ranging from film production to exhibition, therefore, this section will show that the modern woman was not simply a consumer of modern culture but its creator and how the issue of gender was further complicated by other societal aspects such as class and the colonial situation.

The prototypical figure of *gisaeng* can be traced back as far as the Three Kingdom Period (from circa AD 100 to 668) but the practice of *gisaeng* is generally considered a creation of the Joseon dynasty which dates back to at least the fifteenth century. *Gisaeng* were primarily dancers who performed and served for the amusement and pleasure of aristocratic males and, accordingly, the regional governments were in charge of selecting and managing *gisaeng*. Though they belonged to the lowest class (*cheonmin*) in the Joseon dynasty's caste system, they were more than entertainers because they had to develop and nurture their artistic and cultural character to satisfy the male intellectuals for whom they worked. To be a fine *gisaeng*, she must have excelled in calligraphy, dance, poetry and singing. Though sexual service seems to have been an important part of the *gisaeng*'s profession, the relationship to prostitution was rather ambivalent. Despite the fact that the majority of *gisaeng* did not often have the choice to avoid prostitution, those who engaged in it were despised even by their fellow *gisaeng* and called 'third-rate (*sampae*)' *gisaeng*. A romantic relationship with a patron was regarded as the ideal of *gisaeng*, and becoming a concubine was seen as the only way out of the *gisaeng* life, though that was extremely rare.

As Korean society became modernised around the turn of the twentieth century, the *gisaeng* practice underwent major changes. The transformation was prompted by the issuing of the '*Gisaeng* Regulation Order (*Gisaeng Dansokryeong*)' and 'Prostitute Regulation Order (*Changgi Dansokryeong*)' on 28 September 1908.[64] Under this regulation, all *gisaeng* were required to register with the police department and obtain a permit to be in the business. The introduction of the permit system and the disbanding of the official *gisaeng* brought two important changes to the *gisaeng* world. First, although the permit system was designed to control *gisaeng* more strictly, it resulted in a sharp increase in the number of *gisaeng*. After attending newly established *gisaeng* schools and getting a permit, anyone could become a *gisaeng*. Also, as *gisaeng* were regulated along with prostitutes, their public image was gradually affected. Beginning in the 1910s, Japanese immigrants, visitors and tourists emerged as major patrons for the *gisaeng* business but they did not have a historical understanding of *gisaeng* and thus often saw *gisaeng* primarily as sexual objects. During the colonial period, in fact, images of *gisaeng* as sexual objects of the curious imperial male gaze were exhaustively reproduced in many Japanese postcards, photographs, *haiku*, travel guidebooks and travelogues. Even after *gisaeng* officially disappeared in 1947, when the government banned the practice,[65] the legacy of the relationship between *gisaeng* and the imperial male gaze remained in postcolonial Korea and Japan; the notorious so-called sex tours which Japanese men made to South Korea have been commonly referred to as '*gisaeng* tours'.

The second noteworthy change, facilitated by the new *gisaeng* regulation, was that, as the state no longer managed them, *gisaeng* became privatised. As soon as the *Gisaeng* Regulation Order was implemented, *gisaeng* formed private associations to protect their interests and continue their practice. Since 1914, the *gisaeng* guilds (*johab*) transformed into *gwonbeon* (J: *kanban*) which designates an association. *Gisaeng gwonbeon* functioned as a *gisaeng* company as well as a *gisaeng* school; it had investors, hired *gisaeng*, scheduled *gisaeng*'s performances both in the public settings (theatres and expositions) and private locales (restaurants and private parties), and divided the income among its members, including *gisaeng*. In the meantime, women who wanted to be trained to become *gisaeng* could enrol in *gwonbeon* as long as they could afford tuition for the three-year training. In the 1930s, many *gwonbeon* converted to stock companies and, as a result, some owners of *gwonbeon* and a number of the most popular *gisaeng* became millionaires. The privatisation of *gisaeng* and dissolution of the traditional caste system also had an impact on the *gisaeng* patronage because now it was not their class status but their economic capabilities that granted patrons an access to *gisaeng* entertainment. A writer who called for the abolition of the *gisaeng* practice, for example, commented on this transformation by noting:

> It is the age of popularisation. Everything is under popularisation, so why not *gisaeng*? In the past, only high-ranking officials could hang out with *gisaeng*, but ever since the aristocracy collapsed, *gisaeng* has become completely popularised. Now even a bastard could flirt with the finest *gisaeng* if he has the gold.[66]

In the industrialisation of the *gisaeng* practice, *gisaeng*'s artistic heritage was underappreciated; instead, *gisaeng*'s appearances and patrons' money became the major factors that determined the modern *gisaeng* business. Meanwhile, as the employees of *gwonbeon*, *gisaeng* were able to make money although their income varied significantly depending on their popularity. In the 1920s, the average income of *gisaeng* was equal to that of middle-class households, and a *gisaeng*'s income was among the highest in those professions then available to women, thus attracting many women, especially those from poor families.[67]

The advent of theatre played a pivotal role in the rapid transformation of *gisaeng* into a modern business institution and popular entertainment. As explained in previous chapters, indoor theatres began to appear only around 1902 and, because of the lack of a stage drama tradition, dance performances by *gisaeng* became the central attraction of theatre bills. As a result, *gisaeng* became instrumental in the emerging theatre culture. In the 1910s, with the increase in theatres together with the commercialisation of *gisaeng*, more and more people could enjoy *gisaeng*'s performances, resulting in a growing influence of *gisaeng* in the overall culture and entertainment business. The performance of *gisaeng*, once available only to people with certain social classes in limited spaces, became widely available to the masses through theatres. (Figure 5.10) In light of the lack of local film and stage drama productions, it was inevitable that *gisaeng* rose as the first popular celebrities. From 28 January to 11 June 1914, the newspaper *Maeil sinbo* serialised a section called 'One Hundred People in the Entertainment World'[68] that introduced, one person each day, the most powerful and popular

Figure 5.10 *Gisaeng* perform on the stage of the Entertainment Theatre established at the 1929 Joseon Exposition to entertain the exposition attendees. (*Chōsen hakurankai kinen shashinchō* [Keijō (Seoul): *Chōsen Sōtokufu*, 1930])

entertainers in Joseon. Among the list of the ninety-nine people presented by the newspaper are three *byeonsa*, one dramatist, three singers, and ninety-two *gisaeng*. This astonishingly large number of *gisaeng*, listed in the daily over the six months, evinces how crucial the role of the *gisaeng* was in Joseon's nascent entertainment business at the time.

The exposure of *gisaeng* to the general public was not restricted to performance venues because the new generation of *gisaeng*, with their economic power and almost unique ability to gain access to male-oriented public spaces, was eager to enjoy modern culture. Soon, *gisaeng* became the major patrons of mass entertainment including films, expositions, dance halls, museums and cafes, while expanding their business into these new cultural venues. The curriculum of the *gwonbeon* accommodated this change to include courses on Western and Japanese dances and Japanese language in order to attract their new potential patrons.[69] How *gisaeng* emerged as major players in both the production and consumption of the new entertainments can be explained by their unique position in Joseon's class system. On a journey from England, Isabella Bird Bishop, one of the few women among Western adventurers/travellers who visited turn-of-the-century Korea, wrote her travelogue *Korea and Her Neighbours* (1898) in which she expressed her particular interest in the gender issue of Korean society. One of the subjects that most intrigued Bishop during her visit to Korea was the figure of the *gisaeng*. She took particular notice of the *gisaeng*'s mobility:

> Their training and non-secluded position place them, however, outside of the reputable classes, and though in Japan *geishas* often become the wives of nobles and even of statesmen, no Korean man would dream of raising a *gesang* [*gisaeng*] to such a position.[70]

As Bishop pointed out, the *gisaeng*'s unique mobility or 'non-secluded position', which contrasted sharply with other women's containment within the private sphere, stemmed from her place outside the official societal system. Bishop's words indicate that the *gisaeng*'s social position in Joseon dynasty's caste system was below that of even the lowest caste but that her class 'immobility' ironically enabled her to move freely across gender-specific places. Thus, while becoming a *gisaeng* signified a great social fall in the class structure, which made it nearly impossible for *gisaeng* to escape from her social status, the strict gender segregation and roles did not in turn apply to them; like slaves, they were 'sub-human beings' to whom rules of human society did not apply. In addition, *gisaeng*'s expected social function was to become a cultural – and, to some extent, sexual – companion of aristocratic males which meant that her presence in male-dominated spaces, from the royal palace to restaurants, was not only socially accepted but naturally assumed.

This paradoxical mixture of liberty and limitation in mobility of *gisaeng* continued after the advent of the private *gisaeng* business. Though *gisaeng* were a relic of the old caste system, which was gradually being dissembled, their mobility was socially acceptable owing to this very system. The tolerance towards the *gisaeng*'s presence in the male sphere permitted *gisaeng* to roam freely in urban spaces and take full pleasure in modern cultures. Consequently, without being socially criticised, controlled, or restricted for their 'breach' into the public domain, *gisaeng* enjoyed the privilege of surprisingly free access to public spaces, including those cultural institutions in modern Joseon society which were still considered inappropriate for women. *Gisaeng* were even viewed as trendsetters, and thus their appearance per se at certain cultural events attracted people and gave those events more credence. For example, a newspaper report on the successful *Loyal Vengeance* (1919) opening night specifically points out that two hundred *gisaeng* attended the premiere.[71] Similarly, another newspaper report on the 1929 Joseon Exposition notes that a group of *gisaeng* from Pyongyang, a city known for the finest *gisaeng*, had already scheduled a trip to the exposition and this made people more intrigued by the event.[72] Society was not just tolerant towards *gisaeng*'s attendance at modern cultural venues but it was often enthusiastic about it. This is why *gisaeng*'s presence at movie theatres was also naturally accepted while other female spectators were under the constant scrutiny of suspicious and controlling male eyes.

Gisaeng's patronage, however, was only a partial account of their involvement with the film culture. The *gisaeng*'s role in early Korean film culture has been underrated in Korean film history. They have been mainly relegated to anecdotes or footnotes that underline their fandom – the romantic relationships with film-makers, actors, or *byeonsa* – largely because they were the only female patrons who regularly enjoyed movie-going activities. *Gisaeng*, however, influenced the early development of film culture at many levels. First, as *gisaeng* and theatre practices were mutually influential and grew together from the 1910s onward, it was quite natural for *gisaeng* to become an integral part of early film exhibition. Early silent film screenings in Korea/Joseon featured vaudeville-like shows and circuses before and between screenings, and the *gisaeng*'s performance was one of the most popular. This practice did not entirely disappear in the 1920s, as *gisaeng* performances were still employed as popular promotional events for film screenings. Sometimes, *gisaeng* directly leased theatres to put on their performances. Hannam Gwonbeon, one of the so-called Four Great Gwonbeon (*sadae gwonbeon*) of the 1920s, together with Hanseong, Daejeong and Joseon Gwonbeon, for instance, leased and managed the Umigwan Theatre in 1923 for a year,[73] demonstrating the close ties between *gisaeng* and the theatre business.

Secondly, *gisaeng* participated in film-making as actors. Many of the earliest actors starring in films made in the 1920s were *gisaeng* because film-makers tried to take advantage of their established star personas. There was also a practical reason why it was extremely difficult to find female actors, that is acting was considered an indecent profession, especially for women.[74] As *gisaeng*'s influence over the cultural business across the different forms of amusement continued to grow, *gwonbeon* eventually evolved into powerful cultural and economic institutions. *Gwonbeon* even produced films in the mid-1920s.

> As Joseon films are so rare, people go to see them anyway, and thus no Joseon films lose money. As a result, there have been quite a number of Joseon films produced lately. This time *Path at the Twilight*, a film whose title already sounds so sweet, has been made by the Joseon Gwonbeon *gisaeng*'s hands. This film only features *gisaeng*, and they say the production has been completed and will be released at Danseongsa on 16 September.[75]

Before *Path at the Twilight* (*Nakyangui gil*, 1927), which featured some of the most popular *gisaeng* affiliated with Joseon Gwonbeon, such as Kim Ran-ju, Lee Yeon-hyang, Kim Yeong-wol, Kim Do-hwa and Lee Bong-hee,[76] Joseon Gwonbeon had already shot two films in 1925, *Love and Brothers* (*Aewa hyeongje*) and *A Maid and Destiny* (*Cheonyeowa unmyeong*).[77] All these melodramas by Joseon Gwonbeon were chain dramas – hybrids between film and stage drama – the perfect choice for a *gisaeng* film because they could incorporate live *gisaeng* performances into the film showings. This strategic move turned out to be a problem, however, because *gisaeng* actors who starred in these films were already so popular that they could not find time to travel with the films to cities other than Seoul, which generated conflicts between Joseon Gwonbeon and the film promoters who had purchased the rights to the film's exhibition outside Seoul.[78]

As illustrated, *gisaeng*'s contributions to film and other popular cultural entertainment in Joseon defy the common association made between modern woman and modern culture. The discussions in cultural studies of the female presence in modern cultural spaces typically revolve around the figures of new woman or modern girl. The new woman's engagement with modern culture is generally linked to the activities of consumption and leisure activities as well as to consumption spaces, as either a consumer at arcades and department stores or as a spectator at theatres. In a similar vein, the discourse of female *flânerie* and the notion of *flâneuse* (a female who performed *flânerie*) are related either to consumption or to prostitution – in both the actual and allegorical senses – because of women's limited access to male-dominated modern public spaces. Anne Friedberg, for instance, argues 'the female *flâneur*, the *flâneuse*, was not possible until she was free to roam the city on her own. And this was equated with the privilege of shopping on her own.'[79] In other words, the consumerist space functioned as a modern public sphere where women's presence was socially acceptable to some degree and, thus, the empowerment of women was inevitably associated with the power, painstakingly earned, in consumerist activities. The link between modern woman's mobility in urban space and consumerism may be useful in discovering women's *flânerie*, thus unsettling the male-centred definition of *flânerie*. Yet this concept, which is intended to make sense of middle-class women's mobility, tends to obscure the differences across the diverse groups of new women, and the modern-woman-as-consumer discourse also tends to remain inattentive to women's participation in the production of modern culture, as Anke Gleber insightfully points out:

> However, the territories of such preliminary and rudimentary forms of flanerie – the preoccupied strolling and shopping of a female consumer – have to be regarded, in view of the vast terrain of existing real city spaces, as decidedly circumscribed and distinctly derivative. Limited excursions of shopping in a prescribed ghetto of consumption amount to little more than secondhand distraction, never approximating the *flaneur*'s wide-reaching mode of perception, unimpeded by aims, purposes, and schedule. The conflation of shopping and strolling noted by Friedberg necessarily relativizes what initially appears as a first instance of the 'empowered gaze of the *flaneuse*'. Reduced in its potential to the purposefully limited and capitalistically promoted license to shop, the early 'department store *flaneuses*' who 'roam' the interiors of capitalist consumption represent little more than a bourgeois variant of domesticized *flanerie*.[80]

Indeed, many studies of modern womanhood or the concept of new woman are often tied to the upper and/or middle class, often marginalising women from the other classes. Though the original term *new woman* was closely tied to middle-class women, it was eventually contested among various groups of women and thus its definition broadened. In Joseon, the term *new woman* entered into the popular vocabulary when the women's magazine *Sinyeoseong* (*New Woman*) was published in 1923. When the term was first introduced, the new woman was defined as an educated, enlightened and middle-class woman who devoted herself to challenging the traditional gender roles. The term began to carry multiple connotations, however, as its initial definition was contested towards the end of the decade by many new women themselves who were disillusioned with the middle-class, family-oriented 'new woman' ideology. In particular, Marxist feminism, which quickly became a powerful intellectual trend beginning in 1924 when fourteen new women convened to form a socialist feminism organisation called Friendly Society of Joseon Women (*Joseon Dongwuhoe*), defined the new woman in a completely different way. According to Jeong Chil-seong, a Marxist feminist who was previously a *gisaeng*, the new woman was 'a proletarian woman who possesses a class consciousness and will to deny the unreasonable old system and create a new social environment'.[81]

This varied conceptualisation of modern women urges us to reconsider new woman not as a universal and monolithic notion but as heterogeneous constituencies. There were new kinds of women urban workers such as dancers, singers, actresses, secretaries, waitresses, factory workers, office clerks and prostitutes, and their degree of access to modern public spaces varied greatly according to their social, economic and racial backgrounds, and often their urban *flânerie* was even more limited than the upper/middle-class (white) women or by the narrow sense of 'new women'. The figure of *gisaeng* further compounds the conventional configuration of modern woman. *Gisaeng* was the only group of women who were able fully to take advantage of modern metropolitan life, and their mobility in the modern urban milieu stood at the confluence of traditional class system, rapid modernisation and emerging capitalism. It is almost impossible to make sense of *gisaeng*'s uniqueness in terms of their class position, gender politics and *flânerie* with a restricted understanding of new woman or modern girl. *Gisaeng*, as an 'in-between' figure, suggests another possible form of modern womanhood and female *flânerie* in relation to modern urban culture.

Gisaeng were both consumers and producers of modern culture, traditional female figures and modern women at the same time, objects of (imperial) male sexual desire and gaze but also possessors of power in gender relations, labourers in the nascent capitalist social system but also industrialists, and still largely restrained by the old class system but allowed to roam public spaces without restraint by this very class system because their assumed place in society was not the domestic space. Many *gisaeng* actively participated in political activities, challenging the rigid social mores of Joseon. Their deep involvement with the film culture further proves *gisaeng*'s unorthodox social position in colonial Joseon society. They were avid film aficionados but did not just stay in the spectator seat. *Gisaeng* performed pre-screening shows, acted before the camera, produced and promoted the films and managed movie theatres. Some may say *gisaeng* were simply exploited by their male employers who wished to capitalise on the growing popularity of film to promote their *gisaeng* businesses but *gisaeng* did not quietly follow what they were told to do. *Gisaeng*, one of the most culturally enlightened groups at the time, published their own journal (*Janghan*) to showcase their artistic talent and critically analyse the patriarchal hierarchy, capitalism and their own profession.[82] They even went on strike when they were mistreated by their employers.[83] Though they did not wear high heels or short hair, *gisaeng* were at the vanguard of modern Korea.

Conclusion:
Integrating into the Imperial Cinema

In October of 1936, the completion of Meijiza, a new six-storey, giant-sized movie theatre (including two underground floors), which could accommodate fifteen hundred spectators, delighted film aficionados in Seoul. Ishibashi Ryōsuke, a highly successful Japanese businessman based in Seoul who owned the Maru Building, one of the landmark buildings in Meiji-machi that housed the luxurious Maru cafe and many other business entities, initiated the project, when Shochiku studio granted him exclusive distribution and exhibition rights to its films. The establishment of Meijiza was part of the deal made with Japanese Shochiku studio, as detailed in Chapter 3. The theatre was designed by Japanese settler architect Tamata Kitsuji who designed the renovated buildings for Danseongsa (1935) and Koganekan (1936). As a Shochiku-affiliated theatre, Meijiza was primarily a movie theatre but served a variety of purposes, also accommodating stage plays, kabuki and other performing arts. It was located in Meiji-machi (today's Myeong-dong), one of the commercial centres of the Japanese area South Village, to which Japanese settlers popularly referred as 'Ginza of Joseon', and quickly became a landmark of Seoul. The theatre became co-managed by Shochiku and was renamed Shochiku–Meijiza in August 1941.[1] Meijiza remained the largest theatre in Joseon until the end of the Japanese occupation, and the legacy of Meijiza's grand size and elegant European-style facade and interior was sustained long after the colonial period. Meijiza was renamed Sigonggwan in 1947 and brought under the management of the city of Seoul. The theatre survived the Korean War (1950–53) and, after the war, accommodated The National Theatre of Korea from 1957 until 1973 when the National Theatre moved to its current location in the Jangchung-dong area. To finance the construction of a new national theatre, the government sold the theatre to a private business. After being used by private companies for several decades, the Ministry of Culture and Tourism purchased the building in 2004 and announced its plan to restore the building as a national theatre. After years of major renovation, which aimed to restore the original structure and style as much as possible, Myeong-dong Art Theatre opened in June 2009.

The opening of Meijiza in 1936 was an event indicative of a new current in Joseon cinema in the final decade of Japanese colonial rule. Though the theatre was located in a Japanese business area, in his interview with a Korean-language magazine, its owner Ishibashi stated, 'We aim to appeal to all six hundred thousand residents in the great city of Seoul, not just Japanese migrants.'[2] As a first step in this ambitious plan, Ishibashi announced that he had already arranged a performance of Choi Seung-hee, a Korean dance artist, who had become famous throughout Asia, together with Japanese kabuki and *takarazuka* troupes, for the forthcoming opening-day special event.[3] Finally, as Meijiza's case demonstrates, Japanese movie theatres began actively to reach out to Korean film patrons. Around the time Meijiza opened, Japanese and Koreans were no longer segregated at the cinema as before.

In contrast, Korean theatres saw their decline as new theatres started appearing around this time. *Maeil sinbo*'s report on Danseongsa's announcement of its conversion into a stage drama theatre in July 1937 detailed the changing film industry conditions that significantly affected the theatre business. In a concerned tone, the daily reported that this only surviving movie theatre in Seoul's North Village could not compete with the new upmarket theatres built with Japanese film capital that 'is after Joseon entertainment'.[4] In an interview cited by *Maeil sinbo*, the theatre's manager said he had difficulties in acquiring foreign films because of the sharp rise in distribution fees brought about by the competition among Japanese studios and distributors to take over the supply of foreign movies in Joseon.[5] *Maeil sinbo* continued that Danseongsa's exit from the film business meant the end of the Korean-run movie theatre. The overall plight of other Korean movie theatres was similar to that of Danseongsa as they lost patronage from Koreans to the upmarket Japanese theatres. Also importantly, unlike the previous decades, Joseon films were billed at Japanese movie houses. Accordingly, Korean-language newspapers began to run theatre listings, ads and reviews of films screened at these Japanese movie theatres. Right under the above-cited *Maeil sinbo*'s article on the intrusion of Japanese film capital and the unfortunate fate of Danseongsa it triggered, for instance, the film preview section of the newspaper introduced George Cukor's *Romeo and Juliet* (1936, MGM) premiere at Meijiza for Korean readers/filmgoers. (Figure C.1)

Maeil sinbo's concern was reaffirmed when Danseongsa was purchased by Ishibashi to reopen as Daeryuk Geukjang in 1939 and later became affiliated with Shochiku (1941). Danseongsa's departure from the film business in 1937, therefore, heralded the official ending of the film practice of ethnic segregation and also the twilight of Joseon cinema's autonomy. In 1938 in Seoul, where

Integrating into the Imperial Cinema 231

Figure C.1 The preview of *Romeo and Juliet* (1936), located right under the report on Danseongsa's conversion into a stage drama theatre. (*Maeil sinbo*, 15 July 1937)

ethnic segregation had directed the film exhibition business since the late 1910s, movie theatres run by Japanese studios, such as Meijiza, Wakakusa Gekijō and Koganekan, counted half of their clients as being Korean.[6] It should also be noted that Japanese movie theatres managed by Japanese settlers suffered in a similar manner to that of Korean theatres. *Chōsen kōron* reported in 1936 that more than half the movie theatres in Joseon had already been taken over by Japanese studios.[7] Old Japanese settler movie theatres were sold to Japanese studios, became second-run theatres or closed down. By the end of the decade, film exhibition in Joseon was controlled by major Japanese companies, such as Shochiku, Toho, and Shinko, as well as by Yoshimoto Kōgyō (an entertainment company) and Tōwa Shōji (a distribution business).

As *Tokyo eiga shimbun* reported in 1938,[8] Japanese film capital entering Joseon from about 1935 concentrated on the film exhibition business, acquiring theatres or building new upmarket, 'modern' cinemas. Meijiza signalled the introduction of a new type of theatre in conjunction with a new development in the film theatre business in Japan. From around 1930, Japanese film patrons witnessed the rise of new kinds of high-end film theatres. Built with steel and concrete, these theatres, first appearing in Tokyo's Marunouchi area, enhanced and altered film-viewing experiences by introducing a number of new amenities, such as air-conditioning and heating systems, advance ticket sales, in-theatre shops and restaurants, and individual seats. The emergence of lavish cinemas was an obvious consequence of the growing popularity of film, and these cinemas were among the many measures Japanese studios took in order to continue to expand their influence in the midst of fierce competition. In the 1930s, Shochiku emerged as the dominant player; Nikkatsu's decline accelerated; and Teikoku Kinema, Makino Kinema, Tōa Kinema and many other studios shut down. After its ferocious battle against the pack of four major film studios (Shochiku, Nikkatsu, Daito and Shinko), Toho, a new mega-studio, became Shochiku's sole rival towards the end of the decade. Though much smaller in scale, similar changes began to take place in Joseon as well but these changes were initiated by what happened in the Japanese film industry. In 1937 when Shochiku's influence was also felt in Joseon, Kobayashi Ichizō, the founder of Toho, visited Joseon to observe the Joseon entertainment boom.[9] Shortly afterwards, Toho took over the management of Wakakusa Gekijō, a huge cinema in which the studio had invested when it opened in Wakakusa-cho (today's Cho-dong) in 1935, and started directly managing the distribution of its films beginning in November 1937.[10] In addition to Wakakusa Gekijō, the studio eventually ran a number of theatres in Pyongyang, Incheon, Cheongjin, and other cities.[11] In the meantime, in 1941, Shochiku opened its first Seoul office. Conventionally, Japanese studios took out contracts with Japanese settler exhibitors to represent them in Joseon but Shochiku's Seoul office was the first subsidiary that was directly operated by the head office.

Joseon cinema's crisis was also greatly accelerated by the changes in colonial governance. The influx of Japanese film capital into the Joseon film industry in the mid-1930s coincided more or less with the emergence of the coercive policies of the Office of the Governor General which banned the use of the Korean language and publication of Korean cultural products, and forced Koreans to change their names to Japanese style under the newly implemented family registration system (K: *hojeok*; J: *koseki*, 1939). The empire attempted even more aggressively and thoroughly to turn Koreans into imperial subjects. The situation deteriorated as both Japan and Joseon entered the turmoil of World War II. In the 1940s, film culture in Joseon underwent yet another transformation with the authorities' attempts to nationalise the film business. In January 1940, the Joseon Film Directive, modelled after Japan's 1939 Film Law, was introduced. In 1942, the Office of the Governor General closed down all the distribution companies, launching the Joseon Film Distribution Company (K: Joseon Yeonghwa Baegeubsa; J: Chōsen Eiga Haikyūsha) to distribute all films. Soon all film-production companies were forcibly closed down, and Joseon Film Production Corporation (K: Joseon Yeonghwa Jejak Jusikhoesa; J: Chōsen Eiga Seisaku Kabushikigaisha), which was established in September 1942, became the sole production company in the colony. With the establishment of these state-owned film companies, the entire film business in Joseon came under the direct management of the Office of the Governor General,[12] and the entire film culture operated for the empire's propagandist needs. Consequently, whether or not they agreed with the imperialist ideals, Joseon film-makers were obliged to be associates of the empire's propaganda machine if they wished to stay in the film business. In the last few years of the empire, the function of Joseon cinema became quite one-dimensional. As the president of the Joseon Film Distribution Company and the Joseon Film Production Corporation, Tanaka Saburō, the founder of the prominent Japanese film magazine Kinema junpō, emphasised, the new duty of Joseon cinema was to 'sincerely introduce the political achievements of the Governor General and the current state of Joseon to the world' and to 'make a contribution to turning twenty-four million Koreans into imperial subjects (kōminka)'.[13]

As Japanese studios micromanaged the distribution and exhibition of their films in Joseon, and the empire introduced film regulations and laws, Japanese migrants were significantly reduced to minor roles in Joseon cinema. Major players left the film industry after selling off their cinemas to newcomers and quietly disappeared from the Joseon film world or became agents for Japanese studios. Tokunaga Kumaichirō, for example, sold his cinema, Koganekan, to the Joseon branch of Tōwa in 1938 and then represented Toho's Seoul office.[14] When the film industry was completely nationalised in the 1940s, and thus all film-related workers had to register with the authorities, these migrants' names, with the exception of technicians, were hard to find in the registers of the Joseon film workforce. Instead, the lists were filled with the bureaucrats, censors, military personnel or film professionals who represented Japanese studios, most of whom had recently moved to Joseon. In addition, those who replaced the veterans were new players who willingly colluded with the Japanese film industry's takeover of Joseon cinema and/or the authorities' politicisation of Joseon cinema, or what Uchida Jun calls 'the full-fledged partners of the wartime empire'.[15] When Ishibashi took over the contract with Shochiku from Tokunaga by using his family's powerful network in Japan to lobby for securing the contract to open Meijiza, settlers expressed their frustration about this unprecedented move. Referring to the deal made between this business mogul and a major Japanese studio, which shook up the local Joseon film business, settler film critic Mizui Reiko deplored the 'Flames of modern capitalism are scattering here'.[16]

Ishibashi turned out to be the one who led the pack of new players. He expanded his business into film only in the late 1930s but he was instrumental in paving the way for the march of Japanese film studios into the Joseon film industry. As a known advocate of Ichikawa Sai's proposal for the Greater East Asian Cinema,[17] Ishibashi's role in Joseon cinema's integration into Japanese cinema was crucial. Together with Ishibashi, new appointees from the Joseon branches of Toho, Shochiku, and other studios, censors, military personnel, and government officials became the new key figures in the 'new' Joseon cinema. In the meantime, Korean film-makers were considered important for a political purpose: in implementing the *naisen ittai* policy in the field of film-making, the participation of Korean film-makers was absolutely necessary. This arrangement further pushed Japanese emigrants to the margins of Joseon cinema, as any role these figures could play in building a pan-imperial cinema was rather obscure. At this time of rebuilding the empire to emphasise the unity between it and its colonies, what the authorities desired was liaison between 'authentic' Joseon and 'true' Japanese film-makers and, thus, the part of old immigrants in this political manoeuvre was de-emphasised. First by the intrusion of Japanese capital and then by political considerations, therefore, the settlers who had played decisive roles in the development of Joseon cinema for almost four decades were replaced by 'true' Japanese film-makers. With the marginalisation of Japanese immigrants and the political mobilisation of Korean film-makers, the tradition of Joseon cinema suffered a drastic discontinuity.

In 1942, Ishibashi Ryōsuke became the sole owner of Meijiza as he parted ways with Shochiku. Yet this termination of the partnership was neither Ishibashi's nor Shochiku's wish but, instead, it was a new, empire-wide film regulation that granted the Office of the Governor General the role of sole film distributor and exhibitor in Joseon. With the introduction of the new regulation, the entire film culture was placed under the firm, unchallenged control of the authorities. As in Japan, all theatres in Joseon had already been divided into two clusters, the Red Group (*akai-kei*) or the White Group (*shiro-kei*), which screened films alternately. Thus, even before the regulation, screenings were already being handled largely by the authorities. The 1942 film law was primarily designed to drive out any form of intervention from corporate film entities, namely Japanese film studios, from the Joseon film market. Shortly after the implementation of this film law, Shochiku, Toho and other Japanese film businesses cancelled their contracts with cinemas in Joseon, closed their branches and left Joseon cinema entirely. Control by Japanese film studios over Joseon cinema abruptly ended in this way and, from then on, Joseon cinema underwent yet another transformation, as the profit-driven interaction between Joseon and Japanese cinemas was stripped of any future. The authorities began completely to control every aspect of Joseon film culture, from film production to exhibition.

My analysis of Joseon cinema ends here. Too often colonial film history is seen as a monolith, discounting the differences and variations throughout almost four decades of colonial occupation. When approaching the final years of Joseon cinema, however, the new political climate, different imperial policies and politics, new players, and the changing notions of empire, nation, ethnicity, and citizenship must be taken into account, together with the radically altered practices in production, distribution, exhibition, film technologies and aesthetics. From the discursive definition of *Joseon cinema* to its role and function within the empire, the entire system and practice of film culture in Joseon went through radical shifts from around 1940, as outlined above. Joseon cinema in the final stage of colonial occupation was a considerable different entity from the earlier Joseon cinema. Though I have focused on the earlier phases of Joseon cinema, with *Eclipsed Cinema* I have tried to lay a foundation for further studies of this equally critical period, as well as for Korean and Japanese film histories. The exploration of the cinema's convoluted relationship with Korea's colonial modern experiences and the Japanese imperial enterprise, the critical application of national and colonial cinema frameworks, the reassessment of existing film historiography, and the understanding of film history as more than the mode of production – these theoretical backbones of my book can be foundational for subsequent interrogations of this later period. Yet it will also require distinctive theoretical and historiographical paradigms adequately to envisage the alterations in the film culture of this period and their historical, cultural and social implications; hence my belief that the story of such drastic changes deserves its own extensive study.

Notes

Introducing *Joseon Cinema*

1. Jaekil Seo, 'One Film, or Many?: The Multiple Texts of the Colonial Korean Film *Volunteer*', Jongmin Kim and Seulgie Lim (trans.), *Cross-Currents: East Asian History and Culture Review E-Journal*, 5, December 2012, p. 40 (http://cross-currents.berkeley.edu/e-journal/issue-5/Seo). Last accessed 8 August 2015.
2. 'Chōsen Sōtokufu kanseichū kaisei no ken', *kakukō dai 125gō*, 16 August 1927, pp. 41–2.
3. See Hayward, Susan, *French National Cinema* (London and New York: Routledge, 1993), pp. 1–16.
4. Cho Hee-mun, 'Hanguk yeonghwaui gaenyeomjeok jeonguiwa gijeome gwanhan yeongu', in *Hanguk yeonghwaui jaengjeom 1* (Seoul: Jibmundang, 2002), p. 15.
5. In Japan, *rensageki* was banned in the early 1920s for sanitary and safety reasons but in colonial Korea it continued to flourish until the mid-1930s. For more studies on chain drama, see Bernardi, Joanne, *Writing in Light: Silent Scenario and the Japanese Pure Film Movement* (Detroit MI: Wayne State University Press, 2001), Chapter 1; Anderson, J. L., 'Spoken Silents in the Japanese Cinema; or Talking to Pictures', in David Desser and Arthur Nolletti Jr (eds), *Reframing Japanese Cinema* (Bloomington IN: Indiana University Press, 1992), pp. 259–311. For further discussions of chain drama in relation to Joseon cinema, see Jeon Pyeong-guk, 'Uri Yeonghwa giwoneuroseo yeonswaegeuke daehan siron', *Yeonghwa yeongu*, 24, December 2004, pp. 463–89 and Baek Moonim, 'Joseon yeonghwaui punggyeongui balgyeon: yeonswaegeukgua gongganui jeonyu', *Dongbang hakji*, 158, June 2012, pp. 271–310.
6. Choi Chang-ho and Hong Gang-seong, *Na Un-Gyuwa sunangi yeonghwa* (Pyongyang: Pyongyang Chulpansa, 2001), p. 15.
7. See Kim Ryeo-sil, *Tusahaneun jeguk tuyeonghaneun sikminji* (Seoul: Samin, 2006), pp. 9–10.
8. *Chōsen Sōdokufu kanpō dai 1gō*, 29 August 1910, p. 17.
9. Ibid., p. 18.
10. Deocampo, Nick, *Cine: Spanish Influences on Early Cinema in the Philippines* (Manila: National Commission for Culture and Arts, 2003), p. 12.
11. Eckert, Carter J., 'Exorcizing Hegel's Ghosts', in Gi-Wook Shin and Michael Robinson (eds), *Colonial Modernity in Korea* (Boston MA: Harvard University Press, 2001), p. 366.

12. See Yamazaki Yukihiko, 'Chōsen eigakai no genzai to shōrai', *Chōsen kōron*, 283, October 1936, pp. 72–4.
13. Here, in particular, I place my research alongside the works of Michael Baskett (*The Attractive Empire: Transnational Film Culture in Imperial Japan*), James Burn (*Cinema and Society in the British Empire, 1895–1940*), Nick Deocampo (*Cine: Spanish Influences on Early Cinema in the Philippines*), Robert Dixon (*Photography, Early Cinema and Colonial Modernity: Frank Hurley's Synchronized Lecture Entertainments*), Anna Everett (*Returning the Gaze: A Genealogy of Black Film Criticism 1909–1949*), Allyson Nadia Field (*Uplift Cinema: The Emergence of African American Film and the Possibility of Black Modernity*), and Jacqueline Stewart (*Migrating to the Movies: Cinema and Black Urban Modernity*).
14. An Dong-su, 'Yeonghwa sugam', *Yeonghwa yeongeuk*, 1.1, 1939, p. 44.

Chapter 1

1. Chōsen gyōsei (ed.), *Chōsen tōchi hiwa* (Keijō: Teikoku Chihō Gyōsei Kakukai Chōsen Honbu, 1937), p. 2.
2. *Maeil sinbo*, 30 January 1919.
3. Ibid.
4. Chōsen Sōtokufu Keimukyoku, *Chōsen hōeki tōkei* (Keijō: Chōsen Sōtokufu Keimugyoku, 1941), p. 10.
5. *Maeil sinbo*, 3 January 1918.
6. 'Na Un-gyu, Shin Il-seoneurobuteo Mun ye-bong, Sim Yeongdeungui myeongue ireugikkajiui isibnyeonganui Joseon yeonghwa baldalsa', *Samchoelli*, 12.5, 1 May 1940, p. 227.
7. *Hwangseong sunbo*, 10 July 1903.
8. 'News Calendar', *The Korean Review*, 3, June 1903, p. 268.
9. Ibid., p. 268.
10. Ruot, M., 'The Motion Picture Industry in Japan', *Journal of the Society of Motion Picture Engineers*, 18.5, May 1932, p. 632.
11. In 1942, 192 movies theatres, including thirty-two makeshift theatres, were members of the Joseon Entertainment Association. 'Chōsen tsūshin', *Eiga junpō*, 54, July 1942, p. 56.
12. Formed in 1925, Korea Artista Proleta Federatio (Esperanto, KAPF) was a cultural group that aimed for socialist revolution and attempted to use culture for social activism. Its members worked in various cultural fields, including literature, theatre, music, and film. Owing to oppression from the authorities and disputes among its members over their ideological and artistic differences, KAPF disbanded in 1935.
13. Yim Hwa, 'Joseon yeonghwaron', *Chunchu*, 2.10, November 1941, pp. 88–9.
14. Sa Jin-sil, *Hanguk Yeongeuksa Yeongu* (Seoul: Taehaksa, 1997), pp. 281–303.
15. *Mansebo*, 29 June 1907.
16. Holmes, Burton, *The Burton Holmes Lectures Vol. X* (Battle Creek, MI: The Little-Preston Company, Limited, 1901), p. 86.

17. Ibid., p. 106.
18. This term (J: *goran* or *jyōran*; K: *eoram* or *sangram*) originated from Japan where it was used by exhibitors to promote their film programmes. Its usage dates back to 1897 when Kinkikan of Tokyo used the term in its pamphlet to advertise its films. See Ishimaki Yoshio, *Ōbei oyobi Nihon no eigashi* (Osaka: Pratonsha, 1925), pp. 310–12.
19. *Hwangseong sinmun*, 8 March 1908, 14 April 1908, 17 April 1908, and 28 October 1910; *Maeil sinbo*, 15 May 1912 and 6 September 1913; and *Haeyang yeongu sobo*, 14 April 1910.
20. *Maeil sinbo*, 17 May 1912.
21. *Hwangseong sinmun*, 28 March 1908, 10 May 1908, 10 September 1909, 15 December 1909, 28 May 1910; *Maeil sinbo*, 25 November 1922; *Joseon ilbo*, 13 May 1921.
22. *Maeil sinbo*, 2 April 1912. Upon colonisation, the Korean royal family became part of the Japanese imperial family, and Emperor Sunjong was demoted to the kingship and given a new title, 'King Lee', named after the royal family's family name. The kingship was an honorary position without any rights over the governance of Joseon. After Sunjong's death, his son, Prince Uimin (Lee Eun), succeeded to the title 'King Lee' but he did not take up residence at the palace (Changdeokgung) but instead lived in Tokyo with his Japanese wife and continued to serve in the Japanese imperial army until 1945. After the war, Lee Eun and his wife were not allowed to return to Korea by the South Korean government which also refused to grant them Korean citizenship; the couple was finally able to return to South Korea in 1963 when they took up residence at the Changdeok palace.
23. 'The motion pictures will be played at the Electric Company's power plant inside of the East Gate from 8pm to 10pm every day except Sunday and rainy days. The pictures include the stunning scenery of lively cities of Korea and the West. The admission fee is ten cents (*jeon*).' *Hwangseong sinmun*, 24 June 1903.
24. *The Korean Review*, p. 268.
25. 'Hwaldong sajin iyagi', *Byeolgeongon*, 2 December 1926, pp. 90–1.
26. Tsivian, Yuri, *Early Cinema in Russia and Its Cultural Reception*, Alan Bodger (trans.) (Chicago IL: University of Chicago Press, 1998), p. 17.
27. *The Korea Review*, p. 268.
28. *Mansebo*, 8 June 1907.
29. Kim Jong-won and Jeong Jung-heon, *Uri Yeonghwa 100nyeon* (Seoul: Hyeonamsa, 2001), p. 38.
30. Chōsen eiga bunka kenkyūsho, 'Chōsen eiga sanjūnenshi', *Eiga junpō*, 87, 1 July 1943, p. 16.
31. 'Umigwan', *Maeil sinbo*, 21 December 1912. For more information about Hayashida, see *Chōsen zaishū nachijin jitsugyōka jinmeijiten* (Keijō: Chōsen Jitsugyō Shimbunsha, 1913), p. 26 and *Zai-Chōsen naichijin shinshi meikanroku* (Keijō: Chōsen Kōronsha, 1917), p. 59.
32. *Maeil sinbo*, 8 May 1914.
33. *Maeil sinbo*, 2 February 1913 and 15 February 1913.

34. 'Naichi kinkyō tsūshin (News and Notes by Our Own Correspondents: Chōsen)', *The Kinema Record*, 32, 10 February 1916, p. 67.
35. *Chōsen Sōdokufu kanpō dai 247gō furoku*, 29 January 1913, p. 3.
36. For more discussion of this multiple function of theatres in rural areas in Joseon, see Lee Seung-hee, 'Gonggong mediaroseoui geukjanggwa Joseon minganjabonui munhwajeongchi', *Daedongmunhwa yeongu*, 69, March 2010, pp. 219–59.
37. Yim, p. 87.
38. Chōsen Ginkō Chōsafu, 'Shintōchi no ichinen', *Chōsen jijo, hachigatsu gejūnko*, 1920, p. 38.
39. Matsuda Jukkoku, *Saitō Makoto den: Niniroku jikende ansatsusareta teitoku no shinjitsu* (Tokyo: Genshū Shuppansha, 2008), pp. 187–92.
40. Saitō served as the governor general twice, from 1919 to 1927 and again from 1929 to 1931. He became the prime minister of Japan in 1932 and his administration lasted until 1934. Saitō was assassinated at his residence by the rebels during the 2.26 Incident (February 26 Incident) in 1936.
41. *Chōsen Sōtokufu shisei nenpō taishō 11 nen* (Keijō: Chōsen Sōtokufu, 1924), p. 10.
42. Chōsen Ginkō Chōsafu, 'Chōsen shōkai shisetsu', *Chōsen jijo, kugatsu jyōjūngō*, 1920, p. 12; Chōsen Sōtokufu Naimugyoku Shakaika, 'Chōsen Sōtokufu katsudō shashinhan gaikyō', *Chōsen shakai jigyō*, 6.7, July 1928, p. 53.
43. 'Jyōhō Iinkai setchi', *Chōsen*, December 1920, p. 136; 'Jyōhō Iinkai setchi oyobi jyōhō kakari,' *Chōsen*, January 1921, p. 148.
44. See Bae Byoung-wook, '1920nyeondae jeonban Joseon Chongdokbu seonjeon yeonghwa jejakgwa sangyeong', *Jibangsawa jibang munhwa*, 9.2, November 2006, pp. 183–239 and Kang Dong-jin, *Nihon no Chōsen shihai seisakushi kenkyū* (Tokyo: Tokyo Daigaku Shūppankai, 1981), pp. 26–8.
45. Though the Ministry of Education began to commission educational films from 1923, its own film unit was formed in 1927.
46. See Monbushō Shakai Kyōikukyoku, *Chūokanchōni okeru eiga riyō jyōkyō* (Tokyo: Monbushō, 1937).
47. Ibid., pp. 22–31, 40–6 and 47–56.
48. Ching, Leo T. S., *Becoming Japanese: Colonial Taiwan and the Politics of Identity Formation* (Berkeley CA: University of California Press, 2001), pp. 43–4.
49. See, for example, James Burn, *Cinema and Society in the British Empire 1895–1940* (London: Palgrave Macmillan, 2013), Lee Grieveson and Colin MacCabe (eds), *Empire and Film* (London: British Film Institute, 2011) and *Film and the End of Empire* (London: British Film Institute, 2011).
50. Rivers, Chérie, 'Cinema', in F. Abiola Irele and Biodun Jeyifo (eds), *The Oxford Encyclopedia of African Thought* (Volume 1) (London: Oxford University Press, 2010), pp. 232–3.
51. For more information about *Tour of Korea*, see Tanaka Jun'ichirō, *Nihon eiga hattatsushi I* (Tokyo: Chūkō Bunko, 1975), pp. 144–5.
52. *Maeil sinbo*, 17 May 1912.

53. See 'Daikyōjinkai no fuirumu', *Keijo nippō*, 8 October 1915, and 'Hwaldong hwamyeojungui gongjinhoe', *Maeil sinbo*, 8 October 1915.
54. For more information about the magic lantern shows in Korea held in the 1890s, see Brian Yecies and Ae-Gyung Shim, *Korea's Occupied Cinemas, 1893–1948* (London and New York: Routledge, 2011), pp. 20–6. For the earliest Korean records of magic lantern shows, see 'Hoegwan hwandeung', *Hwangseong sinmun*, 8 December 1899, and 'Ilyo hwandeung', *Hwangseong sinmun*, 22 December 1899.
55. 'Wisaeng hwandeung', *Hwangseong sinmun*, 17 November 1906, 'Wisaeng hwandeung', *Hwangseong sinmun*, 14 January 1907, 'Hwandeung gaehoe', *Daehan maeil sinbo*, 15 January 1907, and 'Ongga hwandeung', *Daehan maeil sinbo*, 30 January 1907.
56. 'Nongeob hwandeunghoe', *Hwangseong sinmun*, 8 December 1906.
57. See Shepard, Elizabeth, 'The Magic Lantern Slide in Entertainment and Education, 1860–1920', *History of Photography*, 11.2, April–June 1987, pp. 91–108.
58. 'Hwaldongsajingwa hwandeungeuro wisaengsasangui seonjeoneul handa', *Maeil sinbo*, 17 March 1920.
59. 'Wisaeng hwandeung gwijo', *Maeil sinbo*, 18 April 1920.
60. 'Dōchijini taisuru sōdoku shiji', *Chōsen Sōdokufu kanpō*, 2424, 8 September 1920, p. 95.
61. 'Munhwa hwandeung hoesa saegiguro chulbal', *Maeil sinbo*, 10 October 1942.
62. 'Shōgyō tōki: Chōsen Bunka Gentō Kabushiki Kaisha', *Chōsen Sōdokufu kanpō*, 4748, 27 November 1942, p. 6.
63. Tanaka Jun'ichirō, *Nihon kyōiku eiga hattatsushi* (Tokyo: Kakyūsha, 1979), pp. 29–30 and Yoshihara Junpei, *Nihon tanpen eizōshi* (Tokyo: Iwanami Shoten, 2011), pp. 4–5.
64. Tanaka, *Nihon kyōiku eiga hattatsushi*, p. 47.
65. Ruot, pp. 637–9.
66. Ibid., p. 639.
67. Hideaki Fujiki, 'Creation of the Audience: Cinema as Popular Recreation and Social Education in Modern Japan', in Daisuke Miyao (ed.), *The Oxford Handbook of Japanese Cinema* (Oxford and New York: Oxford University Press, 2014), pp. 79–97.
68. Fujiki, pp. 92–3.
69. *Joseon Wangjo silrok: Sunbu 14 gwon 16 nyeon*, 13 October 1923.
70. Kunii Izumi, 'Kyōiku katsudō shashikan no kyūsetsuo kanametosu', *Chōsen kōron*, 8.10, October 1920, pp. 73–5.
71. Okuyama Sennō, 'Katsudō shashinni taisuru ichikōsatsu', *Chōsen shakai jigyō*, 9.6, June 1931, p. 39.
72. Chōsen Sōtokufu Gakumukyoku Shakai Kyōikuka, *Chōsen shakai kyōka yoran* (Keijō: Sakazawa Shoten, 1937), p. 92.
73. Tanaka, *Nihon kyōiku eiga hattatsushi*, p. 41.
74. Ibid., p. 47.
75. Kang, pp. 27–8.
76. 'Jyōhō Iinkai setchi oyobi jyōhō kakari', p. 148.
77. *Chōsen Sōtokufu shisei nenpō taishō 11 nen*, p. 10.

Notes   241

78. Ibid., p. 19.
79. Chōsen gyōsei, p. 209.
80. In 1920, only 340,000 Koreans out of the total 17 million population were able to speak or understand Japanese. *Chōsen jijo, jyūnigatsu jūjyungō*, 1920, pp. 38–9.
81. Capiro, Mark, *Japanese Assimilation Policies in Colonial Korea, 1910–1945* (Seattle WA: University of Washington Press, 2009), p. 126.
82. 'Jyōhō Iinkai setchi', p. 136.
83. Tsumura Isamu, 'Bunka eiga no tenbō', *Chōsen*, 273, 1 February 1938, p. 144.
84. Chōsen gyōsei, pp. 208–14.
85. 'Naichi shōkai shashin', *Chōsen jijo, kugatsu jūjyungō*, 1920, p. 50.
86. Chōsen gyōsei, p. 141.
87. Chōsen Sōdokufu, *Chōsen Sōdokufu shisei nenpō showa gennen* (Keijo: Chōsen Insatsu Kabushikikaisha, 1928), p. 15.
88. 'Gunshū naichi shisatsu jyōkyōno katsudō shashin eisha', *Chōsen*, November 1920, pp. 167–70.
89. Chōsen gyōsei, p. 141.
90. Chōsen Sōtokufu Kanbō Bunshoka, *Chōsen Sōtokufu Kinema* (Keijō: Chōsen Insatsu Kabushiki Kaisha, 1937), p. 10.
91. JACAR *(Ajia rekishi shiryō senta)* Ref.B03041605100, *Chōsenjinni taisuru shisei kankei zakken/ippanno bu dainikan (1-5-3-15_1_002) (gaimushō gaikōshiryōkan)*
92. Ibid.
93. Tsumura, 'Bunka eiga no tenbō', p. 151.
94. For female attendees at the MPU film screenings, see Tsumura, 'Bunka eigano tenbō', p. 151 and 'Naichi shōkai shashin', *Chōsen jijo, kugatsu jūjyungō*, 1920, p. 50.
95. 'Gunshū naichi shisatsu jyōkyō no katsudō shashin eisha', p. 169.
96. *Tokyo hakurankai jimuhogokushō*, p. 273–4.
97. 'Joseon sajeongui naeji seonjeon sogae', *Joseon*, 74, November 1923, p. 74.
98. Tsumura, 'Bunka eiga no tenbō', p. 146.
99. *Chōsen Sōdokufu Kinema*, pp. 8–9.
100. *Chōsen Sōdokufu shisei nenpō showa gennen*, pp. 14–15.
101. Chosen gyōsei, p. 141.
102. Chōsen Kyōsankai, *Heiwakinen Tokyo hakurankai Chōsen kyōchanshakai jimuhōgoku* (Keijō: Chōsen Kyōsankai, 1922), p. 274.
103. Tsumura, 'Kyōkaeigawa hatashite yukitsutteneruka', *Chōsen shakai jigyō*, 4.7, July 1926, p. 24.
104. *Chōsen Sōtokufu Kinema*, p. 16.
105. See Chosen gyōsei, pp. 187–207 and Kang, pp. 70–86.
106. Capiro, p. 125.
107. JACAR(*Ajia rekishi shiryō senta*) Ref.B03040723700, *senden kankei zakken/ shokutaku oyobi hojokin shikyū sendenmono sonota sendenhi shishutsukankei— hompōjinno bu dainikan (1-3-1-35_1_1_002) (gaimushō gaikōshiryōkan)*
108. *Chōsen Sōdokufu shisei nenpō showa gennen*, p. 15.

109. Mitsunaga Shichō, 'Toradoshi umare suta kondate', *Chōsen kōron*, 154, January 1926, p. 124.
110. Tsumura Isamu, 'Shōwa 5nendo shakaika katsudō shashin sōmaguri', *Chōsen shakai jigyō*, 9.7, July 1931, p. 64.
111. Yamane Mikihito, 'Kyōiku eigakai', *Nihon eiga jigyō sōran shōwa 5 nenhan (1929–30)* (Tokyo: Kokusai Eiga Tsūshinsa, 1930), pp. 53–5.
112. Tsumura, 'Kyōkaeigawa hatashite yukitsutteneruka', p. 23.
113. Okuyama, p. 37.
114. 'Hakgyonaee yeongsagi sangseol: yeonghwaro gyoyuk', *Maeil sinbo*, 22 December 1927.
115. Kim Il-yeong, 'Yeonghwawa minjung', *Maeil sinbo*, 22 February 1925.
116. Tsumura, 'Kyōkaeigawa hatashite yukitsutteneruka', pp. 22-23.
117. Tsumura, 'Shōwa 5nendo shakaika katsudō shashin sōmaguri', p. 65.
118. *Chōsen Sōtokufu Kinema*, p. 1.
119. Ibid., p. 24.
120. Ibid., p. 23.
121. 'Katsudō shashinran no kaisetsu', *Chōsen shakai jigyō*, 9.7, July 1931, p. 64.
122. See my Chapter 4.
123. 'Chōsen Sōdokufurei dai 812gō, Katsudō shashin torishimari kisoku', *Chōsen Sōdokufu kanpō*, 2273, 7 August 1934, p. 49.
124. *Chōsen shakai kyōka yoran*, pp. 93–4.
125. Tsumura, 'Bunka eiga no tenbō', p. 142.
126. 'Yeonghwa tongje ganghwa', *Donga ilbo*, 16 October 1937.

Chapter 2

1. 'Na Un-gyu, Shin Il-seoneurobuteo Mun Ye-bong, Sim Yeongdeungui myeongue ireugikkajiui isibnyeonganui Joseon yeonghwa baldalsa', *Samchoelli*, 12.5, 1 May 1940, p. 228.
2. Hanguk Yesul Yeonguso (ed.), 'Lee Chang-geun', in *Lee Yeong-ilui Hanguk yeonghwareul wihan jeungeonrok: Yu Jang-san, Lee Gyeong-son, Lee Pil-wu, Lee Chang-geun pyeon* (Seoul: Sodo, 2003), p. 127.
3. Cheongryu-saeng, 'Joseon yeonghwagye mundab', *Joseon munye*, 1.1, 1929, p. 97. See also Sai, 'Yōranki no Chōsen eiga', *Kinema junpō*, 296, 21 May 1928, p. 64.
4. Maeda Muro, 'Chōsen eiga no genjyōtai', *Kinema junpō*, 358, 1 March 1930, p. 58.
5. Oka Shigematsu, 'Chōsenni okeru eiga no kenetsuni tsuite', *Chōsen*, 190, March 1931, p. 137.
6. Ibid., p. 137.
7. 'Na Un-gyu, Shin Il-seoneurobuteo . . .', p. 229.
8. Park Min-il, *Hanguk Arirang munhak yeongu* (Chuncheon: Gangwondaehakgyo Chulpanbu, 1990), p. 48.
9. Hanguk Yesul Yeonguso, *Lee Yeong-ilui Hanguk yeonghwasa ganguirok* (Seoul: Sodo, 2006), p. 31.

10. *Hankyoreh sinmun*, 8 February 2002.
11. Cho Hee-mun, 'Yeonghwa *Arirang*ui Jaepyeongga', in *Hanguk Yeongwhaui Jaengjeom 1* (Seoul: Jibmundang, 2002), pp. 204–5 (a reproduced version).
12. For detailed accounts of this debate, see Kim Ryeo-sil, *Tusahaneun jeguk tuyeonghaneun sikminji* (Seoul: Samin, 2006), pp. 88–90 and Kim Gab-ui, *Chunsa Na Un-gyu jeonjib* (Seoul: Jibmundang, 2001), p. 140.
13. See Rhee, Jooyeon, '*Arirang*, and the making of a national narrative in South and North Korea', *Journal of Japanese and Korean Cinema*, 1.1, 2009, pp. 27–43; Kim Ryeo-sil, pp. 88–118; Cho Hye-jung, 'Na Un-gyu sinhwaui jinjeongseong yeongu', *Yeonghwa gyoyuk yeongu*, 6, 2004, pp. 175–92.
14. See Lee Jeong-ha, 'Na Un-gyuui *Arirang* (1926)ui jaeguseong – *Arirang*ui hwalgeukjeok hyogwa hokeun hyogwaui saengsan', *Yeonghwa yeongu*, 26, 2005, pp. 265–90; Kim Yeong-chan, 'Na Un-gyu *Arirang*ui yeonghwajeok geundaeseong', *Hanguk munhak irongwa bipyeong*, 30, March 2006, pp. 177–99; Kim Sang-min, '*Arirang*gwa Hollywood', *SAI*, 14, 2013, pp. 265–96; and Yecies, Brian and Ae-Gyung Shim, *Korea's Occupied Cinemas, 1893–1948* (New York and London: Routledge, 2011), pp. 87–8.
15. *Hwangseong sinmun*'s editorial writing in 1901 reported, 'These days, indecent songs like so-called *Ryukjaegi* and *Arirang* are popular', and 'Men and women are singing them and dancing to their tunes regardless of their class background at parties and feasts.' ('Nonseol', *Hwangseong sinmun*, 13 November 1901).
16. *Donga ilbo*, 1 November 1924.
17. *Kenki dai 1547 gō*, 4 August 1909.
18. Lee Yong-shik, 'Mandeuleojin jeontong: ilje gangjeomgi gigan *Arirang*ui geundaehwa, minjokhwa, yuhaenghwa gwajeong', *Dongyang eumak*, 27, 2005, pp. 127–59.
19. Lee, 'Mandeuleojin jeontong', p. 129.
20. Park, p. 48.
21. Jin Hong-lian, 'Ilje gangjoemgie natanan *Arirang*ui hwaksangwa uimi byeoncheon', *Eumakgwa minjok*, 31, 2006, pp. 238–42.
22. See Cho and Rhee.
23. *Maeil sinbo*, 3 October 1926.
24. Lee Yeong-il, *Hanguk yeonghwa jeonsa* (Seoul: Sodo, 2004), p. 105.
25. Memmi, Albert, *The Colonizer and the Colonized* (London: Souvenir Press, 1974), p. 91.
26. See Lee Gyeong-son, 'Museong yeonghwa sidaeui jajeon', *Sindonga*, 63, December 1964, pp. 320–49.
27. *Jungoi ilbo*, 25 October 1929. Emphasis added.
28. Yun Gi-jeong, 'Joseon yeonghwaui jejak gyeonghyang (4)—Ilban jejakjae goham', *Jungoi ilbo*, 9 May 1930.
29. For the impact of radio and the music industry on Koreans' discovery of their own musical traditions, see Michael Robinson, 'Broadcasting, Cultural Hegemony, and Colonial Modernity', in Gi-Wook Shin and Michael Robinson (eds), *Colonial Modernity in Korea* (Boston MA: Harvard University Press, 2001), pp. 52–69.
30. Kim Gab-ui (ed.), *Chunsa Na Un-gyun jeonjib* (Seoul: Jibmundang, 2001), pp. 139–41.

31. The last theatrical screening recorded indicates that there was a commercial screening of *Arirang* at the Mangyeonggwan Theatre in the city of Daegu in 1952, right in the middle of the Korean War, during which the film is believed to have been lost. Kim Gab-ui, p. 139.
32. An Dong-su, 'Yeonghwa sugam', *Yeonghwa yeongeuk*, 1.1, 1939, p. 45.
33. 'Baegman dokjareul gajin daeyesulgadeul', *Samcheolli*, 9.1, January 1937, p. 138 and Lee, *Hanguk yeonghwa jeonsa*, p. 110.
34. Lee, Yeong-il, *The History of Korean Cinema*, Richard Lynn Greever (trans.) (Seoul: Motion Picture Promotion Corp., 1988), pp. 25–7.
35. Choi Chang-ho and Hong Gang-seong, *Na un-gyuwa sunangi yeonghwa* (Pyongyang: Pyongyang Chulpansa, 2001), p. 89.
36. For a further discussion of *Arirang* and its critical realism, see Kim Ryong-bong, *Joseon Yeonghwasa* (Pyongyang: Sahoe Gwahak Chulpansa, 2013), pp. 16–30.
37. Go Seung-han, 'Sinyeonghwa *Arirang*eul bogo', *Maeil sinbo*, 10 October 1926.
38. *Donga ilbo*, 19 November 1925.
39. Oh Yeong-jin, 'Eiga to Chōsentaishū', *Eiga hyōron*, 3.11, November 1943, p. 38.
40. The only exception to this trend was Joseon Kinema's *A Plaintive Melody of the Sea* (1924), the first Joseon film whose story was original, written by Takasa Kanjo, a Japanese settler film-maker. Though the film was a box-office success, it was criticised as an imitation of sentimentalist Japanese romance literature because the film's tragic love story of a young couple, which ends with their double suicide (J: *shinjū*), looked similar to a common theme found in Japanese *joruri* (puppet theatre) and modern novels. (Lee Gu-yeong, 'Joseon yeonghwaui insang', *Maeil sinbo*, 1 January 1925) In the *Kinema junpō* review, published upon the film's release in Japan, an unforgiving Japanese film reviewer showed no mercy by harshly critiquing the film's unoriginality, 'The plot sounds like a masterpiece that portrays a sturdy fate, but in its execution, it turns out to be pretty messy, weaving familiar elements taken from here and there into it. Everything is below average, and I don't even want to review it.' (Sato Yukio, 'Umi no hikyōku', *Kinema junpō*, 181, 1 January 1925, p. 37) In addition, the film's story takes place against the exotic landscape of the island of Jeju to which it was difficult for most Koreans to travel at the time, so it is hard to imagine Korean filmgoers felt a strong connection to the screened images.
41. Seung Il, 'Radio, Sports, Cinema', *Byeolgeongon*, 2, December 1926, p. 109.
42. See An, pp. 44–5.
43. Oh, pp. 39–40.
44. For further discussions of the film novel, see Jina E. Kim, 'Intermedial Aesthetics: Still Images, Moving Words, and Written Sounds in Early Twentieth-Century Korean Cinematic Novels (*Yeonghwa Soseol*)', *The Review of Korean Studies*, 16.2, December 2013, pp. 45–79 and Kim Ryo-sil, pp. 96–109.
45. 'Nuntteugo motbol *Biryeonui gok*', *Maeil sinbo*, 3 December 1924.
46. 'Jamyeongjong', *Joseon ilbo*, 28 November 1924.
47. Lee Gu-yeong, 'Joseon yeonghwaui insang', *Maeil sinbo*, 1 January 1925.

48. PN-saeng, 'Joseon yeonghwareul sahoejeokeuro gamsihaja', *Joseon ilbo*, 17 November 1927.
49. Ikeda Kunio, 'Chōsenni okeru eiga kenetsu no tokyushūsei', *Kokusai eiga shimbun*, 231, October 1938, p. 3.
50. Sim Hun, 'Uri minjungeun eotteohan yeonghwareul yoguhaneungareul nonhayeo mannyeonseolgunege', *Jungoi ilbo*, 22 July 1928.
51. Cheongryu-saeng, p. 98. The word in capital letters indicates the author's own use of an English word.
52. Yun Gi-jeong, 'Joseon yeonghwaneun jinjeonhaneunga (2)', *Jungoi ilbo*, 21 September 1930.
53. Poyeong, 'Sinyeonghwa *Arirang*eul bogo', *Maeil sinbo*, 10 October 1926.
54. The first Joseon film that employed multiple lighting and fill light was *Bell Sound*. The cinematographer Lee Pil-wu's use of these techniques was deemed 'epoch-making'. ('Geumgang Kinemajak Jongsori – sisapyeong', *Donga ilbo*, 3 April 1929) Also See Yang Ryu-seong, '*Jongsori* insang', *Jungoi ilbo*, 3 April 1929 and A-saeng, 'Jongsorie natanan baeuui yeongiwa chwalyeong gigyo insanggi', *Joseon ilbo*, 4 April 1929.
55. Namgung Ok, '*Arirang* hupyeoneul bogo (1)', *Jungoi ilbo*, 18 February 1930.
56. Seo Gwang-je, '*Arirang* hupyeon-yeonghwa bipyeong', *Joseon ilbo*, 21 February 1930.
57. Seo Gwang-je, 'Wonbanggak jakpum *Cheolindo* bipan (4)', *Jungoi ilbo*, 30 April 1930.
58. Indol, '*Cheolindo*reul bogo', *Donga ilbo*, 16 April 1930.
59. Ibid.
60. Seo Gwang-je, 'Wonbanggak jakpum *Cheolindo* bipan (3)', *Jungoi ilbo*, 28 April 1930.
61. Mun Il, *Cheolindo* (Gyeongseong: Pakmuseogwan, 1931), p. gyeyo.
62. Na Un-gyu, '*Cheolindo* pyeongeul ilgo – jejakjaroseo ileon', *Jungoi ilbo*, 2–4 May 1930.
63. Na Un-gyu, '*Arirang*eul mandeulttae', *Joseon yeongwha*, November 1936, p. 47. Words in capital letters indicate Na's own uses of English words.
64. 'Na Un-gyu jeilhoe *Jal itgeora* 5il Danseongsa sangyeong', *Joseon ilbo*, 5 November 1927.
65. Jeong, Kelly, *Crisis of Gender and the Nation in Korean Literature and Cinema* (Lanham MD: Lexington Books, 2011), p. 22.
66. See Na, '*Arirang*eul mandeulttae', pp. 46–7
67. Ikeda, p. 3.
68. 'Gak sangseolgwan sinpuro', *Donga ilbo*, 14 January 1927.
69. 'Lee Pil-wu', pp. 234–6.
70. Sim Hun, 'Joseon yeonghwain eonpared', *Donggwang*, 23, July 1931, p. 61.
71. Ibid., p. 61.
72. Sim Hun, 'Mobanguel hajimalgo sasiljueuiro nagara (6)', *Joseon ilbo*, 28 January 1931.
73. Seo Gwang-je, '1930nyeon Joseon yeonghwagyeui hyeondangye', *Jungoi ilbo*, 25 March 1930. Also see Park Wan-sik, 'Nokseong Kinemasa yeonghwa *Badawa ssauneun saramdeul*', *Joseon ilbo*, 16 and 18 November 1930.
74. Sojebu, 'Haehak, Pungja, Chungyedaecheonggyeol', *Byeolgeongon*, 28, May 1930, p. 68.

75. A. W.-shōsei, 'Chōsenjin kawa no eigani tsuite', *Chōsen oyobi Manshū*, 252, November 1928, pp. 64–8.
76. See Na Un-gyu, 'Joseon yeonghwainui tujiwa gyeongje', *Joseon jungang ilbo*, 1 January 1936.
77. Na Un-gyu, 'Gamdok euroseo mandeulgo sipeun yeonghwa', *Joseon ilbo*, 7 July 1935 and Na, 'Yeonghwa sigam', *Samcheolli*, 9.1, 1 January 1937, pp. 182–6.
78. Lee, *Hanguk yeongwasa ganguirok*, p. 128.
79. Kim Tae-jin, 'Yeonghwagyeui punguna go Na Un-gyureul nonham (sang)', *Donga Ilbo*, 8 August 1939.
80. Seo Gwang-je, 'Go Na Un-gyuui sangaewa yesul', *Jogwang*, 3.10, October 1937, pp. 310–17.
81. 'Ariran no uta', *Kinema junpō*, 465, 21 March 1933, p. 75.
82. Tajima Yasuhide, 'Ariran kō', *Bunkyō no Chōsen*, 95, July 1933, p. 130.
83. Shirotori Seigo, 'Yanagi', *Samcheonlli*, 5.10, 1 October 1933, pp. 118–19. Translated with the help of Glynne Walley.
84. Atkins, E. Taylor, 'The Dual Career of "Arirang": The Korean Resistance Anthem That Became a Japanese Pop Hit', *The Journal of Asian Studies*, 66.3, August, 2007, p. 663.
85. See the ad for *Arirang*, *Kinema junpō*, 248, 11 December 1926.
86. Kim Hae, '1934nyeon Joseon yeonghwa 2 pyeon', *Yeonghwa sidae*, 5.1, January 1935, p. 59.
87. Na Ung, 'Chōsen eiga no genshō', *Eiga hyōron*, 19.1, January 1937, p. 102.
88. 'Myeong baewu, myeong gamdoki moyeo Joseon yeonghwareul malham', *Samcheolli*, 8.11, 1 November 1936, pp. 82–99.
89. I use the film's original title for the rest of the chapter for consistency.
90. Ōta Tsuneya, 'Chōsen eiga no tenbō', *Kinema junpō*, 644, 1 May 1938, p. 4.
91. 'Zadankai hōkoku: Chōsen eiga no genjyōo ireru', *Nihon eiga*, 1 August 1939, p. 120.
92. Hazumi Tsuneo, 'Joseon yeonghwa jabgam', *Samcheolli*, 10.5, 1 May 1938, p. 185.
93. *Bokjimanli* was co-produced by Goryeo Yeonghwa Hyeobhoe and Manchukuo Film Association.
94. Ōta, p. 4.
95. 'Joseon munhwa geub sanyeongbakramhoe, yeonghwa pyeon', *Samcheolli*, 12.5, 1 May 1940, p. 231.
96. Yim Hwa, 'Joseon yeonghwa baldal sosa', *Samcheolli*, 13.6, 1 June 1941, p. 204.
97. Namgung Ok, 'Joseon yeonghwaui choigobong *Nageune*reul bogo', 22 April 1937.
98. Yim, p. 204.
99. Seo Gwang-je, 'Lee Gyu-hwanjak *Nageune* (sang)', *Joseon ilbo*, 24 April 1937.
100. For a detailed account of the *Nageune* production, see Hanguk Yesul Yeonguso (ed.), 'Lee Gyu-hwan', in *Lee Yeong-ilui Hanguk yeonghwasareul wihan jeungeonrok: Seong Dong-ho, Lee Gyu-hwan, Choi Geum-dong pyeon* (Seoul: Sodo, 2003), pp. 167–77.
101. Ōta, p. 4.
102. 'Zadankai hōgoku', p. 121.

103. Murakami Tadahisa, 'Gunyō ressha', Kinema junpō, 654, 11 August 1938, p. 78.
104. Ishita Yoshinori, 'Tabiji', Nihon eiga, 1 July 1937, p. 104.
105. Shigeno Tatsuhiko, 'Hangang', Kinema junpō, 689, 11 August 1939, p. 81.
106. Ishita, p. 103.
107. Iida Shimbi, 'Hangang', Kinema junpō, 646, 21 May 1938, p. 46.
108. Ibid, p. 46.
109. Byeolranggi, 'Hangang sisareul bogo', Joseon ilbo, 3 May 1938.
110. Iijima Tadashi, 'Chōsen eigaron', Shin eiga, 8.10, October 1938, p. 40.
111. 'Tabiji', Asahi Graph, 28.20, 12 May 1937, p. 23.
112. 'Lee Gyu-hwan', pp. 170–1.
113. Shigeno Tatsuhiko, 'Gyōka', Kinema junpō, 656, 1 September 1938, p. 75. The existing prints of the film seem to be the Japanese-release version, judging from the fact that the film is subtitled in Japanese and includes Japanese credit sequences. The film is available to view at the Korean Movie Database website of Korean Film Archive. (http://www.kmdb.or.kr/)
114. Shigeno, p. 75.
115. Okada Jun'ichi, 'Eiga kenetsu no gaikyō', Keimu ibō, 360, April 1936, p. 60.
116. Kim Tae-jin, 'Eulmyonyeon Joseon yeonghwa chonggwan', Yeonghwa yeongeuk, 2, 1940, p. 32.
117. 'Zadankai hōgoku', p. 127.
118. Mizui Reiko, 'Chōsen eigaseisakuo kaheri mite', Shin eiga, 2.11, December 1942, p. 91.
119. Hazumi Tsuneo, 'Joseon yeonghwawa lyricism', Joseon ilbo, 1 November 1939.
120. Hazumi Tsuneo, 'Chōsen eigao kataru', Modan Nihon, 10.12, October 1939, p. 250. Reprinted by Eomunhaksa (Seoul, 2007).
121. Hames, Peter, Czech and Slovak Cinema: Theme and Tradition (Edinburgh: Edinburgh University Press, 2009), p. 113.
122. Iida, p. 46.
123. 'Young Love', Variety, 121, 11 March 1936, p. 15. Young Love was the title for the US release.
124. Innes, Abby, Czechoslovakia – the Short Goodbye (New Haven CT: Yale University Press, 2001), p. 190.
125. 'Geumhu jumok doineungeokeun Joseonsaek balhui yeobu', Donga ilbo, 21 January 1938.
126. Lee Hyo-suk, 'Munsaga malhaneun yeonghwa', Samcheolli, 10.8, 1 August 1938, p. 244.
127. 'Lee Tae-jun, Park Gi-chae yangsidaedam (ha)', Donga ilbo, 14 December 1938.
128. An, p. 45.
129. Kim Tae-jin, 'Eulmyonyeon Joseon yeonghwa chonggwan', pp. 30–1.
130. Ju Yeong-seob, 'Chōsen eiga no tenbō', Kinema junpō, 659, 1 October 1938, pp. 131-32.
131. Murayama Tomoyoshi, 'Chōsentono kōryū', Asahi shimbun, 2 September 1938.
132. bell hooks, Black Looks: Race and Representation (Boston MA: South End Press, 1992), p. 26.
133. Iida, p. 46.

134. Mizui, 'Chōsen eigaseisakuo kaheri mite', pp. 90–4.
135. Ibid., p. 91.
136. Mizui Reiko, 'Kironi tatsu Chōsen eiga', *Kokusai eiga Shimbun*, 252, August 1939, p. 5.
137. Mizui Reiko, 'Shochiku eigao meguru shomondai', *Chōsen oyobi Manshū*, 336, November 1935, pp. 79–81.
138. Donomura Masaru, 'Sikminjigi Joseon daejungmunhwawa ilbonin', *Ilbon gonggan*, 2, November 2007, p. 110.
139. Uchida Kimiyo, 'Tokushū: Chōsen eiga no genjyōkyō', *Eiga hyōron*, 1.7, July 1941, p. 44.
140. Ōkuro Toyoshi, 'Chosen eigakō (1)', *Eiga hyōron*, 1.9, September 1941, pp. 74–7.

Chapter 3

1. Namiki Satoshi, 'Keijō tsūshin', *Kinema junpō*, 440, 1 July 1932, p. 96.
2. My account of the scandal surrounding the distribution rights to Shochiku films is reconstructed from the following materials: Usami Seiichirō, 'Shochiku eiga katagawari mondai no shinjyū', *Chōsen oyobi Manshū*, 320, July 1934, p. 81; Yamaguchi Torao, 'Chihō tsūshin', *Kokusai eiga shimbun*, 130, July 1934, p. 34; 'Shochiku mondai kaigetsusu Tōao būkirikan toshi', *Keijō nippō*, 1 July 1934; and Mizui Reiko, 'Shochiku eigao meguru shomondai', *Chōsen oyobi Manshū*, 336, November 1935, pp. 79–81.
3. Commonly, distribution rights to Japanese films in Joseon were divided into two regions: Seoul and the rest of Joseon. The distribution rights to Shochiku films, for instance, were shared jointly by Taishōkan, which distributed Shochiku films in Seoul, and Manshō Minejiro, the owner of Zōjyōkan in Busan, who distributed the studio's films outside of Seoul. See Usami, p. 81.
4. Out of the forty-five talkies produced in 1932, thirty were Shochiku's, including *Chushingura*. Anderson, Joseph and Donald Richie, *The Japanese Film: Art and Industry* (Princeton NJ: Princeton University Press, 1982), p. 77. The Tsuchihashi system was named after Tsuchihashi Takeo, its chief inventor. Tsuchihashi worked for Shochiku's Kamata Studio and participated in about forty Shochiku films from 1931 to 1938 as a sound recorder, including Japan's first talkie, *My Neighbor's Wife and Mine* (*Madam to Nyobo*, 1931) directed by Gosho Heinosuke. Lee Pil-wu, a pioneering Korean film-maker/film entrepreneur, was invited to participate in developing the Tsuchihashi system during his stay in Japan. As one of three inventors of the Tsuchihashi system, along with Tsuchihashi Takeo and Nakajima Kyōshi, Lee acquired patent rights for it, though the rights were limited to use in Joseon. He later worked with his brother Lee Myeong-wu to create their own P.K.R. system (1933), a sound-on-film technology. During a production tour of Japan, Joseph von Sternberg was impressed by the P.K.R. system when he briefly stopped in Joseon and watched *The Tale of Janghwa and Hongryeon* (1936), the second talkie to use the Lee brothers' sound system. See Hanguk Yesul Yeonguso (ed.), 'Lee Pil-wu', in *Lee Yeong-ilui*

Hanguk yeonghwareul wihan jeungeonrok: Yu Jang-san, Lee Gyeong-son, Lee Pil-wu, Lee Chang-geun pyeon (Seoul: Sodo, 2003), pp. 271–2.

5. My account of Tokunaga's life and career is collectively drawn from the following materials: Okamura Shihō, *Katsudō shashin meikan: zenpen* (Tokyo: Katsudō Shimbunsha, 1922), p. 71 [reproduced in *Saisentan minshū goraku eiga bunken shiryōshū 5* (Tokyo: Yumani Shobō, 2006), p. 95]; Keijō Nippōsha, *Dai-Keijō kōshokusha meikan* (Keijō: Keijō Nippōsha, 1936), pp. 83–4; and the journals and magazines cited in the following notes.
6. Okamura, p. 71.
7. Wakayagi Rokurō, 'Engeirakuya hanashi – shibai, katsudō, yose', *Chōsen oyobi Manshū*, 243, February 1928, p. 88 and A. W.-shōsei, 'Chōsenjin kawa no eigani tsuite', *Chōsen oyobi Manshū*, 252, November 1928, pp. 64–8.
8. A. W.-shōsei, pp. 64–8.
9. See Tsumura Isamu, 'Showa 5nendo shakaika katsudō shashin sōmaguri', *Chōsen shakai jigyō*, 9.7, July 1931, p. 67 and 'Chōsen Sōtokufu kanbō bunshoka', *Chōsen Sōtokufu Kinema* (Keijō: Chōsen Insatsu Kabushikigaisha, 1937), pp. 24–6.
10. *Dai-Keijō kōshokusha meikan*, pp. 83–4.
11. Takikawa Kiyohiro, 'Chihō tsūshin', *Kinema junpō*, 375, 21 August 1930, pp. 71–2.
12. Yamaguchi Torao, 'Keijō', *Kokusai eiga shimbun*, 118, January 1934, p. 23.
13. Yamaguchi Torao, 'Keijō', *Kokusai eiga shimbun*, 131, August 1934, pp. 16–17.
14. Namiki, p. 96.
15. Yamaguchi Torao, 'Keijō', *Kokusai eiga shimbun*, 122, March 1934, p. 27.
16. 'Keijō', *Kokusai eiga shimbun*, 191, February 1937, p. 34.
17. See Brian Yecies and Ae-Gyung Shim, *Korea's Occupied Cinemas, 1893–1948* (New York and London: Routledge, 2011), pp. 41–2.
18. Jun, Uchida, *Brokers of Empire: Japanese Settler Colonialism in Korea 1876–1945* (Cambridge MA: Harvard University Press, 2011). Especially Chapter 2.
19. Chung Chong-hwa, 'Sikminji Joseon yeonghwaui ilbonindeul', in Hanguk Yeongsang Jaryowon Hanguk Yeonghwasa Yeonguso (ed.), *Ilboneo jabjiro bon Joseon yeonghwa 2* (Seoul: Korean Film Archive, 2011), pp. 346–7.
20. Kim Seung-gu, 'Tajaui siseone bichin sikminji Joseon yeonghwagye', *Hangukhak yeongu*, 48, 30 March 2014, pp. 71–3.
21. Sim Hun, 'Joseon yeonghwa chonggwan (1)', *Joseon ilbo*, 1 January 1929, and Son Wi-bin, 'Joseon Yeonghwasa-sibnyeonganui byeoncheonsa', *Joseon ilbo*, 28 May 1933.
22. Ichikawa Sai, *Ajia eiga no sōzō oyobi kensetsu* (Tokyo: Tairiku Bunka Kyōkai, 1941), p. 99.
23. See Hong Seon-yeong, '1910nyeon jeonhu Seouleseo hwaldonghan ilbonin yeongeukgwa geukjang', *Ilbon hakbo*, 56.2, September 2003, pp. 243–52 and Kim Sung-su, 'Keijō shimbuno toshite miru nipponjin kyoryūchi no engeki-Sakurazao chūshinni', *Engeki kenkyū senta kiyō*, 2, 2004, pp. 207–11.
24. Hong, p. 252.

25. Edokko, 'Keijō katsudō shashinkai no naimaku', *Chōsen oyobi Manshū*, 103, February 1916, p. 122.
26. 'Katsudō nyūjōryō nimangosen yen', *Busan (Fuzan) nippō*, 18 February 1917.
27. Hong, p. 247.
28. 'Ōgekijō no kensetsuhō', *Keijō shimbun*, 5 January 1909.
29. Nitta Ryujiro, 'Eigaya geki no setsuhikara mita Keijō', *Chōsen oyobi Manshū*, 333, August 1935, pp. 55–6.
30. Kitamura Kachō, 'Tokusha rondan', *Chōsen kōron*, 18, September 1914, pp. 91–2.
31. Ibid., p. 92.
32. Hanamura Shinjiro, 'Chōsen no naniwabushitō katsudō shashin kai', *Chōsen kōron*, 3.3, March 1915, pp. 95–7.
33. See Wakayagi, p. 88.
34. *Zai-Chōsen naichijin shinshi meikanroku* (Keijō: Chōsen Kōronsha, 1917), p. 60 and *Chōsen zaishū nachijin jitsugyōka jinmeijiten dai ichi hen* (Keijō: Chōsen Jitsugyō Shimbunsha, 1913), p. 269.
35. There is conflicting information about his role at Koganekan. He is generally known as the owner of the theatre but I follow the *meikan* documents that record him as the manager.
36. Wakayagi, pp. 86–7 and Tsukuda Jiro, 'Kinemakyō jidaika', *Chōsen kōron*, 16.3, March 1928, pp. 19–20.
37. See Shirogin Bakufu, 'Eigamachi sanpō', *Chōsen kōron*, 16.4, April 1928, pp. 7–10.
38. 'Sakurai-cho', *Keijōfu machi naichijinbutsu to jigyō annai* (Keijō: Keijō Nippō, 1921), p. 4.
39. Ibid., p. 4.
40. Ibid., p. 4.
41. See the Nitta Shōten ad, *Keijō nippō*, 10 March 1925.
42. *Zai-Chōsen naichijin shinshi meikanroku*, p. 71.
43. Okamura, p. 54.
44. For a more detailed account of the Nitta family's film business in Joseon, see Sasagawa Keiko, 'Keijōni okeru Teikoku Kinema engei no kōgyō', *Kansai toshi isan kenkyū*, 3, March 2013, pp. 19–31.
45. Ino Kenji, *Kōgyōkai no kaoyaku* (Tokyo: Sakuma Shobō, 2004), pp. 475–6.
46. See Sim Hun, 'Joseon yeonghwain eonpared', *Donggwang*, 23, July 1931, p. 61.
47. Kim Ryeo-sil, *Tasahaneun jeguk, tuyeonghaneun sikminji* (Seoul: Samin, 2006), p. 136.
48. *Donga ilbo*, 16 September 1923.
49. *Donga ilbo*, 18 August 1925.
50. Based in Busan, Sakuraba Fujio's Sakuraba Shōkai distributed Paramount Pictures and Makino films for more than a dozen movie theatres in Joseon and Manchuria and directly managed four theatres in Joseon. After working as a manager for a real estate company for a few years, Sakuraba left his job to run Saiwaikan in Busan. While running his film distribution business and movie theatres, Sakuraba engaged in a number of businesses, including soy sauce manufacturing, newspaper publication, electricity distribution, and an insurance agency, becoming one of the wealthiest businessmen in Busan. See Kim Seung and Yang Mi-suk (eds), *Sinpyeon Busan daegwan* (Seoul: Seonin,

2010), pp. 590–3 and Ueda Koichirō, *Busan [Fuzan] no shōkōkai annai* (Busan: Busan Shōkōkaigisho, 1935), pp. 38–9.

51. For Toyama Mitsuru's career in Joseon, see Tanaka Norihiro, 'Zai-Chōsen Nihonjin no eiga seisaku kenkyū', *Mediashi kenkyū*, 17, 2004, pp. 122–42 and Dong Hoon Kim, 'Segregated Cinemas and Intertwined Histories', *Journal of Japanese and Korean Cinema*, 1.1, 2009, p. 13.
52. See Kokusai Eiga Tsūshinsha (ed.), *Zengoku kōgyō torishmari kitei oyobi kōgyōzei ichiran* (Tokyo: Kokusai Eiga Tsūshinsha, 1927), pp. 517–19.
53. The name of the theatre Keiryūkan (*Kei* came from Keijō [Seoul] and *Ryū* from Ryūzan [Yongsan]) demonstrates its location on the border between the two areas.
54. Okamura, p. 14.
55. Momoyama Long, 'Arubenshi shibō no seinenni', *Chōsen kōron*, 137, August 1924, p. 106.
56. See, for example, Matsumoto Teruka, 'Keijō kinema kai', *Chōsen kōron*, 102, September 1921, p. 135, Matsumoto Teruka, 'Eigakai tsūshin', *Chōsen kōron*, 111, June, 1922, p. 101, 'Fuirumu fan no tsubuyaki', *Chōsen kōron*, 117, December 1922, p. 109, 'Fuirumu fan no ryōiki', *Chōsen kōron*, 123, June 1923, p. 128, and Mr Y., 'Fan no koe', *Keijō nippō*, 5 June 1925.
57. Miyagawa Hayanosuke is mistakenly known in Korea as Miyagawa Sōnosuke.
58. An Jong-hwa, *Hanguk yeonghwa cheumyeon bisa* (Seoul: Hyeondai mihaksa, 1998), pp. 37–41. New information about him surfaced recently and, according to this source, Miyagawa, a Totori Prefecture native (born in 1884) started his film career when he joined M. Pathé, one of the film companies merged into Nikkatsu studio, in 1908. He moved to Tenkatsu's film photography team in 1913 and then migrated to Joseon in May 1921 because of the economic recess. This information, provided by a self-claimed grandchild of Miyagawa, needs further verification. Nagasawa Masaharu, 'Chōsen eiga reimeiki no satsueigishi – Miyagawa Heinosuke no koto, nado', *Kengōno yohaku* (Seikyusha, 4 March 2014), last accessed 30 August 2015, http://www.seikyusha.co.jp/wp/rennsai/yohakuni/blank125.html
59. 'Yeonghwa danggukja hyeobui', *Donga ilbo*, 20 July 1926.
60. 'Yeonghwaro bakeun Jeonjuui bongchuk', *Maeil sinbo*, 21 November 1928.
61. 'Jinhae jonanja wirogeum (3)', *Maeil sinbo*, 19 March 1930.
62. Other notable Japanese DPs include Kato Kyōhei (*A Bird in the Cage* [1926], *Golden Fish* [1927], *Wild Rat* [1927], and *Hornless Bull* [1927]) and Ōta Hitoshi (*Song of the Unforgettable* [1927], and *A Plaintive Song of Crimson Love* [1927]).
63. 'Dongtteuneun Joseon yeonghwagye (7)', *Maeil sinbo*, 27 October 1927.
64. Sim, p. 59.
65. Lee Pil-wu, 'Joseon chwalyeong gisaui gosim', *Daejung yeonghwa*, 4, July 1930, pp. 18–19.
66. *Hwangseong sinmun*, 28 February 1910.
67. In 1927, of the sixty-eight projectionists, twenty-two were Japanese. *Katsudō shashin fuirumu keiretsu gaiyō* (Keijō: Chōsen Sōtokufu Keimukyoku, 1931), pp. 148–9.

68. See Sakai Masao, 'Keijō no katsudō shashinkai', *Chōsen oyobi Manshū*, 170, January 1922, pp. 118–20.
69. See 'Lee Pil-wu', *Lee Yeong-ilui Hanguk yeonghwareul wihan jeungeonrok*, pp. 230–1.
70. Koszarski, Richard, *An Evening's Entertainment: The Age of the Silent Feature Picture, 1915–1928* (Berkeley CA and Los Angeles CA: University of California Press, 1994), p. 166.
71. See 'Kinemakai ōrai', *Chōsen kōron*, 131, February 1924, p. 116, Kurozukin-sei, 'Kinemakai ōrai', *Chōsen kōron*, 132, March 1924, p. 46, and 'Fuirumu fan no sakebi', *Chōsen kōron*, 137, August 1924, p. 107.
72. The theatre's business was further restricted by its neighbouring business entities which submitted a petition to the authorities proposing a restriction on the number of film screenings at the theatre. Fearing a potential fire at the cinema, a common problem for movie theatres at the time, shops and banks petitioned that a movie theatre should not be open in one of the busiest streets in Seoul. In the end, the authorities allowed the theatre to open for only two weeks a month. See Edokko, 'Keijō katsudō shashinkai no naimaku', *Chōsen oyobi Manshū*, 103, February 1916, pp. 122–4.
73. Edokko, p. 122.
74. Matsumoto, 'Keijō kinemakai', p. 136.
75. Ishimaki Yoshio, *Ōbei oyobi Nihon no eigashi* (Osaka: Pratonsha, 1925), p. 380.
76. 'Kyōmishinshin zen – Chōsen eigakai jinbutsu sōmaguri', *Chōsen kōron*, 139, October 1924, p. 106.
77. *Katsudō shashin fuirumu keiretsu gaiyō*, p. 44.
78. See Tomita Mika (ed.), *Senzenki eiga fan zasshi shūsei dai ichi ki Makino 1–13* (Tokyo: Yumani Shobō, 2014).
79. 'Keijō tsūshin', *Kinema junpō*, 96, 21 March 1932, p. 96.
80. Mizui Reiko, 'Chōsen jyōsei to eiga', *Shin eiga*, May 1942, p. 82.
81. Toyoichi, 'Busan tsūsin', *Kinema junpō*, 246, 21 November 1926, p. 66.
82. 'Chōsen Incheon tsūsin', *Kinema junpō*, 203, 21 August 1925, p. 52.
83. *Katsudō shashin fuirumu keiretsu gaiyō*, pp. 144–5.
84. Sawada Taketo, 'Keijō eigakai zasshin', *Kinema junpō*, 265, 21 June 1927, p. 74.
85. *Katsudō shashin fuirumu keiretsu gaiyō*, pp. 145–7.
86. Yoshio-sei, 'Eiga shunjū', *Chōsen kōron*, 15.9, September 1927, p. 104.
87. Kim Gyeong-il, *Nodong Undong*, The History of Korean Independence Movement Online (https://search.i815.or.kr/Degae/DegaeView.jsp?nid=927), last accessed 30 March 2015.
88. *Katsudō shashin fuirumu keiretsu gaiyō*, pp. 147–8.
89. 'Keijō no saimatsu fūkeio sagasu', *Chōsen oyobi Manshū*, 361, December 1937, p. 82.
90. Wi Gyeong-hae, 'Sikminji gaehangdosi geukjangui jangsoseong – Gunsaneul jungsimeuro', *Daedong munhwa yeongu*, 72, 2010, pp. 37–77.
91. 'Kukusai eiga shimbuno tsūjite chihōkan keieisha no kyōshin', *Kokusai eiga shimbun*, 62, September 1931, p. 31.
92. *Donga ilbo*, 4 June 1927.

93. 'Mansegwan ibjang singyu', *Maeil sinbo*, 30 November 1918.
94. 'Senjin to Nihongo,' *Chōsen jijo, jyūnigatsu jūjyungō*, 1920, pp. 38–9.
95. Takasaki Soji, *Sikminji Joseonui Ilbonildeul (Shokuminchi Chōsen no Nihonjin)*, Lee Kyu-su (trans.) (Seoul: Yeoksa Bipyeongsa, 2006), pp. 39–54.
96. 'Sōdokufu chihōkan kansei', *Chōsen Sōdokufu kanpō*, 28, 30 September 1910, pp. 125–6.
97. *Chōsen Sōdokufu tōkei nenkan* (Keijō: Chōsen Sōdokufu, 1928), pp. 24–5.
98. *Maeil sinbo*, 6 May 1917.
99. See Rōkankō, 'Fuirumu fan no ryōiki', *Chōsen kōron*, 119, February 1923, p. 108, and ABC, 'Fuirumu fan no ryōiki', *Chōsen kōron*, 120, March 1923, p. 116.
100. Uta Neko, 'Okite kudasai, Chōsen no hanashio', *Kinema junpō*, 345, 11 October 1929, p. 157.
101. 'Kinemakai ōrai', *Chōsen kōron*, 138, September 1924, p. 83.
102. Matsumoto Teruka, 'Eiga shunjū (1)', *Chōsen kōron*, 157, April 1926, p. 88.
103. Maeda Muro, 'Chōsen eiga no genjyōtai', *Kinema junpō*, 358, 1 March 1931, p. 57. Also see 'Moukaruwazu no Chōsen kinema jyōsetsukan', *Chōsen oyobi Manshū*, 232, March 1927, p. 95.
104. Yamazaki Yukihiko, 'Chōsen eigakai no genzaito shōrai', *Chōsen kōron*, 283, October 1936, p. 73.
105. Maeda, p. 57.
106. Ikeda Kunio, 'Chōsenni okeru eiga kenetsu no tokyushūsei', *Kokusai eiga shimbun*, 231, October 1938, p. 3.
107. Muraoka, 'Eiga to mandan – Keiretsu shunin Oka no yokogao', *Chōsen oyobi Manshū*, 304, March 1933, p. 101.
108. See 'Kinemakai ōrai', *Chōsen kōron*, 138, September 1924, p. 83.
109. 'Fuirumu kenetsuyori mita Chōsen eigakai no kinkyō', *Chōsen kōron*, 244, July 1933, p. 109.
110. Sawada, p. 74.
111. Ching, Leo, *Becoming Japanese: Colonial Taiwan and the Politics of Identity Formation* (Berkeley CA, Los Angeles CA and London: University of California Press, 2001), p. 23.
112. Morris-Suzuki, Tessa, 'Becoming Japanese: Imperial Expansion and Identity Crises in the Early Twentieth Century', in Sharon A. Minichiello (ed.), *Japan's Competing Modernities: Issues in Culture and Democracy, 1900–1930* (Honolulu HI: University of Hawai'i Press, 1998), p. 159.
113. Ibid., p. 159.
114. Ching, p. 6.
115. 'Chōsende eiga no zeisakuokaishi', *Kastudō zasshi*, 10, July 1924, pp. 70–1.
116. Ibid., pp. 70–1.
117. 'Nikkatsu to Chōsen Kinema no teikei', *Kinema junpō*, 179, 1 December 1924, p. 33.
118. Kim Jong-wook (ed.), *Sillok Hanguk yeonghwa chongseo, sang* (Seoul: Gukhakjaryowon, 2002), pp. 166–7.
119. Sato Yukio, '*Umi no hikyōku*', *Kinema junpō*, 181, 1 January 1925, p. 7.

254 Eclipsed Cinema

120. See *Maeil sinbo*, 13 December 1924, and Yun Yong-gab, '*Unyeongjeon*eul bogo', *Donga ilbo*, 26 January 1925.
121. *Keijō nichinichi nippō*, 29 January 1930.
122. Matsumoto Teruka, 'Keijō kinemakai', pp. 135-36 and Cho Pung-yeon, *Seoul jabhak sajeon* (Seoul: Jeongdong Chulpansa, 1989), p. 154.

Chapter 4

1. Kang So-cheon, 'Joseon yeonghwaga geoleoon gil I', *Yeonghwa sidae*, 1.1, 1 April 1946, p. 38.
2. *Katsudō shashin fuirumu keiretsu gaiyō* (Keijo: Chōsen Sōtokufu Keimukyoku, 1931), p. 45.
3. Ibid., p. 29.
4. Jacqueline Najuma Stewart, *Migrating to the Movies: Cinema and Black Urban Modernity* (Berkeley CA and Los Angeles CA: University of California Press, 2005), p. 94.
5. Ibid., p. 110.
6. 'Receives Scenario from Korea', *Motography*, 18.5, 4 August 1917, p. 246.
7. 'Los Angeles Brevities', *The Moving Picture World*, 33, 11 August 1917, p. 948.
8. This film preview format, which was common in Japanese and Joseon film magazines, introduces a film mainly in words, often with several accompanying images from a film, by rewriting the film's narrative in short-story style.
9. *Maeil sinbo*, 19 December 1919.
10. See A. W.-shōsei, 'Chōsenjin kawa no eigani tsuite', *Chōsen oyobi Manshū*, 252, November 1928, pp. 64–8.
11. *Donga ilbo*, 31 July 1923.
12. *Donga ilbo*, 14 May 1927, *Jungoi ilbo*, 15 May 1927, and 'Chōsen keijōni Gisin Yanghaeng setsuritsu', *Kinema junpō*, 264, 11 June 1927, p. 6.
13. A. W.-shōsei, pp. 64–8.
14. *Jungoi ilbo*, 30 August 1927.
15. Ibid.
16. *Donga ilbo*, 20 January 1934.
17. *Donga ilbo*, 1 June 1937.
18. Lee Gu-yeong, 'Yeonghwagye ilnyeon (1)', *Donga ilbo*, 2 January 1926.
19. Hanguk Yesul Yeonguso (ed.), 'Lee Pil-wu', in *Lee Yeong-ilui Hanguk yeonghwareul wihan jeungeonrok: Yu Jang-san, Lee Gyeong-soon, Lee Pil-wu, Lee Chang-geun pyeon* (Seoul: Sodo, 2003), pp. 233–5.
20. Lee Gu-yeong, 'Joseon yeonghwagyeui gwageo, hyeonjae, jangrae (4)', *Joseon ilbo*, 26 November 1926.
21. 'Hwaldong gwangaek sodong', *Donga ilbo*, 11 May 1923.
22. *Katsudō shashin fuirumu keiretsu gaiyō*, p. 48.
23. 'Chōsen Sōtokufu eiga kenetsu tsūkeihyō', *Kokusai eiga shimbun*, 226, July 1939, p. 32.
24. Okada Jun'ichi, 'Eiga kenetsu no gaikyō', *Keimu ibō*, 360, April 1936, p. 59.

25. Ikeda Kunio, 'Chōsenni okeru eiga kenetsu no tokyushūsei', *Kokusai eiga shimbun*, 231, October 1938, p. 2.
26. Ibid., p. 3.
27. See 'Chōsen Sōtokufu eiga tōsei', *Kinema junpō*, 506, 21 May 1934 and 'Chōsen no eiga tōseian', *Kinema junpō*, 515, 21 August 1934, p. 35.
28. *Joseon ilbo*, 9 May 1926.
29. Wallerstein, Immanuel, *After Liberalism* (New York: New Press, 1995), pp. 108–10.
30. Saldaña-Portillo, Maria Josefina, *The Revolutionary Imagination in the Americas in the Age of Development* (Durham NC: Duke University Press, 2003), pp. 19–20.
31. *Donga ilbo*, 24 August 1920.
32. Chōsen Kinko Chōsafu, 'Beigiindan nyūsen', *Chōsen jijō, hachigatsu gejūnko*, 1920, p. 41.
33. Jang Sin-seong, 'Yeonghwaui minjokseong', *Yeonghwa sidae*, 1.3, 1931, p. 17.
34. 'Tongyeong cheongnyeondan chonghoe', *Donga ilbo*, 5 May 1921.
35. 'Tongyeong hwaldong sajindae', *Maeil sinbo*, 14 August 1921.
36. 'Tongyeong hwaldongsajin', *Joseon ilbo*, 27 August 1921.
37. 'Tongyeong hwalsadae gwihyang', *Donga ilbo*, 30 October 1923.
38. See 'Tongyeong hwaldong sajindae', *Maeil sinbo*, 16 August 1921; 'Hwaldong sajindan Pyongyang yangchak', *Donga ilbo*, 26 August 1921; 'Hwalsadae Boseong chakbal', *Donga ilbo*, 2 October 1922.
39. 'Yunyeon gyoyukeul wihayeo', *Donga ilbo*, 9 September 1921.
40. See 'Gukje cheongnyeondaywa gakji gyeongchalui gangap', *Donga ilbo*, 11 September 1925; 'Ginyeom gangyeon geumji', *Donga ilbo*, 18 January 1926; 'Tongyeongseodo seongto geumji', *Donga ilbo*, 11 September 1926; 'Siwi haengryeol geumji', *Donga ilbo*, 17 May 1927; and 'Tongyeong cheongnyeonhoe hoewon sibmyeong dolyeon geomsok', *Donga ilbo*, 13 May 1927.
41. 'Cheongnyeondan hwaldongdae raejin', *Donga ilbo*, 28 July 1921.
42. 'Tongyeong cheongnyeonhoe juchoiui hwaldongsajin seonghwang', *Joseon ilbo*, 9 September 1921.
43. 'Tongyeong hwaldong sajindae', *Maeil sinbo*, 14 August 1921.
44. 'Cheongyododange *Myeonggeum* sangyeong', *Maeil sinbo*, 1 December 1924.
45. *Donga ilbo*, 29 September 1926.
46. 'Fuirumu kenetsu yori mita Chōsen eigakai no kinkyō', *Chōsen kōron*, 244, July 1933, pp. 108-9.
47. Here I turn to Henry Jenkins's critical concept of *textual poaching* that validates media consumers' active interpretation of media texts, developed in his seminal work on media fandom, *Textual Poachers: Television Fans and Participatory Culture* (London and New York: Routledge, 1992).
48. 'Chōsen Sōtokufu eiga kyōsei no enkakuto tōsei keii', *Eiga junpō*, 11 July 1943, p. 22.
49. Oka Shigematsu, 'Eiga kenetsu zakkan', *Chōsen oyobi Manshū*, 305, April 1933, p. 78
50. Ibid., p.78.
51. *Katsudō shashin fuirumu keiretsu gaiyō*, p. 145.
52. 'Chōsen Sōdokufurei dai 812gō, Katsudō shashin torishimari kisoku', *Chōsen Sōdokufu kanpō*, 2273, 7 August 1934, p. 49.

53. The fifth clause of 'Chōsen Sōdokufurei dai 812gō, Katsudō shashin torishimari kisoku'. Also see 'Yeonghwa tongje gyuchik', *Donga ilbo*, 2 August 1934, and 'Yeonghwa sangyeongui jongryu sigan jehan', *Donga ilbo*, 16 August 1934.
54. See 'Chōsen Sōtokufu kankyōnandōrei dai nijūgō', *Chōsen Sōtokufu kanpō*, 2301, 8 September 1934, 'Hwaldong sajin chwiche', *Donga ilbo*, 4 September 1934, and Tetsuya Mori, 'Dubbing Test Goes Over in Japan Houses', *Motion Picture Daily*, 7 October 1935.
55. Before the introduction of the screen quota, Suzuki Shigeyoshi's *What Made Her Do It?* (*Nani ga kanojo o sōsaseta ka*, 1930), a leftist-tendency film, was officially acknowledged as the sole Japanese film released at Korean cinemas. 'Fuirumu kenetsu yori mita Chōsen eigakai no kinkyō', p. 106.
56. 'Chōsen no eiga tōsei jisshi', *Kinema junpō*, 489, 21 November 1933, p. 15.
57. Ikeda, pp. 2–3.
58. See the seventh clause of 'Chōsen Sōdokufurei dai 812gō, Katsudō shashin torishimari kisoku'.
59. Yamaguchi Torao, 'Kenetsuo meguru dabitotsu', *Chosen kōron*, 290, May 1937, pp. 60–1.
60. T. Y-sei, 'Kenetsu jiji henpen', *Chosen kōron*, 292, July 1937, p. 74.
61. OGS-sei, 'Chihō tsūshin', *Kinema junpō*, 687, 21 July 1939, p. 97.
62. See Mori, 'Dubbing Test Goes Over in Japan Houses', *Motion Picture Daily*, 7 October 1935, 'Japanese Quota for Korea', *The Film Daily*, 13 May 1936, Chikushi Tani, 'Korea's Quota Strengthens', *Motion Picture Herald*, 122, 8 February 1936, p. 64, and 'Japanese edict to raise Korean quota', *Motion Picture Herald*, 123, 20 June 1936, p. 82.
63. 'Japanese edict to raise Korean quota', p. 82.
64. 'Guksan yeonghwa dokmudae guga', *Joseon ilbo*, 22 December 1937. Also see the editorial writing of *Joseon ilbo*, 27 January 1938.
65. 'Chōsen eiga yakushin', *Tokyo eiga shimbun*, in *Kokusai eiga shimbun*, 223, June 1938, p. 3.
66. *Donga ilbo*, 3 January 1938.
67. Yecies, Brian and Ae-Gyung Shim, *Korea's Occupied Cinema, 1893–1948* (New York: Routledge, 2011), p. 41.
68. Deocampo, Nick, *Cine: Spanish Influences on Early Cinema in the Philippines* (Manila: National Commission for Culture and Arts, 2003), p. xv.
69. Higson, Andrew, 'Limiting Imagination of National Cinema', in Mette Hjort and Scott Mackenzie (eds), *Cinema and Nation* (London and New York, Routledge, 2000), p. 69.
70. Lee Gu-yeong, 'Sagyeonuirobon yeonghwasa', *Yeonghwa yesul*, December 1970, pp. 80–1.
71. *Maeil sinbo*, 22 August 1919.
72. *Maeil sinbo*, 18 January 1919.
73. Sato Tadao, 'Benshini tsuite', *Katsudō benshi* (Tokyo: Urban Connections, 2001), p. 4 and Anderson, J. L., 'Spoken Silents in the Japanese Cinema; or, Talking to Pictures',

in Arthur Nolletti and David Desser (eds), *Reframing Japanese Cinema* (Bloomington IN: University of Indiana Press, 1992), p. 261.
74. Kim Jong-won and Jeong Jung-heon, *Uri Yeonghwa 100nyeon* (Seoul: Hyunamsa, 2001), p. 142.
75. Choi Chang-ho and Hong Gang-seong, *Na un-gyuwa sunangi yeonghwa* (Pyongyang: Pyongyang Chulpansa, 2001), p. 191.
76. An Jong-hwa, *Hanguk yeonghwa cheukmyeonbisa* (Seoul: Hyeondae Mihaksa, 1998), p. 33.
77. Jang Han-ki, *Hanguk yeongeuksa* (Seoul: Dongguk University Press, 2000), pp. 199–213.
78. Eckert, Carter J., *Offspring of Empire: The Koch'Ang Kims and the Colonial Origins of Korean Capitalism, 1876–1945* (Seattle WA and London: University of Washington Press, 1996), p. 34.
79. *Byeonsa* literally signifies 'orator', and it did not solely designate film narrator, since the term was employed to describe orators and public lecturers even before the advent of the film-narrator practice. Though *byeonsa* was the most common term used to indicate narrators, *hwalbyeon* (*katsuben* in Japanese), a term shortened from *hwaldongsajin byeonsa*, was also in frequent use. Today the word *byeonsa* is no longer a part of everyday vocabulary – the term gradually disappeared coming into the 1950s – and it is now solely associated with film narrators of the silent-film era.
80. Musei Eiga Kanjōkai (ed.), *Katsudō benshi* (Tokyo: Urban Connections, 2001), p. 11.
81. See *Mansebo*, 12 May 1907 and *Maeil sinbo*, 17 May 1912.
82. Cho Hee-moon, 'Museong yeonghwaui haeseolja, byeonsa yeongu', in *Hanguk yeonghwaui Jaengjeom 1* (Seoul: Jibmundang, 2002), p. 130.
83. *Maeil sinbo*, 9 June 1914.
84. See Misono Kyōhei, *Katsubenjidai* (Tokyo: Iwanami Shoten), 1990, p. 34 and Fujiki, Hideaki, 'Benshi as Stars: The Irony of the Popularity and Respectability of Voice Performers in Japanese Cinema', *Cinema Journal*, 45.2, 2006, p. 71.
85. Cho, p. 134.
86. Hun, 'Chōsen eiga no shiteki kōsatsu (1)', *Kokusai eiga shimbun*, 48, January 1931, p. 35.
87. An, pp. 31–2. An Jong-hwa, a film-maker from the colonial period, described Wu's career negatively in his book which recounts the colonial film culture primarily through his personal experiences. Because of An's portrayal, Wu is considered to have been quickly pushed out of his profession. An's account appears to have been inaccurate, however, as, according to the sources below, Wu continued to work as a *byeonsa* for Danseongsa until the early 1930s. See 'Sucheon dokja hwanho', *Sidae ilbo*, 10 July 1925; 'Radio bangsong', *Donga ilbo*, 15 November 1927; 'Jinjue hwalsa jeonggi sangseol', *Jungoi ilbo*, 29 April 1928; 'Radio bangsong', *Donga ilbo*, 15 October 1928; and Hun, p. 35.
88. Hun, 'Chōsen eiga no shiteki kōsatsu (2)', *Kokusai eiga Shimbun*, 49, February 1931, p. 7.

89. *Maeil sinbo*, 3 June 1914.
90. *Maeil sinbo*, 24 April 1915.
91. *Donga ilbo*, 28 June 1922. Not all *byeonsa/benshi* applied for this permit at first and only a handful of those who did actually passed the test. In response, the police department of Gyeonggi Province, which was in charge of film censorship at the time, decided to pass all *byeonsa* who applied, acknowledging that the hasty implementation of this new regulation required more time for adjustment.
92. *Donga ilbo*, 8 July 1920.
93. 'Katsudō shashin kenetsu kisoku', *Chōsen Sōdokufu kanpō*, 4162, 5 July 1926, p. 41.
94. Gerow, Aaron, *Visions of Japanese Modernity: Articulations of Cinema, Nation, and Spectatorship, 1895–1925* (Berkeley CA and Los Angeles CA: University of California Press, 2010), pp. 210–11.
95. *Donga ilbo*, 28 June 1922.
96. *Joseon ilbo*, 24 July 1929.
97. Gerow, p. 214.
98. Baekpa-saeng, 'Yeonghwa haeseoljaui pyeoneo', *Jungoi ilbo*, 24 July 1927.
99. Hanguk Yesul Yeonguso (ed.), 'Seong Dong-ho', in *Lee Yeong-ilui Hanguk yeonghwasareul wihan jeungeonrok: Seong Dong-ho, Lee Gyu-hwan, Choi Geum-dong pyeon* (Seoul: Sodo, 2003), p. 2.
100. 'Hwaldong sajin byeonsa jwadamhoe', *Jogwang*, 4.4, April 1938, pp. 292–3.
101. Lee Gu-yeong, 'Sagyeoneurobon yeonghwasa', pp. 80–1.
102. Lee Seung-wu, 'Yeonghwa haeseolgwa gwangaekui simri', *Yeonghwa sidae*, 1.1, February 1931, p. 21.
103. Kim Il-yeong, 'Yeonghwawa minjung', *Maeil sinbo*, 2 February 1925. See also 'Yeonghwa haeseolgwa yeohak', *Joseon ilbo*, 1 January 1926.
104. G-saeng, 'Meondongi teulttaereul bogo', *Donga ilbo*, 2 November 1927.
105. Kim Yeong-hwan, 'Yeonghwa haeseolui sogo', *Daejung yeonghwa*, 4, July 1930, pp. 10–11.
106. Yun Chi-ho, *Journal 9*, 16 January 1929, n.p. Yun has been a controversial historical figure after his collaboration with the Office of the Governor General during the later years of the Japanese Empire. Yun began to write his journal in English in 1899 when he studied in the United States.
107. Hanguk Yesul Yeonguso (ed.), 'Lee Gu-yeong', in *Lee Yeong-ilui Hanguk yeonghwasareul wihan jeungeonrok: Kim Seong-chun, Bok Hye-suk, Lee Gu-yeong pyeon* (Seoul: Sodo, 2003), pp. 283–6.
108. Yoo Heung-tae, 'Dangdae ingi byeonsa Seo Sang-ho ildaegi', *Jungang*, 4.10, October 1938, pp. 120–1.
109. Kinema Junpōsha Chōshabu, *Zenkoku eigakan mokuroku* (Tokyo: Kinema Junpōsha, 1936), pp. 40–1.
110. See 'Zengoku eigakan roku', *Eiga junpō*, 11 July 1943, pp. 42–6.
111. Wi Gyeong-hye, *Honamui geukjang munhwasa* (Seoul: Dahal Media, 2007), pp. 21–44.

Chapter 5

1. *Daehan maeil sinbo*, 6 June 1907.
2. Christ, Carol Ann, 'The Sole Guardians of the Art Inheritance of Asia: Japan at the 1904 St. Louis World's Fair', *Positions*, 8.3, winter 2000, p. 683.
3. Shin Myeong-jik, *Modern boy Gyeongseongeul geonilda* (Seoul: Hyeonsil Munhwa Yeongu, 2003), p. 15.
4. Min Yeong-hwan, *Minchungjeonggong yugo 3 gwon: haecheon chobeom*, 17 June 1896; 7 May by lunar calendar, p. 96.
5. Mizui Reiko, 'Chōsen jyōsei to eiga', *Shin eiga*, May 1942, pp. 81–2.
6. Chatterjee, Partha, *Nationalist Thought and the Colonial World* (Minneapolis MN: University of Minnesota Press, 1993), p. 10.
7. Yu Gwang-yeol, 'Modern girl, modern boy daenonjaeng', *Byeolgeongon*, 10, December 1927, p. 113. Words in capital letters indicate Yu's own uses of English words.
8. Park Yeong-hee, 'Yusanja sahoeui sowi geundaenyeo, geundanamui teukjing', *Byeolgeongon*, 10, December 1927, p. 115–16. Words in capital letters indicate Park's own uses of English words.
9. For a discussion of the development of the *new woman* discourse from the 1910s through the 1940s, see Suh, Jiyoung, 'The "New Woman" and the topography of modernity in colonial Korea', *Korean Studies*, 37, 2013, pp. 11–43.
10. Cho Hye-jeong, *Hangukui yeoseonggwa namseong* (Seoul: Munhakgwa Jiseongsa, 1991), pp. 97–8.
11. 'Modern girliran', *Jungoi ilbo*, 25 July 1927.
12. Chaplin, Sarah, 'Interiority and the "Modern Woman" in Japan', in Shoma Munshi (ed.), *Images of the 'Modern Woman' in Asia: Global Media, Local Meanings* (New York: Routledge, 2001), p. 57.
13. Kim Ki-rim, 'Miss Koreayeo danbalhasio', *Donggwang*, 37, 1 September 1932, pp. 61–2.
14. Ibid., p. 62.
15. 'Chonggak jwadamhoe', *Sinyeoseong*, 7.2, February 1933, p. 50.
16. 'Modanrangui gyeolhongwan', *Jungoi ilbo*, 26 August 1927.
17. Cheonrian, 'Clara Bow-yang', *Yeonghwa sidae*, 1.5, July 1931, p. 14.
18. 'Sineo haeseol', *Donga ilbo*, 13 March 1931.
19. Chu Jeong-hyang, '*It-girl*ui daetongsa', *Yeonghwa sidae*, 1.3, May 1931, p. 26.
20. 'Modern girlui wonjo Claraui bigeuk', *Jungoi ilbo*, 23 December 1927.
21. See Shimizu Iso, *Okamoto Ippei manga manbunshū* (Tokyo: Iwanami Shoten, 1995).
22. An Seok-yeong, 'Gasangsogyeon (2) modern boyui sanbo', *Joseon ilbo*, 7 February 1928.
23. Mr A, 'Manchu Punggyeong', *Joseon ilbo*, 26 October 1930.
24. An Seok-yeong, 'Eunmaketteun chosaengdale yeonaegeolsinbyeong hwanja', *Joseon jungang ilbo*, 24 September 1933.
25. Choi Seung-il, 'Dae Gyeongseong panorama', *Joseon munye*, 1.1, 1929, pp. 85–6. Words in capital letters indicate Choi's own uses of English words.

26. *Hwangseong sunbo*, 5 May 1906.
27. *Joseon wangjo silok: Gojong 47*, 17 April 1906, n.p. During the later years of the Spring and Autumn Period, the Chinese feudal era (772 BC–481 BC), whose name came from Confucius's book *Spring and Autumn Annals*, music from the Cheng country (*Chengyīn*) was considered the most 'lewd' entertainment. In his conversation with his disciple Yan Hui, Confucius used *Chengyīn* as a metaphor standing for all forms of base popular amusement which must be expelled from the ideal country he envisioned. Lee Pil-wha employed this famous Confucian teaching to underscore Hyeobryulsa's negative social function.
28. Ibid., n.p.
29. Kim Won-geuk, 'Agukui yeongeukjang sosik', *Daehan heunghakbo*, 1, 20 March 1909, pp. 19–20.
30. See *Maeil sinbo* 27 April 1913, 8 January 1915 and 9 January 1915.
31. An Seok-yeong, 'Gasangsogyeon (2) modern boyui sanbo', *Joseon ilbo*, 7 February 1928.
32. Benjamin, Walter, 'The Paris of the Second Empire in Baudelaire', *Charles Baudelaire: A Lyric Poet in the Era of High Capitalism*, Harry Zohn (trans.) (London: NLB, 1973), pp. 35–66.
33. Lee Sang, 'Sanchon yeojeong', *Lee Sang seonjib* (Seoul: Eulyu Munhwasa, 1994), p. 160. Words in capital letters indicate Lee's own uses of English words.
34. Lee Sang, 'Gwontae', *Lee Sang seonjib*, p. 232.
35. Benjamin, Walter, *The Arcade Project*, Howard Eiland and Kevin McLaughlin (trans.) (Cambridge MA and London: The Belknap Press of Harvard University Press, 1999), p. 106.
36. Ibid., pp. 105–6.
37. Kracauer, Siegfried, 'Boredom', *The Mass Ornament: Weimar Essays*, Thomas Y. Levin (trans.) (Cambridge MA and London: Harvard University Press, 1995), p. 334.
38. Stewart, Jacqueline N., *Migration to the Movies: Cinema and Black Urban Modernity* (Berkeley CA and Los Angeles CA: University of California Press, 2005), p. 106.
39. See Chen, Ching-chih, 'Police and Community Control System in the Empire', in Ramon H. Myers and Mark R. Peattie (eds), *The Japanese Colonial Empire 1895–1945* (Princeton NJ: Princeton University Press, 1984).
40. *Chōsen Sōdokufu tōkei nenkan 1928* (Keijō: Chōsen Sōdokufu, 1930), pp. 334–5.
41. Ibid., pp. 334–5.
42. Nahm, Andrew, 'Korea under Japanese Colonial Rule', *Korea: Tradition and Transformation* (Elizabeth NJ: Hollym, 1996), p. 226
43. Starr, Frederick, 'Buin haebangui gyeonghyang', *Donga ilbo*, 10 June 1921. For Starr's personal and scholarly engagement with colonial Korea, see Oppenheim, Robert, '"The West" and the Anthropology of Other People's Colonialism: Frederick Starr in Korea, 1911–1930', *The Journal of Asian Studies*, 64.3, August 2005, pp. 677–703.
44. Ibid.
45. Ibid.

46. 'Guekjang mandam,' *Byeolgeongon*, 5, March 1927, p. 95.
47. Mizui, 'Chōsen jyōsei to eiga', p. 82.
48. McKenzie, Frederick Arthur, *The Tragedy of Korea* (London: Hodder and Stoughton, 1908), p. 30.
49. 'Naichi kinshin: Chōsen', *The Kinema Record*, 40, 10 October 1916, p. 442.
50. Aozawa Yōrō, 'Eigakan no murasaki no yamini mitsukani ikihareru zaiaku', *Chōsen kōron*, 120, March 1923, p. 124.
51. Bukdae gija SS, 'Jeonyulhal daeakmagul yeohaksaeng yuindan tamsagi', *Byeolgeongon*, 5, March 1927, pp. 76–89.
52. Ibid., p. 78.
53. Seo Gwang-je, 'Yeoseonggwa yeonghwa: Joseon yeoseongi badneun yeonghyang', *Joseon ilbo*, 22 June 1931.
54. Lee Tae-jun, 'Modern girlui manchan', *Lee Tae-jun danpyeon jeonjib 1* (Seoul: Garam Gihoik, 2005), pp. 59–63.
55. Cha Bu-rim, 'Yeonghwa gamsangbeob', *Yeoseong*, 1.6, August 1936, p. 24.
56. Yim Eul-cheon, 'Yeonghwawa saenghwal', *Yeoseong*, 2.6, June 1937, pp. 54–5.
57. 'Zadankai', *Eiga hyōron*, 1.7, July 1941, p. 57.
58. '*Mimong*', *Maeil sinbo*, 4 July 1936.
59. 'Myeongranghago yesuljeokin gyotong yeonghwa jejak', *Maeil sinbo*, 28 January 1937.
60. 'Gisaengsileun jadongcha jeonchawa jeongmyeon chudol', *Joseon ilbo*, 27 April 1928.
61. 'Geudeului bomtaryeong: manhwagyeong back mirror', *Joseon ilbo*, 20 April 1934.
62. Kang Suk-jeong, 'Baekhwajeomui ojeon', *Yeoseong sidae*, 1.2, September 1930, p. 53.
63. Bukdae gija SS, p. 78.
64. 'Gisaeng Dansokryeong' and 'Changgi Dansokryeong', *Gwanbo*, 4088, 28 September 1908.
65. *Gwonbeon* and *gisaeng* were banned in 1942 by the Office of the Governor General. They were briefly revived in South Korea after the colonial occupation but officially disappeared in 1947.
66. Han Cheong-san, 'Gisaeng cheolpyeron', *Donggwang*, December 1931, p. 56.
67. Kawamura Minato, *Malhaneun kkot gisaeng*, Yoo Jae-Sun (trans.) (Seoul: Sodam Chulpansa, 2002), pp. 177–84.
68. See 'Yedan ilbaekin', *Maeil sinbo*, 28 January to 11 June 1914.
69. For further discussions of the impact of modern entertainment on the content and style of the *gisaeng* performance, see Kang In-suk and Oh Jeong-im, 'Geundae seogusik geukjang seollibe ttareun gisaeng gongyeonui byeonmo yangsang', *The Korean Research Journal of Dance Documentation*, 19, 2010, pp. 1–27.
70. Bishop, Isabella Bird, *Korea and Her Neighbours: A Narrative of Travel, with an Account of the Recent Vicissitudes and Present Position of the Country* (London: John Murray, 1898), p. 166.
71. *Maeil sinbo*, 29 October 1919.
72. *Joseon ilbo*, 28 June 1929.

73. Hanguk Yesul Yeonguso (ed.), 'Seong Dong-ho', in *Lee Yeong-ilui Hanguk yeonghwasareul wihan jeungeonrok: Seong Dong-ho, Lee Gyu-hwan, Choi Geum-dong pyeon* (Seoul: Sodo, 2003), p. 39.
74. The *gisaeng*'s involvement with film as actors resulting from the strict social gender and class structures displays a striking similarity to *kalavantins* in India, performing artists who belonged to the lowest caste just like *gisaeng*. As acting and performing arts were widely considered to be demeaning careers in India in a similar fashion to Korea, many *kalavantins* became movie actors and a few of them became the earliest stars of Indian cinema. For further discussion of *kalavantins*, see Jaikumar, Priya, *Cinema at the End of Empire: A Politics of Transition in Britain and India* (Durham NC and London: Duke University Press, 2006), pp. 97–8.
75. *Maeil sinbo*, 3 July 1927.
76. *Maeil sinbo*, 23 July 1927.
77. *Sidae ilbo*, 12 May 1925.
78. Hanguk Yesul Yeonguso (ed.), 'Lee Pil-wu', in *Lee Yeong-ilui Hanguk yeonghwareul wihan jeungeonrok: Yu Jang-san, Lee Gyeong-son, Lee Pil-wu, Lee Chang-geun pyeon* (Seoul: Sodo, 2003), pp. 205–8.
79. Friedberg, Anne, *Window Shopping: Cinema and the Postmodern* (Berkeley CA, Los Angeles CA and London: University of California Press, 1994), p. 36.
80. Gleber, Anke, 'Female Flanerie and the Symphony of the City', in Katharina von Ankum (ed.), *Women in the Metropolis: Gender and Modernity in Weimar Culture* (Berkeley CA, Los Angeles CA and London: University of California Press, 1997), p. 71.
81. Jeong Chil-seong, 'Sinnyeoseongiran mueot', *Joseon ilbo*, 4 January 1926. See also Park Yong-ok, 'Sinnyeoseonge daehan sahoejeok suyonggwa bipan', in Mun Ok-pyo (ed.), *Sinnyeoseong* (Seoul: Cheongnyeonsa, 2003), pp. 71.
82. See *Janghan*, 1.1, January 1927, and *Janghan*, 1.2, February 1927. Reprints are also available in Son Jung-heum, Park Gyeong-u and Yu Chun-dong (eds), *Geundae gisaengui munhwawa yesul: jaryopyeon 1* (Seoul: Bogosa, 2009).
83. For detailed reports on the strikes by *gisaeng*, see *Maeil sinbo*, 9 October 1925, *Jungoi ilbo*, 24 May 1927, *Jungoi ilbo*, 25 July 1927, and *Maeil sinbo*, 27 December 1927.

Conclusion

1. 'Eigakan no page: Keijō', *Eiga junpō*, 23, 21 August 1941, p. 66.
2. 'Dae Gyeongseong yuksibmanbumineul bureuneun yeonghwa yesul jeondang Meijiza', *Samcheolli*, 8.6, June 1936, p. 103.
3. Ibid., p. 103.
4. 'Pukchon yuilui yeonghwageukjang Danseongsa yeongeukeuro jeonhwan', *Maeil sinbo*, 15 July 1937.
5. Ibid.
6. 'Gimilsil, Joseonsahoe naemak ilramsil', *Samcheolli*, 10.5, May 1938, p. 25.
7. Yamazaki Yukihiko, 'Chōsen eigakai no genzai to shōrai', *Chōsen kōron*, 283, October 1936.

8. *Tokyo eiga shimbun*, 118, in *Kokusai eiga shimbun*, 226, July 1938, p. 2.
9. 'Keijōni shinshūtsusuru Kobayashi Ichizō', *Chōsen kōron*, 291, June 1937, p. 81.
10. 'Toho Chōsenni', *Tokyo eiga shimbun*, 104, in *Kokusai eiga shimbun*, 210, November 1937, p. 3.
11. Kim Jeong-hyuk, 'Joseon yeonghwa jinheungui mokpyo', *Samchoelli*, 13.1, 1 January 1941, p. 162.
12. 'Chōsen Eiga Seisaku Kabushikigaisha gaikyō' and 'Chōsen Eiga Haikyūsha gaikyō', *Eiga junpō*, 11 July 1943, pp. 35–8.
13. Tanaka Saburō, 'Daitōa to Chōsen eiga', *Eiga junpō*, 100, 21 November 1943, p. 18.
14. 'Keijō eigamachi ōrai', *Chōsen kōron*, 299, February 1938, p. 120. After the deal with Shochiku was over, Tokunaga partnered up with Makino but the studio that had dominated 1920s Japanese cinema disolved in 1937 after years of struggle. Frustrated by a series of short-lived partnerships with Japanese studios, Tokunaga finally sold his theatre. In 1940 Koganekan was sold to Yoshimoto Kōgyō which opened its business in Seoul with the acquisition of the theatre. ('Gimilsil', *Samcheolli*, 12.5, 1 May 1940, p. 21)
15. Jun, Uchida, *Brokers of Empire: Japanese Settler Colonialism in Korea 1876–1945* (Cambridge MA: Harvard University Press, 2011), p. 358.
16. Mizui Reiko, 'Shochiku eigao meguru shomondai', *Chōsen oyobi Manshū*, 336, November 1935), pp. 79–81.
17. See Ishibashi Ryōsuke, 'Tokui jidaio keikaiseyo', in Ichikawa Sai, *Waga eiga jigyōron*, (Tokyo: Kokusai Eiga Shimbun Tsūshinsha Shuppanbu, 1941), pp. 327–8.

Appendix

This appendix lists the film-makers, cinemas and film companies discussed in the book. I have added additional individuals, entities and organisations that I was not able fully to engage with in the book but thought their inclusion would further benefit the reader. Note that the following lists are by no means comprehensive. They are intended as rudimentary guides for information and research.

1. Film Professionals

An Cheol-yeong (1909[?]–?) — Director of *Fishing Fires* (*Eohwa*, 1938); emigrated to Hawaii, United States, in the late 1940s.

An Seok-yeong (1901–50) — Essay cartoonist; debuted as a director in 1937 (*Tale of Sim Cheong* [*Sim Cheong joen*]).

Bang Han-jun (1906–?) — Director of *Han River* (*Hangang*, 1938), *A Village Shrine* (*Seonghwangdang*, 1938), and *Tuition* (*Sueobryo*, 1940).

Choi Byeong-ryong (?–?) — Korean *byeonsa* affiliated with Danseongsa.

Choi In-gyu (1911–?) — Director/screenwriter who was active in the 1940s; directed *Border* (*Gukgyeong*, 1939), *Tuition* (1940, co-director), and *Homeless Angels* (*Jibeobneun cheonsa*, 1941); directed propaganda films as a key member of Joseon Film Production Corporation; directed *Hurrah for Freedom* (1946), the film considered the first South Korean film.

Choi Wan-gyu (1905–?) — President of Goryeo Yeonghwasa; worked as an executive of Joseon Cultural Magic Lantern Company; older brother of Choi In-gyu.

Hayakawa Jōtaro (1879–?) — Founder of Hayakawa Entertainment Company; directed films from the early 1920s while managing Joseon Geukjang; used the name 'Hayakawa Koshū' for film credits; emigrated from Tokyo to Joseon in 1905.

Hayashida Kinjiro (1861–?)	Owner of Hayashida Trading Company that distributed films and sold film stock; owner of Umigwan; from Nagasaki.
Ikeda Kunio (?–?)	Film censor.
Ikoma Tenrai (?–?)	Japanese *benshi* affiliated with Koganekan; earned fame with his performances for Universal serials.
Im Su-ho (?–?)	One of the most prominent film exhibitors during the colonial era; specialised in mobile screenings.
Ishibashi Ryōsuke (?–?)	Founder of Meijiza.
Ishida Akika (1893–?)	Japanese *benshi* initially hired by Kirakukan; soon moved to Koganekan; considered the best *benshi* in Joseon; from Osaka.
Iwasaki Takeji (1892–?)	Founder of Hōraikan (Busan); migrated from Ibaraki Prefecture in 1914.
Kato Kyōhei (?–?)	Cinematographer; director of photography for *A Bird in the Cage* (*Nongjungjo*, 1926), *Golden Fish* (*Geumbungeo*, 1927), *Wild Rat* (*Deuljwi*, 1927), and *Hornless Bull* (*Ppuleubneun Hwangso*, 1927).
Kim Deok-gyeong (?–?)	One of the early *byeonsa* stars in the 1910s; became the chief *byeonsa* for the Second Taishōkan Theatre in 1914 and moved to Danseongsa after the theatre's closure.
Kim Do-san (1891–1921)	Director of *Loyal Vengeance* (*Eurijeok guto*, 1919), a chain drama generally credited as the first Korean film.
Kim Sin-jae (1919–98)	Actress who rose to stardom in the 1940s; starred in such films as *Tale of Sim Cheong* (1937), *Dosaengrok* (1938), *Heartless* (*Mujeong*, 1939), *Homeless Angels* (1941), and *You and Me* (*Gimi to boku*, 1941).
Kim Tae-jin (1905–?)	Screenwriter; began his career as an actor and used the name 'Namgung Un' for his actor credit; a co-star of *Arirang* (1926).
Kim Yeon-sil (1911–97)	Actress/singer; sang the *Arirang*'s theme song for the gramophone record.
Kim Yeong-hwan (?–?)	Korean *byeonsa* affiliated with Danseongsa.
Kim Yu-yeong (1907–40)	Directed *Vagabond* (*Yurang*, 1928) and *Honga* (1929); a KAPF (Korea Artista Proleta Federatio) member.

Kubo Junkichi (?–?)	Founder of Daidō Katsuei Company based in Pyongyang.
Lee Chang-yong (1907–61)	Cinematographer; became the president of Goryeo Yeonghwa Hyeobhoe (1937); was instrumental in the Joseon–Japan propaganda co-productions in the last phase of colonial occupation.
Lee Gu-yeong (1901–73)	Head of the promotion department for Danseongsa; screenwriter for *Tale of Janghwa and Hongryeon* (*Janghwa Hongryeon jeon*, 1924).
Lee Gyeong-son (1905–77)	Director/critic; migrated to Shanghai, China, in the early 1930s and made *The Yangtze River* (*Yangjagang*, 1931) there.
Lee Gyu-hwan (1904–82)	Director of *A Ferry Boat that Has No Owner* (*Imja eobneun nalusbae*, 1932) and *The Wayfarer* (*Nageune*, 1937); trained at Teikoku Kinema of Japan under Suzuki Shigeyoshi.
Lee Han-gyeong (?–?)	Early *byeonsa* star; worked for Umigwan.
Lee Myeong-wu (1903–?)	Cinematographer/sound technician; co-invented with his older brother Lee Pil-wu PKR system, a Korean sound system.
Lee Pil-wu (1897–78)	Considered the first professional Korean cinematographer; worked also as producer, distributor and exhibitor; participated in the invention of Tsuchihashi sound system; co-invented Korean PKR sound system.
Maeda Muro (?–?)	Japanese settler film critic; regularly contributed to *Kinema Junpō*.
Manshō Minejiro (?–?)	Owner of Zōjyōkan (Busan); moved to Joseon in 1927 from Fukuoka, Kyūshū.
Martin, L. (?–?)	Considered the first professional film exhibitor in Korea (1907); nothing specific is known about this French film exhibitor.
Matsumoto Teruka (?–?)	Long-standing film reviewer for *Chōsen kōron*.
Minami Toshio (?–?)	Japanese *benshi* affiliated with Koganekan; specialised in melodrama.
Miyagawa Hayanosuke (1884[?]–?)	Cinematographer; came to Joseon when hired by Danseongsa to film *Loyal Vengeance* [1919] and *View of Seoul City* [*Gyeongseongui gyeong*, 1919].
Mizui Reiko (?–?)	Settler film critic who wrote extensively on Joseon cinema for Joseon and for Japanese film magazines.

Momoyama Long (?–?)	Japanese *benshi* affiliated with Koganekan; specialised in serials and costume dramas; from Fukuoka.
Morris, G. H. (?–?)	Head of Morris Trading Company.
Mun Ye-bong (1917–99)	The most popular female star actor in the 1930s and 1940s; starred in more than two dozen films such as *A Ferry Boat that Has No Owner* (1932), *Sweet Dream* (1936), *The Wayfarer* (1937) *Military Train* (1938), *You and Me* (1941); moved to North Korea in 1948.
Muraya Bisui (?–?)	Music director of Taishōkan.
Na Un-gyu (1902–37)	Most prominent director/screenwriter/actor; best known as the creator of *Arirang* (1926).
Nango Kimitoshi (?–?)	One of the first Japanese *benshi* in Joseon; later became the manager of Koganekan.
Nishikawa Hidehiro (?–?)	Cinematographer; *Tale of Unyeong* (*Unyeong jeon*, 1925), *Tale of Sim Sheong* (1925), *The Pioneer* (*Gaecheokja*, 1925), *Janghanmong* (1926), and *The Secret of Chinese Street* (*Jinagaui bimil*, 1928).
Nitta Byōhei (1888–?)	Youngest of the Nitta brothers; managed Hisagokan Theatre in Incheon and also worked there as *benshi*.
Nitta Hideyoshi (?–?)	In charge of the Nitta Entertainment Company on behalf of his brother Kōichi.
Nitta Kōichi (1882–?)	Founder of Nitta Shōten and Nitta Entertainment Company; owner of Taishōkan (Seoul); from Shimonoseki, Yamaguchi Prefecture.
Nomura Shirotori (1883–?)	Hired by the Nitta Entertainment (1915); moved to Busan to become the chief manager of Saiwaikan (Busan) in 1922; from Yamaguchi Prefecture.
Oka Shigematsu (?–?)	Chief censor of the film censorship board.
Oka Tengo (?–?)	Japanese *benshi* affiliated with Chūokan.
Okada Jun'ichi (?–?)	Film censor.
Ōta Hitoshi (?–?)	Cinematographer; *Song of the Unforgettable* (*Bulmanggok*, 1927) and *A Plaintive Song of Crimson Love* (*Hongryeon biga*, 1927).
Park Gi-chae (1906–?)	Cinematographer/director; a founding member of Joseon Yeonghwa Jusikhoesa (Joseon Cinema Corporation, 1937).
Park Jeong-hyeon (1893–1939)	Manager of Danseongsa; became the new head of the theatre after Park Seung-pil's demise (1932).

Park Seung-pil (1875–1932)	Head of Gwangmudae and Danseongsa; one of the first professional theatre exhibitors in Korea; producer of *Loyal Vengeance* (1919).
Sakuraba Fujio (1892–?)	Owner of Sakuraba Shōkai; from Beppu, Ōita.
Seo Gwang-je (1901–?)	Pioneering film critic; later debuted as director (*Military Train*, 1938).
Seo Sang-ho (?–1937)	One of the most popular Korean *byeonsa*.
Seo Sang-pil (?–?)	Korean *byeonsa* affiliated with Danseongsa.
Seong Dong-ho (1904–85)	Famed *byeonsa* affiliated with Joseon Geukjang; started distributing films around 1940 and turned film producer after the end of colonial occupation.
Shin Il-seon (1912–99)	Female lead of *Arirang* (1926).
Suzuki Shigeyoshi (1900–76)	Producer of *The Wayfarer* (1937); trained Lee Gyu-hwan when they worked together at Teikoku Kinema; best known as director of the tendency film *What Made Her Do It?* (*Nani ga kanojo o sōsaseta ka*, 1930).
Takasa Kanjo (?–?)	One of the founders of Joseon Kinema (1924); directed *A Plaintive Melody of Sea* (*Haeui bigok*, 1924), *God's Decoration* (*Sinui Jang*, 1925), and *Hero of the Village* (*Dongriui Hogeol*, 1925).
Takemoto Kunio (?–?)	One of the earliest Japanese *benshi* in Joseon; worked for Taishōkan.
Tamata Kitsuji (?–?)	Architect who designed Meijiza and the renovated buildings for Danseongsa (1935) and Koganekan (1936).
Tanaka Saburō (1899–1965)	President of Joseon Film Distribution Company and the Joseon Film Production Corporation; founder of the prominent Japanese film magazine *Kinema junpō* (first published in 1919).
Tokunaga Kumaichirō (1887–?)	Owner of Tokunaga Moving Picture Shop; from Fukuoka, Kyūshū.
Toyama Mitsuru (1893–1952)	Japanese actor; founded Toyama Mitsuru Production in Joseon in 1931.
Tsumura Isamu (1884–?)	Adviser for the Moving Picture Unit of the Office of the Governor General (MPU) as well as the film censorship board (from 1923); migrated to Joseon as a police captain in 1910.
Wakejima Shujirō (?–?)	One of the most powerful exhibitors in colonial Korea; founder of Gyeongseong Film Productions (1934).

Wu Jeong-sik (?–?)	Considered the first professional *byeonsa* (Gwangmudae Theatre); later worked for Danseongsa.
Yamaguchi Torao (?–?)	Film reviewer for *Chōsen kōron* and Seoul correspondent for *Kokusai eiga shimbun*.
Yang Se-ung (1906–?)	Director of photography for *Military Train*; trained in Japan's Tōa Kinema.
Yim Hwa (1908–53)	Poet/literary and film theorist who was a member of KAPF; involved in film production as screenwriter and actor.
Yokoyama Fumio (1889–?)	Film technician of Bankoku Katsudō Shashin Shōkai, Nagasaki, Japan; came to Joseon in 1918 as the Seoul branch manager of Bankoku and Nikkatsu; originally from Hiroshima Prefecture.
Yun Gi-jeong (1903–55)	Film critic and screenwriter; a core member of KAPF in charge of its film-making section.

2. Cinemas

Aegwan	Korean theatre in Incheon (est. 1926); purchased by Gisin Yanghaeng in 1928.
Chūokan	Japanese theatre in Seoul (est. 1921).
Danseongsa	Korean theatre in Seoul; converted to a cinema in 1919; later purchased by Ishibashi Ryōsuke to reopen as Daeryuk Geukjang (1939).
Gyeongseong godeung yeonyegwan	Korea's first cinema (est. 1910); purchased by the Taishōkan Theatre to become the Second Taishōkan Theatre (1914); permanently closed in 1915.
Hisagokan	Japanese theatre in Incheon (est. 1914).
Hōraikan	Japanese theatre in Busan (est. 1914); screened Tenkatsu, Kokugatsu films (1910s) and Nikkatsu and Teikoku films (1920s).
Jeilgwan	Korean theatre in Pyongyang (est. 1923).
Joseon Geukjang	Korean theatre in Seoul (est. 1922); burnt down in 1936.
Kairakukan	Japanese theatre in Pyongyang (est. 1923); screened Nikkatsu films.
Keiryūkan	Japanese theatre located on the border between Seoul and Yongsan (est. 1921).

Kirakukan	Japanese theatre located in Seoul; established in 1916 as Yūrakukan; changed its name to Kirakukan in 1919.
Koganekan	Japanese theatre in Seoul (est. 1913); screened Kokugatsu films and Universal films (1910s) and Shochiku films (from 1922).
Mangyeonggwan	Korean theatre in Daegu (est. 1922).
Meijiza	Shochiku-affiliated theatre (est. 1936).
Mokpo Geukjang	Korean theatre in Mokpo (est. 1926).
Saiwaikan	Japanese theatre in Busan (est. 1915); screened Nikkatsu films but switched to Makino films from the late 1920s.
Shichiseikan	Japanese theatre in Daegu; screened Nikkatsu films (est. unknown).
Taishōkan	Japanese theatre in Seoul (est. 1912); screened Nikkatsu films but switched to Shochiku films in the early 1920s.
Umigwan	The first cinema to target Korean spectators (Seoul; est. 1912).
Wakakusa Gekijō	Toho-affiliated theatre (Seoul; est. 1935).
Zōjyōkan	Japanese theatre in Busan; became a key partner of Shochiku in the 1920s (est. 1916).

3. *Film Companies*

Allen Trading Company	Distributed Hollywood films through Japan's Daikatsu; and then served as Paramount's Seoul Office (1922).
Daeryuk (Tairiku) Kinema	Film production business established by filmmakers from Japan in 1928.
Daidō Katsuei Company	Film distribution and exhibition company established by Japanese settler businessmen in Pyongyang (1922); ran Kairakukan.
Fujii Shōten	Distributed Fox films.
Geukgwang Yeonghwasa	Film production company established by An Cheol-yeong (1938); co-produced *Fishing Fires* (1938) with Shochiku.

Gisin Yanghaeng	The first Korean-owned distribution and exhibition firm established by the painter/art critic Kim Chan-yeong (1927); distributed films of MGM, United Artists, Paramount, and European films; managed Aegwan theatre of Incheon (1927) and Joseon Geukjang (1934); formed its own film production wing in 1937.
Goryeo Yeonghwa Hyeobhoe	Goryeo Film Association; film production and distribution company established in 1937, headed by Lee Chang-yong; produced such films as *Tuition* (1940), *Homeless Angels* (1941), and *Miles Away from Happiness* (*Bokjimanli*, 1941).
Goryeo Yeonghwasa	Production company established in 1935 by Choi Wan-gyu.
Gyeongseong Yeonghwa Chwalyeongso	Gyeongseong Film Productions; production company established in 1934 by Wakejima Shujirō.
Hayakawa Engeibu	Hayakawa Entertainment Company; established in 1913 by Hayakawa Jōtaro; primarily distributed Tenkatsu films in the 1910s.
Hwaldong Sajinban	Moving Picture Unit (J: *Katsudō Shashinhan*); A film unit run by the colonial government of Korea; the first film production entity in Korea (1920).
Joseon Kinema	The first film company of Joseon established by four Japanese settler merchants in Busan (1924); went bankrupt after the production of only four films in 1925.
Joseon Munhwa Hwandeung Hoesa	Joseon Cultural Magic Lantern Company (J: Chōsen Bunka Gentō Kaisha); established in 1942 to produce, distribute, and exhibit wartime propaganda magic lantern slides.
Joseon Yeonghwa Baegeubsa	Joseon Film Distribution Company (J: Chōsen Eiga Haikyūsha); established and managed by the colonial government (1942) to distribute all films in Joseon.
Joseon Yeonghwa Jejak Jusikhoesa	Joseon Film Production Corporation (J: Chōsen Eiga Seisaku Kabushikigaisha); the state-run production entity established in 1942.

Mansen Motion Picture Trading Co.	Educational film company (est. unknown).
Morris Sanghoe	Morris Trading Co.; served as Universal agency from 1915.
Nitta Engeibu	Nitta Entertainment Company; established in 1912 by Nitta Kōichi; distributed Nikkatsu films (1910s) and Teikoku Kinema films (1920s) and managed theatres in a number of cities, including Taishōkan and Hisagokan.
Sakuraba Shōkai	Largest film distribution company in Joseon and Manchuria based in Busan, owned by the settler businessman Sakuraba Fujio; distributed Paramount, Makino, and Nichibei films for cinemas in Joseon and Manchuria; and managed four theatres and ran two mobile film exhibition units.
Tokunaga Katsudō Shashin Shōkai	Tokunaga Motion Picture Shop; distributed Warner Brothers', FBO's and Ufa films for both Korean and Japanese theatres; managed such theatres as Tōa Club and Yūaikan (Yūaikan); its production wing (Tokunaga Productions) focused on producing educational films.
Toyama Mitsuru Production	Film production company established by Wakejima Shujirō and Japanese actor Toyama Mitsuru (1930); produced *Sadness at Geungang* (*Geumganhan*, 1931) as well as *My Husband is a Guard* (*Otto wa keibida*, 1931), a film commissioned by the colonial government of Joseon.

Bibliography

Note: This bibliography does not include periodical sources for reports, articles, reviews, statistics, cartoons, photographs, advertisements, and theatre listings that are included in the texts, captions and notes.

Archives, Libraries and Special Collections

Busan Metropolitan Simin Municipal Library, Busan, South Korea.
Cinema Library, University of Southern California. Los Angeles CA, United States.
Digital Library from the Meiji Era, National Diet Library, Tokyo, Japan. (kindai.ndl.go.jp).
East Asia Library, Stanford University, Palo Alto CA, United States.
Filmmuseum, Amsterdam, Holland.
Korean Digital Library, Seoul, South Korea. (www.dlibrary.go.kr).
Korean Film Center, Seoul, South Korea.
Korean Heritage Library, University of Southern California. Los Angeles CA, United States.
Korean Movie Database (www.kmdb.or.kr).
National Archives of Japan, Tokyo, Japan.
National Diet Library, Tokyo, Japan.
National Film Center, The National Museum of Modern Arts, Tokyo, Japan.
National Library of Korea, Seoul, South Korea.
Setagaya Literary Museum, Tokyo, Japan.
Tsubouchi Memorial Theatre Museum, Waseda University, Tokyo, Japan.

Books and Articles

1. Korean-language Sources

An Jong-hwa, *Hanguk yeonghwa cheukmyeonbisa* (Seoul: Hyeondai Mihaksa, 1998).
Bae Byoung-wook, '1920nyeondae jeonban Joseon chongdokbu seonjeon yeonghwa jejakgwa sangyeong', *Jibangsawa jibang munhwa*, 9.2, November 2006, pp. 183–239.
Baek Moonim, 'Joseon yeonghwaui punggyeongui balgyeon: yeonswaegeukgua gongganui jeonyu', *Dongbang hakji*, 158, June 2012, pp. 271–310.
Cho Hee-mun, *Na Un-gyu* (Seoul: Hangilsa, 1997).

— 'Yeonghwaui daejunghwawa byeonsaui yeokhal yeongu', *Design Yeongu*, 6, February 1998, pp. 227–46.
— 'Geukyeonghwa Gukyeongui yeonghwasajeok wisange daehan yeongu', *Sahoe jeongchaek nonchong*, 14.1, June 2002, pp. 221–41.
— *Hanguk yeonghwaui jaengjeom I* (Seoul: Jibmundang, 2002).
Cho Hye-jeong, *Hangukui yeoseonggwa namseong* (Seoul: Munhakwa Jiseongsa, 1991).
Cho Hye-jung, 'Na Un-gyu sinhwaui jinjeongseong yeongu', *Yeonghwa gyoyuk yeongu*, 6, 2004, pp. 175–92.
Cho Pung-yeon, *Seoul jabhak sajeon* (Seoul: Jeongdong Chulpansa, 1989).
Choi Chang-ho and Hong Gang-seong, *Na Un-gyuwa sunangi yeonghwa* (Pyongyang: Pyongyang Chulpansa, 2001).
Choi Yeol, *Hanguk manhwaui yeoksa* (Seoul: Yeolhwadang, 1995).
Choi Yeong-cheol, 'Ilbon sikminchihaui yeonghwa jeongchaek', *Hangukhak nonjib*, 11, February 1987, pp. 245–64.
Donomura Masaru, 'Sikminjigi Joseon daejungmunhwawa ilbonin', *Ilbon gonggan*, 2, November 2007, pp. 94–113.
Goh Mi-suk, 'Ilje gangjeomgi geukyeonghwa 4pyeoni balguldoeda', *Yeonghwa eoneo*, summer 2005, pp. 180–201.
Han Sang-il, *Ilbonui gukgajuui* (Seoul: Katchi, 1988).
Hanguk Yesul Yeonguso (ed.), *Lee Yeong-ilui Hanguk yeonghwasareul wihan jeungeonrok: Seong Dong-ho, Lee Gyu-hwan, Choi Geum-dong pyeon* (Seoul: Sodo, 2003).
— *Lee Yeong-ilui Hanguk Yeonghwareul uihan Jeungeonrok: Kim Seong-chun, Bok Hye-suk, Lee Gu-yeong pyeon* (Seoul: Sodo, 2003).
— *Lee Yeong-ilui Hanguk yeonghwareul wihan jeungeonrok: Yu Jang-san, Lee Gyeong-son, Lee Pil-wu, Lee Chang-geun pyeon* (Seoul: Sodo, 2003).
— *Lee Yeong-ilui Hanguk yeonghwasa ganguirok* (Seoul: Sodo, 2006).
Hong Yeong-cheol, *Busan yeonghwa 100 nyeon* (Seoul: Hanguk Yeonghwa Jaryo Yeonguwon, 2001).
— *Busan geundae yeonghwasa: yeonghwa sangyeon jaryo* (Busan: Sanjini, 2009).
Jang Han-ki, *Hanguk yeongeuksa* (Seoul: Dongguk University Press, 2000).
Jeon Pyeong-guk, 'Uri yeonghwa giwoneuroseo yeonswaegeuke daehan siron', *Yeonghwa yeongu*, 24, December 2004, pp. 463–89.
Jeong Jae-hyeong (ed.), *Hanguk chochanggiui yeonghwairon* (Seoul: Jibmundang, 1997).
Jin Hong-lian, 'Ilje gangjoemgie natanan aririangui hwaksangwa uimi byeoncheon', *Eumakgwa minjok*, 31, 2006, pp. 227–54.
Kang In-suk and Oh Jeong-im, 'Geundae seogusik geukjang seollibe ttareun gisaeng gongyeonui byeonmo yangsang', *The Korean Research Journal of Dance Documentation*, 19, 2010, pp. 1–27.
Kang Man-gil (ed.), *Ilbongwa seoguui sikmin tongchi bigyo* (Seoul: Seonin, 2004).
Kang Shim-ho, 'Iljesikminjichiha Gyeongseongbuminui dosijeok gamsuseong hyeongseong yeongu', *Seoulhak yeongu*, 21, September 2002, pp. 101–47.
Kawamura Minamoto, *Malhaneun kkot, gisaeng*, Yoo Jae-Sun (trans.) (Seoul: Sodam Chulpansa, 2002).

Kim Baek-yeong, *Jeguk Ilbongwa sikminji Joseonui geundae dosi hyeongseong* (Seoul: Simsan, 2013).
Kim Gab-ui, *Chunsa Na Un-Gyu jeonjib* (Seoul: Jibmundang, 2001).
Kim Gi-ho, Yang Seung-wu, Kim Han-bae, Yun In-seok, Jeon Wu-yong, Mok Su-hyeon and Eun Gi-su (eds), *Seoul namchon: sigan, jangso, saram* (Seoul: Seoulhak Yeonguso, 2003).
Kim Gyeong-il, *Yeoseongui geundae, geundaeui yeoseong* (Seoul: Pureun Yeoksa, 2007).
Kim Jin-song, *Seoule dancehalleul heohara: geundaeseongui hyeongseong* (Seoul: Hyeonsil munhwa yeongu, 2002).
Kim Jong-il, *Juche Munyeron* (Pyongyang: Jeseon Rodongdang Chulpansa, 1992).
Kim Jong-won and Jeong Jung-heon, *Uri yeonghwa 100nyeon* (Seoul: Hyeonamsa, 2001).
Kim Jong-wook (ed.), *Silok hanguk yeonghwa chongseo (sang)* (Seoul: Gukhakjaryowon, 2002).
— (ed.), *Silok hanguk yeonghwa chongseo (ha)* (Seoul: Gukhakjaryowon, 2002).
Kim Ryeo-sil, *Tusahaneun jeguk tuyeonghaneun sikminji* (Seoul: Samin, 2006).
Kim Sang-min, 'Aranggwa Hollywood', *SAI*, 14, 2013, pp. 265–96.
Kim Seung and Yang Mi-suk (eds), *Sinpyeon Busan daegwan* (Seoul: Seonin, 2010).
Kim Seung-gu, 'Tajaui siseone bichin sikminji Joseon yeonghwagye', *Hangukhak yeongu*, 48, 30 March 2014, pp. 71–98.
Kim Su-nam (ed.), *Museong yeonghwa scenario moeumjib* (Seoul: Jibmundang, 2003).
Kim Tae-su, *Kkotgachi pieo maehokehara* (Seoul: Hwangsojari, 2005).
Kim Yeong-chan, 'Na Un-gyu *Arirang*ui yeonghwajeok geundaeseong', *Hanguk munhak irongwa bipyeong*, 30, March 2006, pp. 177–99.
Kim Yeong-hee, *Gaehwagi daejungyesului kkot, gisaeng* (Seoul: Minsokwon, 2006).
Kim Yeong-mu, *Yumyeong byeonsa haeseol moeumjib* (Seoul: Changjak Maeul, 2003).
Korean Culture Research Institute of Ewha Woman's University (ed.), *Daehan jeguk yeongu* (Seoul: Baeksan Jaryowon, 1998).
Kwon Bodre, *Yeonyeoui sidae* (Seoul: Hyeonsil Munhwa Yeongu, 2003).
Lee Jeong-ha, 'Na Un-gyuui *Arirang* (1926)ui jaeguseong – *Arirang*ui hwalgeukjeok hyogwa hokeun hyogwaui saengsan', *Yeonghwa yeongu*, 26, 2005, pp. 265–90.
Lee Sang, *Lee Sang seonjib* (Seoul: Eulyu Munhwasa, 1994).
Lee Seung-hee, 'Gonggong mediaroseoui geukjanggwa Joseon minganjabonui munhwajeongchi', *Daedongmunhwa yeongu*, 69, March 2010, pp. 219–59.
Lee Tae-jun, *Lee Tae-jun danpyeon jeonjib 1* (Seoul: Garam Gihoik, 2005).
Lee Yeong-il, *Hanguk yeonghwa jeonsa* (Seoul: Sodo, 2004).
Lee Yeong-jae, *Jeguk Ilbonui Joseon yeonghwa* (Seoul: Hyeonsil Munhwa, 2008).
Lee Yong-shik, 'Mandeuleojin jeontong: ilje gangjeomgi gigan arirangui geundaehwa, minkokhwa, yuhaenghwa gwajeong', *Dongyang eumak*, 27, 2005, pp. 127–59.
Mun Il, *Yeonghwa soseol Arirang* (Gyeongseong: Pakmunseogwan, 1929).
— *Cheolindo* (Gyeongseong: Pakmuseogwan, 1931).
Mun Oak-pyo (ed.), *Sinyeoseong* (Seoul: Cheongnyeonsa, 2003).
Park Chun-hong, *Maehokui jilju, geundaeui hoengdan* (Seoul: Sancheoreom, 2003).
Park Ji-hyang, *Ingreureojin geundae* (Seoul: Pureun Yeoksa, 2003).

Park Min-il, *Hanguk Arirang munhak yeongu* (Chuncheon: Kangwondaehakgyo Chulpanbu, 1990).
Park Tae-won, *Soseolga gubossiui ilil* (Seoul: Munhakgwa Jiseongsa, 2005).
Sa Jin-sil, *Hanguk yeongeuksa yeongu* (Seoul: Taehaksa, 1997).
Seo Jeong-ju, *Naui munhak, naui insaeng* (Seoul: Sejong Chulpan Gongsa, 1997).
Shin Hyeon-gyu, *Kkoteul jabgo* (Seoul: Deokgyeong, 2005).
— *Gisaeng iyagi: iljesidaeui daejung star* (Seoul: Salim, 2007).
Shin Myeong-jik, *Modern boy Gyeoseongeul geonilda* (Seoul: Hyeonsil Munhwa Yeongu, 2003).
Son Jong-heum, Park Gyeong-wu, and Yu Chun-dong (eds), *Geundae gisaengui munhwawa yesul jaryopyeon 1* (Seoul: Bogosa, 2009).
Suyo Yeoksa Yeonguhoe (ed.), *Sikminji Joseongwa maeil sinbo – 1910nyeondae* (Seoul: Sinseowon, 2003).
Takasaki Soji, *Sikminji Joseonui ilboindeul* [*Shokumichi Chōsen no nihonjin*], Lee Gyu-Su (trans.) (Seoul: Yeoksa Bipyeongsa, 2002).
Yoo Hyeon-mok, *Hanguk yeonghwa baldalsa, 1900-1945* (Seoul: Chaeknuri, 1997).
Yoo Yeong-mi, '1910 nyeon jeonhu Seouleseo hwaldonghan ilbonin geukjang', *Ilbon Hakbo*, 56.2, September 2003, pp. 244–53.
Wi Gyeong-hye, *Honamui geukjang munhwasa* (Seoul: Dahal Media, 2007).
— 'Sikminji gaehangdosi geukjangui jangsoseong- Gunsaneul jungsimeuro', *Daedong munhwa yeongu*, 72, 2010, pp. 37–77.

2. Japanese-language Sources
Asahi Shimbun (ed.), *Nihon eiga renkan: taishō 13, 14nen* (Tokyo: Asashi Shimbunsha, 1925).
Chōsen gyōsei (ed.), *Chōsen tōchi hiwa* (Keijō: Teikoku Chihō Gyōsei Kakukai Chōsen Honbu, 1937).
Chōsen Jitsugyō Shimbunsha, *Chōsen zaishū nachijin jitsugyōka jinmeijiten* (Keijō: Chōsen Jitsugyō Shimbunsha, 1913).
Chōsen Kōronsha, *Zai-Chōsen naichijin shinshi meikanroku* (Keijō: Chōsen Kōronsha, 1917).
Chōsen Kyōsankai, *Heiwakinen Tokyo hakurankai Chōsen kyōchanshakai jimuhogoku* (Keijō: Chōsen Kyōsankai, 1922).
Chōsen Sōtokufu Gakumukyoku Shakai Gyōikuka, *Chōsen shakai kyōka yoran* (Keijō: Sakazawa Shoten, 1937).
Chōsen Sōtokufu Kanbō Bunshoka, *Chōsen Sōtokufu Kinema* (Keijō: Chōsen Insatsu Kabushiki Kaisha, 1937).
Chōsen Sōtokufu Keimukyoku, *Chōsen hōeki tōkei* (Keijō: Chōsen Sōtokufu Keimugyoku, 1941).
— *Katsudō shashin fuirumu keiretsu gaiyō* (Keijō: Chōsen Sōtokufu Keimukyoku, 1931).
Chung Choong-sil, '1920nendai-1930nendai, Keijō no eigakan', *Ricks Korea kenkyū*, 4, March, 2013, pp. 77–92.
Fujita Motohiko, *Nihon eiga gendaishi: shōwa jūnendai* (Tokyo: Hanagamisha, 1977).

Ichikawa Sai, *Ajia eiga no sōzō oyobi kensetsu* (Tokyo: Gokusei Eiga Tsūshinsha, 1941).
— *Waga eiga jigyōron* (Tokyo: Kokusai Eiga Shimbun Tsūshinsha Shuppanbu, 1941).
Imamura Shohei (ed.), *Nihon eiga no tanjō* (Tokyo: Iwanami Shoten, 1985).
— (ed.), *Musei eiga no kansei* (Tokyo: Iwanami Shoten, 1986).
— (ed.), *Tōkki no jidai* (Tokyo: Iwanami Shoten, 1986).
— (ed.), *Sensō to Nihon eiga* (Tokyo: Iwanami Shoten, 1986).
Ino Kenji, *Kōgyōkai no kaoyaku* (Tokyo: Sakuma Shobō, 2004).
Ishimaki Yoshio, *Ōbei oyobi nihon no eigashi* (Osaka: Pratonsha, 1925).
Itakura Fumiaki, 'Beikoku nikkei imin no Nihon eiga juyō', *Art Research*, 3, 2003, pp. 189–97.
Iwamoto Kenji (ed.), *Nihon eiga to modanizumu 1920–1930* (Tokyo: Ripuropotosha, 1991).
— (ed.), *Gentō no seiki: eiga zenya no shikaku bunkashi* (Tokyo: Shinwasha, 2002).
— (ed.), *Nihon eiga to nashonalizumu 1931–1945* (Tokyo: Shinwasha, 2004).
— (ed,), *Eiga to dai tōa kyōeiken* (Tokyo: Shinwasha, 2004).
Kang Dong-jin, *Nihon no Chōsen shihai seisakushi kenkyū* (Tokyo: Tokyo Daigaku Shūppankai, 1981).
Keijō Nippōsha (ed.), *Keijōfu machi nachijinbutsu to jigyō annai* (Keijō: Keijō Nippōsha, 1921).
— (ed.), *Dai-Keijō kōshokusha meikan* (Keijō: Keijō Nippōsha, 1936).
Kim Jeong-min, 'Shokuminchi Chōsenni okeru "Katsudō shashin [fuirumu] kenetsu kisoku" ni kansuru ichikōsatsu', *Mediashi kenkyū*, 30, 2011, pp. 109–133.
— 'Shokuminchi Chosenni okeru eiga kenetsu saikō', *Mediashi kenkyū*, 32, 2012, pp. 1–21.
Kokusai Eiga Tsūshinsha (ed.), *Nihon eiga jigyō sōran: shōwa 2nen* (Tokyo: Kokusai Eiga Tsūshinsha, 1927).
— (ed.), *Nihon eiga jigyō sōran: shōwa 3, 4nen* (Tokyo: Kokusai Eiga Tsūshinsha, 1928).
— (ed.), *Nihon eiga jigyō sōran: shōwa 5nen* (Tokyo: Kokusai Eiga Tsūshinsha, 1930).
— (ed.), *Zengoku kōgyō torishimari kitei oyobi kōgyōzei ichiran* (Tokyo: Kokusai Eiga Tsūshinsha, 1927).
Makino Mamoru (ed.), *Nihon eiga kenetsushi* (Tokyo: Bandō, 2003).
Matsuda Jukkoku, *Saitō Makoto den: Niniroku jikende ansatsusareta teitoku no shinjitsu* (Tokyo: Genshū Shuppansha, 2008).
Misono Kyohei, *Katsuben jidai* (Tokyo: Iwanami Shoten, 1990).
Monbushō Shakai Kyōikukyoku (ed.), *Chūokanchōni okeru eiga riyō jyōkyō* (Tokyo: Monbushō, 1937).
Musei Eiga Kanjōkai (ed.), *Katsudō benshi* (Tokyo: Urban Connections, 2001).
Nagasawa Masaharu, 'Chōsen eiga reimeiki no satsueigishi—Miyagawa Heinosuke no koto, nado', *Kengō no yohaku*, Seikyusha, March 4, 2014. Last accessed 30 August 2015. http://www.seikyusha.co.jp/wp/rennsai/yohakuni/blank125.html
Okamura Shiho, *Katsudō shashin meikan: zenpen* (Tokyo: Katsudō Shimbunsha, 1922), reprinted in Makino Mamoru (ed.), *Saisentan minshū goraku eiga bunken shiryōshū 5* (Tokyo: Yumani Shobō, 2006).

Sasagawa Keiko, 'Keijōni okeru Teikoku Kinema engei no kōgyō', *Kansai toshi isan kenkyū*, 3, March 2013, pp. 19–31.
Sato Tadao, *Nihon eigashi I, 1896-1940* (Tokyo: Iwanami Shoten, 1995).
Tanaka Jun'ichirō, *Nihon eiga hattatsushi I* (Tokyo: Chūkō Bunko, 1975).
— *Nihon kyōiku eiga hattatsushi* (Tokyo: Kakyūsha, 1979).
— *Hiroku: Nihon no katsudō shashin* (Tokyo: Wise Shutsuban Shūppan, 2004).
Tanaka Norihiro, 'Zai-Chōsen Nihonjin no eiga seisaku kenkyū', *Mediashi kenkyū*, 17, 2004, pp. 122–42.
Takashima Kinji, *Chōsen eiga tōseishi*, Makino Mamoru (ed.) (Tokyo: Yumani Shobō, 2003).
Terakawa Shin, *Eiga oyobi eigageki* (Osaka: Osaka Mainichi Shimbun, 1925).
Ueda Koichirō, *Busan [Fuzan] no shōkōkai annai* (Busan: Busan Shōkōkaigisho, 1935).
Yang In-sil, '1920nendai shikakumeida no ichidanmen Daichiwa bishōmu to Chōsen', *Ritsumeikan sangyōshakai ronshū*, 43.1, June 2007, pp. 35–57.
Yoshihara Junpei, *Nihon tanpen eizōshi* (Tokyo: Iwanami Shoten, 2011).
Yoshishige Yoshida, Michio Yamguchi, and Nawahuki Kinoshita (eds), *Cinematograph to Meiji Nihon* (Tokyo: Iwanami Shoten, 1995).

3. English-language Sources

Abel, Richard, *The Red Rooster Scare: Making Cinema American, 1900–1910* (Berkeley CA: University of California Press, 1999).
Anderson, Joseph and Donald Richie, *The Japanese Film: Art and Industry* (Princeton NJ: Princeton University Press, 1982).
Ankum, Katharina von, *Women in the Metropolis: Gender and Modernity in Weimar Culture* (Berkeley CA: University of California Press, 1997).
Atkins, E. Taylor, 'The Dual Career of "Arirang": The Korean Resistance Anthem That Became a Japanese Pop Hit', *The Journal of Asian Studies*, 66.3, August 2007, pp. 645–87.
— *Primitive Selves: Koreana in the Japanese Colonial Gaze, 1910–1945* (Berkeley CA: University of California Press, 2010).
Baskett, Michael, *The Attractive Empire: Transnational Film Culture in Imperial Japan* (Honolulu HI: University of Hawai'i Press, 2008).
Benjamin, Walter, *Charles Baudelaire: A Lyric Poet in the Era of High Capitalism* (London: NLB, 1973).
— *The Arcade Project*, Translation edited by Howard Eiland and Kevin McLaughlin (Cambridge MA and London: The Belknap Press of Harvard University Press, 1999).
Bernardi, Joanne, *Writing in Light: The Silent Scenario and the Japanese Pure Film Movement* (Detroit MI: Wayne State University Press, 2001).
Bishop, Isabella Bird, *Korea and Her Neighbours: A Narrative of Travel, with an Account of the Recent Vicissitudes and Present Position of the Country* (London: John Murray, 1898).
Bruno, Giuliana, *Streetwalking on a Ruined Map: Cultural Theory and the City Films of Elvira Notari* (Princeton NJ: Princeton University Press, 1993).

Buck-Morss, Susan, *The Dialectics of Seeing: Walter Benjamin and the Arcades Project* (Cambridge MA: MIT Press, 1989).
Burch, Noël and Annette Michelson, *To the Distant Observer: Form and Meaning in the Japanese Cinema* (Berkeley CA: University of California Press, 1979).
Burn, James, *Cinema and Society in the British Empire 1895–1940* (London: Palgrave Macmillan, 2013).
Capiro, Mark, *Japanese Assimilation Policies in Colonial Korea, 1910–1945* (Seattle WA: University of Washington Press, 2009).
Cazdyn, Eric M, *The Flash of Capital: Film and Geopolitics in Japan* (Durham NC: Duke University Press, 2002).
Charney, Leo and Vanessa R. Schwartz, *Cinema and the Invention of Modern Life* (Berkeley CA: University of California Press, 1995).
Chatterjee, Partha, *Nationalist Thought and the Colonial World* (Minneapolis MN: University of Minnesota Press, 1993).
Ching, Leo T. S., *Becoming 'Japanese': Colonial Taiwan and the Politics of Identity Formation* (Berkeley CA: University of California Press, 2001).
Conor, Liz, *The Spectacular Modern Woman: Feminine Visibility in the 1920s* (Bloomington IN: Indiana University Press, 2004).
DeBoer, Stephanie, 'Sayon no Kane (Sayon's Bell)', in Justin Bowyer (ed.), *The Cinema of Japan and Korea* (London: Wallflower Press, 2005), pp. 23–31.
Deocampo, Nick, *Cine: Spanish Influences on Early Cinema in the Philippines* (Manila: Cinema Values Reorientation Program, National Commission for Culture and the Arts, 2003).
Dixon, Robert, *Photography, Early Cinema and Colonial Modernity: Frank Hurley's Synchronized Lecture Entertainments* (London: Anthem Press, 2012).
Duara, Prasenjit, *Rescuing History from the Nation: Questioning Narratives of Modern China* (Chicago IL: University of Chicago Press, 1996).
Duus, Peter, *The Abacus and the Sword: The Japanese Penetration of Korea, 1895–1910* (Berkeley CA: University of California Press, 1998).
Eckert, Carter J., *Offspring of Empire: The Koch'ang Kims and the Colonial Origins of Korean Capitalism, 1876–1945* (Seattle WA: University of Washington Press, 1996).
Elsaesser, Thomas and Adam Barker, *Early Cinema: Space, Frame, Narrative* (London: BFI Publishing, 1993).
Everett, Anna, *Returning the Gaze: A Genealogy of Black Film Criticism, 1909–1949* (Durham NC: Duke University Press, 2001).
Field, Allyson Nadia, *Uplift Cinema: The Emergence of African American Film and the Possibility of Black Modernity* (Durham NC and London: Duke University Press, 2015).
Friedberg, Anne, *Window Shopping: Cinema and the Postmodern* (Berkeley CA: University of California Press, 1993).
Fujiki, Hideaki 'Benshi as Stars: The Irony of the Popularity and Respectability of Voice Performers in Japanese Cinema', *Cinema Journal*, 45.2, winter 2006, pp. 68–84.
— *Making Personas: Transnational Film Stardom in Modern Japan* (Cambridge MA: Harvard University Asia Center, 2013).

— 'Creation of the Audience: Cinema as Popular Recreation and Social Education in Modern Japan', in Daisuke Miyao (ed.), *The Oxford Handbook of Japanese Cinema* (Oxford and New York: Oxford University Press, 2014), pp. 79–97.

Fujitani, Takashi, *Race for Empire: Koreans as Japanese and Japanese as Americans during World War II* (Berkeley CA: University of California Press, 2011).

Fujitani, Takashi, Geoffrey M. White, and Lisa Yoneyama (eds), *Perilous Memories: The Asia–Pacific War(s)* (Durham NC: Duke University Press, 2001).

Gerow, Aaron, *Visions of Japanese Modernity: Articulations of Cinema, Nation, and Spectatorship, 1895–1925* (Berkeley CA and Los Angeles CA: University of California Press, 2010).

Gluck, Carol, *Japan's Modern Myths: Ideology in the Late Meiji Period* (Princeton NJ: Princeton University Press, 1985).

Grieveson, Lee and Peter Krämer (eds), *The Silent Cinema Reader* (London and New York: Routledge, 2004).

Grieveson, Lee and Colin MacCabe (eds), *Film and the End of Empire* (London: Palgrave Macmillan, 2011).

Grieveson, Lee and Colin MacCabe (eds), *Empire and Film* (London: Palgrave Macmillan, 2011).

Hames, Peter, *Czech and Slovak Cinema: Theme and Tradition* (Edinburgh: Edinburgh University Press, 2009).

Hansen, Miriam, *Babel and Babylon Spectatorship in American Silent Film* (Cambridge MA: Harvard University Press, 1991).

— 'Fallen Women, Rising Stars, New Horizons: Shanghai Silent Film as Vernacular Modernism', *Film Quarterly*, 54.1, fall 2000, pp. 10–22.

Harootunian, Harry D, *Overcome by Modernity History, Culture, and Community in Interwar Japan* (Princeton NJ: Princeton University Press, 2000).

Hayward, Susan, *French National Cinema* (London and New York: Routledge, 1993).

High, Peter B, *The Imperial Screen: Japanese Film Culture in the Fifteen Years' War, 1931–1945* (Madison WI: University of Wisconsin Press, 2003).

Higson, Andrew, 'The Concept of National Cinema', *Screen*, 30.4, 1989, pp. 36–44.

Hjort, Mette and Scott MacKenzie (eds), *Cinema and Nation* (London and New York: Routledge, 2000).

Holmes, Burton, *The Burton Holmes Lectures X* (Battle Creek MI: The Little-Preston Co., Limited, 1901).

hooks, bell, *Black Looks: Race and Representation* (Boston MA: South End Press, 1992).

Innes, Abby, *Czechoslovakia – the Short Goodbye* (New Haven CT: Yale University Press, 2001).

Jaikumar, Priya, *Cinema at the End of Empire: A Politics of Transition in Britain and India* (Durham NC: Duke University Press, 2006).

Jeong, Kelly, *Crisis of Gender and the Nation in Korean Literature and Cinema* (Lanham MD: Lexington Books, 2011).

Jun, Uchida, *Brokers of Empire: Japanese Settler Colonialism in Korea 1876–1945* (Cambridge MA: Harvard University Press, 2011).

Kasza, Gregory James, *The State and the Mass Media in Japan, 1918–1945* (Berkeley CA: University of California Press, 1988).
Kenji, Iwamoto, 'Japanese Cinema until 1930: A Consideration of its Formal Aspects', *Iris*, 16, spring 1993, pp. 9–22.
Kim, Jina E, 'Intermedial Aesthetics: Still Images, Moving Words, and Written Sounds in Early Twentieth-Century Korean Cinematic Novels (*Yeonghwa Soseol*)', *The Review of Korean Studies*, 16.2, December 2013, pp. 45–79.
Kim, Jong-Il, *On the Art of the Cinema* (Pyongyang: Foreign Languages Publication House, 1989).
Kirby, Lynne, *Parallel Tracks: The Railroad and Silent Cinema* (Durham NC: Duke University Press, 1997).
Komatsu, Hiroshi, 'From Natural Colour to the Pure Motion Picture Drama: The Meaning of Tenkatsu Company in the 1910s of Japanese Film History', *Film History*, 7.1, spring 1995, pp. 69–86.
— 'Japan: Before the Great Kantō Earthquake', in Geoffrey Nowell-Smith (ed.), *The Oxford History of World Cinema* (Oxford: Oxford University Press, 1996), pp. 177–82.
— 'The Foundation of Modernism: Japanese Cinema in the Year 1927', *Film History*, 17, 2005, pp. 363–75.
Komatsu, Hiroshi and Charles Musser, 'Benshi Search', *Wide Angle*, 9.2, 1987, pp. 72–90.
Koszarski, Richard, *An Evening's Entertainment: The Age of the Silent Feature Picture, 1915–1928* (Berkeley CA and Los Angeles CA: University of California Press, 1994).
Kracauer, Siegfried and Thomas Y. Levin, *The Mass Ornament: Weimar Essays* (Cambridge MA: Harvard University Press, 1995).
Lee, Leo Ou-fan, *Shanghai Modern: The Flowering of a New Urban Culture in China, 1930–1945* (Cambridge MA: Harvard University Press, 1999).
Lee, Yeong-il, *The History of Korean Cinema*, Richard Lynn Greever (trans.) (Seoul: Motion Picture Promotion Corp., 1988).
Loomba, Ania, *Colonialism–Postcolonialism* (London and New York: Routledge, 1998).
Lu, Hanchao, *Beyond the Neon Lights: Everyday Shanghai in the Early Twentieth Century* (Berkeley CA and London: University of California Press, 2004).
McKenzie, Frederick Arthur, *The Tragedy of Korea* (London: Hodder and Stoughton, 1908).
Mayo, Marlene J., J. Thomas Rimer, and H. Eleanor Kerkham (eds), *War, Occupation, and Creativity: Japan and East Asia, 1920–1960* (Honolulu HI: University of Hawai'i Press, 2001).
Memmi, Albert, *The Colonizer and the Colonized* (London: Souvenir Press, 1974).
Minichiello, Sharon, *Japan's Competing Modernities: Issues in Culture and Democracy, 1900–1930* (Honolulu HI: University of Hawai'i Press, 1998).
Morris-Suzuki, Tessa, 'Northern Lights: The Making and Unmaking of Karafuto Identity', *The Journal of Asian Studies*, 60.3, August 2001, pp. 645–71.
Myers, Ramon Hawley, Mark R. Peattie, and Jingzhi Zhen (eds), *The Japanese Colonial Empire, 1895–1945* (Princeton NJ: Princeton University Press, 1987).

Nahm, Andrew C, *Korea: Tradition & Transformation: A History of the Korean People* (Elizabeth NJ: Hollym International Corp., 1996).

Nolletti, Arthur and David Desser (eds), *Reframing Japanese Cinema: Authorship, Genre, History* (Bloomington IN: Indiana University Press, 1992).

Nornes, Markus, *Japanese Documentary Film: The Meiji Era through Hiroshima* (Minneapolis MA: University of Minnesota Press, 2003).

Nornes, Markus and Fukushima Yukio (eds), *The Japan/America Film Wars: World War II Propaganda and Its Cultural Contexts* (Chur, Switzerland and Langhorne, PA: Harwood Academic Publishers, 1994).

Ogihara, Junko, 'The Exhibition of Films for Japanese Americans in Los Angeles during the Silent Film Era', *Film History*, 4.2, 1990, pp. 81–7.

Oksiloff, Assenka, *Picturing the Primitive: Visual Culture, Ethnography, and Early German Cinema* (New York: Palgrave, 2001).

Oppenheim, Robert, '"The West" and the Anthropology of Other People's Colonialism: Frederick Starr in Korea, 1911–1930', *The Journal of Asian Studies*, 64.3, August 2005, pp. 677–703.

Peiss, Kathy Lee, *Cheap Amusements: Working Women and Leisure in Turn-of-the-Century New York* (Philadelphia PA: Temple University Press, 1986).

Petro, Patrice, *Joyless Streets: Women and Melodramatic Representation in Weimar Germany* (Princeton NJ: Princeton University Press, 1989).

Rhee, Jooyeon, '*Arirang*, and the making of a national narrative in South and North Korea', *Journal of Japanese and Korean Cinema*, 1.1, 2009, pp. 27–43.

Richie, Donald, *Japanese Cinema: An Introduction* (Hong Kong and New York: Oxford University Press, 1990).

Rivers, Chérie, 'Cinema', in F. Abiola Irele and Biodun Jeyifo (eds), *The Oxford Encyclopedia of African Thought* (Volume 1) (London: Oxford University Press, 2010).

Robinson, Michael Edson, *Cultural Nationalism in Colonial Korea, 1920–1925* (Seattle WA: University of Washington Press, 1989).

Rony, Fatimah Tobing, *The Third Eye: Race, Cinema, and Ethnographic Spectacle* (Durham NC: Duke University Press, 1996).

Ross, Steven Joseph, *Working-Class Hollywood: Silent Film and the Shaping of Class in America* (Princeton NJ: Princeton University Press, 1998).

Said, Edward, *Culture and Imperialism* (New York: Knopf, 1993).

Saldaña-Portillo, María Josefina, *The Revolutionary Imagination in the Americas and the Age of Development* (Durham NC: Duke University Press, 2003).

Schmid, Andre, *Korea between Empires, 1895–1919* (New York: Columbia University Press, 2002).

Seo, Jaekil, 'One Film, or Many?: The Multiple Texts of the Colonial Korean Film *Volunteer*', Jongmin Kim and Seulgie Lim (trans.), *Cross-Currents: East Asian History and Culture Review E-Journal* 5, December 2012. http://cross-currents.berkeley.edu/e-journal/issue-5/Seo (Last Accessed 8 August 2015).

Shepard, Elizabeth, 'The Magic Lantern Slide in Entertainment and Education, 1860–1920', *History of Photography*, 11.2, April–June 1987, pp. 91–108.

Shin, Gi-Wook, 'Agrarianism: A Critique of Colonial Modernity in Korea', *Comparative Studies in Society and History*, 41.1, October 1999, pp. 784–804.
— *Ethnic Nationalism in Korea: Genealogy, Politics, and Legacy* (Stanford CA: Stanford University Press, 2006).
Shin, Gi-Wook and Michael Edson Robinson (eds), *Colonial Modernity in Korea* (Cambridge MA: Harvard University Asia Center, 1999).
Singer, Ben, *Melodrama and Modernity: Early Sensational Cinema and Its Contexts* (New York: Columbia University Press, 2001).
Slavin, David Henry, *Colonial Cinema and Imperial France, 1919–1939: White Blind Spots, Male Fantasies, Settler Myths* (Baltimore MD: Johns Hopkins University Press, 2001).
Standish, Isolde, 'Mediators of Modernity: "Photo-interpreters" in Japanese Silent Cinema', *Oral Tradition*, 20.1, 2005, pp. 93–101.
Stewart, Jacqueline Najuma, *Migrating to the Movies: Cinema and Black Urban Modernity* (Berkeley CA: University of California Press, 2005).
Stollery, Martin, *Alternative Empires: European Modernist Cinemas and the Cultures of Imperialism* (Exeter: University of Exeter Press, 2000).
Thompson, Kristin, *Exporting Entertainment: America in the World Film Market, 1907–34* (London: BFI Publishing, 1985).
Tipton, Elise K., *Society and the State in Interwar Japan* (London and New York: Routledge, 1997).
Tipton, Elise K. and John Clark (eds), *Being Modern in Japan: Culture and Society from the 1910s to the 1930s* (Honolulu HI: University of Hawai'i Press, 2000).
Tsivian, Yuri, *Early Cinema in Russia and its Cultural Reception*, Alan Bodger (trans.) (Chicago IL and London: The University of Chicago Press, 1998).
Vasey, Ruth, *The World According to Hollywood, 1918–1939* (Madison WI: University of Wisconsin Press, 1997).
Wallerstein, Immanuel Maurice, *After Liberalism* (New York: New Press, 1995).
Ward, Janet, *Weimar Surfaces Urban Visual Culture in 1920s Germany* (Berkeley CA: University of California Press, 2001).
Watanabe, Naoki, 'The Colonial and Transnational Production of Suicide Squad at the Watchtower and Love and the Vow', Rhee Jooyeon (trans.), *Cross-Currents: East Asian History and Culture Review*, 2.1, 2013, pp. 89–115.
Weisenfeld, Gennifer, 'Touring Japan-as-Museum: NIPPON and Other Japanese Imperialist Travelogues', *Positions*, 8.3, winter 2000, pp. 747–93.
Yecies, Brian, 'Lost Memories of Korean Cinema: Film Policies during Japanese Colonial Rule, 1919–1937', *Asian Cinema*, fall/winter 2003, pp. 75–90.
Yecies, Brian and Ae-Gyung Shim, *Korea's Occupied Cinemas 1893–1948* (New York and London: Routledge, 2011).
Young, Louise, *Japan's Total Empire: Manchuria and the Culture of Wartime Imperialism* (Berkeley CA: University of California Press, 1999).
Zhang, Zhen, *An Amorous History of the Silver Screen: Shanghai Cinema, 1896–1937* (Chicago IL: University of Chicago Press, 2005).

Index

Note: **bold** indicates illustrations

action films, 70, 77–8, 79–80, 91, 135, 153
admission fees, 26, 27, 105, 130–1, 211
Aegwan Theatre, 151
aesthetics *see* film aesthetics
Africa, 33–4
African American audiences, 146–7, 208
Age of Singing, The (1930), 75–6
All-Japan Motion Picture Education Society, 38
Allen, George, 150
Allen Trading Company, 150
Ambrosio Film, 133
American films
   censorship of, 160–2
   distribution, 9, 80, 105–6, 124, 140, 150–3
   exhibition, 1–2, 28, 105–6, 124, 126, 127–8, 134–6, 140, 179–81, 182–3
   film studios, 105, 106, 124, 147–53
   genre conventions, 62, 70, 77–82
   influence of, 62, 70, 77–82
   and Korean audiences, 11, 23, 80, 134–5, 140, 144–67
   political aspects of, 153–67
   and sexuality, 157, 160, 197–200, 214
   spectatorship, 11, 23, 80, 127–8, 134, 144–67, 179–81, 182–3
   see also United States
An Cheol-yeong, 94
An Dong-su, 98
An Seok-yeong, 205
Anderson, Joseph L., 171
Arirang (film, 1926), 58–87, **66**, **79**, **81**, 136
Arirang (folk song), 59, 61, 63–7, 68–9, **69**, 82–5
Arirang, The Sequel (1930), 68
Arirang – The Third Installation (1936), 78
art films, 86, 95–8
Asahi Shimbun, 38
assimilation policies, 31, 67, 100–2, 136–43, 161–3, 232, 234; *see also* hegemony
Association of Gyeongseong Exhibitors (AGE), 103–4, 106, 117
audience reception
   of American films, 11, 23, 80, 134–5, 140, 144–67
   of *Arirang*, 59, 65–7, 70, 71
   of *A Hero of the Troubled Times*, 70
   of Japanese films, 126–7
   of local films, 71–2
   of *A Song of Sad Love*, 73–4
Awaya Noriko, 83

Bandō Tsumasuburō, 127, **128**
Baudelaire, Charles, 206
Belgium, 34
Bell Sound (1929), 76
Ben-Hur: A Tale of the Christ (1925), 179–81
Benjamin, Walter, 205–6, 207
benshi/byeonsa, 43–4, 48–9, 62, 72, 116, 120–2, 131, 134, 167–83, **170**, **175**, 224
bicycle boys, 140–3
Bishop, Isabella Bird, 224
Bluebird Photoplays, 124, 148, 149
Border, The (1923), 3
Border, The (1940), 87, 96
boredom, 207–8, 209–10
Bostwick, H. R., 26
Bow, Clara, **197**, 197–9
Brady, Jasper E., 147
British Empire, 33–4; *see also* United Kingdom
Broken Coin (1915), 124, **125**, 160
Brokers of Empire (Jun), 108
Bureau of Agriculture, Commerce and Industry, 35
Bureau of Educational Affairs, 39
Busan, 30, 112, 113, 116, 124, 126, 131, 139
Busan nippō, 113
Byeolgeongon, 72–3, 75, 81, 191–4, 211, 213, 219
byeonsa *see* benshi/byeonsa

Cabinet of Dr. Caligari (1919), 80
Canada, 49
capitalism, 104, 109, 156, 194, 205–6, 228, 234
cars, 217–18
censorship *see* film censorship
Chae Gyu-yeob, 83
chain dramas, 3, 29, 122, 173, 226
Chaney, Lon, 148
Chaplin, Charlie, 105–6, 148

Chaplin, Sarah, 194–5
Chatterjee, Partha, 193
Cheongjin, 232
China, 5, 13, 86, 116, 207; *see also* Manchuria
Ching, Leo, 33, 137–8
Cho Hee-mun, 62
Cho Taek-won, 218–19
Choi Byeong-ryong, 176
Choi In-gyu, 37
Choi Seung-hee, 230
Choi Wan-gyu, 37
cholera, 14, 36
Chōsen kōron, 114, 121–2, 134, 135, 231
Chuncheon, 60, 106
Chūokan Theatre, 121, 133, 140, 143
Chushingura (1932), 103
cinemas *see* movie theatres
cinematographers *see* directors of photography (DPs)
City Lights (1931), 105–6
City of Iron Man, The (1930), 77–8
class segregation, 22–7; *see also* social class
Collbran, Henry, 26–7
Colonial Film Unit (UK), 33–4
comedy films, 158
Confucianism, 21, 64, 196, 203–4, 212
consumerism, 193, 205, 206, 214, 218, 220, 226–7
co-production, 85, 87–95, 98–102
critical reception
 of *The Age of Singing*, 75–6
 of American films, 154–7, 160–7
 of *Arirang*, 72–3, 75, 76–7
 of *The City of Iron Man*, 77–8
 of *Fishing Fires*, 93, 94
 of *Han River*, 92
 of Hollywood-influenced films, 80–1
 of Joseon films in Japan, 90, 91–3, 95–6, 98
 of representations of the rural, 75–6
 of *The Wayfarer*, 90, 91–3, 100–1
 see also film critics
Cukor, George, 230
culture films, 50; *see also* educational films
cultural appropriation, 83–5
cultural imperialism, 166
Cultural Rule, 31, 41–2, 53, 138, 161, 208–9
Czech films, 86, 95–8, 101; *see also* European films
Czech identity, 96–8

Daegu, 16, 105, 116
Daejeong Gwonbeon, 225
Daeryuk Geukjang, 230; *see also* Danseongsa Theatre
Daeryuk Kinema, 118
Dai-Nippōn Kokusuikai, 117
Daito studio, 232
Danseongsa Theatre, 13–17, **15**, 27, 29, 72, 105, 122, 131–3, 150, 153, 174, 179–81, 204, 226, 229, 230
democracy, 154–7
Deocampo, Nick, 8, 165–6
Department of Sanitation, 36

Department of Social Affairs, 50
DeVry projectors, **40**, 40–1
directors of photography (DPs), 122–3
'Dissemination and Publicity' campaign, 31–2
distribution *see* film distribution
documentaries, 25, 35, 122; *see also* educational films
Donga ilbo, 73, 98, 156, 165, **198**, 210
Dongyang Guekjang theatre, 114
Dosaengrok (1938), 87
'Dream of Butterfly' (Zhuang Zi), 207

East Gate Moving Picture Site, 19, 27, 203
Eckert, Carter J., 8, 173
Ecstasy (1932), 96
educational films, 2, 10, 30, 33–52, 105, 122, 157–60, 163; *see also* documentaries; propaganda films; social edifice films
Educational Magic Lantern Association, 37
Eiga junpō, 161–2
eolgaehwakkun, 190–3, **191**, **192**
epidemics, 14, 36
essay cartoons, 199–202, **200**, **201**, 205, 206, 210
ethnic segregation, 17, 28, 129–43, 161–3, 175–6, 230–1
Eulsa Restriction Treaty, 185
European films
 art films, 86, 95–8
 distribution, 80, 124, 151–3
 exhibition, 1–2, 28, 124, 127–8, 133
 influence of, 76–7, 86, 95–8
 lack of availability during First World War, 150
 spectatorship, 80
 see also Czech films; French films; German films; Italian films; Russian films
exhibition *see* film exhibition
Exhibition and Exhibition Sites Regulation, 177
expositions and fairs, 46, **47**, 184–6, 225
expressionist films, 76–7
extras, 78–9

fan magazines, 127, 148
fan reviews, 154
fashion, 193–202
Fast Company (1929), 140, **142**
Faust (1926), 80
FBO studio, 105, 150
female actors, 226
female audiences, 44, 118, 199–204, 210–28
feminism, 194, 196–7, 227–8
film aesthetics, 57, 70–4, 86, 95–8, 172
Film and Photo Bureau (Belgium), 34
film censorship, 1, 52, 56, 67, 80, 95, 126, 146–7, 153–4, 160–4, 176–81, 209
film critics, 9, 11, 50, 68, 72–3, 75–8, 80–1, 90, 91–6, 98, 100–2, 108, 139–40, 157, 163; *see also* critical reception
film distribution
 of American films, 9, 80, 105–6, 124, 126, 140, 150–3

film distribution (*cont.*)
  of educational films, 30, 37–8, 51–2, 105
  of European films, 80, 124, 151–3
  in Japan, 85, 87–8, 90, 153
  of Japanese films, 9, 88–9, 103–5, 106, 123–7
  by Japanese settlers, 9, 103–6, 123–6, 150, 229–32
  by Japanese studios, 88–9, 229–32, 233–4
  by Korean distributors, 150–1
  nationalisation of, 232–3, 234–5
  of propaganda films, 30, 37–8
film exhibition
  of American films, 1–2, 28, 105–6, 124, 126–8, 134–6, 140, 179–81, 182–3
  and assimilation policies, 136–43, 161–3
  benshi/byeonsa, 43–4, 48–9, 72, 120–2, 131, 134, 167–83
  bicycle boys, 140–3
  commercialisation of, 27–9
  early screenings, 19–27, 110–13
  of educational films, 30, 35–6, 37–8, 51–2, 157–60
  emergence of movie theatres, 14–18, 19–21, 27–9, 112–13, 115–17
  and ethnic segregation, 17, 28, 129–36, 140–3, 161–3, 175–6, 230–1
  of European films, 1–2, 28, 124, 127–8, 133
  at expositions and fairs, 46, **47, 48**
  film programmes, 11, 28, 105, 114, 118–20, 124–9, 131, 140, 160–1
  by government and social organisations, 25, 157–60
  for international audiences, 49–50
  in Japan, 19–20, 40–1, 42–3, 46, **47**, 118–20, 136
  of Japanese films, 1–2, 88–9, 103–4, 124–8, 136, 144–5, 162
  for Japanese settler audiences, 9, 28, 110–13, 123–36, 140–3, 229–32
  by Japanese settlers, 9, 11, 27–8, 103–6, 115–20, 123–9, 229–32
  by Japanese studios, 88–9, 101, 229–32, 233–4
  for Korean audiences, 15, 16–17, 28–9, 43–5, **45**, 129–36, 140–3, 230
  by Korean exhibitors, 28–9
  of Korean films, 1–2, 29, 110
  by the MPU, 42–50, **45, 47**, 51
  nationalisation of, 234–5
  by newspapers, 160
  private screenings in Japanese residential areas, 110–11
  projection technology, 40–1
  projectionists, 123
  of propaganda films, 20, 30, 38, 42–50
  at royal palaces, 21–2, 23–5
  screen quotas, 52, 88, 136, 153–4, 161, 163–5
  at temporary venues, 16, 20, **20**, 21–3, 25–7
  in the United States, 40
  see also movie theatres
film-makers *see* film production; film studios

film novels, 73
film production
  co-productions with Japanese studios, 85, 87–95, 98–102
  directors of photography, 122
  early production, 3–4, 17–18, 29–30
  educational films, 30, 33–4, 35, 37–8, 50–2, 105
  by *gwonbeon*, 226
  involvement of movie theatres, 30
  by Japanese settlers, 9, 29–30, 52, 71–2, 105, 116, 117, 122–3, 138–40
  Joseon films, 3–4, 17–18, 52, 55–102, 151
  Korean and Japanese settler collaborations, 9, 107, 138–40
  lack of funding, facilities and equipment, 55–6, 73, 123
  by the MPU, 18, 30–54
  nationalisation of, 233
  by newspapers, 38
  production companies, 30, 51–2, 55–6, 105, 117, 151, 233
  propaganda films, 30, 31–5, 37–8, 41–6
  see also film studios
film programmes, 11, 28, 105, 114, 118–20, 124–9, 131, 140, 160–1
film reception *see* audience reception; critical reception
film reformist movement, 50–2
film regulations, 52, 163–5, 177–81, 232–3
film serials, 124, 150
film spectatorship
  admission fees, 26, 27, 105, 130–1, 211
  of American films, 11, 23, 80, 127–8, 134, 144–67, 179–81, 182–3
  and assimilation policy, 136–43, 161–3
  and *benshi/byeonsa*, 43–4, 48–9, 72, 120–2, 131, 134, 167–83
  demand for local films, 71–2
  as emotional comfort, 17
  and ethnic segregation, 17, 28, 129–36, 140–3, 161–3, 175–6, 230–1
  of European films, 80
  female audiences, 44, 118, 199–204, 210–28
  and gender, 11, 44, 118, 197–204, 210–28
  and hegemony, 160–7
  and identity formation, 67–70
  in Japan, 42–3, 46, 82–102
  Japanese settler audiences, 11, 16–17, 28, 108, 110–13, 123–36, 230–1
  Korean audiences, 11, 15, 16–17, 28–9, 43–5, 71–2, 129–36, 144–67, 230–1
  and modernity, 23, 187–9, 197–210
  and police surveillance, 147, 177–8, 208–9
  reception of films *see* audience reception; critical reception
  reconstructive spectatorship, 146–7
  by the royal family, 21–2, 23–5
  and screen quotas, 52, 88, 136, 153–4, 161, 163–5

Index

and sexuality, 11, 197–204, 211–14
and social class, 22–7, 130–1
in the United States, 23, 146–7
urban audiences, 70, 75–6, 131–4, 183
viewing experience, 11, 15–16, 17
see also movie theatres
film studios
American, 105, 106, 124, 147–53
Japanese, 3, 35, 85, 87–95, 98–102, 103–4, 105, 106, 116, 123–7, 229–34
film theatres *see* movie theatres
films-in-a magazine, 148, **149**, 216
First National Pictures, 153
First World War, 150
Fishing Fires (1938), 87, 93–4
flânerie, 205–10, 226–8
folk songs, 59, 61, 63–67, 68–9, **69**, 82–5
Four Feathers, The (1929), 140, **141**, **142**
Fox Movies, 150
France, 34, 49, 188
French films, 27, 28, 86, 124; *see also* European films
Friedberg, Anne, 226–7
Friendly Society of Joseon Women, 227–8
Fujii Shōten, 150
Fujiki, Hideaki, 38–9
Fukuoka, 105, 121

Gabo Gyeongjang, 190
Gabsin Jeongbyeon, 190
gaehwakkun, 190–3
gaehwapa, 190–3
Gance, Abel, 80, 153
Ganghwa Island Treaty, 111
gender
and acting, 226
feminism, 194, 196–7, 227–8
and film spectatorship, 11, 44, 118, 197–204, 210–28
and *flânerie*, 226–8
gisaeng, 211, 213, 219–28, **223**
and mobility, 210, 216–19, 224–5, 226–8
and modernity, 193–204, 210–28
new woman discourse, 193, 194, 220, 226–8
women's movement, 194, 196–7
gender segregation, 118, 203, 212–13, 219, 224
genre conventions, 62, 70, 77–82
German films, 76–7, 80, 150; *see also* European films
Gerow, Aaron, 178
Geukgwang Yeonghwasa, 93
Geumganggwan Theatre, 28–9
gisaeng, 211, 213, 219–28, **223**
Gisin Yanghaeng, 150–1, **152**
Gleber, Anke, 227
Gojong, Emperor, 5, 13, 23–5, 187, **195**, 195–6, 203–4
Golden Fish (1927), 78
Gongju, 28–9
government and social organisations, 25, 36, 157–60

government reform, 14, 30–2, 41–3, 138
gramophones, 65, 68, 83
Great March of Hinomaru (1937), 53
Griffith, D. W., 176
Gunsan, 16, 130
Gwangmudae Theatre, 27, 174
gwonbeon, 221–5
Gyeongseong Film Productions, 117

hairstyles, 193–4, 196–8, **198**
Hamheung City, 131
Han River (1938), 87, 92, **92**, 96
Hannam Gwonbeon, 225
Hanseong Electric Company, 19, 26–7, 110
Hara Satoshi, 31
Hasegawa Yoshimichi, 14, 31
Hanseong Gwonbeon, 225
Hayakawa Entertainment Company, 29, 115–16, 123
Hayakawa Jōtaro, 29–30, 71–2, 73–4, 115–16
Hayward, Susan, 3
Hazumi Tsuneo, 90, 96
Heartless (1938), 87
hegemony, 51, 64, 67–8, 95, 147, 156, 160–7; *see also* assimilation policies
Heo Jeong-suk, 196
Hero of the Troubled Times, A (1927), 70, 78, 160
High Entertainment Theatre, 28, 112, 116–17, 123–4, 167, 174
Higson, Andrew, 166
Hisagokan Theatre, 116, **117**
Hoeryeong, 70
Hollywood *see* American films
Holmes, Elias Burton, 23–4
Hong Seon-yeong, 112
hooks, bell, 100
Hunchback of Notre Dame, The (1923), 148
Hwangseong sunbo, 203
hybridity, 4, 56–8
Hyeobryulsa Theatre, 19, 21, 23, 188, 203–4, 213

Ichikawa Sai, 111, 234
Iida Shimbi, 92
Iijima Tadashi, 90, 92–3
Ikeda Kunio, 163
Im Su-ho, 69
imperialism, 10, 33–4, 136–8, 160–7, 171, 184–7
Incheon, 16, 112, 116, 151, 232
Incident News (1937), 53
Independence Movement, 13, 30–1, 71, 156–7
Information Committee, 32, 41–2, 50
Inspection Tour of County Magistrates to Japan Proper (1920), 43
international audiences, 49–50
Ishibashi Ryōsuke, 106, 229, 230, 233–4
Ishida Akika, 121
It (1927), 198–9
Italian films, 133; *see also* European films
Itō Hirobumi, 35

Janghanmong (1926), 122
Japan
  co-production of Joseon films, 85, 87–95, 98–102
  expositions, 46, **47**, 184–6
  film censorship, 177–8
  film distribution, 85, 87–8, 90, 153
  film exhibition, 19–20, 40–1, 42–3, 46, **47**, 118–20, 136
  film spectatorship, 42–3, 46, 82–102
  film studios, 3, 35, 85, 87–95, 98–102, 103–4, 105, 106, 116, 123–7, 229–34
  Joseon films exported to, 82–102, 139
  movie theatres, 19–20, 46, **48**, 118, 232
Japan–Korea Trading Treaty, 132
Japanese Affairs (1920), 42–3
Japanese audiences, 42–3, 46, 82–102
Japanese films
  distribution, 9, 88–9, 103–5, 106, 123–7
  exhibition, 1–2, 88–9, 103–4, 124–8, 136, 144–5, 162
  seen as inferior to Hollywood films, 135
Japanese settlers
  as *benshi*, 120–2
  collaboration with Korean film-makers, 9, 107, 138–40
  concentrated in Seoul, 110–11, 132–3, **133**
  development of mass entertainment, 112–15
  as directors of photography, 122
  and ethnic segregation, 17, 28, 129–43, 161–3, 230–1
  film criticism, 9, 11, 81, 100–2, 108, 164
  film culture, 8–9, 11, 103–43
  film distribution, 9, 103–6, 123–7, 150, 229–32
  film exhibition by, 9, 11, 27–8, 103–4, 105–6, 115–20, 123–9, 229–32
  film exhibition for, 9, 28, 110–13, 123–36, 140–3, 229–32
  film production, 9, 29–30, 52, 71–2, 105, 116, 117, 122–3, 138–40
  film spectatorship, 11, 16–17, 28, 108, 110–13, 123–36, 230–1
  identity, 9, 108–9, 137–8
  marginalised by Japanese studios, 89, 104, 233–4
  movie theatres for, 9, 28, 112–13, 123–36, 140–3, 229–32
  movie theatres owned/managed by, 9, 16, 28, 103–4, 105–6, 115–17, 229–32
  as projectionists, 123
  theatres, 112–15, 173
Je-am Village Massacre Incident, 49
Jeong Chil-seong, 228
Jeong Han-seol, 176–7
Jeong, Kelly, 80
Joseon magazine, 46
Joseon Affairs (1920), 42–3
Joseon at the Home Front (1937), 53, **54**
Joseon colour, 85–6, 90–102
Joseon Cultural Magic Lantern Company, 37
Joseon Exposition (1929), 225

Joseon Film Directive, 232–3
Joseon Film Distribution Company, 53, 233
Joseon Film Production Coroporation, 53, 233
Joseon Filmmakers' Association, 53
Joseon Geukjang theatre, 115–16, 132, 133, 134, 140, 143, 150–1, **151**, 209
Joseon Gwonbeon, 225, 226
Joseon identity, 5, 56–8, 63–70, 83–6, 217; *see also* Korean identity
Joseon ilbo, 154
Joseon Kinema, 30, 139–40
Joseon munye, 202
Joseon Public Welfare Corporation, 51–2
Journal of the Society of Motion Picture Engineers, 38
Ju Sam-son, 140
Juche, 61, 71
Jun, Uchida, 108
Jungoi ilbo, 178, 194

kabuki, 28, 112, 113, 114, 229, 230
Kang So-cheon, 144–6
Kang U-gyu, 14
Karafuto, 121
Kato Seichi, 139
Kawakami Otojiro, 113
Keiryūkan Theatre, 106, 121, 124, 133
kengeki see sword drama
Kido Shiro, 103
Kim Deok-gyeong, 173, 174, 176
Kim Do-hwa, 226
Kim Do-san, 3
Kim Do-san Theatre Group, 3, 29
Kim Gap-sun, 29
Kim Hong-jib, 190, 196
Kim Il-sung, 61
Kim Ki-rim, 196–7
Kim Ok-gyun, 190
Kim Ran-ju, 226
Kim Tae-jin, 82
Kim Yeon-sil, 65, 86
Kim Yeong-hawn, 179
Kim Yeong-wol, 226
Kim Yu-yeong, 86
Kinema junpō, 56, 82–3, 85, 87, 94, 98, 129, 163, 182, 233
Kinkikan Theatre, 35
Kirakukan Theatre, 115, 121, 124, 133
Kobayashi Ichizō, 232
Kobe, 40, 43
Koga Masao, 83, 84
Koganekan Theatre, 28, 105–6, 115–16, 133, 175–6, 229, 231, 233
Koizumi Yoshisuke, 127
Kokusai eiga shimbun, 105–6, 111, 131, 135, 163, 165
Kokusaikan Theatre, 131
Komada Kōyō, 50
Korea Artista Proleta Federatio (KAPF), 20, 82
Korea–Japan Treaty, 185

Korean audiences
   and American films, 11, 23, 80, 134–5, 144–67
   demand for local films, 71–2, 165
   and ethnic segregation, 17, 28, 129–36, 140–3, 161–3, 230–1
   film exhibition for, 15, 16–17, 28–9, 43–5, **45**, 129–36, 140–3, 230
   film spectatorship, 11, 15, 16–17, 28–9, 43–5, 71–2, 129–36, 144–67, 230–1
   films produced for, 42–5, 138–40
   living overseas, 44
   movie theatres for, 15, 16–17, 28–9, 105, 115–16, 128–36, 140–3, 150–3, 230
   reception of films *see* audience reception
Korean distributors, 150–1
Korean Empire, 5, 196
Korean exhibitors, 28–9
Korean films
   designation of first Korean film, 3–4, 110
   lack of surviving film texts, 1
   scholarly overemphasis upon, 1–2, 7–8, 109
Korean identity, 4, 8, 57–8, 67; *see also* Joseon identity
Korean language, 25, 42, 102, 232
Korean Literary Arts Association, 139
Korean Review, 19, 26
Korean War, 229
Kotobukiza Theatre, 124, 173
Kracauer, Siegfried, 207
Kuboda Orō, 139
Kunii Izumi, 39
Kyoto, 53, 102

landscape, 74–8, 84, 90–6, 100
League of Nations, 38, 154–5
Lee Bong-hee, 226
Lee Byeong-wu, 123
Lee Chang-yong, 123
Lee Gu-yeong, 180–1
Lee Gyeong-son, 68
Lee Gyu-hwan, 89–90, 101
Lee Han-gyeong, 174, **175**
Lee Jae-sun, 24
Lee Myeong-wu, 86
Lee Pil-wha, 203–4, 213
Lee Pil-wu, 80, 123, 176
Lee Sang, 206–8
Lee Seung-wu, 179
Lee Tae-jun, 98, 214
Lee Yeon-hyang, 226
Lee Yeong-il, 60
Lee Yong-shik, 64
lighting, 55–6, 76
literary adaptations, 72, 74
local colour, 85–6, 90–102
Love and Brothers (1925), 226
Loyal Vengeance (1919), 3, 29, 122, 225
Lumière brothers, 188
lyricism, 95–8

McKenzie, Frederick Arthur, 212–13
Maeda Muro, 135
Maeil sinbo, 13, 14–15, 222–4, 230
maesetsu, 174, 179
magic lantern shows, 26, 35–7
Maid and Destiny, A (1925), 226
Makino Kinema, 106, 126–7, 232
Makino Teruko, 127, **128**
Manchuria, 44, 86, 106, 116, 121
Mansegwan Theatre, 131
Mansen Motion Picture Trading Company, 122
Marata Masao, 127
Martin, L., 27
Marxist feminism, 227–8
Mask Dance, The, 73
mass entertainment, 16, 17–18, 29–30, 68–9, 112–15, 189, 224
Matsumoto Teruka, 134
Matsuura Tsukie, 127
Meijiza Theatre, 106, 229–30, 231–2, 233–4
melancholy, 84–5, 90–1
melodramas, 87, 91, 153, 158, 226
Memmi, Albert, 67
Metro-Goldwyn-Mayer (MGM), 150, 179
Mexico, 49
Miles Away from Happiness (1941), 87
Militant Rule, 31, 138, 208
military police, 208, 209
Military Train (1938), 87, 89, 93
Min Won-sik, 35
Minami Jirō, 161
Ministry of Agriculture, 32
Ministry of Culture and Tourism, 229–30
Ministry of Education, 32–3, 37–8, 41
Ministry of Home Affairs, 177
Ministry of Navy, 38
Ministry of Railway, 32–3, 38
minjok cinema, 2, 56–7, 60
Miyagawa Hayanosuke, 122, 123
Mizui Reiko, 100–2, 127, 188, 234
Mizuno Rentarō, 14, 41–2, 49
mobility, 208, 210, 216–19, 224–5, 226–8
modern boys, 193–4, 197–205, **200**, 209–10, 217
modern drama, 58, 74, 126
modern girls, 193–205, **198**, 209–10, 214, 217–18, 226–8
modernity, 5, 11, 19, 23, 43, 45, 68, 132, 137, 173, 184–228
Mokpo, 16
Momoyama Long, 121
monster films, 78
Monte Cristo (1922) 160
Morris, G. H., 150
Morris-Suzuki, Tessa, 137
Motion Picture Film Censorship Regulation, 177–8
Motion Picture Herald, 164
Motography, 147–8

movie theatres
  emergence of, 14–18, 19–21, 27–9, 112–13, 115–17
  and ethnic segregation, 17, 28, 129–36, 140–3, 161–3, 175–6, 230–1
  female audiences, 118, 199–204, 210–28
  and gender segregation, 118, 203, 212–13, 219
  involvement in production, 30
  in Japan, 19–20, 46, **48**, 118, 232
  for Japanese settler audiences, 9, 28, 112–13, 123–36, 140–3, 229–32
  Japanese settler owned/managed, 9, 16, 28, 103–4, 105–6, 115–17, 229–32
  Japanese studio owned/managed, 88–9, 101, 229–32
  for Korean audiences, 15, 16–17, 28–9, 105, 115–16, 128–36, 140–3, 150–3, 230
  Korean owned/managed, 28–9
  and modern boys and girls, 199–204
  pictured, **15**, **48**, **117**, **151**
  and police surveillance, 147, 177–8, 208–9
  and sexuality, 197–204, 211–14
  and sound technology, 8, 103, 106, 182
  see also film exhibition; film spectatorship
Moving Picture Band (Tongyeong Youth Association), 158–60, **159**
Moving Picture Unit (MPU)
  renamed Cinema Unit, 53
  educational films, 33–4, 41–52, 53, 157
  establishment of, 18, 30–2
  film exhibition by, 42–50, **45**, **47**, 51
  and the film reformist movement, 50–2
  final years, 52–4
  as first unit of its kind, 32–4
  propaganda films, 30, 31–5, 41–50, 53
  representational politics, 41–50
  social edifice films, 50–2, 53
  wartime films, 53, **54**
Moving Picture World, 148
Mun Ye-bong, 86
Murayama Tomoyoshi, 99–100
Myeong-dong Art Theatre, 230
mystery films, 78, 127

Na Un-gyu, 60–1, 68, 70, 71, 73, 74, 76, 77–9, 80, 81–2, 86
Nade Otoichi, 139
Naeoebeob, 212
Nagoya, 42, 43
naisen ittai, 53, 161, 234
naisen yūwa, 136, 138
Nakamura Shōtaro, 123
Nakane Ryūtaro, 127
nakasetsu, 174, 179
naniwabushi, 114–15
Naniwakan Theatre, 127
narrators see benshi/byeonsa
national cinema, 2–4, 17, 33, 56–7, 60–3, 109, 166

national identity see Czech identity; Japanese settlers: identity; Joseon identity; Korean identity
National Theatre of Korea, 229
nationalisation, 232–3, 234–5
nationalism, 2–3, 8, 13–14, 44, 49, 56–7, 60–8, 71, 96–8, 138, 144–5, 153, 156–60, 165–6, 168, 171, 189, 209
New School, 172–3; see also shimpa/sinpa
new woman discourse, 193, 194, 220, 226–8; see also modern girls
newsreels, 1, 20, 38, 50, 53, 158, 160
Nikkatsu Studio, 35, 116, 123, 124–6, 139, 232
Nipton sound system, 106
Nishikawa Hidehiro, 122, 123
Nitta Byōhei, 116
Nitta Entertainment Company, 116, 123
Nitta Hideyoshi, 116
Nitta Kōichi, 116
Nitta Ryujiro, 114
Nitta Shōten, 116
Noh, 112, 114
Nokseong, 148, **149**
North Korea, 3–4, 61, 71

Office of the Governor General (OGG), 3, 25, 31–2, 35, 43, 46, 50, 138, 153, 163, 177, 232–3, 234; see also Information Committee; Moving Picture Unit (MPU)
Oka Shigematsu, 42, 43, 56, 161–2
Okada Jun'ichi, 95
Okamoto Trading Company, 40
Onoe Marsunosuke, 127
Osaka, 8, 102, 103, 116, 121
Osaka Mainichi Shimbun, 38
otherness, 10, 100, 109, 184, 185

Paramount Studios, 140, 150–1, 153, 154, 198
Park Eung-myeon, 179
Park Gi-chae, 86
Park Seung-pil, 27, 29, 122, 174
Path at the Twilight (1927), 226
Pathé films, 27, 28, 124
Patriotic Women's Association, 35
period dramas, 72, 74, 126, 127, 164
Peter Pan (1924), 154, **155**
Phantom of the Opera, The (1925), 148
Philippines, 165–6
Pioneer, The (1925), 122
Plaintive Melody of Sea, A (1924), 139
Plaintive Song of Crimson Love, The (1927), 105
Please Take Care (1927), 79
police surveillance, 147, 177–8, 208–9
Polo, Eddie, 124, 148
production see film production
production companies, 30, 51–2, 55–6, 105, 117, 151, 233
programmes see film programmes
projection technology, 40–1

Index

projectionists, 123
propaganda films, 1, 2, 10, 20, 30, 31–50, 53, 102, 217, 233; *see also* educational films
propaganda magic lantern shows, 35–7
Provisional Government of the Republic of Korea, 13
Pudovkin, Vsevolod, 209
purity, discourse of, 3–4
Pyongyang, 16, 84, 225, 232

radio, 68
realism, 70–9
recommended films, 51–2
reconstructive spectatorship, 146–7
Red Cross Society, 38
rensageki see chain dramas
reviews *see* critical reception; fan reviews; film critics
Richie, Donald, 171
River, The (1933), 96, **97**
Romeo and Juliet (1936), 230, **231**
royal palace film screenings, 21–2, 23–5
Rue, La (1923), 80, 153
rural settings, 74–8, 90–1
Russia, 27, 44, 137, 187–8
Russian films, 153, 160, 209; *see also* European films
Russo-Japanese wars, 37, 185

Sa Jin-sil, 21–2
Saitō Makoto, 14, 30, 31–2, 36, 49
Sakai Yoneko, 127
Sakuraba Fujio, 118, **119**
Saldaña-Portillo, Maria Josefina, 156
Samcheolli, 55, 59, 86–7, 95
scenery *see* landscape
screen quotas, 52, 88, 136, 153–4, 161, 163–5
Second Sino-Japanese War, 52–3, 88, 165
Second Taishōkan Theatre, 174, 176; *see also* Taishōkan Theatre
Second World War, 97, 100, 102, 232
Secret of Chinese Street, The (1928), 122
segregation *see* class segregation; ethnic segregation; gender segregation
Sekaikan Theatre, Seoul, 124; *see also* High Entertainment Theatre
Sekaikan Theatre, Shinuiju, 131
Seo Gwang-je, 82, 89, 214
Seo Sang-ho, 167, 174, **175**, 179, 181
Seong Dong-ho, 179
Seongbong Yeonghwawon, 87, 90
Seoul
  and *Arirang*, 60–1, 69
  film regulation, 177
  film studio offices in, 150, 153
  Hangseong Electric Company film screening, 19, 26
  Japanese settlers in, 110–17, 132–3, **133**
  magic lantern shows, 35, 36
  and modernity, 187, 206–8

movie theatres, 15, 27–8, 103–6, 114–17, 121, 124, 126, 127, 131–4, 140–3, 150, 176, 182, 229–32
street demonstrations, 157
theatres, 16, 19, 112, 113, 173
serials *see* film serials
settlers *see* Japanese settlers
sexuality, 11, 157, 160, 197–204, 211–14, 221
Shakai kyōiku jigyō, 52
Shimazu Yasujiro, 94
shimpa/sinpa, 28, 112, 113, 114, 172–3
Shin Il-seon, 67, 68
Shin Myeong-jik, 187
Shinko Kinema, 87, 89–90, 93, 123, 231, 232
Shinuiju, 131
Shirotori Seigo, 83–4
Shochiku studio, 3, 90, 93–4, 103–4, 106, 123, 126, 176, 229, 230, 231, 232, 233–4
Shochikuza Theatre, 106; *see also* Koganekan Theatre
Shoes (1916), **149**
Sigonggwan Theatre *see* Meijiza Theatre
Sim Cheong (1937), 74
Sim Hun, 73, 75, 80–1
Singajeong, 215
sinpa see shimpa/sinpa
Sinyeoseong, 227
Sir Min Yeong-hwan, 187–8
social class, 22–7, 77, 130–1, 220–1, 222, 224, 227–8
social edifice films, 50–2, 53
social organisations, 25, 36, 157–60
socialism, 153, 160, 209, 227–8
Society for the Study of Joseon Music and Dance, 102
Song of Arirang, The (film, 1933), 82–3
Song of Arirang, The (song), 83–5
Song of Sad Love, A (1924), 73–4
Song of the Unforgettable, The (1927), 105
sound technology, 74, 86, 88, 103, 106, 182; *see also* talkies
South Korea, 3, 60–2, 71, 182–3, 221
South Manchurian Railway Company, 32
Soviet Union *see* Russia
Spanish flu, 14, 36
spectatorship *see* film spectatorship
stage drama, 21, 112, 114, 172–3, 229, 230; *see also* theatres
Stallich, Jan, 96
Starr, Frederick, 210, 211
Stewart, Jacqueline, 146–7, 208
Storm of Asia (1928), 209
studios *see* film studios
sugupa, 190
Sunjong, Emperor, 5, 25
Suzuki Shigeyoshi, 89–90, 101
swashbucklers, 70, 78, 80
Sweden, 49–50
Sweet Dream (1936), 216–19, **218**
sword drama, 118, 127, 135

Taishō democracy, 31, 137
Taishōkan Theatre, 28, 103–4, 116, 133, 175–6; see also Second Taishōkan Theatre
Taiwan, 32, 35, 121, 171
Takarazuka Kinema, 83, 106, 123
Takasa Kanjo, 139–40
Tale of Chun-hyang (1923), 30, 72
Tale of Chun-hyang (1935), 74, 182
Tale of Honggildong (1936), 74
Tale of Janghwa and Hongryeon (1924), 72, 116
Tale of Janghwa and Hongryeon (1936), 74
Tale of Sim Cheong (1925), 122
Tale of Sim Cheong (1937), 151
Tale of Unyeong (1925), 122
talkies, 74, 86, 89, 103, 106, 140, 181–2; see also sound technology
Tamata Kitsuji, 229
Tanaka Saburō, 233
Taoism, 207
technology, 40–1, 45, 68–9, 74, 86, 88, 103, 106, 182, 184, 187–9
Teikoku Kinema, 89, 121, 123, 126, 232
temporary venues, 16, 20, **20**, 21–3, 25–7
Tenkatsu studio, 116, 122, 123
Terauchi Masatake, 31
Thailand, 171
theatres, 19, 21–2, 23, 28, 112–15, 172–3, 188, 222, 230; see also movie theatres
Three Penny Opera (1931), 80
Tōa Club, 105–6; see also Koganekan Theatre
Tōa Kinema, 105, 106, 232
Tōgatsu studio, 105
Toho studio, 89, 90, 93, 231, 232, 233, 234
Tokunaga Kumaichirō, 103–7, **104**, 118, 150, 233
Tokunaga Moving Picture Shop, 105, 150
Tokunaga Productions, 52, 105
Tokyo, 35, 42, 43, 46, 93, 139, 153, 184, 185, 232
Tokyo eiga shimbun, 231–2
Tokyo Exposition (1922), 46, **47**
Tokyo Geijutsu Eigasha studio, 123
Tokyo Industrial Exposition (1907), 184, 185
Tongyeong Youth Association, 158–60, **159**
Tour of Korea (1908), 35
Tōwa Shōji, 231, 233
Toyama Mitsuru, 118
Tōyō Katsudō Shashinkan, 46, **48**
tradition, 23, 61, 63–5, 86, 93, 160, 162, 189, 193–4, 196, 203–4
tragedy, 59, 90–1
Treaty of Versaille, 154–5
Tsivian, Yuri, 27
Tsuchihashi sound system, 103
Tsumura Isamu, 44, 49, 51

Uchida Jun, 108, 233
Uchida Kimio, 102
Umigwan Theatre, 16, 28, 29, 132, 133, 150, 153, 169, 174, 176–7, 181–2, 225

United Artists, 150
United Kingdom, 33–4, 49
United States
  African American audiences, 146–7, 208
  and democracy, 154–7
  film exhibition, 40
  film spectatorship, 23, 146–7
  film studios, 105, 106, 124, 147–53
  propaganda film screenings, 49
  see also American films
Universal Studios, 124, 144, 147–50, 153
urban audiences, 70, 75–6, 131–4, 183
urbanisation, 16–17, 131–2, 205–6

Variety, 96
Venice film festival, 96
View of Seoul City, A (1919), 29
Village Shrine, A (1939), 87
violence, 79–80, 160
Vow Made Under the Moon, The (1923), 3–4

Wakakusa Gekijō Theatre, 231, 232
Wakejima Shujirō, 103, 116–17
Warner Brothers, 105, 106, 150
wartime films, 53, **54**
Watanabe Tatsuchiru, 139
Way Down East (1920), 176
Wayfarer, The (1937), 87–96, **99**, 100–1
westerns, 77–8, 80, 153, 158, 199
White, Pearl, 148
Wi Gyeong-hae, 130, 182
Wild Rat (1927), 79
Willow (Shirotori), 83–4
Wilson, Woodrow, 154–6
women's magazines, 215–16
women's movement, 194, 196–7
Wonsan, 116
Wu Jeong-sik, 174

yakuza organisations, 116–17
Yamaguchi Torao, 164
Yamamoto Kaichi, 127
Yamamoto Tadami, 49
Yamane Mikihito, 50
Yamani Trading Company, 85, 136
Yang Se-ung, 123
Yim Hwa, 20–1, 30
Yokoda Shōkai, 35
Yongsan, 106, 121
yose, 28, 112, 118
Yoshimoto Kōgyō, 231
Yūaikan Theatre, 106
Yun Baek-nam, 3
Yun Chi-ho, 180
Yun Gi-jeong, 75–6
Yūrakukan Theatre, 124; see also Kirakukan Theatre

Zhuang Zi, 206–7
Zigomar, 38

EU representative:
Easy Access System Europe
Mustamäe tee 50, 10621 Tallinn, Estonia
Gpsr.requests@easproject.com

www.ingramcontent.com/pod-product-compliance
Lightning Source LLC
Chambersburg PA
CBHW061707300426
44115CB00014B/2588